The AIRFIELDS OF LINCOLNSHIRE SINCE 1912

Opposite: **Lancaster LM326 of 207 Sqn seen over Barkston Heath during a photographic sortie from Spilsby on 18th October 1943.** *(IWM CH12115)*

The AIRFIELDS OF LINCOLNSHIRE SINCE 1912

Ron Blake · Mike Hodgson · Bill Taylor

First published in 1984 by
Midland Counties Publications
24 The Hollow, Earl Shilton,
Leicester, LE9 7NA, England.

ISBN 0 904597 32 6

Editorial layout by Keith Woodcock

Printed in the United Kingdom by
Nene Litho and bound by Woolnough
Bookbinding, Sanders Road,
Wellingborough, Northants, England.

Contents

Preface 6
Acknowledgements 8
Notes on using this Book 9
Grid References 9
Popular Sheet Numbers 10
Other Locational Data 10
Airfield Terminology 11
Abbreviations 15

Part One:
The Development of
Airfields in Lincolnshire 17

Evolution 18
Military Development 20
Civil Development 25

Part Two:
The Airfields 29

Anwick 31
Bardney 31
Barkston Heath 34
Binbrook 37
Blyborough 41
Blyton 41
Boston (Wyberton Fen) 42
Bracebridge Heath 43
Braceby 44
Buckminster 44
Bucknall 45
Caistor 46
Cammeringham/Ingham 47
Cleethorpes Beach 49
Cockthorne 49
Coleby Grange 49
Coningsby 51
Cranwell (North) 55
Cranwell (South) 55
Crowland/Postland 63
Cuxwold 63
Digby/Scopwick 63
Donna Nook 71
Dunholme Lodge 72
East Kirkby 75
Elsham 78

Elsham Wolds 78
Faldingworth 82
Fiskerton 82
Folkingham 84
Freiston 85
Fulbeck 87
Gainsborough 88
Gosberton 88
Goxhill 88
Greenland Top 89
Grimsby (Waltham) 89
Harlaxton 95
Hemswell/Harpswell 97
Hibaldstow 103
Holbeach Range 104
Holbeach St Johns/Fenland 104
Immingham 104
Kelstern (1) 105
Kelstern (2) 105
Killingholme 107
Kirmington/Humberside 112
Kirton in Lindsey (1)/Manton 115
Kirton in Lindsey (2) 116
Leadenham 120
Lincoln (Handley Page Field) 121
Lincoln (West Common) 121
Ludborough 123
Ludford Magna 123
Manby 125
Market Deeping 131
Metheringham 131
Moorby 132
New Holland 132
North Coates 132
North Killingholme 139
North Witham 141
Sandtoft 143
Scampton/Brattleby 144
Scunthorpe (Emmanuel) 154
Skegness (Burgh Road) 154
Skegness (Winthorpe) 154
Skegness (Ingoldmells) 156
Skellingthorpe 159
South Carlton 162
Spalding (Weston Marsh) 164
Spilsby 164

Spitalgate/Grantham 167
Strubby 172
Sturgate 175
Sutton Bridge 177
Swinderby 180
Swinstead 184
Theddlethorpe 184
Tydd St Mary 184
Waddington 185
Wellingore 193
Wickenby 194
Willoughby Hills 195
Winterton 196
Woodhall Spa 196
General Bibliography 199

Part Three:
Military Airfields and the
Lincolnshire Landscape 201

Part Four:
Appendices 217

A Location Details
    of Main Airfields 218
B Index of Military Flying Units 222
C Bomber Command
    Base Organisation 243
D Airfield Defence and the Royal
    Air Force Regiment 245
E Unusual and Experimental
    Devices 248
F Decoy Airfields 253
G Bombing and Gunnery
    Ranges 257
H Sundry Air Force Sites 262
I Principal Civil Operators 266
J Notable Airstrips 273
K Air Memorials 278
L Aviation Museums 283
M Airfield Names 289
N Essendine: The Airfield That
    Never Was 291
O Source Material and
    Research Methods 293
Notes/Addenda 296

Preface

The past decade has seen a growing interest in the origin, development and decline of British airfields. Ten years ago not a single book was available on the subject and the magazines of the day contained only brief histories of individual stations selected without apparent reference to any overall scheme of study. By the mid-seventies however, three regional airfield surveys had been published, respectively covering Yorkshire, Scotland and Hampshire, each of which contained valuable ideas as to how the rest of the country might eventually be tackled (see General Bibliography). Since then the numbers and substance of works has expanded quite dramatically. In 1978, an elaborately illustrated survey of American Eighth Air Force bases, *Airfields of the Eighth - Then and Now*, received critical acclaim and within two years had been complemented by a copiously researched work on the Battle of Britain and the principal airfields of that period. The publishers of these two works have since contributed further to the study of British airfields with the release, in association with the RAF Museum, of an expanding series of facsimile reproductions of original airfield plans. In 1979 the first truly regional airfield history was published, in the form of *Action Stations 1* which covered the Second World War airfields of East Anglia, and this has already been followed up with equivalent surveys of Lincolnshire and the East Midlands, of Wales and North-West England, Yorkshire, the South-West, the Cotswolds and Central Midlands. Ultimately the whole of the United Kingdom will have been covered in the style set by the publishers concerned.

Airfield monographs have also proliferated over the past few years and detailed profiles of particular stations are now a regular feature of several aeronautical journals. At the broader scale, comprehensive listings and mapped distributions are beginning to appear in specially compiled registers designed to satisfy the more regionally and nationally-minded aero historian. Two books on the subject of aviation archaeology have made a feature of airfield buildings and within the last few years an 'Airfield Research Group' has been formed to co-ordinate and promote investigation in this field. In a number of counties, for example Cornwall, Cumbria and Kent, there are societies and dedicated individuals working towards definitive records of their local airfields and it is at this level that the present Lincolnshire project fits into the picture.

But why this new-found interest in airfields? To start with, many relevant wartime documents were simply not accessible a decade ago due to the 'thirty-year rule' governing their release, whereas today there is an almost embarrassing amount of material to work through. Secondly, with the continued run-down and disposal of RAF stations, it is now possible to explore a more representative selection of premises without fear of trespass or indiscretion. Thirdly, many ex-airmen are reaching a stage in their lives when nostalgia is drawing them back to old haunts and in some cases to inspect official archives where forgotten technical details can be checked out. As the passage of time threatens to erase much of the physical evidence, there is a growing sense of mission that the histories of wartime airfields should be recorded before memories inevitably fade. For the younger enthusiast growing up in an age of nuclear deterrence and electronic warning systems, it must seem amazing that so many airfields were ever required at all and there is a great deal of active interest being shown by persons who clearly were not yet born when the stations concerned were in their heyday. Finally, there seems at long last to be a general recognition that aviation history was not made solely by the designers of aircraft and the personnel who flew in them, but also by the land and buildings which made aviation possible yet which have been largely unsung to date. Many groups not traditionally interested in aviation, including local historians, town planners and industrial archaeologists, are also beginning to show a real concern for the fate of old airfields and these people represent both an interested audience and a source of expertise for continued studies in the field.

The present book has been compiled with these various interest groups very much in mind and is intended as a contribution to both local history and aviation archaeology. For all the recent publications on airfield subjects, we believe this to be the first full-length survey of an English county to encompass all types of airfields, at all periods and from all points of view. In finalising its structure and content we have been conscious of the parallel research carried out by Terry Hancock for his *Bomber County: A History of the RAF in Lincolnshire*, which was appropriately published a few years before this present study, and all along we have seen the two projects as complementary rather than overlapping in their aims. Whereas *Bomber County* has successfully examined the role and organisation of military aviation in Lincolnshire and its impact on the life and times of the local population, *The Airfields of Lincolnshire since 1912* is intended to focus much more on the individual history and geography of each station and what has physically happened to it since closure. We are also mindful of, and grateful for, Bruce Halpenny's recently published *Action Stations 2* which covers both our county and adjacent areas from the military point of view. Some duplication of wartime material has been inevitable, but there is always room for a variety of approach and illustration, and on the civil side in particular we believe that we have ploughed fresh territory. In short we have set out to produce a definitive guide to all the military and civil airfields which have existed in the county since organised flying began in 1912, and we hope this will encourage others to undertake local research into some of the less familiar aspects.

To assist the reader, the study is divided into four parts. Part One deals in turn with the evolution of military and civil airfields as a whole in Lincolnshire within the context of broad national trends. A special effort has been made to avoid repetition of published material on the military side, but space has been generously devoted to the development of civil aviation in view of the fact that virtually nothing has been written, in books at least, on Lincolnshire's role in this respect. Part Two, which represents the main body of the book, consists of individual profiles of eighty-six airfields arranged alphabetically regardless of their main function. The qualifications for inclusion in the main list are: for military airfields, whether an airfield is mentioned in wartime records as an aircraft operating base; for the civil side, whether an airfield has ever been listed in the *UK Air Pilot* (the official manual of civil aeronautical information). Private airstrips which are not located on former RAF stations have been listed separately and included in Appendix J. Part Three is devoted to an analysis of military airfields as a feature of the landscape, including their construction, architecture and the geographical factors influencing site selection. The opportunity is also taken here to draw out themes relating to the pattern of after-uses, environmental planning and industrial re-development potential. Finally, Part Four comprises some fifteen appendices which supply facts, figures and explanations that would be repetitive or unwieldy within any of the three preceding parts.

Throughout the study we have taken particular care to be geographically precise. As a whole, the survey covers the historic County of Lincolnshire, comprising the three administrative Parts of Holland, Kesteven and Lindsey including the sizeable portion which in 1974 was transferred into the new County of Humberside. One airfield *outside* historic Lincolnshire is included (an early landing ground near Gainsborough) but this is offset by the exclusion of parts of Bottesford and Saltby aerodromes which actually straddle the county boundary with Leicestershire. In describing the eighty-six airfields individually we have been successful in pin-pointing every one on the ground and in all but a few cases we have also determined their original boundaries. A grid reference and a popular Ordnance Survey sheet number for every airfield is provided under its name in

Part Two and is repeated with further location details, such as parishes, in Appendix A. Where minor establishments, such as sundry sites or decoy airfields, are not described by a grid reference it can be taken that the precise sites have remained uncertain to the compilers.

Another aspect highlighted in the study is the question of airfield names. A great deal of confusion has been caused in the past by the fact that certain airfields have either changed their names or have borne concurrent alternatives. In other cases the same name has applied to quite separate airfields and these relationships have been fully explained in Appendix M. Finally, we have prepared some twenty maps and diagrams which are designed to illustrate patterns not evident from the text or photographs. These include airfield distributions, typical layouts and technical equipment associated with airfields in Lincolnshire.

Despite almost ten years of continuous research it has still not been possible to assemble consistent information for every airfield. Experienced readers will possibly spot errors and omissions and we would welcome feedback on any aspect of the book. Since we have also included the present state of each airfield, some of the last reported uses may well have changed since the survey went to press and observations would be equally appreciated here. We know from our many contacts that studies on further aspects of Lincolnshire aviation are at a formative stage and we sincerely hope that this book has contributed in some way to a balanced understanding of the way airfields have evolved in this premier aeronautical county.

R.N.E. Blake   September 1983
M. Hodgson
W.J. Taylor

Acknowledgments

In writing this book the authors have been greatly helped and encouraged by the many individuals and organisations who have willingly given of their valuable time: to all we tender our grateful thanks.

How to record the names of those kind individuals who have helped in many different ways is a problem and listing by country and in alphabetical order is the only convenient way to express our heartfelt thanks for such valuable help. *United Kingdom:* D.Ashley, Sqn Ldr R.C.B.Ashworth, Bill Baguley, Malcom Bills, Chaz Bowyer, Sqn Ldr A.J.Brookes, Jeff Brown, Jack Bruce, Cyril Chaney, O.P.Chandler, Warrant Officer F.R.Clarke, Peter Corbell, Peter Claydon, Cliff Clover, Lt Cdr L.A.Cox, R.Durran, Sid Finn, Neville Franklin, Roger Freeman, Geoff Gardiner, Sqn Ldr J.I.Gilson, Eric Gledhill, Terry Hancock, Vernon Hawley, Geo D.Hay, Jim Halley, Rod Houldsworth, Sqn Ldr C.G.Jefford, D.Jones, Flt Lt E.Longhurst, Daphne Lansdown, George Maplethorpe, Brian Martin, Martin Middlebrook, Denis I.Newman, Archer Osbourne, Mrs K.Peace, Arthur Pearcy, Roy Pickworth, Stephen Piercy, Peter Pountney, Eric Redshaw, Flt Lt E.M.C.Rowe, P.M.Sharman, Trevor Simpson, P.J.Small, D.J.Stennett, Ray Sturtivant, Wg Cdr K.H.Wallis, Bernard Ward, Peter Wilson, Ron Winton. *Australia:* Gerald Muir, the staff of the Australian War Memorial. *Canada:* Dr Fred Hatch, Bud Stevenson and W.A.B.Douglas, the Director of History at the National Defence Headquarters. *United States:* Brigadier Brian S.Gunderson USAF (Rtd), Colonel Peter L.Smith USAF (Rtd), Colonel Fred D.Stevens USAF (Rtd), Colonel Donald L.Wilkinson USAF, Lieutenant Colonel Raymond F.Hunter USAF, Major John P.Seeley USAF (Rtd), Flight Lieutenant Seymour B.Feldman DFC RAF (Rtd), Robert L.Cloer, Charles S.Herman, Jack Ilfrey, Daniel B. Potochniak and Bill Woodward.

We should like to thank the many departments within the Ministry of Defence which have been of considerable assistance: the staff of the Air Historical Branch, the Inspectorate of Recruiting, C1 (Ceremonial), Reprographic Services, S4C (Air), Lands 2J, the Royal Air Force Museum, the Commanding Officers of several current RAF stations - in particular, those at Coningsby and Digby, and the Community Relations Officers at the few Royal Air Force stations still active in the County. The Royal Air Force Establishment at Bedford has provided considerable help, as has the Air Photographs Unit of the Department of Environment and the former Grantham Sub-District of the Defence Lands Agent, Property Services Agency.

Other organisations who gave help included the Office of History, Headquarters US Third Air Force; the US Naval Historical Centre; the Imperial War Museum; the Lincolnshire Aviation Museum; the College of Arms; Lincolnshire Library Services and its various Branch Libraries - in particular those at Cleethorpes, Skegness and Stamford; Airwork Services Ltd; British Steel Corporation; Eastern Air Executive Ltd; Fairey Surveys Ltd; Management Aviation Ltd; plus the chairman and clerks of many parish councils; various departments of Humberside County Council and Lincolnshire County Council and many District Councils; environmental bodies and firms not connected with aviation which now occupy airfield premises. We should also like to thank the staff of the Public Records Office who have faithfully produced for inspection the official documents on which of this book is based.

Also, we must record our grateful thanks for the co-operation of the many newspaper and magazine editors both at home and overseas who published letters seeking assistance with our research.

Lastly, but most of all, we should like to record our indebtedness to three good friends - Peter Green, Roy Bonser and John Walls, who have been a regular source of useful information and sound advice. Peter's lifelong interest in aviation has been of particular value to us, and his vast collection has been a profuse source of photographs. We should also like to thank Peter and Roy for proof reading early drafts of the manuscript.

Notes on using this book

Any study which is based on the inter-disciplinary approach is bound to contain some terms with which the reader is unfamiliar. Whilst every effort has been made to avoid technical jargon, it is not possible to be either accurate or concise without borrowing some terminology from the fields of aeronautics, civil engineering, regional geography, architecture and town planning. In most cases the terms used are self-explanatory or clear from their context, but because the study of airfields is still a comparatively new specialism, it was felt necessary to include notes on those aspects of interpretation most likely to present difficulties to the general reader.

The correct rendering of locations is considered most crucial to a study of this detail and is explained in relation to the Ordnance Survey grid, distances from local landmarks and site elevations. Airfield terminology is similarly of central importance and an attempt is made to define the most common terms used to differentiate main sub-types of establishment.

Equally important is that the dating of airfields should be historically faithful: Part Two in particular contains many dates, some of which may differ from those previously published. These differences occur for two reasons: firstly, material gleaned from such official sources as the Form 540 Operational Record Book(s) for station and unit histories has occasionally been at variance with published versions to date; secondly, unit moves were often spread over a number of days with advance, main and rear party movements and intended plans were often affected by unexpected weather and by delays with completion of airfield installations. Throughout this work, quoted movements relate to the main party of the unit. A consolidated list of military aircraft operating units including movement dates indexed to the airfields within the county, plus a separate selection of representative aircraft, appear in Appendix B.

In keeping with most factual compilations today, a list of standard abbreviations is also provided to help the reader cope with condensed parts of the text.

GRID REFERENCES

All known locations in this study are specified by a numeric code derived from the Ordnance Survey national grid. This method is considered preferable to using co-ordinates of longitude and latitude which are intended primarily for navigation purposes and are not shown as lines across popular topographical maps. Whereas 'long-lat' references provide an accuracy of only about one mile using two letters and eight digits, e.g.

53°22'N/00°05'E (Manby aerodrome), the Ordnance Survey grid enables any place in Great Britain to be uniquely expressed to an accuracy of 100 metres with two letters and only six digits, e.g. TF 386 867 (same aerodrome). As a significant proportion of Lincolnshire's historic airfields are now physically obscure and indeed may never have been shown on published maps, precise grid references are clearly essential to any reader who wishes to either visit sites or to reflect on their geographical positions. To avoid misleading the reader, approximations (such as the nearest village) are avoided and wherever a site is obscure this fact is noted.

The derivation of OS grid references is explained on the margin of current 1 : 50 000 sheets. Briefly, the lettered prefixes relate to the 100 x 100 km supergrid, of which four squares — SE, SK, TA and TF — are represented in Lincolnshire (meeting in the vicinity of Hibaldstow). Each supersquare itself comprises one hundred 10 x 10 kms squares which are published at 1 : 25 000 scale and bear two-digit codes, e.g. TF 38 (Louth area). The latter are sub-divided into quadrants for publication at 1 : 10 000 scale, e.g. TF 38 NE (which includes Manby aerodrome). Inevitably certain airfields fall onto a number of sheets, e.g. Spilsby (on all 1 : 10 000 quadrants of TF 46) and Scampton (which straddles 1 : 25 000 sheets SK 97 and 98).

To register a particular site it is standard practice to quote eastings before northings. Eastings are derived by taking the vertical grid line (two digits) which lies immediately west of the site in question and estimating tenths of a kilometre (one digit) until the site is reached. Likewise northings are derived from the horizontal line immediately south of the site plus an estimate of the number of 100-metre steps up to the site. As an example, the intersection of the two runways at Manby lies 600 metres east of vertical 38 (hence 386) and 700 metres north of horizontal 86 (hence 867). It is also useful to note that the first and fourth digits of any six-figure grid reference always relate back to the code for the published 1 : 10 000 and 1 : 25 000 OS sheets. Thus once a grid reference is known it is possible to find the relevant map should more geographic detail be required.

To simplify map reading, grid references for all Second World War airfields are rounded off here to the nearest 500 metres (ending in 0 and 5), e.g. TF 390 865 (Manby), the point normally lying between the landing surface and the main technical site. This 'centroid' is considered a truer way of describing a whole airfield than the alternative practice of pinpointing the station gates. Where a First World War site lies eccentrically within a more modern aerodrome, as at Harpswell/Hemswell

(SK 940 905), a common grid reference is employed which may be some distance from the hub of the enlarged establishment. In the case of certain early landing grounds, grid references are expressed down to the last 100 metres, e.g. Gosberton (TF 167 297), because rounding off to a 500-metre mesh would have missed the field altogether.

POPULAR SHEET NUMBERS

Although cast onto the national grid the 1 : 63 360 and 1 : 50 000 OS maps, which most people buy folded, have an independent numbering system which is purely for commercial convenience and is quite unrelated to the metricated grid. In some cases popular maps coincide exactly with a set of medium scale (1 : 25 000 and 1 : 10 000) sheets but this is exceptional in Lincolnshire. Most readers will acquire the popular scales in the first instance for reference, field work and as a means to ordering the correct larger scale sheets from libraries and bookshops (see previous sub-section). For this reason relevant popular sheet numbers are provided in the book in addition to site grid references. Due to the slight change of publication scale (from 1 : 63 000 to 1 : 50 000), it has been necessary to include two separate, and again unrelated, numbering systems; these appear side by side in Appendix A but only the current 1 : 50 000 sheets are quoted alongside airfield references in Part Two and in Appendices G, I, J, and K, which also specify locations. The defunct 'One Inch' numbers will be useful to readers with older map collections and as a substitute for the 1 : 50 000 series where this is not available on request in libraries.

OTHER LOCATIONAL DATA

As a back-up to grid references, and to provide a measure of choice for the reader, each airfield location is also described in terms of its distance from a local landmark and its site elevation above sea level.

With regard to landmarks, the obvious choice is normally the nearest parish church which can be clearly identified on any popular OS sheet. In certain cases, for example where an airfield lies a long way from a church or where a cluster of town churches confuses the picture, a railway station is used instead as the identification base. Distances are rendered in kilometres to an accuracy of 100 metres (one decimal place), as the OS

grid provides a ready measuring device. The finishing point in each case is the 'centroid' of the airfield defined in the above sub-section. Directions from a stated landmark are generalised to one of sixteen compass points (E, ESE, SE, etc).

Elevations are provided as a further safeguard that sites have been correctly pin-pointed. These relate to the airfield 'centroids' and are quoted to an accuracy of 10 feet (about 3 metres) above mean sea level where this information is known from published sources. In cases where no official elevations are available, e.g. First World War landing grounds, estimates have been made from spot heights and 25ft contours as shown on the 1 : 25 000 and 1 : 10 000 OS sheets.

Airfield Terminology

A wide variety of terms have been used over the years to denote premises laid out for aircraft operations. Some of these terms overlap in meaning, a few are virtually synonymous but others have quite distinct meanings and need to be used advisedly to avoid confusion. Aeronautical dictionaries have devoted minimal space to the nuances between different classes of flying establishments and there is no known official source which sheds light on the matter. The opportunity is therefore taken to define the main terms used in the study, in the hope that the reader may better comprehend the diversity of airfield types, both in Lincolnshire and more widely. Absolute precision is not claimed, but a special effort has been made to apply each term consistently within the confines of the present study.

AERODROME (Greek: 'aerial racecourse') normally denotes an airfield possessing facilities such as hangars, workshops, stores, offices and domestic accommodation. The term may be applied equally to military and civil stations, though most laymen agree that it tends to evoke wartime activity. During the First World War it denoted a station where aeroplane squadrons or technical units were based (in contrast to a landing ground which saw only sporadic use). In the Second World War an aerodrome was normally distinguishable from a landing ground by the possession of a control tower. The actual landing surface of an aerodrome may be paved or all-grass and a category of 'water aerodrome' is retained by the CAA for flying-boat stations. For reasons which are not altogether clear, the CAA persists in using the term as an umbrella for all kinds of airfield, regardless of size and complexity, in spite of today's popular preference for 'airfield'. The Ordnance Survey for its part has chosen to confine the term to civil establishments, e.g. Boston Aerodrome, and normally describes a military aerodrome as 'airfield'. A certain inconsistency between official bodies is apparent here although today the RAF uses the term 'aerodrome' to denote its flying stations in order to conform to the 'Safeguarding of Aerodromes' Direction contained in the Town and Country Planning Acts.

AIRCRAFT ACCEPTANCE PARK was a term peculiar to the First World War and denoted a military aerodrome where aircraft manufactured by private companies were officially tested before acceptance into the squadrons of the RFC and RNAS, later the RAF.

AIRFIELD is a term of American origin which entered the vocabulary of this country during the Second World War.

Although it is popularly considered synonymous with 'aerodrome', it is fact a generic term which covers any area of land or water, with or without facilities, set aside for the take-off and landing of aircraft. It therefore has the widest possible meaning and embraces all the other terms here defined, with the exception of decoys and sundries which were never used for flying purposes. It has proved useful to invoke when a variety of sub-types are being referred to collectively, as in the title of the present study, but for the most part it is avoided in the description of individual establishments since each of these will belong to a specific category, e.g military aerodrome, private airstrip or seaplane station.

AIRFIELD CLOSURE can prove an ambiguous term. Frequently an airfield is described as having 'closed' when regular military flying has ceased, even when some other defence function or Service gliding has continued. In this study the expanded term 'closed to flying' is used to distinguish the first stage of run-down from complete military evacuation and subsequent land disposal.

AIRPORT is frequently used in error to mean any kind of civil airfield, and sometimes even as a substitute for military air bases. Strictly, an airport should possess immigration controls and customs facilities for passengers and cargo arriving from abroad, on the precise analogy of a seaport. In practice, however, it is commonly used for any airfield handling regular civil air traffic, whether from outside or within the United Kingdom. A proper airport has a control tower, terminal buildings and technical facilities which may include repair shops, overnight accommodation and car parks. In Lincolnshire's case only one genuine civil airport has existed — Kirmington/Humberside — but the term was also applied to Grimsby's pre-war municipal airfield and, in more recent times, to Skegness (Ingoldmells). Despite the CAA's adherence to 'aerodrome', minor civil flying establishments are better referred to collectively as 'civil airfields' and individually as private 'airstrip', 'helipad', or whatever specific category is involved.

AIRSHIP STATION appears self-explanatory but, to avoid any confusion, this study preserves a distinction between bases for powered airship and those for kite balloons. In Lincolnshire there was only one airship station, being located on what is now the North Aerodrome at RAF Cranwell. This site is shown on the map in Part One as being exclusively devoted to airships during the First World War even though aeroplanes may on occasions have also landed there.

AIR STATION is mainly a Naval term of Second World War origin denoting a land base used by ship-borne aircraft. During the First World War, however, the kindred term 'aeroplane station' was employed in official documents to distinguish a combat aerodrome from other types of flying establishment.

AIRSTRIP is confined in this study to small private airfields which are not listed in *Air Pilot* (the CAA's official manual of flying facilities in the UK). There are no military airstrips in Lincolnshire, though in other parts of the country, such as Army training areas, a number are still used for communications flights. Civil airstrips normally consist of one or two elongated landing areas, typically no longer than 600 metres, hence the term 'strip'. Most are equipped with a small hangar, office and wind-sock for the use of farmers, businessmen or club members. The majority of airstrips have all-grass surfaces though several are based on the concrete runways of abandoned aerodromes. When an airstrip becomes sufficiently busy it is usually upgraded by the CAA into a 'civil aerodrome', e.g. Sturgate and Wickenby, and as such takes a place in the eighty-six main airfields in Part Two. Minor airstrips which have not achieved this status are listed in Appendix J.

CATEGORY OF AERODROME is the term used by the RAF since the early 1960s to denote the role for which all of its permanent aerodromes were either designed or primarily intended. Generally the specification of a particular category was based upon the performance characteristics of the aircraft for which it was intended. The tables show the categories of aerodrome in use before and after March 1981 and their main features.

From March 1981, simplified aerodrome categories were introduced by the RAF, these being based on runway length and width instead of role.

RAF Permanent Aerodrome Categories (March 1981 to date)

Category	Main Runway Length	Main Runway Width
1.	9000 ft and over	200 ft
2.	7500 ft to 9000 ft	150 ft
3.	6000 ft to 7500 ft	150 ft
4.	4500 ft to 6000 ft	150 ft
5.	Grass	–

CLASS OF AIRFIELD was a designation introduced during 1938 when it was decided that new bomber airfields should be built to set standards. The specification of the Class 'A' bomber airfield was initially set at one 1400 yards (1280 metres) main runway and two 1100 yard (1006 metre) subsidiary runways, all interconnected by a fifty feet (15 metres) wide perimeter taxiway (or 'peri-track'). The specification of the Class 'B' bomber airfield was set at one 1400 yard (1280 metres) main runway and two 900 yard (825 metres) subsidiary runways. Fighter airfields were to have two 800 yard (730 metre) runways each fifty feet (15 metres) wide.

In 1939 the length of fighter runways was increased to 1000 yards (915 metres) and by the end of 1940 the main runway length at all new airfields was set at 1600 yards (1465 metres). Finally, the specification of the Class 'A' operational airfield was increased to a main runway length of 2000 yards (1830 metres) and two subsidiary runways of 1400 yards (1280 metres). The width of all runways was set at fifty yards (45 metres).

A few Very Heavy Bomber and a few Transport airfields featured 3000 x 100 yard (2740 x 90 metres) runways but none was represented in Lincolnshire. Three emergency landing runways were constructed to still larger proportions, at Carnaby (Yorkshire), Manston (Kent) and Woodbridge (Suffolk). Although none of the emergency runways was located in Lincolnshire many Lincolnshire-based aircraft made emergency landings on them when returning from operations with heavy damage due to enemy action or with one or more engines out of action.

Following the Second World War the term 'Class A Airfield' seems to have been replaced by 'Class 1 Bomber Airfield' but the precise date of this change is unknown. However, by the mid-1960s use of the term 'class' was dropped in favour of the term 'category'. Much confusion still surrounds the precise airfield classifications used by the Royal Air Force and this is added to by frequent changes of policy and the use of 'class' and 'category' to describe other features such as the type of airfield lighting or the extent of the crash rescue facilities provided at a particular airfield.

CLASS OF LANDING GROUND was a concept peculiar to Home Defence organisation during the First World War. Landing grounds were graded into three classes according to the quality of their aerial approaches. Class 1 landing grounds were unrestricted from any direction, Class 2 subject to hazards (usually trees and buildings) from one direction while Class 3 were

Royal Air Force Permanent Aerodrome Categories (mid 1960s to March 1981)

Category	Role	Main Runway	Subsidiary Runway	Taxiway Width	Dispersal Access Track Width
1.	Medium Bomber, Strategic Transport, Strategic Reconnaissance, Long Range Maritime Patrol (Jet), Tankers, Long Range Strike/Attack.	3000 x 67 yds	Not provided	20 yds	20 yds
2.	Light Bomber, Tactical Transport.	2000 x 50 yds	1600 x 50 yds	17 yds	17 yds
3.	Fighter, Offensive Support, Tactical Reconnaissance.	2500 x 50 yds	Not provided	17 yds	17 yds
4.	Long Range Maritime Patrol (Piston).	2500 x 50 yds	Not provided	20 yds	17 yds
5.	Advanced Flying Schools.	2000 x 50 yds	1800 x 50 yds	17 yds	10 yds
6.	Basic Flying Schools	1500 x 50 yds	1300 x 50 yds	17 yds	10 yds

obstructed on more than one side. In very broad terms the Class 1 fields tended to be the largest but the relationship between size and quality was not a very hard and fast one. Landing grounds were also sub-divided on another basis - lit and unlit. This denoted which were suitable for night use and official records specifiy Night Landing Grounds and Day Landing Grounds in addition to their approachability class. Changes of class and day/night designation were quite frequent during the operational life of a landing ground.

The term 'Emergency Landing Ground' is often associated with First World War landing grounds. The origin of this term is obscure as it is not used in official documents and aerodrome directories of the period.

DECOY AIRFIELD is fully explained in Appendix F but may be briefly defined here as an imitation (dummy or spoof) airfield designed to lure enemy aircraft away from genuine aerodromes. Since they had no aircraft movements they cannot be classed as airfields proper and in consequence are excluded from Part Two. They are, however, too distinctive to be classed under 'Sundry Sites' and have for that reason been listed separately.

DISUSED AIRFIELD applies in general to any site where powered aircraft no longer operate on a regular basis. Aeronautical Charts today depict those which were once fully-fledged aerodromes with a cross inside a circle. The term is somewhat ambiguous, however, since certain officially disused sites may retain aeronautical functions such as gliding, missiles or radar. These latter are therefore sometimes described as 'inactive' or 'dormant' where they remain serviceable and could conceivably be re-activated. Only those already relinquished by the government and converted to alternative land uses should be classed as genuinely 'disused', a criterion which has been observed in the study. Terms such as 'surplus', which implies continued government ownership during obsolescence, and 'abandoned', which evokes vacancy or dereliction, are avoided unless those precise conditions apply.

FLIGHT STATION was a term applied during the First World War to an aerodrome at which a Flight (A, B or C) of aeroplanes was deployed by a Home Defence Squadron. It was analogous to a Second World War fighter aerodrome and had servicing facilities, domestic accommodation (huts and tents) and administrative offices. The term was coined at the time to differentiate the operational aerodromes from their parent squadron's HQ which in many cases was at a house with no airfield alongside. It may also have been derived from 'aeroplane station' which was in use before the expansion of the Home Defence programme during 1916.

FLYING FIELD is an archaic term with connotations of aeronautical experiment. In Part Two it is restricted to one private site which was used for ferrying new aeroplanes from an adjacent factory to nearby RFC stations. The essence of a flying field was *outward* movement of aeroplanes (in contrast to a landing ground), though machines obviously landed there occasionally on pre-meditated journeys. Between the wars the term was used loosely to denote a minor civil airfield, such as Louth (Kenwick Road), similar to a private modern airstrip.

GRASS AERODROME refers to any well equipped aeroplane base which retains an unclad and vegetated landing area, whether for civil or military purposes. During the Second World War several grass aerodromes in Lincolnshire were fitted with paved perimeter tracks and dispersals, but their actual landing areas remained soft. In other parts of the country it was common for grass-based fighter aerodromes to have temporary steel tracking laid as a substitute for concrete. In the map in Part One the term 'grass aerodrome' is confined to military stations, grass civil aerodromes being merged for simplicity with the paved type.

HELIPAD is a small installation, often within urban premises, and with a capacity for handling only a limited number of private helicopters.

HELIPORT denotes a base from which commercial helicopters operate in substantial numbers with full servicing arrangements and space for take-off runs. Lincolnshire's only current heliport is located at Strubby, an ex-RAF aerodrome which was sold in March 1980.

KITE BALLOON STATION was a peculiarity of the First World War. Kite balloons were manned, engineless, airships towed behind naval vessels for spotting enemy shipping and submarines. As such aircraft were mobile, the places where they were serviced and connected up to ships are rightly considered by aero historians as a bona fide category of airfield (unlike barrage balloon sites). Kite balloon stations were almost invariably located at or close to traditional harbours, such as Milford Haven, Lowestoft and, in Lincolnshire's case, Immingham.

LANDING GROUND refers to an airfield without any buildings or facilities to service aircraft or accommodate personnel. The term is essentially military in its connotation, though between the wars there were civil landing grounds, mostly in southern England, for emergency use by airliners and private pilots under a scheme organised by the Automobile Association. In Lincolnshire there were no such civil landing grounds, though during the First World War the military equivalent had proliferated as part of the Home Defence patrol system (see Class of Landing Ground). During the Second World War there were comparatively few in the eastern counties due to the predominance of heavy bomber aerodromes, though Theddlethorpe and Holbeach ranges had LGs for communications and emergency use. As the term implies, the purpose was for *landings* rather than planned outward missions.

MASTER DIVERSION AERODROME is the term applied to a number of the RAF's major airfields which remain open twenty four hours a day in order to provide alternatives should an aircraft have to divert from its planned destination due to bad weather or in the event of an airborne emergency. Leeming, Leuchars, Lossiemouth, Lyneham, Manston, St Mawgan, Valley, Waddington and Wattisham, are each provided with radio aids and facilities necessary to handle all types of RAF aircraft. Up to mid-1980 Leeming and Manston were also provided with runway foam laying equipment. Lincolnshire's only MDA is Waddington although Coningsby has undertaken the commitment on occasions when the former has been closed for such reasons as runway re-surfacing. Following a rationalisation of its requirements, the RAF dropped the use of the term 'MDA' and diversion aerodromes were renamed 'Military Emergency Diversion Aerodromes' with effect from 1st May 1982.

MILITARY AIRFIELD is sometimes used to distinguish an RAF station from a Royal Naval Air Station (or Naval Airfield). During the First World War the terms 'military aerodrome' and 'military landing ground' were used to denote RFC stations as opposed to those operated by the RNAS ('naval aerodrome', etc). By the Second World War however, the 'military' epithet was generally accepted as encompassing all three Armed Services. Today the term has been further extended to include experimental airfields such as RAE Farnborough.

MILITARY EMERGENCY DIVERSION AERODROME was the term introduced by the RAF on 1st May 1982 following a rationalisation of its requirements for diversion aerodrome facilities.

MISSILE SITE is fairly self-explanatory though opinion is divided as to whether it should be considered a genuine airfield sub-category. Some argue that missiles are not aircraft because they are unmanned. The reason for including missile sites in the map in Part One derives from the fact that they were all placed on former aerodromes which thereby enjoyed an extension of their active lives. With the exception of North Coates, the main operational period of missile sites in Lincolnshire was from 1957 until 1963.

PAVED AERODROME refers to any airfield possessing concrete, bitumen or other hard runways. Paved perimeter tracks and aprons alone do not allow an airfield to be considered 'paved'. In this study the definition embraces about two-thirds of all Second World War military airfields, a minority of which survive as active RAF bases, CAA-licensed civil aerodromes and gliding sites.

RELIEF LANDING GROUND is a coinage of the inter-war period when flying training began to cause congestion. RLGs proliferated during the Second World War though Lincolnshire had few at that stage. Today the term denotes an aerodrome retained as an overspill landing area for an extra-busy RAF base. The RAF College, for example, has its main RLG at Barkston Heath which in former days enjoyed independent station status. Modern RLG's have usually inherited paved runways, hangars and control towers but are not permanently manned and are very much demoted establishments.

SATELLITE AIRFIELD was a characteristic phenomenon of the Second World War when the density of active flying reached its historic peak. Many bomber and fighter bases had one or two 'satellites' which helped in the deployment of aircraft which could not be accommodated in the numbers required at a single base. Satellites were fully manned aerodromes and separately equipped with runway lighting, etc., and should not be confused with the more subordinate RLGs referred to immediately above. They were also quite different from 'satellite landing grounds' which served as dispersed fields for Maintenance Units mainly located in the Wessex region.

SEAPLANE STATION in the Lincolnshire context is a category peculiar to the First World War. Seaplane (and flying boat) stations are classed as a sub-category of airfield only where they possess proper slipways, hangars, sheds and technical facilities, otherwise they are better described as 'SP/FB anchorages'. Today the term 'marine airfield (or aerodrome)' is used by the CAA in its publications. At RNAS Killingholme the slipways etc had a landing ground alongside for amphibious aeroplanes.

STATION is a term commonly used to alleviate repetition when referring to any shore-based military site that is broadly of a size that necessitates an establishment of a Commanding Officer and substantial personnel (see also Flight Station, Kite Balloon Station and Seaplane Station).

SUNDRY SITE is used in this study to embrace any military establishment connected with aerial warfare which was neither an active airfield (within Part Two), missile site or decoy. The several functions which fall within this residual classification are set out in Appendix H.

TRAINING DEPOT STATION was used during the First World War for an aerodrome devoted to the training of pilots for active service. It was very similar in function to a modern Flying Training School but, because the training process was then so much less sophisticated, it also combined the role of an Operational Conversion Unit. Compared with Home Defence or Naval Flight Stations, a TDS had quite elaborate facilities for the period, including numerous hangars (or 'aeroplane sheds') and accommodation for a large personnel.

REFERENCES

Air Ministry, *AP3024: Flying Control in the Royal Air Force*, First edition, August 1944.
Gunston, Bill, *Jane's Aerospace Dictionary*, Jane's, 1980.
Ministry of Defence, *AP3384 Volume 1: RAF Layout Specifications and Safeguarding Criteria for Permanent Aerodromes* Third Edition, March 1981.
Wragg, David, *A Dictionary of Aviation*, Osprey: Reading, 1973.

Abbreviations

AA	Anti-Aircraft
AACU	Anti-Aircraft Co-operation Unit
AADA	Advance Air Depot Area (USAAF)
A & AEE	Aeroplane & Armament Experimental Establishment
AAP	Aircraft Acceptance Park
AAS	Air Armament School
ABG	Air Base Group (USAF)
ABS	Air Base Squadron (USAF)
ACS	Aircrew School
ADV	Air Defence Variant
AEU	Aircrew Educational Unit
AFB	Air Force Base (USAF)
AFC	Air Force Cross
AFDS	Air Fighting Development Squadron
AFM	Air Force Medal
AFS	Advanced Flying School
AFU	Advanced Flying Unit
AGLT	Automatic Gun Laying Turret
AMSL	Above mean sea level
AMU	Aircraft Modification Unit
AOS	Air Observers School
ARS	Air Rescue Squadron (USAF)
ASV	Air to Surface Vessel
ATA	Air Transport Auxiliary
ATS	Armament Training School
ATU	Aircrew Transit Unit
AWJRU	All Weather Jet Refresher Unit
BAPC	British Aircraft Preservation Council
BAT	Beam Approach Training
BBMF	Battle of Britain Memorial Flight
BD	Bomb Disposal
BDT	Bomber Defence Training
BFTS	Basic Flying Training School
BG	Bombardment Group (USAAF)
BGA	British Gliding Association
(B)G	(Bomber) Gunnery
CAA	Civil Aviation Authority
CAG	Civil Air Guard
CAW	College of Air Warfare
CFE	Central Fighter Establishment
CFS	Central Flying School
CGS	Central Gunnery School
Comm	Communications
Conv	Conversion

CTU	Conversion Training Unit
CU	Conversion Unit
Det	Detachment
DFC	Distinguished Flying Cross
DFM	Distinguished Flying Medal
EAAS	Empire Air Armament School
ECAS	Empire Central Armament School
EGS	Elementary Gliding School
ELG	Emergency Landing Ground
E & RFTS	Elementary and Reserve Flying Training School
E & WS	Electrical and Wireless School
FCTU	Fighter Command Trials Unit
FG	Fighter Group (USAAF)
FIDO	Fog Investigation and Dispersal Operation
FIS	Flying Instructors School
Flt	Flight
FRS	Flying Refresher School
FS	Fighter Squadron (USAAF)
FSS	Flying Selection School
FTG	Fighter Training Group (USAAF)
FTS	Flying Training School
GAS	Ground Armament School
GC	Gliding Centre
GCA	Ground Controlled Approach
GCI	Ground Controlled Interception
GDGS	Ground Defence Gunnery School
Gp	Group
GS	Gliding School
HAS	Hardened Aircraft Shelters
ha	Hectare(s) [2.47 acres]
HCB	Heavy Conversion Base
HCU	Heavy Conversion Unit
HD	Home Defence
HGCU	Heavy Glider Conversion Unit
HSL	High Speed Launch
IRBM	Intermediate Range Ballistic Missile
ITS	Initial Training School
IWM	Imperial War Museum
JSTU	Joint Services Trials Unit
LACW	Leading Aircraftwomen
LAM	Lincolnshire Aviation Museum
LAPS	Lincolnshire Aircraft Preservation Society
LC	Lincoln Conversion
LFS	Lancaster Finishing School
LRPTE	Long Range Pilot Training Element
MAP	Ministry of Aircraft Production
MDA	Master Diversion Aerodrome
MEDA	Military Emergency Diversion Aerodrome
MSU	Major Servicing Unit
MT	Mechanical Transport
MU	Maintenance Unit
OCU	Operational Conversion Unit

ORP	Operational Readiness Platform
OS	Ordnance Survey
OTU	Operational Training Unit
(P)AFU	(Pilot) Advanced Flying Unit
PFA	Popular Flying Association
PFF	Pathfinder Force
PRO	Public Records Office
PRU	Photographic Reconnaissance Unit
RAAF	Royal Australian Air Force
RAE	Royal Aircraft Establishment
RAF	Royal Air Force
RAFC	Royal Air Force College
RAF FC	Royal Air Force Flying College
RAFGSA	Royal Air Force Gliding and Soaring Association
RCAF	Royal Canadian Air Force
Res	Reserve
RFC	Royal Flying Corps
RLG	Relief Landing Ground
RMLI	Royal Marines Light Infantry
RNZAF	Royal New Zealand Air Force
RS	Radio Shool
RTP	Recruit Training Pool
SAC	Strategic Air Command (USAF)
SAM	Surface to Air Missile
SAMOTS	Surface to Air Missile Operational Training School
SCBS	Strike Command Bombing School
SD	Special Duty
SFTS	Service Flying Training School
SFW	Strategic Fighter Wing (USAF)
SoRF	School of Refresher Flying
S of RT	School of Recruit Training
S of TT	School of Technical Training
Sqn	Squadron
SS	Submarine Scout
STC	Strike Command
SU	Signals Unit
TAD	Tactical Air Depot
TCG	Troop Carrier Group (USAAF)
TCS	Troop Carrier Squadron (USAAF)
TCW	Troop Carrier Wing (USAAF)
TDS	Training Depot Station
Trg	Training
TS	Training Squadron
TT	Target Tow
USAAC	United States Army Air Corps
USAAF	United States Army Air Force
USAF	United States Air Force
VC	Victoria Cross
WRAF	Women's Royal Air Force
WT	Wireless Telegraphy

PART ONE

THE DEVELOPMENT OF AIRFIELDS IN LINCOLNSHIRE

Cranwell's airship station under construction during 1917 (*RAF Museum P1065*)

THE EVOLUTION OF AIRFIELDS
IN LINCOLNSHIRE SINCE 1914

● Military Aerodrome (Paved) ⬢ Airship Station ▼ Kite Balloon Station

◐ Military Aerodrome (Grass) ⊡ Factory Flying Field ⊗ Gliding Site

○ Military Landing Ground + Missile Site

△ Seaplane Station ⊙ Civil Aerodrome

0 10 50 Kms

0 10 30 Miles

1	ANWICK	44	KELSTERN (1)
2	BARDNEY	45	KELSTERN (2)
3	BARKSTON HEATH	46	KILLINGHOLME
4	BINBROOK	47	KIRMINGTON/HUMBERSIDE
5	BLYBOROUGH	48	KIRTON IN LINDSEY (1)/MANTON
6	BLYTON	49	KIRTON IN LINDSEY (2)
7	BOSTON (WYBERTON FEN)	50	LEADENHAM
8	BRACEBRIDGE HEATH	51	LINCOLN (HANDLEY PAGE FIELD)
9	BRACEBY	52	LINCOLN (WEST COMMON)
10	BUCKMINSTER	53	LUDBOROUGH
11	BUCKNALL	54	LUDFORD MAGNA
12	CAISTOR	55	MANBY
13	CAMMERINGHAM/INGHAM	56	MARKET DEEPING
14	CLEETHORPES BEACH	57	METHERINGHAM
15	COCKTHORNE	58	MOORBY
16	COLEBY GRANGE	59	NEW HOLLAND
17	CONINGSBY	60	NORTH COATES
18	CRANWELL (NORTH)	61	NORTH KILLINGHOLME
19	CRANWELL (SOUTH)	62	NORTH WITHAM
20	CROWLAND/POSTLAND	63	SANDTOFT
21	CUXWOLD	64	SCAMPTON/BRATTLEBY
22	DIGBY/SCOPWICK	65	SCUNTHORPE (EMMANUEL)
23	DONNA NOOK	66	SKEGNESS (BURGH ROAD)
24	DUNHOLME LODGE	67	SKEGNESS (WINTHORPE)
25	EAST KIRKBY	68	SKEGNESS (INGOLDMELLS)
26	ELSHAM	69	SKELLINGTHORPE
27	ELSHAM WOLDS	70	SOUTH CARLTON
28	FALDINGWORTH	71	SPALDING (WESTON MARSH)
29	FISKERTON	72	SPILSBY
30	FOLKINGHAM	73	SPITALGATE/GRANTHAM
31	FREISTON	74	STRUBBY
32	FULBECK	75	STURGATE
33	GAINSBOROUGH	76	SUTTON BRIDGE
34	GOSBERTON	77	SWINDERBY
35	GOXHILL	78	SWINSTEAD
36	GREENLAND TOP	79	THEDDLETHORPE
37	GRIMSBY (WALTHAM)	80	TYDD ST MARY
38	HARLAXTON	81	WADDINGTON
39	HEMSWELL/HARPSWELL	82	WELLINGORE
40	HIBALDSTOW	83	WICKENBY
41	HOLBEACH RANGE	84	WILLOUGHBY HILLS
42	HOLBEACH ST JOHNS/FENLAND	85	WINTERTON
43	IMMINGHAM	86	WOODHALL SPA

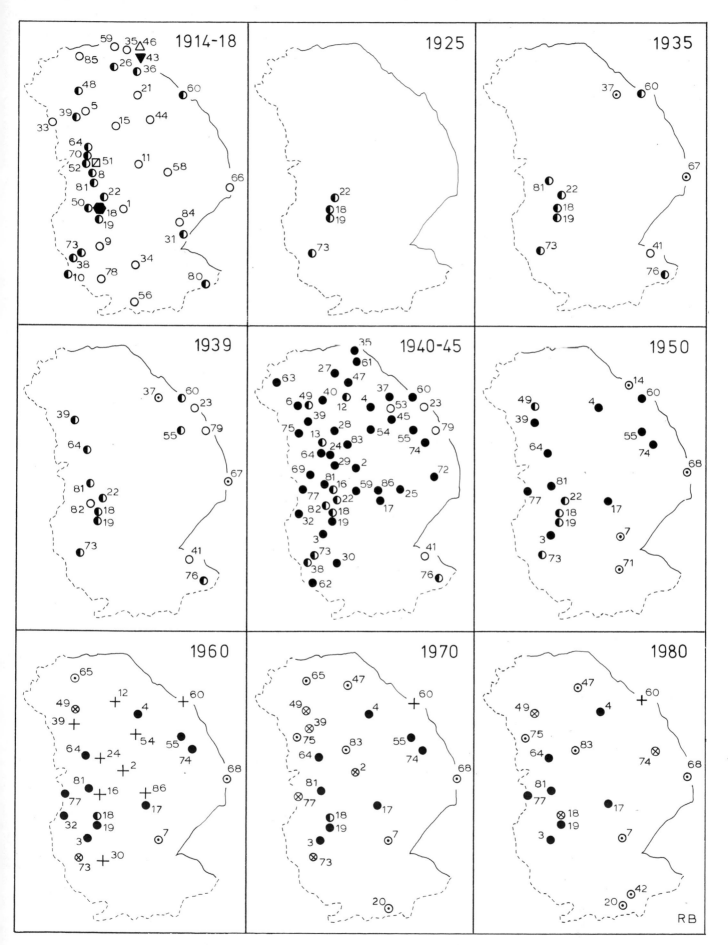

Military Development

When the Royal Flying Corps was formed, on 13th May 1912, there were only a handful of military airfields in Britain, all of them in the south of England. It was the expansion of military flying in 1913 which brought the essentially rural county of Lincolnshire into the permanent realm of aviation when officers of the Royal Flying Corps began to make flights from the home of military aviation at Farnborough, Hampshire, to a new base at Montrose in eastern Scotland. This journey could take anything up to nine days to accomplish due to frequent stops for refuelling and servicing, and ground crews would have to travel in advance of the aeroplanes to prepare landing places. Once the aeroplanes had taken off again the ground staff would move on by road and the sites could revert to their former use. The pattern of staging posts was clearly quite fluid at that period, pilots often having to make unscheduled landings because of unforeseen difficulties. It is definitely known that a field to the east of Lincoln (probably off Nettleham Road) was used by RFC pilots during some of these up-country flights and it seems likely that they had prior knowledge of its suitability as a landing ground.

By the time the First World War broke out in August 1914 only a rudimentary plan had been evolved for the protection of Britain from aerial attack, and after much argument between the War Office and the Admiralty, the task of Home Defence formally passed to the latter in September 1914. However, with the apparent failure of the Royal Naval Air Service to cope with the Zeppelin raids of 1915, Home Defence duties were handed back to the Royal Flying Corps early in 1916. In March 1916 ten new squadrons were formed specifically for Home Defence purposes and by July a barrage line of search-lights, anti-aircraft guns and aerodromes had been established throughout the Eastern Counties.

Home Defence squadrons normally had their headquarters in a spacious house commandeered by the War Office, with three Flights detached at aerodromes known as 'Flight Stations'. Because the aeroplanes in use at that time had limited range, it was found necessary to establish a system of relief landing grounds at convenient intervals throughout a particular squadron's territory. No. 33 Squadron, for example, whose HQ was in the Lincolnshire town of Gainsborough, had aerodromes at Brattleby, Elsham and Kirton in Lindsey; plus some twenty landing grounds, nine of which were in Lincolnshire and the remainder in Yorkshire and Nottinghamshire.

The landing grounds mostly consisted of a single field, or perhaps two or three combined, for which the owner was paid a small retainer by the War Office to keep the site under grass. An airman was sometimes billeted with the farmer and supplied with a telephone link to the nearest Flight Station so that when an aeroplane was likely to land, the fields could first be cleared of livestock. Some of the better-used landing grounds boasted a permanent staff of three and a couple of wooden huts for living quarters and stores such as fuel, flares and spare parts. Flight Stations had somewhat larger grass surfaces and were equipped with canvas 'Bessoneau' hangars and a few smaller buildings accommodating pilots and technical assistants. It was only at training aerodromes that stoutly-built hangars (known then as 'aeroplane sheds') became commonplace.

By the middle of 1916 the need for front-line aircrews had grown to such an extent that training aerodromes began to spring up throughout the country. In many cases a Home Defence Flight Station was enlarged for training purposes, the best example being Brattleby (later renamed 'Scampton'). It was normal for a training aerodrome at that time to house three training squadrons and with the formation of the Royal Air Force in April 1918 training aerodromes were re-organised into 'Training Depot Stations'. To simplify administration these were grouped into 'Wings' each comprising two aerodromes with their HQ and repair shops at the larger of the two stations. With the decrease in Zeppelin activity in 1918 Home Defence Squadrons themselves began to undertake training duties and many of Lincolnshire's aerodromes ended the War in essentially non-combatant roles.

It would be misleading, however, to think of Lincolnshire as being exclusively occupied by the RFC between 1914 and 1918. Along the coast the Royal Naval Air Service had a seaplane base, a kite balloon base, an air gunnery school and several patrol aerodromes, while inland at Cranwell it had a huge airship training station. Of a very different character, there were also two Aircraft Acceptance Parks on the outskirts of Lincoln where aeroplanes manufactured by firms in the town were officially tested. Over the four years Lincolnshire in fact acquired representatives of every main category of military airfield known at that period, which in retrospect has made it a most instructive, as well as a prolific, county for the aero-historian to study. There were thirty-seven military airfields within the county boundary during the First World War, plus one just inside Nottinghamshire adjacent to Gainsborough.

At the end of the hostilities in November 1918 the Royal Air Force began to run down, most of the Home Defence Squadrons soldiering on as training units until the middle of 1919 when they were finally disbanded. The canvas and wooden buildings at the Flight Stations were soon removed and all obvious traces quickly disappeared. By late 1919 the Training Depot Stations also began running down but, as their hangars and other buildings were more numerous and more permanently built, they took rather longer to erase and a few have even survived to this day. By 1925 only four aerodromes remained active: Cranwell's twin fields and Digby used for flying training,

and Spitalgate as the county's sole representative of aerial defence. This was the period of the 'Geddes Axe' when cuts on government spending had savagely reduced the Air Ministry's budget, leaving fewer than fifty stations active on home soil out of more than 400 in 1918. `

For the next ten years there was little change in Lincolnshire apart from the formation of a Special Reserve Bomber Squadron at Waddington in 1926 and the adoption of North Coates and Sutton Bridge as Armament Training Camps in 1928. However, by the early 1930s the menace of Nazi Germany, combined with high unemployment in Britain, brought this static period in military aviation to an effective close. In 1935 the government announced the RAF Expansion Scheme which heralded Lincolnshire's second great epoch of airfield construction.

As the expansion gathered pace several of the county's older airfields, for example Waddington, were modernised; others such as Hemswell and Scampton were re-occupied after years under the plough, while totally new sites were taken over at Manby and Kirton in Lindsey. RAF stations built during this period are easily recognised by their stout brick hangars and

Page 20: **The standard hangar designs of the First World War featured 'Belfast' style roof trusses, as in this view of DH.4s at Harlaxton on 13th April 1917.** *(Crown copyright/RAF photo H2379)*

Right: **One of the first military aircraft to operate in the County, Bristol TB.8 No.153 formed part of Commander Samson's Eastchurch Squadron and was based at Skegness (Burgh Road) in 1914.** *(via M. Hodgson)*

Below: **Armament Practice Camps were located at North Coates and Sutton Bridge from the 1920s. Aircraft of 35 and 207 Sqns are parked in front of the Bessoneau hangars at North Coates in the early 1930s.** *(Flt Lt S. Fine via Roy Bonser)*

Above: **Expansion: 'C' type hangars and the technical site nearly complete at Scampton, 1938.** *(via P.H.T.Green)*

Centre: **A typical pre-Second World War scene at an expansion airfield - Gladiators of 73 Sqn parked in front of one of Digby's 'C' type hangars during 1938.** *(via E.Longhurst)*

Below: **This 50 Sqn Hampden was photographed on the day that the Second World War began, 3rd September 1939, at Waddington.** *(W.Baker via P.H.T.Green)*

Above: **One of the many squadrons to operate Spitfires from Lincolnshire was 65 (East India), represented by P8147 at Kirton in Lindsey in June 1941.** *(IWM CH2920)*

Centre: **During the 1950s, the station emblem was often applied to aircraft as well as the usual squadron markings. Scampton's aircraft carried a 'speedbird', as on this 18 Sqn Canberra B.2.** *(Air-Britain)*

Below: **The nuclear deterrent-Vulcans of 27 Sqn armed with the Blue Steel stand-off bomb lurk in early morning mist at Scampton.** *(via M.Hodgson)*

communal sites and their generally compact layouts. At the outbreak of the Second World War in September 1939 the number of military aerodromes in Lincolnshire had reached ten, plus four landing grounds. Kirton in Lindsey was still under construction and a small civil airport near Grimsby was awaiting requisition.

Just prior to the war Lincolnshire contained a fair mixture of bomber, fighter and training units but, with the commencement of hostilities, some of the training units were moved 'behind the lines' to bases over on the west coast. During the Battle of Britain fighter aircraft operated from Digby and Kirton in Lindsey, though the limelight at that stage was naturally stolen by stations in Kent and Essex. By 1941, however, when the British counter-offensive against industrial Germany was gathering momentum, Lincolnshire's strategic location for bomber aerodromes began to realise its full potential. Out of some three dozen new aerodromes commisioned during the war itself, the great majority were operational Bomber Command stations, the remainder being mostly fighter stations lending support to bomber formations. By the end of hostilities in 1945 Lincolnshire contained forty-nine military airfields, more than any other county in Britain. Although lacking the obvious variety of functions present in 1918, it could nevertheless boast units engaged in coastal patrol, armament practice and flying training as well as guests from the United States Army Air Force.

One important innovation during the Second World War was the introduction of the paved runway arrangement. In 1939 even the largest bomber aircraft could operate from all-grass aerodromes provided that the soil was not too heavy. With the conversion of bomber squadrons to four-engine aircraft, and the inevitable construction of new aerodromes in zones of inferior drainage, the paved runway became a necessity. Many of the aerodromes built during the 1935-39 Expansion were enlarged and retrospectively equipped with paved runways, bringing their surfaces up to the standard of aerodromes conceived during the war itself. Because Lincolnshire had such a preponderance of Bomber Command stations, more than three-quarters of all its airfields gained paved runways and of the remaining grass type the majority had a concrete perimeter track. Another distinctive feature of bomber stations built during the war was the steel 'T2' type hangar, some of which were added to the older stations, thereby producing interesting comparisons of architectural style in the landscape.

As soon as the Second World War ended, a massive contraction immediately took place in the RAF and virtually all the aerodromes constructed under the wartime emergency were vacated by flying units, though still kept under 'Care and Maintenance'. Broadly the pattern of active stations returned to what it had been just before the war, with the RAF concentrating its flying at places with permanently built hangars and well-appointed domestic accomodation. In the early 'fifties the RAF was expanded somewhat but this did not result in the re-activation of many of the aerodromes which had already been closed to flying. As front-line squadrons gradually converted to jet aircraft, the main runways at principal aerodromes, notably V-Bomber bases at Scampton and Waddington, were extended to around 3,000 yards and their domestic sites greatly increased in capacity. Even some of the less important aerodromes, e.g. Spilsby and Sturgate, had runway extensions in anticipation of the giant American Boeing B-52 bomber which in the event was never permanently based in Great Britain.

Probably the most memorable change during this period was the controversial Defence White Paper of 1957 which involved a substantial reduction in both fighter and training strength. Between 1958 and 1963 nine disused airfields in Lincolnshire were converted to house 'Thor' and 'Bloodhound' missiles in place of the traditional fighter cover, two of the airfields concerned — Hemswell and North Coates — only recently having closed as operational flying stations. Although the missile programme itself became obsolete after five years, none of the aerodromes concerned was re-opened to regular flying and during this turbulent phase a gradual run-down took place at other active stations such as Kirton in Lindsey, Spitalgate and Swinderby as part of the planned rationalisation of the RAF.

During the late 'sixties and early 'seventies all Lincolnshire's surviving operational airfields managed to stay active, but after further re-appraisals of defence costs, Strubby and Manby were closed down in 1972 and 1974 respectively, and Service gliding wound up at Spitalgate and Hemswell. Today, only eight stations remain officially on the active flying list compared with nearly three times that number in 1955. Since the early 'sixties there has also been a major disposal of surplus airfield land with the result that many sites have ceased to be maintained and in some cases have been substantially demolished. Nevertheless, Lincolnshire still has more active RAF stations than any other county (Yorkshire has seven) and, if non-flying establishments such as Digby and North Coates are included, then unquestionably, it can still claim to hold the premier position it enjoyed in 1945.

With some seventy-seven military airfields to its credit, Lincolnshire has justly become legend in the history of British aviation. Though only a handful of stations remain active, the county still contains a substantial strike capability and the nation's most important air training establishment, both of which roles seem certain to remain for a long time to come. In spite of progressive reductions of manpower over the years, the concentration of forces at a few very large stations has ensured that the RAF remains a major employer of labour in Lincolnshire and, through the trade it brings to shops and building contractors, an important element in the county's economy.

(W. J. Taylor)

Desolate and forlorn — a runway and hangar at Spilsby in 1971

24

Right: **Ascent of a coal gas balloon at the King's Great Gala, Gainsborough, on 13th July 1874.** *(via Mrs E.H.Rudkin)*

Below: **The DH.6 G-EAWT of Martin Aviation on the beach at Cleethorpes - note Capt. Martin in the centre.** *(via P.H.T.Green)*

Civil Development

As a predominantly agricultural county situated clear of the main conurbations, Lincolnshire has never attracted a permanent aerospace industry or required busy commercial airports. Civil airfields have instead tended to be small, scattered and specialised and related to the needs of farmers, local business men, aero clubs and holiday-makers, rather than regular air links with the outside world. Since 1930 more than a dozen airfields have been listed in *Air Pilot*, the majority of which had no RAF associations whatsoever, while scores of private flying fields and airstrips are on record within the county over a somewhat longer period. The full story of civil aviation in Lincolnshire requires a book of its own and there is only space here to summarise its development and to give some indication of the locations of the airfields which it has generated.

The first known landing by an aeronaut in Lincolnshire took place at Heckington, near Sleaford, in October 1811. On that occasion James Sadler, who in 1784 had been the first English-man to ascend in a balloon, was blown 112 miles in a gale from Birmingham in just eighty minutes. Two years later Sadler made an aerial journey from Nottingham, also in a hydrogen-filled balloon, and landed at Dekin Lodge, near Stamford, where spectators paid for the privilege of watching the craft being re-inflated. The first planned ascent within the county did not take place, however, until 2nd July 1825 when Charles Green rose in his 'Royal Coronation Balloon' accompanied by a Miss Stocks, from a site known then as the 'Gas Enclosure' in Stamford. This was to be the beginning of a whole series of ascents by Green in Lincolnshire, including Stamford's Burghley Park and sites in Boston, Louth and Gainsborough. Richard Gypson, another aeronaut, made ascents at Spalding and Sleaford in 1841, whereas in 1855 J. W. Charnock of Leeds was rather less successful at Boston and incurred the anger of disappointed spectators. The latter half of the nineteenth century saw little aeronautical activity in Lincolnshire except for a gas-filled balloon which appeared at the Louth Flower Show, probably in 1898.

There is some confusion as to who was the first man to land an aeroplane in Lincolnshire, though it was probably one W. H.

Ewen (who had been issued with Royal Aero Club Aviator's Certificate No.63 on 14th February 1912) during the 'Daily Mail' circuit of Britain Race in 1912 and the site is believed to have been near the Grammar School, off Wragby Road in Lincoln. In the same year B. C. Hucks, a motor racing driver of the day, gave exhibition flights in a 70hp Bleriot Monoplane on West Common Race Course, Lincoln, which was later to be adopted as an aerodrome, and at Burghley Park, Stamford, which already had an aeronautical tradition. In the north of the county Gustav Hamel flew over from Hull to land in the People's Park at Grimsby in 1912 and also gave exhibition flights at the Lincolnshire Agricultural Show which that year was held at Skegness. In 1913 it was the turn of Hucks to give exhibitions at Skegness.

Lincolnshire's first native aviator was Montague F. Glew, second son of Walter Glew of Wittering and previously of South Kelsey. In 1913 Glew gave a demonstration in a Blackburn Monoplane at Market Rasen using a field off Legsby Road, while later the same summer he was employed to give exhibition flights at Horncastle, another of Lincolnshire's market towns. Today the very aeroplane which Glew used may be seen in the Shuttleworth Collection at Old Warden, Bedfordshire, where it often flies when weather conditions are suitable. It is believed that a site off Nettleham Road, Lincoln, was used during 1913 by both Ewen and Hucks but with the onset of war there was something of a decline in civil flying in Lincolnshire.

Despite these various activities, Lincolnshire possessed no organised flying ground when war eventually broke out. Only Lincoln's West Common race course proved suitable for use by military aeroplanes, the remainder of the flying fields having already reverted to public open spaces or farmland. During the war itself civil flying was, of course, not permitted, though several of Lincoln's established engineering firms were involved in the manufacture and test flying of aeroplanes under sub-contract from larger companies. These are described briefly under the appropriate airfields in Part Two and further details may be obtained from published works by John Walls. When the Armistice was eventually signed in November 1918 there was renewed enthusiasm for civil aviation and many surplus RAF stations were listed in *Flight* magazine as being available for private pilots by 1919. A map published in that magazine

for 1st May 1919 showed a proposed domestic air route with intermediate landing places at Harlaxton, South Carlton and New Holland, but this proposal apparently never came to fruition and none of the First World War stations in Lincolnshire was formally adopted as a permanent civil aerodrome from that time on.

For most of the 'twenties, civil flying was at a low ebb, both in Britain as a whole and especially in Lincolnshire. Pleasure trips were given from the beach in Skegness in 1919, from Lincoln's 'Handley Page Field' in 1920 and at Cleethorpes in 1921 but none of these ventures survived the first season. Some indication of Lincolnshire's aeronautical decline at that period is evident from the history of Alan Cobham's Berkshire Aviation Company which in 1919 toured thirty-four towns in Britain, not one of them in the county which recently had possessed over thirty aerodromes and landing grounds. Towards the end of the 'twenties, however, there were signs of a revival in civil activity in Lincolnshire, with Sir Alan Cobham (knighted in 1926) providing joy rides from Skegness Beach in 1928, and T. M. and G. H. Worth, the 'Flying Farmers', using a private hilltop strip at East Keal, near Spilsby, from 1927 until about 1930. During the early 'thirties Cobham organised a series of National Aviation Days, with the idea of educating the public in aviation matters, and over the four seasons 1932-35 he gave displays at Boston, Bourne, Grantham, Grimsby, Holbeach, Horncastle, Lincoln, Louth, Scunthorpe, Skegness, Sleaford, Stamford and Sutton on Sea. Unfortunately his recently published autobiography lists only the towns and leaves the locations of the actual fields to the aero historian to trace. From 1934-39 an organisation called Lincolnshire Flying Services was engaged in joy-riding and banner-towing from a field off Kenwick Road, just south of Louth, while Alex Henshaw, later of Cape Flight record fame and a well-known Second World War test-pilot, used fields at Hagnaby and Bar Fen near Mable-thorpe, his home town.

Perhaps the most significant development in this period was the establishment of permanent civil aerodromes as an alternative to casually adopted fields. Cobham was a pioneer in this move-ment and gave advice to Skegness Council on the feasibility and siting of an aerodrome. Skegness was in fact the first town in Lincolnshire to acquire a civil aerodrome, developed privately at Winthorpe, on the landward side of the Roman Bank, in 1930. This enabled more elaborate air pageants to be held and air services were operated as far as Hunstanton in Norfolk and Nottingham. The other civil aerodrome of the period was established at Waltham in 1933 and became the county's first and only pre-war municipal airport, serving the nearby town of Grimsby. From here services operated across the Humber to Hull where a number of domestic airlines regularly flew. These were, however, the only two proper aerodromes to be set up in the county before war broke out again, the county town of Lincoln remaining conspicuous by its lack of such a facility. Grimsby airport, the superior of the two, was taken over as an RAF station in 1939, while Skegness aerodrome was closed for the duration of hostilities and never re-opened for flying.

After the Second World War it was again possible for civil flying to expand, though there were several obstacles to its development. First, the RAF decided to hold on to the majority of its wartime stations indefinitely and it was unclear whether Lincoln would achieve its own airport, both for economic and military reasons. A proposal to convert Skellingthorpe aerodrome for civil flying in 1948 came to nought through a combination of costs, closeness to the built-up area (which has since consumed the site) and the high density of RAF activity around the city. The earliest post-war aerodromes to open for civil use were in fact in the extreme south-east of the county, at Boston and Spalding in 1948. Boston aerodrome, on the site of pre-war displays, was mainly used for crop-spraying activities, while Spalding was the base of a small and short-lived airline. The third new aerodrome to open in 1948 was Skegness (Ingoldmells), serving a town which had quickly revived as a popular day resort and holiday camp centre. Joy riding was revived on

Cleethorpes Beach during the early 'fifties, as it had existed between the wars, but fell out of fashion by the end of the decade.

For much of the 'sixties, civil aviation in Lincolnshire remained at a plateau, with flying and gliding clubs moving quite frequently from site to site as RAF stations changed roles. Some hint of industrial revival in the north of the county was given by the construction of airstrips at Scunthorpe in 1959, but it was not until the late 'sixties that the needs of local business executives began to express themselves in the establishment of new civil aerodromes. By this time most of the ex-RAF bomber stations had been declared surplus and disposed of and some of these provided ideal sites for small air transport firms. Wickenby, Sturgate and Kirmington, all lying between Lincoln and Humberside, each re-opened around 1970 and remain active today, the last of the three now operating as Humberside Airport, the only civic development within historic Lincolnshire since 1945. With entry into the European Economic Community, and the exploitation of North Sea oil and gas, Lincolnshire and Humberside are well placed for light industrial aviation, one interesting recent development being the establishment of a busy helicopter base at Strubby, an RAF diversion airfield which closed in 1972.

Elsewhere in the county there have been quieter changes over the last ten years or so. Entirely new civil aerodromes have been established at Crowland and Holbeach St. Johns, both in the Fens where disused military airfields are virtually non-existent. Private airstrips, mainly belonging to farmers, have grown up in all districts, from the busy RAF flying zone in the south-west to the coastal marshlands. A hill-side gliding site, a rare phenomenon in Lincolnshire, was in use at Careby, near

Left: **Mr Troop's Flying Flea at Wellingore. This aircraft is now displayed in the Lincolnshire Aviation Museum at Tattershall.** *(via M.Hodgson)*

Below: **Scheduled services from Kirmington were initially undertaken by Fokker F.27s of Air Anglia. These aircraft later operated the services in the colours of Air UK.** *(MAP).*

Stamford, contrasting with old aerodromes such as Bardney where glider launching was practised until 1978.

Looking back over nearly seventy years of civil flying in Lincolnshire two things become apparent. On the one hand, the civil side has been completely overshadowed by the presence of the RAF and it is quite understandable that relatively little is known about it outside the county. At the same time, on closer examination, the civil operations are found to have been quite prolific and without the RAF alongside these would probably have gained as much recognition as the activities of many smaller counties. As to the future, the question of an airport for Lincoln has still to be resolved, especially with the new county of Humberside developing a thriving airport which is helping to draw industrial investment northwards. Recent proposals to invest public money into Sturgate as an airport for the Lincoln area have not met with much success and have rather reinforced the idea that central and south Lincolnshire is basically a rural region which is best served by a number of smaller airfields rather than a prestigious centralised airport.

REFERENCES

Cobham, Sir A.J., *A Time to Fly,* Shepheard-Walwyn, 1978.

Davis, A., 'Swifts, biplanes and cloth caps: when Skegness went air racing', *Lincolnshire Life,* July 1974, pp 42-44.

Green, P.H.T., 'Joyride flying in Lincolnshire', *Lincolnshire Life,* August 1963, p 32.

Green, P.H.T., 'The revival of Kirmington Airfield', *Lincolnshire Life,* October 1973, pp 30-33.

Green, P.H.T., 'Kirmington: A New Airport for Hull and Grimsby', *Aviation News,* Vol.2, No.23, 12 25 April 1974, pp 6.

Henshaw, A., *The Flight of the Mew Gull,* John Murray, 1980.

Leckonby, D.P., 'British Isles Airports No.7': Humberside Airport' (in two parts), *Aircraft Illustrated,* Vol.12, November 1979, pp 523-7 and December 1979, pp 574-7.

Robinson, D.N., 'Ballooning in Lincolnshire' (in two parts), *Lincolnshire Life,* April 1971, pp 25-28 and May 1971 38-39.

Rolt, L.T.C., *The Aeronauts: A History of Ballooning 1783-1903,* Longman 1966.

G-BCDD

AIR ANGLIA

PART TWO

THE AIRFIELDS

Air-to-ground view of most of Spilsby, 28 March 1962.(*RAF Museum P3395*)

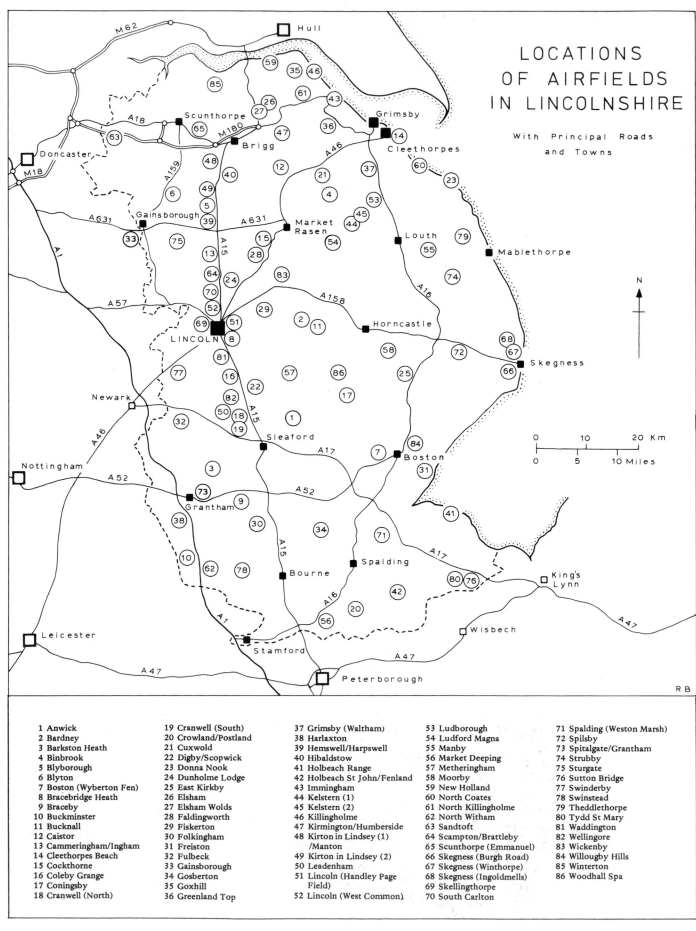

LOCATIONS OF AIRFIELDS IN LINCOLNSHIRE

With Principal Roads and Towns

1 Anwick
2 Bardney
3 Barkston Heath
4 Binbrook
5 Blyborough
6 Blyton
7 Boston (Wyberton Fen)
8 Bracebridge Heath
9 Braceby
10 Buckminster
11 Bucknall
12 Caistor
13 Cammeringham/Ingham
14 Cleethorpes Beach
15 Cockthorne
16 Coleby Grange
17 Coningsby
18 Cranwell (North)

19 Cranwell (South)
20 Crowland/Postland
21 Cuxwold
22 Digby/Scopwick
23 Donna Nook
24 Dunholme Lodge
25 East Kirkby
26 Elsham
27 Elsham Wolds
28 Faldingworth
29 Fiskerton
30 Folkingham
31 Freiston
32 Fulbeck
33 Gainsborough
34 Gosberton
35 Goxhill
36 Greenland Top

37 Grimsby (Waltham)
38 Harlaxton
39 Hemswell/Harpswell
40 Hibaldstow
41 Holbeach Range
42 Holbeach St John/Fenland
43 Immingham
44 Kelsham (1)
45 Kelstern (2)
46 Killingholme
47 Kirmington/Humberside
48 Kirton in Lindsey (1)
   /Manton
49 Kirton in Lindsey (2)
50 Leadenham
51 Lincoln (Handley Page
   Field)
52 Lincoln (West Common)

53 Ludborough
54 Ludford Magna
55 Manby
56 Market Deeping
57 Metheringham
58 Moorby
59 New Holland
60 North Coates
61 North Killingholme
62 North Witham
63 Sandtoft
64 Scampton/Brattleby
65 Scunthorpe (Emmanuel)
66 Skegness (Burgh Road)
67 Skegness (Winthorpe)
68 Skegness (Ingoldmells)
69 Skellingthorpe
70 South Carlton

71 Spalding (Weston Marsh)
72 Spilsby
73 Spitalgate/Grantham
74 Strubby
75 Sturgate
76 Sutton Bridge
77 Swinderby
78 Swinstead
79 Theddlethorpe
80 Tydd St Mary
81 Waddington
82 Wellingore
83 Wickenby
84 Willougby Hills
85 Winterton
86 Woodhall Spa

R B

Anwick

1 km NNW of Anwick Church
121/TF 110 515   30 ft (10 m) AMSL

A class 2 landing ground was established at Anwick for the use of 38 (Home Defence) Squadron during the time it operated over South Lincolnshire, from September 1916 to May 1918. Originally unlit, suggesting day use only, lighting was installed later, and from August 1918 to June 1919 it was used by 90 (Home Defence) Squadron. The landing ground as a whole covered 54 acres (22 ha), its two strips measuring 530 and 550 yards. Today it is farmland.

Bardney

2.5 km NE of Bardney Church
121/TF 140 710   40 ft (12 m) AMSL

Construction of this station began during 1942, but completion was delayed due to a shortage of materials, and it was eventually opened in early 1943 under the control of 5 Group, Bomber Command. The first operational unit to arrive was 9 Squadron whose Avro Lancasters landed for the first time at Bardney upon return from operations on 14th April. No. 53 Base was formed at Waddington on 15th November of that year with Bardney as one of its sub-stations, although it was quickly upgraded to full station status. The station's first Commanding Officer, Group Captain A C Evan-Evans, was succeeded by Group Captain Pleasance who

was tragically posted missing while flying on operations with Flying Officer Manning of 9 Squadron during the night of 22-23rd March 1944.

The first 12,000 lb 'Tallboy' bomb to be delivered to the station arrived on 31st August 1944, and it was with this weapon that 9 Squadron combined with 617 Squadron from Woodhall Spa to sink the German battleship the *Tirpitz*. In a raid on Munich on 26th November all 9 Squadron aircraft carried the 'Tallboy', the first time that the new weapon had been dropped on a city and, in order to accomplish the mission, all Squadron aircraft took off at 3,000 lb above maximum all-up weight.

While 9 Squadron was engaged in the *Tirpitz* operations the Headquarters unit

Above: **A 12,000 lb 'Tallboy' bomb on its trolley in the bomb store at Bardney during 1945.** *(Bill Baguley/Rod Houldsworth)*

Below: **Lancaster ED856 of 9 Sqn preparing to take off from Bardney.** *(IWM HU2353)*

and 'A' Flight of 227 Squadron formed at Bardney. After a short work-up the new squadron moved to Balderton in Nottinghamshire on 21st October to join 'B' Flight which had been attached to Strubby. At the same time 189 Squadron formed at Bardney, became operational on 1st November and moved to Fulbeck the next day. 1945 began with the honour of a posthumous Victoria Cross on 20th Feburary, awarded to Flight Sergeant George Thompson for gallantry during a daylight attack on the Dortmund—Ems Canal on New Years Day.

The Bomber Command Film Unit formed at Bardney on 21st March 1945 and moved to Fulbeck on 8th April, the day that 189 Squadron returned to Bardney. A short time later preparations commenced within 5 Group for Operation *Tiger,* the aerial offensive against Japan by the RAF. It was decided that all *Tiger Force* units would concentrate at stations which offered full facilities; as a result 9 Squadron moved to Waddington on 6th July. Before preparations were complete the *Tiger Force* was disbanded and the ground element of 551 Wing, one of the *Tiger Force* contingents, moved to Bardney from Woodhall Spa, whereupon it disbanded.

The main body of the last resident unit, 189 Squadron, moved to Metheringham on 15th October and the station started to run down. Placed on Care and Maintenance from 10th December 1945, the War Office took over the station and the 53rd (Field) Holding Regiment Royal Artillery formed there. A further sub-tenant of the station was a Ministry of Supply unit.

Although closed to all flying, the main runway remained open for emergency use, but in 1949 the station was handed to the Ministry of Agriculture for letting to local farmers. Lincoln Aero Club started activities from the aerodrome in 1955 but in 1958 was forced to leave because part of the runway was needed for a Douglas Thor missile site. To this end 106 Squadron reformed in July 1959

and moved in with three missiles as part of the Hemswell Missile Wing within 1 Group Bomber Command, operating at Bardney until May 1963 when the missiles were withdrawn.

In October 1964 the initial meeting of the Lincolnshire Gliding Club was held at Bardney and flying commenced with EoN Baby BGA1252. However, although the club received the permission of Bardney's tenant it was unable to gain the permission of the landowners, the Air Ministry, and was forced to cease gliding activities at Bardney. The club then moved to Swinderby and during 1965 and 1966 the 680 acre (270 ha) airfield was sold to the existing tenants.

The Lincolnshire Gliding Club returned to Bardney in the summer of 1966, taking over the former watch office as a clubhouse. A blister hangar was erected adjacent to the clubhouse during 1967 and by the end of 1971 eight gliders were based at Bardney. However, gradual deterioration of the former taxiway used by the club as a runway and encroachment of the agricultural activities made gliding from Bardney too dangerous. The club very reluctantly decided to cease operations from Bardney at the end of May 1978. The clubhouse was closed and the blister hangar was dismantled and sold. Fortunately gliding facilities were later obtained at Strubby where some of the former Lincolnshire Gliding Club members formed another group with aircraft formerly used at Bardney.

Despite the demise of the former

gliding club aircraft continued to use Bardney. On the site of a former T2 hangar on the northern edge of the airfield Sprayfields (Scothern) Ltd set up an operating base for its own crop spraying operations. The site, formerly used by a number of other operators, became the summer base for two Piper Pawnee aircraft G-AXED and G-BDCT. Crop spraying operations were undertaken in and around north Lincolnshire and South Yorkshire, and in 1980 G-AXED was replaced by a new aircraft, G-BGPP.

As the crop spraying aircraft continued to operate from a grass runway demolition of the concrete runways,

taxiways and dispersals commenced, much of the hardcore going to various housing developments in and around Lincoln. Today the former Thor site in the centre of the airfield continues to house an intensive poultry unit and the two remaining hangars, a Ministry of Aircraft Production B1 and a standard T2, continue in use as warehouses for a food manufacturer. Demolition of the former dispersed domestic sites has now commenced and a second crop spraying contractor, Omnia, uses part of the former technical site for his fleet of conventional tractor-drawn equipment and road tankers.

Left: **Bardney, 19th April 1948. Note the equipment stored on the runways and hardstandings.** *(DOE, Crown Copyright)*

Upper right: **A Lancaster and crew of 189 Sqn at Bardney in March, 1945.** *(J.Clark via P.H.T.Green)*

Right: **Typical of the crop-sprayers which use Bardney during the spring and summer is Pawnee G-AXED of Sprayfields (Scothern) Ltd, seen in July, 1978.** *(W.J.Taylor)*

Barkston Heath

3.5 km E of Barkston Church
130/SK 970 415   350 ft (110 m) AMSL

Barkston Heath was in use by late 1936 as a Relief Landing Ground for nearby Cranwell. It received attention from the Luftwaffe on the night of 8th May 1941 when several bombs were dropped on it. The Aircrew Commando School moved to Barkston Heath from Winthorpe, Nottinghamshire, during December 1942 and continued to give its one week course of physical fitness, discipline and morale building to aircrew of 5 Group, Bomber Command, who were between OTU and HCU training.

The formal opening of the station took place on 12th December 1942, at which time the only resident unit was the ACS, though this unit moved out to Morton Hall near Swinderby shortly afterwards, in March 1943. Barkston Heath became a satellite of Swinderby on 1st April 1943, but the next day aircraft arrived from Cranwell to operate from Barkston Heath while runways were being constructed at their home base. On completion of the work at Cranwell the aircraft of the RAF College SFTS left and Barkston Heath was closed for construction of its own runways.

After the paved runways had been laid, Barkston Heath was allocated to the US Ninth Army Air Force and assigned to the 52nd Troop Carrier Wing. The first American unit to arrive was the 61st Troop Carrier Group which brought its Douglas C-47s from Sicily and arrived at Barkston Heath on 13th February 1944. The four squadrons within the Group then began a period of intensive training in preparation for the Invasion, which involved the dropping of parachutists and supplies and towing gliders such as the Airspeed Horsa and the General Aircraft Hamilcar. The Group took part in the D-Day landings on 6th June 1944 when it dropped parachutists of the 507th Parachute Infantry, and in the following September helped carry the 1st Parachute Brigade of the British 1st Airborne Division by glider during the Arnhem operation.

The 61TCG left Barkston Heath for France on 13th March 1945 and was replaced by the 349TCG which arrived from the United States later that month, operating Curtiss C-46 as well as C-47 aircraft. The new Group remained at Barkston Heath only until 18th April when it too went to France, and the station was then returned to the RAF to be placed on Care and Maintenance.

No. 40 Group, Maintenance Command took over the station on 1st June 1945 and 7 Equipment Dispersal Depot then formed under 55 (Maintenance) Wing. However, this was renumbered 256 Maintenance Unit two weeks later and on 1st September, No. 2 RAF Regiment Sub-Depot formed there. Under the control of the RAF Regiment Depot at Belton Park this sub-depot carried out the primary training of RAF Regiment personnel until it closed in mid-1946.

In 1948 flying training at Cranwell was re-organised and with effect from 1st May Barkston Heath was allocated to Cranwell for North American Harvard flying. No. 256 MU disbanded on 31st December 1948 and Barkston Heath reverted to Care and Maintenance. In early 1949 discussions took place with a view to housing a jet aircraft Operational Conversion Unit at Barkston Heath. However, the plan was dropped and Cranwell continued to use Barkston as a Relief Landing Ground. Aircraft of the RAF College continued to be based at Barkston Heath until July 1966 when the latter ceased to be permanently manned, although the runways and air traffic control facilities remained in use by the RAF College for circuit training.

As originally built, Barkston Heath took the form of a standard RAF heavy bomber airfield with three hangars (two T2 and one MAP B1). However, as a major troop carrier base considerable hangarage was required both for the resident transport aircraft and for the erection and storage of the many gliders that would be required. As a result, four more T2 hangars were built side by side on the eastern side of the Roman Road *Ermine Street* which runs along the eastern boundary of the airfield. The addi-

Right: **Barkston Heath, 1st April 1976. Note the B6403** *Ermine Street* **running across this photograph. Just one aircraft is visible, a Harvard parked on the grass to the west of the signals square.** *(DOE, Crown Copyright)*

Below: **A row of T2 hangars at Barkston Heath which are now in use for storage.** *(W.J.Taylor)*

tional hangars were connected to the airfield by concrete taxiways and housed the many Waco CG4A Hadrian gliders used by the Americans.

As the flying training task at Cranwell began to increase in 1979 more use began to be made of the RAF College's Relief Landing Ground facilities at the 600 acre (240 ha) aerodrome. Further development of facilities at Barkston Heath will take place during 1983 when a flight of British Aerospace Bloodhound missiles of 25 Squadron arrives. Presently based at RAF airfields in Germany, 25 Squadron is being withdrawn to the UK to reinforce our home defences, providing protection for the nearby Panavia Tornado base at Cottesmore, Leicestershire.

Unlike most of the Second World War airfields, Barkston Heath still retains all of its hangars. Apart from one T2 hangar close to the control tower which is used by the RAF for storage, all of the hangars are used for the bulk storage of commodities such as paper and fertiliser. The former watch office has been modified and now sports a modern 'glasshouse' local control room on its roof. Many of the buildings in the remote domestic sites remain, most being used as farm stores. For a number of years Barkston Heath has also been the venue of the British National Model Aircraft Championships.

Since 1982 the hangars have housed a number of civil aircraft often seen at Cranwell North, including a Pilatus P.2 G-BJAX and CAP.10 G-SLEA. In May 1983 Max Holst MH1521 Broussard G-BKPU seemed to be in residence and in mid-83 Spitfire MH434/G-ASJV was repainted here.

Above: **USAAF Dakotas over Barkston Heath, 21st July 1944.** *(IWM H39683)*

Below: **Members of the 1st Parachute Battalion before take-off at Barkston Heath, 17th September 1944.** *(Humberside APS via P.H.T.Green)*

Bottom: **Provost T.1s of the RAF College, including XF612/JV at Barkston Heath.** *(via N.Franklin)*

Binbrook

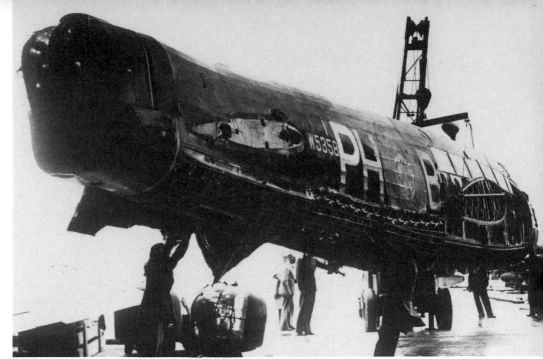

Above: Wellington W5358 of 12 Sqn, Binbrook after a mishap. *(MAP)*

Below: Binbrook's most famous Lancaster, W4783 G-George of 460 Sqn is now displayed in the Australian War Memorial, Canberra. Note how the censor has obliterated the H2S radomes from under the rear fuselage of both aircraft. *(IWM CH13246)*

Description: On a mound a lion statant guardant charged on the shoulder with a fleur de lys.

Motto: United we Strike.

Authority: King George VI, July 1951.

This unit, which is situated on a hill, has adopted a lion on a mound, indicative of this country and the fighting spirit. The fleur de lys shown charged on the lion's shoulder is taken from the Arms of Lincoln in reference to the station's situation.

Crown Copyright / RAF Photograph

2.5 km NW of Binbrook Church
113/TA 190 960 370 ft (120 m) AMSL

When 1 Group Bomber Command reformed in England on 18th June 1940 it was allocated the new station then under construction at Binbrook. On 3rd July the Fairey Battle aircraft of 12 and 142 Squadrons arrived, being bombed up immediately after arrival and placed on standby. The following month 12 Squadron moved to Thorney Island, Sussex, and 142 Squadron moved to Eastchurch, Kent, whilst the airfield was completed. Also during August the airfield was bombed and the NAAFI strafed but the squadrons returned in September although the airfield was still barely complete and during the winter the grass landing area was continually becoming waterlogged due to rain and snow.

Re-equipment of the two squadrons with the Vickers Wellington began on 9th November when the first four aircraft arrived; others followed in rapid succession. In late 1941 Binbrook took over the newly reconstructed satellite aerodrome at Grimsby, and aircraft from Binbrook made their first operation from Grimsby on 15th November, with both 'A' and 'B' Flights of 142 Squadron moving there on 26th November. The 1 Group Target Tow Flight had moved to Binbrook with its Westland Lysanders on 10th November; four days later it was renumbered 1481 Target Tow Flight and received a dual control Lysander two weeks later for pilot training. In the spring of 1942 the Flight received four Armstrong Whitworth Whitleys and one Wellington for air gunner training and, as a reflection of its change of role, was renamed 1481

Target Tow and Gunnery Flight. The name was changed yet again a few months later to 1481 (Bomber) Gunnery Flight. To give the gunners a close look at enemy aircraft, a captured Junkers Ju 88, Heinkel He 111 and Messerschmitt Bf 109 of the Enemy Aircraft Flight visited the station on 11th April 1942.

The Cologne operation on the night of 30th May was a notable achievement for Bomber Command when for the first time over 1,000 aircraft were despatched on a raid. Of these Binbrook supplied twenty-eight Wellingtons from 12 Squadron and three Whitleys from 1481 Flight. On 25th September 12 Squadron began to move to Wickenby and 1481 Flight to Blyton. On the following day Binbrook closed for runway construction.

RAF Base Binbrook was formed on 25th March 1943 though the runway

Above: **Early deliveries of Canberras went to 100 Sqn in January 1952, where they were flown at 2-3 times normal usage for intensive trials.** *(Flight 26724)*

Right: **Lincoln SX384 of 9 Sqn taking off from Binbrook to participate in the King's birthday flypast, 8 June 1950.** *(LAM)*

work was not complete. This was the first of the Bomber Command Bases within 1 Group and it served as a model for the others to follow. Later re-numbered 12 Base, it had been intended that completion of the runway work would allow the return of 1481 Flight on 1st May and the arrival of 460 (RAAF) Squadron on 7th May. However, poor weather and the Easter holiday combined to delay the arrivals until 6th and 14th May respectively, accomplished by using Airspeed Horsa gliders towed by the Whitley and Armstrong Whitworth Albemarle tugs of 269 Squadron from Thruxton, Wiltshire. Six Horsas were used, moving 125 men and 25 tons of equipment for 1481 Flight, and 868 men and 90 tons of equipment for 460 Squadron. Shortly after the two units had arrived the station was

visited by King George VI and Queen Elizabeth, on 27th May. During that month Binbrook was also host to the Indent Party which was formed to undertake the opening of nearby Ludford Magna.

Drama overtook the station on 3rd July when incendiary bombs from one aircraft were inadvertently released and ignited during bombing-up operations. Despite the prompt action of the ground-crew and fire crew the aircraft was engulfed in flames and the fuel tanks exploded. The explosion destroyed two other aircraft and a further seven were damaged. After the runway and perimeter track had been cleared of debris, seventeen aircraft took off on operations.

It was planned to move 1481 Flight to Ingham on 1st March 1944 but bad

weather delayed the move of the main party until the 15th. On 18th April 1 Group Special Duties Flight was formed at Binbrook with six Avro Lancasters and crews, commencing training as a Path-finder unit for 1 Group on 22nd April and carrying out its first operation on 30th April, these operations continuing until 11th August when it disbanded. The war in Europe was nearing an end when 12 Base disbanded on 31st March 1945, so 460 Squadron was reduced to two flights, and, having been selected to form part of the *Tiger Force*, moved to East Kirkby to join 5 Group on 27th July.

No.12 Squadron returned to Binbrook on 24th September, receiving in the process five Lancaster aircraft from 153 Squadron at Scampton. One week later 101 Squadron arrived from Ludford Magna, concurrent with a reduction in strength to two flights. In early 1946, 9 and 617 Squadrons arrived from India and in mid-1947 the Binbrook squadrons began conversion to the Avro Lincoln: 9 and 12 Squadrons re-equipped during July at Waddington and Lindholme in Yorkshire respectively and returned to Binbrook in September; 101 Squadron remained at Binbrook and began its conversion during August; 617 Squadron

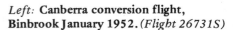

Left: **Canberra conversion flight, Binbrook January 1952.** *(Flight 26731S)*

Right: **A Canberra B2 of 101 Sqn being towed from a hangar on 22nd April 1952. Note the derelict fuselage of a white painted Lancaster in the background.** *(Crown Copyright PRB4479)*

began to follow suit in the following month, also at Binbrook.

When all of the squadrons had become fully operational with the Lincoln the Binbrook Wing took its place in the peacetime Royal Air Force. The Lincoln remained in use until, on 25th May 1951, the RAF's first English Electric Canberra, WD936, was delivered to 101 Squadron at Binbrook by Wing Commander R. P. Beamont. The squadron completed conversion to the twin jet bomber by the end of the year and as such became the first bomber unit to be equipped with jet aircraft.

A Canberra conversion flight was also formed at Binbrook during 1951 to assist pilots to convert to the new type. It operated a single Canberra B.2 (WD951), two Gloster Meteor F.4 and two Meteor T.7 aircraft. The training sequence commenced with the Meteor T.7, progressed to the Meteor F.4 and eventually the Canberra. The flight was absorbed into 231 OCU when it formed at Bassingbourn in Cambridgeshire during January 1952 as the Canberra Operational Conversion Unit.

Also in January 1952 617 Squadron started to convert to the Canberra; 12 Squadron followed in March and 9 Squadron in May. 50 Squadron re-formed at Binbrook on 15th August 1952, also equipped with the jet bomber. In June 1954 101 Squadron became the first to receive the Canberra B.6, followed later that year by 617 and 12 Squadrons. 9 Squadron did not receive this improved version until December 1955.

Also during that month 617 Squadron was disbanded and 50 Squadron started

to move out to Upwood, Huntingdonshire. These changes provided sufficient space at Binbrook for the arrival of 109 and 139 Squadrons from Hemswell in January 1956. During 1956 many aircraft from Binbrook took part in operations over Suez while detached to airfields in Cyprus and Malta.

No.101 Squadron disbanded on 1st February 1957 and at the same time 109 Squadron merged into 139 Squadron. During June 1959, 9 Squadron moved to Coningsby, followed by 12 Squadron on 2nd July. No. 139 Squadron disbanded on 31st December 1959 and the station was closed down.

Binbrook was allocated to Fighter Command on 1st April 1960 but it was not until 1st June 1962 that the first unit arrived; this was 64 Squadron which was operating the Gloster Javelin. It was joined in October 1962 by the Air Fighting Development Squadron from West Raynham, Norfolk, tasked with developing fighter techniques, evaluating new armament and advising on the design, layout and performance of new fighter aircraft: to this end it operated Hawker Hunter and English Electric Lightning aircraft. A functional part of the Central Fighter Establishment, the AFDS carried out a great many of the trials, including in 1963, those between a Lightning and a Spitfire in order to determine the effectiveness of a modern supersonic jet fighter against a piston-engined fighter.

During May 1963, 85 Squadron also moved to Binbrook from West Raynham. This squadron was the first within Fighter Command to operate the Canberra and was at one stage the largest squadron in

the RAF. Also during 1963 twelve Javelins of 64 Squadron were deployed to India to participate in Exercise 'Shiksha', an air defence exercise conducted in conjunction with the RAAF and the USAF in support of the Indian Air Force in an effort to counter the ambitions of China which had just occupied Tibet. Seven aircraft returned home on 15th November, another, XH765/A, having run off the end of the runway. The remaining four aircraft continued eastward to Tengah to strengthen 60 Squadron, and in September 1964 eight more Javelins followed them, at the time of the Indonesian Confrontation. The squadron headquarters and the remaining aircraft stayed at Binbrook until early 1965, the aircraft slowly going to other units. On 1st April, the Tengah detachment, now at full strength, took over the squadron number.

No.5 Squadron re-formed at Binbrook on 8th October 1965 and became the first squadron to operate the Lightning F.6. On 1st February 1966 the CFE disbanded and the AFDS was renamed the Fighter Command Trials Unit, operating a small number of Lightning F.1 aircraft to provide high speed target facilities for the pilots of 5 Squadron. Exactly two months later, the station received the Freedom of the Borough of Grimsby. The following year, on 30th June, the FCTU was disbanded to form the Binbrook Target Facilities Flight.

The Meteors of 85 Squadron were gradually phased out of service and during 1970 the Meteor flight was disbanded. On 28th January 1972, No.85 Squadron returned to West Raynham, a move

brought about by the re-distribution of air defence units which also saw the arrival of the Lightnings of 11 Squadron from Leuchars in Fife, on 22nd March.

From 1973, the Sepecat Jaguar was brought into service in the ground attack role, releasing McDonnell Douglas Phantoms for use in the air defence role. The Phantom was due to replace the ageing Lightning and rundown of the Lightning force commenced; an early casualty being 226 OCU at Coltishall, Norfolk. Binbrook then undertook the training of pilots destined to fly the Lightning. Initially, this work was carried out by 'C' Flight of 11 Squadron, but on 1st October 1974, the Lightning Training Flight was formed as a separate pilot training unit. High speed target facilities for the Binbrook squadrons continued to be provided by the Binbrook TFF until it ceased flying on 31st December 1973.

Throughout most of its operational life the Lightning flew in natural metal colours. However, in the early 1970s a camouflage colour scheme of dark green and dark grey upper surfaces were introduced following some experimentation on time-expired decoy airframes. Eventually, all aircraft of 5 and 11 Squadrons and the LTF were finished in the new colours as Binbrook became the RAF's sole Lightning base.

Many more aircraft were retained in service at Binbrook than were needed to equip the three units, the surplus aircraft being placed in temporary storage in one of the station's large hangars. It then became normal practice for aircraft to be taken into and out of storage in order to spread flying hours and fatigue consumption across the fleet. The aircraft retained were a mix of F.3 and F.6 single-seaters and T.5 two-seaters. Of the many aircraft phased out of use during the transition phase, one F.3 XP748 which was placed on a pole at the main gate in 1977, alongside Spitfire F.22 PK664.

In mid-1979 plans were announced that a third Lightning squadron would be formed to be based at Binbrook from

Above: **Javelins of 64 Sqn leaving Binbrook on 27 October 1963 for India to take part in EXERCISE SHIKSHA.** *(Crown Copyright PRB26170)*

Below: **Lightning F6 XS898 of 5 Sqn at Binbrook in July 1967.** *(D.M.Sargent)*

Bottom: **Lightning F3 XP750 of the LTF seen in its 1977 camouflaged colour scheme.** *(W.J.Taylor)*

early 1982 in order to strengthen the flagging air defences of the UK. However, in early 1981, the Government again found it necessary to revise its defence expenditure plans and formation of the new squadron was cancelled. To achieve the same effect as the formation of a third squadron, but at substantially less cost, a Lightning Augmentation Flight was formed in early 1982 to hold a small number of aircraft in immediate readiness reserve. In times of tension these aircraft would be brought into

service and pooled with the aircraft of the LTF, forming in effect, a third squadron.

As Binbrook moves into the 1980s it retains its vital role in the defence of the UK. From mid-1981 the Lightnings have begun to appear in two-tone grey colours, now internationally accepted as the most effective camouflage for fighters. The Lightning is expected to remain in service until the late 1980s when it will be replaced by the air defence variant of the Tornado, the Tornado F.2.

Blyborough

2 km ENE of Willoughton Church
112/SK 953 937   150 ft (45 m) AMSL

A class 1 night landing ground was established at Blyborough for the use of 33 (Home Defence) Squadron during the period it operated in north Lincolnshire, between December 1916 and early 1918. Records suggest that the ground had already been given up by the Armistice. Plans indicate that it covered some 50 acres (20 ha) which today are still farmed.

Blyton

2 km ENE of Blyton Church
112/SK 870 955   70 ft (22 m) AMSL

Examination of an aerodrome site at Blyton began during 1941 and construction was completed in time to allow the station to open on 20th April 1942 under the control of Lindholme in Yorkshire, in 1 Group Bomber Command. Hemswell took over control on 6th July and on 10th July 'B' Flight of 18 (Polish) OTU arrived from Bramcote in Warwickshire with Vickers Wellingtons to operate in conjunction with the Polish squadrons which were then operating from Hemswell.

On 26th September 1481 (B) G Flt arrived from Binbrook, operating a mixture of aircraft which included the Armstrong Whitworth Whitley, Boulton Paul Defiant, Westland Lysander and the Wellington; their arrival was quite spectacular as one of the Defiants crashed on landing. On 3rd November the Flight was moved to Lindholme, as Blyton was required for the formation of 199 Squadron, accomplished on 7th November, with the first Wellington for the squadron arriving on the 10th. The aircraft for the new squadron came from 12 Squadron at Wickenby which was in the process of converting to the Avro Lancaster. Becoming operational the following month, the squadron commenced bombing and mine-laying operations.

The New Year saw a change of role for the station when 1662 HCU started to form on 1st February 1943. Initially established for twelve Lancasters and twenty Handley Page Halifax or Avro Manchester aircraft, the unit was equipped only to half strength when it concentrated at Blyton on 16th February. The Lancasters were allocated to 'A'

Flight and the Halifaxes and Manchesters to 'B' and 'C' Flights. The following month a build-up to full strength commenced, at which time 18 OTU returned to Bramcote. The station was then returned to the control of Lindholme and its status was upgraded from satellite to that of sub-station. This change preceded the formation of 1 Group Heavy Conversion Base at Lindholme on 1st July 1943, of which Blyton became a sub-station. The 1 Group HCB was renamed 11 Base on 18th September 1943.

A further revision came in November 1943 when a shortage of Lancasters was being felt by the operational squadrons. It was decided to concentrate those Lancasters that were available for training within one unit, and accordingly the establishment of the HCU was amended to thirty-two Halifaxes on 21st November. The Flight of Lancasters thus released was designated 'B' Flight of 1 Lancaster Finishing School which was formed that day with its Headquarters at Lindholme. Problems began to be experienced with the runways and paved surfaces at Blyton which necessitated the Lancasters moving to Hemswell on 12th February 1944, although the problems continued to be experienced until the end of the war.

In common with other Groups, 1 Group had its training concentrated within one Base, in this case No.11. In late 1944, 7 Group was formed to control all Bomber Command training and as part of this re-organisation 11 Base was transferred to 7 Group as 71 Base with effect from 5th November, although it still supplied crews to 1 Group. At about the same time sufficient Lancasters had become available to allow the conversion units to re-equip, and the first course to

pass through 1662 HCU on the Lancaster commenced training on 6th November.

With the end of the war approaching, 1662 HCU was disbanded on 6th April 1945 and all training had ceased by the 15th. The station then became the home of 7 Aircrew Holding Unit which received aircrew prior to their allocation for release or further training; when it disbanded in January 1946, some 5,000 aircrew had passed through the unit. With effect from 6th June the station became self-accounting and was placed on Care and Maintenance, returning to the control of 1 Group in December 1945. In September 1951 Blyton was re-activated as a Relief Landing Ground for 101 Refresher Flying School at Finningley, Yorkshire, which operated a mixture of Wellington and Gloster Meteor aircraft. No. 101 RFS was renamed 215 Advanced Flying School in February 1952 and it continued to operate Meteors from Blyton until May 1954 when the station was closed.

Following closure the 690 acres (260 ha) airfield reverted to agricultural uses and was sold between 1961 and 1963. Since the station's closure a number of buildings including the hangars have been demolished but many, including the unusual watch office, remain intact. Much of the runways, taxiways and dispersal areas remain, often being used as a race track by local karting and motorcycle enthusiasts.

Below: **Still standing in July 1980 was Blyton's watch office, but note that its design differs from that of the standard austerity pattern.** *(W.J.Taylor)*

Left: **Pawnee G-ATYA at rest in the Boston hangar with a bare Pawnee frame hanging from the wall.** *(W.J.Taylor)*

Below: **The combined Auster and Pawnee fleets of Lincs Aerial Spraying and Skegness Air Taxi Service lined up in front of the hangars in 1967.** *(D.Stennett)*

Bottom: **Hornet Moth G-ADKK was restored at Boston during 1974 and has since won many prizes in concours d'elegance competitions.** *(W.J.Taylor)*

Boston (Wyberton Fen)

3 km W of Boston Church
131/TF 297437   10 ft (3 m) AMSL

Boston Aerodrome was opened in late 1948 and became the base of Boston Air Transport Ltd., which was an extension of the activities of the Boston Haulage Company. The varied aircraft fleet of Boston Air Transport provided for the flying training needs of the Boston Aero Club. Charter work, plus pleasure flying and flying training, kept the aircraft of Boston Air Transport busy until 1954 when the company's operations ceased at the end of the summer season.

In the early months of 1950 Aerial Spraying Contractors Ltd amassed at Boston a fleet of Auster aircraft equipped for crop spraying. The company was the post-war pioneer of aerial crop spraying and its operations took the Austers throughout the country and as far as the Sudan. In 1956 the company was absorbed by the Skegness Air Taxi Service Ltd, which owned and operated Skegness aerodrome as well as taking over operation of Boston aerodrome. Ownership of the Austers was also transferred and the aircraft continued to give sterling service in their arduous role until replaced in the mid-1960s by Piper Pawnees.

That many of the original crop spraying Austers remain airworthy today is a tribute to the high maintenance and operating standards of the Lincs Aerial Spraying Company, a subsidiary of Skegness Air Taxi Service, which operates the crop sprayers and the maintenance fac-

ilities at Boston today. In addition to maintaining the company fleet, the Lincs Aerial Spraying Company also maintains the aircraft of a number of private owners who are mainly 'flying farmers' from the

Boston area.

The airfield, which has changed its configuration somewhat since 1948, occupies some 44 acres (18 ha) of which the periphery is in agricultural use.

Right: Aerial view of Bracebridge Heath taken in 1958 during reconstruction of the Lincolnshire Road Car depot. *(via J.Walls)*

Below: The Robey-Peters No.2 in front of Robey's aerodrome shed, Bracebridge Heath, 1917. *(via N.Franklin)*

Bracebridge Heath

2 km ESE of Bracebridge Church
121/SK 986 673   210 ft (65 m) AMSL

At the beginning of 1915 the Lincoln firm of Robey & Co were awarded an Admiralty contract to build a limited number of Sopwith Type 806 Gunbuses. By the time the prototypes were ready for testing the firm had purchased land at Bracebridge Heath and were erecting two aeroplane workshops and establishing a drawing office under the leadership of Mr. J. A. Peters. The first design from the company drawing board was a single seater scout biplane which is believed to have been built in the Bracebridge workshops, though it is doubtful if it ever flew. A pusher biplane design followed but it seems likely that this model was not actually built. Peters then produced a design in early 1916 and in September of that year the prototype emerged from the workshops for flight testing. This aircraft, 9498, was designed to an Admiralty specification for an anti-Zeppelin and U-boat patrol aircraft.

The aeroplane was a large biplane with unequal wingspans and nacelles for the gunners mounted in the upper wing; it carried Lewis guns, plus an unsuccessful Davis gun installation in the starboard nacelle, and the pilot was seated to the rear of the fuselage. The Robey Peters fighting machine made a successful first flight and circuit of the aerodrome but was damaged when taking off for a second time. Three days later the machine was again ready for test flying, but shortly after take-off it caught fire and crashed onto the roof of a nearby mental hospital.

Although the Admiralty cancelled the order for two aeroplanes, a second prototype was eventually completed. This time the aircraft was built with upper and lower wings of equal span, a larger fin and was powered by a Rolls Royce Eagle III engine instead of the previous 250 hp Rolls Royce V12. Success again eluded the enterprise for in January 1917 the aircraft stalled on take-off and crashed badly. Soon after this Peters left the Robey Company and the design office closed down. However, the firm did continue to build Short seaplanes until the end of the war.

During 1916 Robey's Aerodrome, as it had become known, was enlarged to 125 acres (50 ha) and taken over by the Air Ministry for use as an Aircraft Acceptance Park, to which end Bessoneau hangars were erected and RFC ground and air personnel were moved in. The park was used until the end of the war for accepting aeroplanes built by the various Lincoln contractors: Sopwith Camels and Triplanes from Clayton and Shuttleworth, and Handley Page O/400s from Clayton's by the end of the war.

During the later part of 1917 and early 1918 three large hangars were erected, suitable for housing large Handley Page O/400s and designed for use by the newly independent Royal Air Force. In October 1918 121 Squadron started to re-form at Bracebridge Heath and equip with the de Havilland D.H.9. The Squadron had not fully equipped by the end of the war and was eventually disbanded in November 1919 without becoming operational.

During the inter-war years the establishment was leased out to various private companies until May 1941 when the site, except for one hangar occupied by the Lincolnshire Road Car Company, was requisitioned by the Ministry of Supply and allocated to A.V.Roe and Company for use as a repair and salvage depot. The A.V.Roe repair organisation expanded rapidly and a second site was opened at Langar in Nottinghamshire in 1942 to re-assemble aircraft from components recovered at Bracebridge and by other sub-contractors throughout the country.

By this time all flying had long ceased

from Bracebridge Heath and the lesser damaged aircraft which were repaired here, mainly Avro Lancasters, were moved by road the short distance to Waddington with their outer wing sections removed. At Waddington they were re-assembled and flight tested before return to the front-line units. New buildings were erected during this period to enable the company to set up the Repair Co-ordinating Stores Depot, operated on behalf of the Ministry of Aircraft Production and later the Ministry of Supply, which was responsible for the supply of all repair group factories and sub-contractors. Many of the spares held in the stores came from crashed aircraft.

Early in 1942 the White Hart Garage in Lincoln was also requisitioned for use by A.V.Roe and this unit was employed solely in the salvage of nuts and bolts from aircraft wreckage. The sorting of such things as rivets and screws from factory floor sweepings was also carried out. By the time the war ended over 4,000 aircraft had been salvaged and put back into the air by the A.V.Roe Repair Organisation.

After the war Bracebridge Heath was retained by A.V.Roe and became the centre for the repair and modification of Lancasters, Avro Lincolns and Avro Yorks, many of which were destined to be used by foreign air forces while during the early 1950s Avro Ansons were also taken to the factory for repair and conversion into flying classrooms for the Royal Navy. The last of the experimental Avro 707 Series of delta-winged aircraft was assembled at Bracebridge Heath from

components manufactured in Avro's Manchester factories, and when complete the two-seater Avro 707C (WZ744) was towed to Waddington where it made its first flight on 1st July 1953.

A.V. Roe was later absorbed into the Hawker Siddeley organisation which has, in turn, been absorbed into British Aerospace, Aircraft Group, Manchester Division. Throughout these changes Bracebridge Heath has been the head-quarters of the company's repair and servicing organisation, retaining spare parts storage facilities for all of the Division's products and other BAe aircraft. BAe employs some 200 people at Brace-bridge Heath which is also the administrative centre for working parties operating on many RAF stations throughout the UK.

The other hangars are put to a variety of uses, mainly storage and warehousing. For many years the centre three-bay 1917 'Belfast' pattern hangar has been used as the main engineering base of the Lincolnshire Road Car company. In 1958 two of the three bays of the hangar were demolished and a modern purpose-built workshop complex was constructed on the same foundations. Today a new company, Amalgamated Passenger Transport Ltd., operates the engineering base, taking in work from most of the subsidiary companies of the National Bus Company.

Unfortunately, much of the British Aerospace work at Bracebridge Heath was carried out in support of the RAF Vulcan force and, due to its demise, BAe announced in March 1982 that the

facility would be run down and closure expected in September 1982. Most of the workforce were likely to be made redundant although alternative employment might be available in other BAe factories at Chadderton (Lancashire) and Woodford (Cheshire).

Braceby

1.5 km W of Haceby Church
130/TF 016 358   260 ft (80 m) AMSL

A class 2 night landing ground was established at Braceby for the use of 38 (Home Defence) Squadron during its period of operation over south Lincolnshire, from October 1916 until May 1918. From August 1918 until June 1919 it was administered by 90 (Home Defence) Squadron. Its two strips measured 450 and 500 yards and the site occupied 38 acres (15 ha) which today are farmed.

Buckminster

1.5 km ENE of Buckminster Church
130/SK 895 235   480 ft (150 m) AMSL

Although the village of Buckminster is in the county of Leicestershire the area occupied by the former aerodrome lay

Below: **Two bays of the remaining three-bay Belfast hangar at Bracebridge Heath in July 1982. In the foreground lie engines and transmissions removed from buses scrapped by APT.** *(W.J.Taylor)*

within Lincolnshire and is for that reason included in this study.

With the increase in German Zeppelin activity in late 1915 and early 1916 several new Home Defence Squadrons were formed for the protection of the industrial Midlands. One of these was 38 which had existed for a short time at Thetford in Norfolk before being re-formed as a Home Defence unit in July 1916 at Castle Bromwich, Warwickshire. Commencing patrols with Royal Aircraft Factory B.E.2s, the unit soon began to re-equip with Royal Aircraft Factory F.E.2bs, and with this type the squadron transferred to South Lincolnshire for Home Defence duties. In September 1916 the Headquarters of the squadron was established at Melton Mowbray, in Leicestershire, and 'B' Flight was resident at the newly-constructed Flight Station near Buckminster by 1st October of that year.

With its eight F.E.2bs the Flight operated unsuccessfully against every Zeppelin raid within its patrol area until May 1918, the month when it began to convert to a night bombing role and on the 31st was transferred to Dunkirk, whence it undertook its first operational bombing mission on the night of 13-14th June 1918.

Prior to the departure of the Home Defence Flight, Buckminster had been selected as an Aircraft Acceptance Park and a programme of expansion work was put in hand. Much of the labour used in the construction of the permanent hangars and buildings was obtained by using prisoners-of-war from an adjacent German PoW Camp. No. 90 Squadron was re-formed at Buckminster as a Home Defence unit on 14th August 1918 and, equipped with Avro 504 night fighters and a few Sopwith Camels, began defensive patrols from the aerodrome.

The Zeppelin threat had by this late stage of the war diminished and as a result the squadron saw no action. After the Armistice was signed in November 1918 90 Squadron remained at Buckminster, until in June 1919 it became a casualty of the post-war disarmament and was disbanded.

The Aircraft Acceptance Park was destined for storage use only but was still under construction when the war ended. It would appear that further work was abandoned and Buckminster was finally closed down during 1919. The permanent buildings which had been erected remained for several years but as far as can be ascertained the RAF made no further use of them. From September 1918 until the final closure of the aerodrome 1 POW Mechanical Transport Repair Depot was located at Buckminster. In more recent times the 125 acre (50 ha) site has been largely transformed by ironstone workings.

Bucknall

2 km N of Bucknall Church
121/TF 170 705   60 ft (20m) AMSL

A class 2 night landing ground was established at Bucknall for 33 (Home Defence) Squadron during the period it operated from Lincolnshire, between December 1916 and June 1919. During this period the Squadron's main equipment was the Avro 504 NF, but Royal Aircraft Factory F.E.2b, F.E.2d and Bristol F.2Bs were also operated. The field, which had strips of 600 and 300 yards, covered 32 acres (13 ha) and is today farmed.

N

Stainby
Lodge

County Boundary

Buckminster
Village

B 676

RB

BUCKMINSTER
AERODROME

0   100   300   500 Metres

0   500 1000 Feet

Left: **Old WW1 concrete foundation blocks at Buckminster in 1977.**
(W.J.Taylor)

45

Caistor

3.5 km WNW of Caistor Church
112/TA 085 020   80 ft (25 m) AMSL

The all grass aerodrome at Caistor opened on 6th September 1940 as a satellite of Kirton in Lindsey in 12 Group, Fighter Command, the first unit, 'A' Flight of 264 Squadron, arriving on 12th September. Equipped with the Boulton Paul Defiant, the squadron was instructed to operate only at night, and so the following night it stood-to for night operations. During October the squadron was moved to Martlesham Heath, Suffolk, and the following month 'A' Flight of 85 Squadron spent some time training at Caistor. Although remaining a satellite of Kirton in Lindsey, with effect from 15th May 1942 Caistor was passed to the control of 15(P)AFU at Kirmington.

When later relinquished by Kirmington, Caistor was placed in Care and Maintenance until control was passed to Manby on 9th December 1942. The staff of the RAF College SFTS visited the station on 31st March 1943 with a view to its use for night flying, which was agreed and the following day Caistor was loaned to Cranwell; the first Airspeed Oxford arrived on 6th April. The normal routine involved aircraft arriving in the early evening, flying during the night, and then returning to Cranwell in the morning, although this routine was later modified and a full flight each of Oxfords and Miles Masters were detached to Caistor.

In late 1943 concern was expressed for the safety of aircraft night flying from Caistor due to its proximity to the coast and the consequent risk of enemy action, which was thought to have caused the loss of a Master on the night of 4th September 1943. The decision to cease night flying from Caistor was made that day and the following day authority to night-fly from Fulbeck was received, Caistor remaining in use thereafter for day flying only.

American personnel of the 346th Company US Engineering Corps arrived during November and the 'Stars and Stripes' was hoisted at a special parade on 4th December. The Engineers stayed until 4th February 1944, and were replaced by the 948th Ordnance Corps on 11th March. During March the RAF College SFTS was renumbered 17 SFTS and in September a flight of North American Harvard aircraft was moved in.

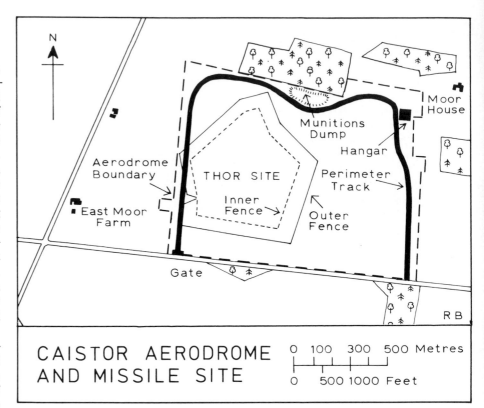

CAISTOR AERODROME AND MISSILE SITE

0 100 300 500 Metres

0 500 1000 Feet

Coleby Grange was then taken over as a satellite of Cranwell and the Caistor aircraft moved there on 16th November.

The aerodrome was then again placed on Care and Maintenance and became the home of 5354 Airfield Construction Wing with 43 (Maintenance) Wing taking over control of the station on 21st February 1945 for the use of 233 MU at Market Stainton. At the end of the war the station was transferred to the Ministry of Agriculture for allocation to local farmers.

In 1958 part of the wartime airfield was returned to Air Ministry control for the construction of a site for three Douglas Thor missiles to be operated by 269 Squadron (see map), which re-formed during July 1959 as part of the Hemswell Missile Wing within 1 Group Bomber Command. The missiles were withdrawn during 1963 and the squadron disbanded in May.

Above: **A blister hangar, in use as a farm store, at Caistor in October 1971.** *(W.J.Taylor)*

With the demise of Thor the missile enclave was dismantled and the tons of high quality scrap metal were eagerly bought by local scrap merchants. The whole of the former airfield's 310 acres (125 ha) was sold during 1964 and 1965 and became a major production unit of Cherry Valley Farms Ltd, a company famous throughout the the world for its ducklings. Within the perimeter of the Thor site the company built a number of intensive rearing houses and the grass of the aerodrome is harvested to provide grass pellets on which the ducklings are fed. Few other buildings remain but those that do are in use as farm stores. One blister hangar remains on the eastern edge of the airfield and this has been converted into a barn.

Right: **Cammeringham (Ingham), 6th December 1946** *(DoE, Crown Copyright)*

Cammeringham/ Ingham

1.5 km E of Ingham Church
121/SK 965 840   200 ft (60 m) AMSL

Ingham aerodrome was constructed as an all-grass satellite for Hemswell and was ready for use as such on 20th March 1940, at which time it was not occupied. It was eventually decided to build a concrete perimeter track which was started in April 1942. The first aircraft to arrive from Hemswell on 18th May 1942 (variously reported as 20th March) were the Vickers Wellingtons of 300 (Polish) Squadron, which operated from Ingham until 31st January 1943 when the squadron returned to Hemswell. The replacement unit was 199 Squadron which moved in from Blyton on 3rd February.

No.199 Squadron stayed only a short time and left on 20th June, to be replaced two days later by 300 Squadron, which returned in the company of 305 (Polish) Squadron because of runway construction at Hemswell. The two Polish squadrons operated together from Ingham for

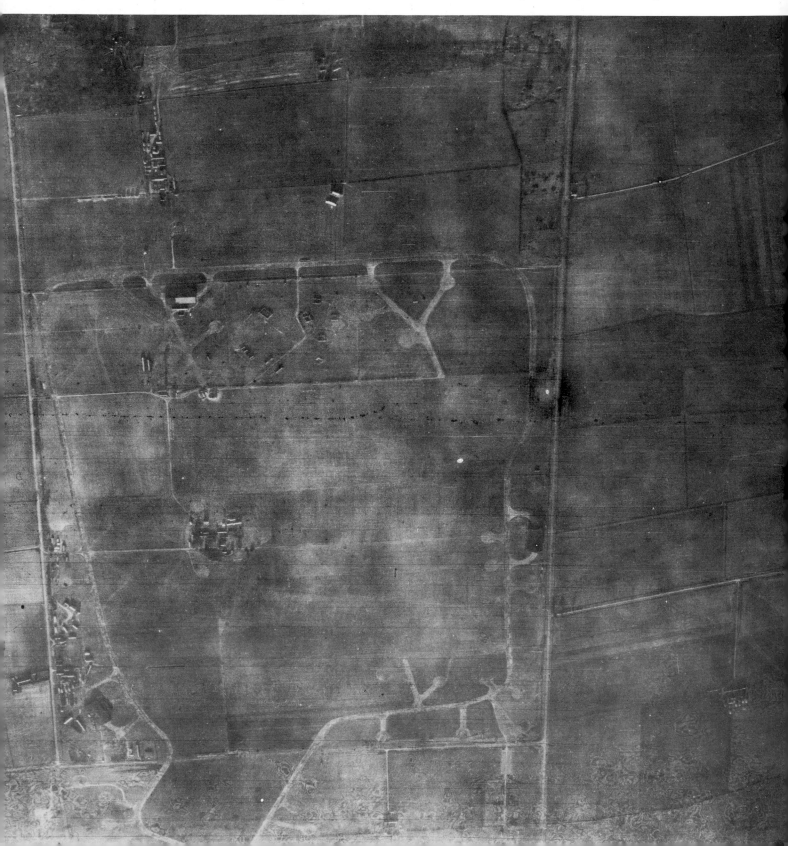

less than two months because on 9th August 305 Squadron was withdrawn from operations and left Ingham for 2 Group on 5th September. During December 1943 16 Service Flying Training School started to use the facilities at Ingham due to the unserviceability of its base airfield at Newton, Nottinghamshire.

No.300 Squadron was reduced in strength on 15th December to eight Wellingtons and twelve experienced crews who continued to operate the squadron while the remaining crews were attached to 11 Base to convert to the Avro Lancaster. When conversion was almost complete the squadron was moved to Faldingworth on 1st March 1944, the day that 1687 Bomber Defence Training Flight was formed at Ingham and 1481 (Bomber) Gunnery Flight was due to move in from Binbrook. The move of the latter was delayed by poor weather until 15th March, by which time Ingham was operating a variety of aircraft including the Miles Master, Miles Martinet, Spitfire, Hurricane and Wellington. With the increase in activity the station was upgraded from satellite to sub-station status on 3rd July, which was followed on 24th November by the renaming as Cammeringham due to confusion with a station in Suffolk also called Ingham. 1481 Flight was disbanded the following day and its aircraft and personnel were absorbed by 1687 Flight.

Cammeringham became a sub-station of 15 Base at Scampton on 1st December and was immediately placed on Care and Maintenance. No 1687 Flight was moved to Scampton two days later, leaving its few remaining Wellingtons at Cammeringham for future disposal. The Night Bomber Training School moved in on 1st March 1944 and stayed for the remainder of the year, leaving for Worksop in Nottinghamshire on 20th January 1945. From 1st March the station was allocated for the use of various non-operational units and the first of these to form was the 1 Group (Armament) Salvage Pool on 12th March, followed on 23rd March by 4791 Works Flight which was based at Cammeringham while carrying out work at Faldingworth. From 10th April the hangars were brought into use to store food and 24 Group Technical Training Command took the station over on 18th June 1945 and closed it to all flying.

In July 1945 16 School of Technical Training (Polish) was moved in from Locking in Somerset whilst on 26th November 4 Personnel Holding Unit (Polish) took the station over with 16 SoTT being granted lodger facilities. The Polish Air Force Film Unit arrived from Pinewood, Middlesex, and to help with the resettlement of the large numbers of Polish airmen in the area, 1 Resettlement Unit was formed on 1st November 1946, and operated until 7th December when it was disbanded and the station closed.

Today much of the 650 acres (265 ha) has been returned to agricultural use. The one remaining T2 hangar has been extensively modified and is now used by a haulage contractor as a storage and distribution centre. Much of the concrete perimeter track and the dispersal areas have been removed.

Upper: **A battered and torn blister hangar at Cammeringham, 1945.** *(Bill Baguley/Rod Houldsworth)*

Lower: **Cammeringham's watch office was still standing in 1980, although surrounded by vegetation.** *(Bill Baguley/ Rod Houldsworth)*

Cleethorpes Beach

2 km SE of Cleethorpes Railway Station
113/TA 320 080   *At sea level*

Civil aviation records indicate that a licensed airstrip was in existence on Cleethorpes Beach by 1950, its largest runway being 2,150 feet (approximately 700 metres). Municipal records reveal that it was used during the mid-1950s by Mr. J. Crampton, later Managing Director of Air Anglia (now part of Air UK), who operated pleasure flights in the summer season from a point in front of the boating lake.

During 1954 two Auster J/1 Autocrats (G-AGWY and G-AIBY) operated from the beach. At night both aircraft were hangared at Waltham and G-AIBY was equipped with an aerial loudspeaker system used to advertise the flights. Later an Auster 5 (G-AKWS) was used. Pleasure flights ceased in the early 1960s and there is no surviving structure.

Cockthorne

3.5 km WSW of Market Rasen Church
121/TF 075 875   *80 ft (25 m) AMSL*

A class 2 landing ground was established at Cockthorne Farm for the use of 33 (Home Defence) Squadron during its period of operation over north Lincolnshire, between December 1916 and June 1919. Originally it was unlit, suggesting day use only, but later on lighting was provided. The ground, which had strips of 600 and 450 yards and covered 56 acres (22 ha), is today farmed.

Below: **Beaufighter IIf T3145 of 409 Sqn at Coleby Grange.** *(W. Woodward)*

Below right: **C.O. of 409 Sqn., W/Cdr P.Y. Davoud, with the Squadron mascot.** *(Bill Baguley / Rod Houldsworth)*

Coleby Grange

3 km E of Coleby Church
121/TF 005 605   200 ft (60 m) AMSL

Constructed shortly after the outbreak of the Second World War, Coleby Grange was initially allocated to Digby as a satellite station but as a temporary measure was taken over by Kirton in Lindsey on 18th May 1940 due to the non-completion of Hibaldstow. The first of the Kirton in Lindsey units to arrive was 253 Squadron which sent two sections of Hawker Hurricanes on 8th July for a short stay, leaving for Ringway in Cheshire the following day. Between 2nd and 21st August the Boulton Paul Defiants of 264 Squadron were in residence, but the station was returned to the control of Digby on 9th September.

The first unit to take up a permanent residency was 409 (RCAF) Squadron, which moved in on 25th July 1941 to complete its work-up on the Defiant. The squadron, nicknamed the 'Nighthawks', had been formed at Digby the previous month and was the second Canadian squadron in the RAF. With the work-up completed, the Squadron began active operations on 3rd August, and conversion to the Bristol Beaufighter started late in the year. Tragedy struck during this period when the Commanding Officer, Wing Commander N.P. Petersen, was killed in a Beaufighter crash, the first fatal accident experienced by the squadron.

The new Commanding Officer was Squadron Leader (later Wing Commander) P.Y. Davoud, who claimed 409 Squadron's first enemy aircraft destroyed, following combat with a Dornier on 1st November. By the end of the month, the squadron was once more fully operational. During the next year only limited operations took place, although several more enemy aircraft were shot down. With the gradual decline of enemy activity

in early 1943 a re-shuffle of fighter squadrons took place and the 'Nighthawks' were replaced by 410 (RCAF) Squadron from Acklington in Northumberland, who were equipped with the de Havilland Mosquito. The new squadron flew many sorties in support of the Allied bomber offensive as well as several intruder missions before a move to West Malling in Kent was made in October 1943. With its departure Coleby Grange became a transit station for several squadrons in rapid succession until it was transferred to 27 Group on 30th October 1944.

By now a satellite of 17 SFTS at Cranwell, Coleby Grange received two flights of Cranwell aircraft which moved from Caistor on 16th November. No.1515 BAT Flight also arrived from Peplow in Shropshire with three of its Oxfords on 28th February 1945. Then, on 3rd March the main party of the unit arrived and training began on the 14th. Also at around this time 107 Elementary Gliding School started to give gliding experience to Air Cadets at Coleby Grange.

Concurrently with a move to Spitalgate, 17 SFTS was transferred to 21 Group, although it retained its facilities at Coleby Grange. An open day was held on 8th May 1946 at which a Meteor was on display and later in the year, on 10th August, the station was visited by the globe-trotting Avro Lancaster 'Aries', when its crew gave lectures about flights over the North Pole. Towards the end of the year a rundown in training commenced and the aircraft were gradually taken out of service. With the exception of a few Airspeed Oxfords, the spare aircraft were flown out to Enstone in Oxfordshire on 10th November and the remaining aircraft were moved the following day to Spitalgate. The station was then closed and placed on Care and Maintenance, though the gliding function continued until 1947.

During 1958 the Air Ministry stepped in again and began the construction of a Douglas Thor missile site, to which end 142 Squadron was formed to operate three missiles as part of the Hemswell Missile Wing of 1 Group Bomber Command. The squadron was disbanded in May 1963 following the withdrawal of the missiles, the 400 acre (160 ha) aerodrome being finally sold during 1964 and 1965.

Having been a grass airfield, little remains today of the airfield site itself. Part of the perimeter taxiway remains but all of the eight Blister hangars once dispersed around the perimeter have long since vanished. However, the lone 'T1' hangar built here still stands by the side of a wood on the other side of the main A15 Sleaford to Lincoln road which runs along the eastern boundary of the airfield. The former watch office also remains, in relatively sound condition.

STATION BADGE CONINGSBY

Crown Copyright/RAF Photograph

Description: A representation of the mighty Keep of Tattershall.
Motto: Loyalty Binds Me.
Authority: Queen Elizabeth II, December 1958.

Tattershall Castle is a well known landmark which dominates the low lying country in which the airfield is situated. The motto is the English translation of the family motto of the Earl of Ancaster who, at the time the Badge was designed, was the Lord of the Manor of Coningsby.

Coningsby

1.5 km S of Coningsby Church
122/TF 225 565   25 ft (8 m) AMSL

Work started on the construction of Coningsby aerodrome in 1937 but was not completed until 1st January 1941, when it opened as a heavy bomber base within 5 Group, Bomber Command. No. 106 Squadron, equipped with Handley Page Hampdens, moved in from Finningley in Yorkshire on the 23rd February. The squadron commenced operations from Coningsby on the night of 1st-2nd March when five aircraft successfully carried out a bombing raid on Cologne. A second squadron, 97, arrived from Waddington on 15th March, equipped with Avro Manchesters to join in the bombing and mine-laying missions.

On 1st April 1941 the 5 Group Towed Target Flight arrived at Coningsby to work on flying training using Westland Lysanders and Fairey Battles until its posting to Scampton in August 1941. Early the next year 97 Squadron started to receive Avro Lancasters and a Conversion Flight of two Avro Manchesters and two Lancasters was established to assist the aircrew in converting to these four-engined aircraft. In March 97 Squadron moved to Woodhall Spa, leaving the Conversion Flight to continue to operate from Coningsby.

At the same time 106 Squadron exchanged its Hampdens for Manchesters and 106 Conversion Flight was formed in May when the squadron began to accept its first Lancasters; operations with these aircraft commenced at the end of the month. In late September the two Conversion Flights were transferred to Skellingthorpe before they joined to become 1660 Heavy Conversion Unit at Swinderby. No. 106 Squadron moved to Syerston in Nottinghamshire at the end of the month and all operational flying from Coningsby ceased while paved runways were laid.

During the next twelve months several ground schools were established at Coningsby. The 5 Group Training School started up in October 1942 and was followed by the 5 Group 'Gee' Equipment

School and the Bomber Command Field Cookery School. In March 1943 part of the airfield housed 1514 Beam Approach Training Flight equipped with Avro Ansons and Airspeed Oxfords.

The station was declared operational again at the end of August 1943, and on the 30th 617 Squadron arrived from Scampton. It was during its stay at Coningsby that the famous squadron undertook its most disastrous raid of the whole war when, supported by a flight of de Havilland Mosquitos drawn from 11 Group, eight Lancasters attempted the breaching of the Dortmund—Ems canal on the night of 16-17th September. Only three of the eight aircraft returned to base at the end of this unsuccessful raid.

On 1st January 1944 Coningsby became the Headquarters of 54 Base, controlling all activites from Woodhall Spa and Metheringham aerodromes. No. 1514 BAT Flight left the station on 2nd January, making room for 61 Squadron which arrived with Lancasters from Skellingthorpe. No.617 Squadron then moved to Woodhall Spa and 619 Squadron took its place. During February a flight of three Hawker Hurricanes was added to the strength of 54 Base at Coningsby; these were used for fighter affiliation and radar calibration duties within the Base. The two Lancaster

squadrons remained at Coningsby until April when 61 Squadron returned to Skellingthorpe and 619 Squadron moved to Dunholme Lodge.

In 1944 it was considered that 5 Group should have its own small Pathfinder force and 54 Base was selected to house these and the other special duty squadrons of 5 Group. To this end 83 and 97 Squadrons transferred to Coningsby in April 1944 from bases within 8 (PFF) Group, and the new marker force achieved outstanding results, the skill of its crews being largely responsible for 5 Group's bombing successes during the last year of the war.

As hostilities ended in Europe a long-range bomber force — named 'Tiger Force' — was planned to operate in the Pacific theatre against Japan. Training began and 551 Wing was formed at Con-

ingsby on 25th May 1945 comprising 83, 97 and 627 Squadrons, the last of which remained at its home base of Woodhall Spa where a huge tented camp was set up to accommodate the extra personnel. On 26th July the composition of 551 Wing was changed and the Coningsby units were transferred to become part of 553 Wing. Training continued until September 1945, but with the surrender of Japan, Tiger Force disbanded in October, followed by 54 Base in November 1945. Following the disbandment of 5 Group, Coningsby was transferred to 1 Group, Bomber Command, and 83 and 97 Squadrons, by now equipped with Avro Lincolns, moved to Hemswell in November 1946, to be replaced by 109 and 139 Squadrons, operating the Mosquito B.16. No. 231 OCU was formed on the airfield in June 1947 and also equipped with Mosquito B.16s. These Mosquito units operated from Coningsby until March 1950 when all three moved to Hemswell.

Between April and September 1950 the station was placed on Care and Maintenance, and in October 149 Squadron arrived with the Boeing B-29 Washington, soon to be joined by three more Washington units: 15 Squadron arrived in February 1951; 44 Squadron in April; a year later 57 Squadron arrived. Shortly after the arrival of 40 Squadron, all five resident units began conversion to the English Electric Canberra. No. 40 Squadron moved to Wittering, near Peterborough, in the spring of 1954 and the other units transferred to Cottesmore in Rutland.

Coningsby was then closed for two years from June 1954 to allow for extension and strengthening of the runway and general refurbishment of the station, re-opening under the command of 3 Group in November 1956. The Canberras of 57 Squadron returned, still carrying yellow and black identification stripes worn in the Suez operations of that year. No. 249 Squadron re-formed at Coningsby in August 1957 and moved to Akrotiri in Cyprus two months later. No. 57 Squadron disbanded in December 1957 and Coningsby became the home of the Canberra Holding Unit for the next two years, the primary role of the station being the continuation training of Canberra crews. Several squadrons visited the station, some to convert to the Canberra, others to disband.

Front-line units returned in June 1959

when 9 Squadron moved in from Binbrook, followed one month later by 12 Squadron, also from Binbrook. Both squadrons operated their Canberras from Coningsby until they disbanded in July 1961. The station was again placed on Care and Maintenance until the re-formation of 9 Squadron with the Avro Vulcan in March 1962. No. 12 Squadron followed suit in July. A third unit, 35 Squadron, arrived at the station in December, and all three squadrons operated from Coningsby until 1964 when they were moved to Cottesmore in Rutland. It was during this period that the station received the Freedom of the Borough of Boston.

From November 1964 to December 1967 the station was under Care and Maintenance while further expansion was undertaken, in anticipation of the arrival of the first BAC TSR 2s. However, as is now well known, production of this type was cancelled and in December 1967 the first training course on McDonnell Douglas Phantom aircraft systems was started at 5 School of Technical Training, which was absorbed into 228 OCU in August 1968. In May 1969, 6 Squadron became the first RAF unit to be formed to operate the Phantom FGR.2, followed in September by 54 Squadron, which also re-formed at Coningsby with the Phantom. By July 1970 the OCU was allocated 64 Squadron as its reserve unit title and in order to operate the Phantom in the tactical reconnaissance role 41 Squadron re-formed at Coningsby on 1st April 1972.

With the introduction of the Sepecat Jaguar ground-attack aircraft during 1974

Page 52 upper: **Aerial view of Coningsby in 1947 showing villa-type control tower, Bellman hangar (left), two J/K hangars and T2 in background.** *(via M.Hodgson)*

Page 52 lower: **Mosquito B35 VR758 of 109 Sqn at Coningsby in 1948.** *(V.Hawley)*

Right: **Part of a formation of Washingtons of 149 Sqn airborne from Coningsby during 1951.** *(J.Brown)*

Upper right: **The faithful Anson served for many years as station 'hack' at most of Lincolnshire's larger stations. Typical of such use was Anson C19 TX176 which was operated by Coningsby.** *(MAP)*

and 1975, many Phantom squadrons re-equipped with new aircraft, their 'cast off' aircraft being used to re-equip former English Electric Lightning air defence squadrons. No.54 Squadron disbanded at Coningsby on 23rd April 1974, its aircraft passing to 111 Squadron, which re-formed at the same base with the Phantom on 1st July. No.6 Squadron disbanded on 1st October 1974, the day Coningsby was transferred from 38 Group to 11 Group, and its aircraft passed to 29 Squadron which reformed at Coningsby on 1st January 1975.

The changeover continued into 1975, with 23 Squadron re-forming at Coningby with the Phantom during December and 111 Squadron moved to Leuchars in Fife to make room. In 1976 56 Squadron re-formed at Coningsby with the Phantom and on 23rd February 23 Squadron moved to Wattisham, Suffolk, followed by 56 Squadron on 8th July. 41 Squadron disbanded as a Phantom unit at Coningsby on 1st April 1977.

Today the aerodrome, which covers more than 1000 acres (400 ha) is a very active Phantom base, and is often visited by aircraft from other friendly air forces for training and joint exercises. It is also host to the Spitfires, Hurricanes and Lancaster of the RAF's Battle of Britain Memorial Flight, which moved to Coningsby from Coltishall, Norfolk, on 1st March 1976, and whose aircraft are a familiar and welcome sight at many air displays.

Construction of the first hardened aircraft shelters within Lincolnshire began at Coningsby in June 1981 in preparation for the station being equipped with the Tornado F.2 fighter. The Ministry of Defence announced in early February 1982 that Coningsby would house the Tornado F.2 OCU. This is likely to operate alongside an operational squadron, as is the case with the Phantom at present.

In late 1982 29 Squadron was sent to provide air defence in the Falkland Isles and its first Phantom arrived at RAF Stanley on 17th October. However, by March 1983 29 Squadron had returned from the South Atlantic and in April 50 Squadron arrived on detachment with its Vulcan K.2 tankers whilst the Waddington runway was resurfaced.

Training of Tornado F.2 aircrew is expected to start at Coningsby in mid-84 but 29 Squadron is expected to continue Phantom operations from the station for some time thereafter.

Below: **XV486, the reserve aircraft for the July 1979 Alcock and Brown commemorative non-stop Atlantic flight, seen at its Coningsby base.** *(MAP)*

Below centre: **Phantom FGR.2 XV481 of 29 Sqn., active in the September 1976 'Exercise Priory'.** *(David M Sargent)*

Bottom: **Battle of Britain Memorial Flight.** *(W.H.Bushell)*

54

Aerial view of Cranwell, 9th April 1952 on the occasion of graduation parade. Lord De L'Isle and Dudley VC, officiated and the ceremony was watched by a party of Swedish AF officers, whose Mustangs, Ju 86 and Dakota are in the foreground. *(Flight 26989S)*

Cranwell (North)

2 km WNW of Cranwell Church
121/TF 010 510   200 ft (60 m) AMSL

Cranwell (South)

2 km WSW of Cranwell Church
130/TF 015 490   220 ft (70 m) AMSL

Though generally considered as a single establishment, Cranwell has from its inception contained two physically separate aerodromes and these are registered as two stations in the present survey. At the same time it has been difficult to trace their histories separately so it is necessary to describe them jointly in the following section.

Following a visit made by an Admiralty survey party in 1914, the owners of a tract of farmland to the west of Cranwell village were informed that their property was required under the Defence of the Realm Act for an aerodrome. Construction parties began to move in at the end of 1915 and were billeted at 'The Lodge' and adjoining cottages. When the station actually opened, 'The Lodge' became the official residence of the Commandant, and apart from a period between 1939 and 1945, has been used as such ever since. The Admiralty proposed that this new station would be used to train pilots to fly aeroplanes, kite balloons, free balloons and dirigible airships. In addition, instruction would be given in dropping bombs, gunnery and torpedo work, as well as wireless and navigation training. The first sod was cut on 28th December 1915 and the construction of the first workshops, hangars and living accomodation began.

During the autumn of 1915 Captain Godfrey M. Paine CB, MVO, was promoted to Commodore First Class and appointed to command the Central Depot and Training Aerodrome then being constructed at Cranwell. Instruct-

ions were issued that a hulk be selected in the Medway and commisioned under the name *HMS Daedalus*, upon which Commodore Paine's pennant was hoisted and flown for one day, after which it was hauled down, transferred to the shore and thence to Cranwell. Commodore Paine's appointment as Commandant was to take effect from 10th December 1915.

HMS Daedalus opened on 1st April 1916 and with its opening came a scheme to standardise the training of Naval pilots. All cadets underwent their basic training at Crystal Palace, London, and later (from the summer of 1917) at Greenwich, London. Aeroplane pilots were then sent to Eastchurch in Kent, Chingford in Essex or Eastbourne in Sussex for preliminary training before being drafted to Cranwell for cross-country navigation, aerial gunnery, bombing, photography and wireless

training. Seaplane pilots, after preliminary training, were sent to Calshot in Hampshire, Felixstowe in Suffolk or Killingholme for flying training. Successful pilots were then posted to Cranwell to graduate in all subjects except flying.

Airship and kite balloon pilots underwent their training at Wormwood Scrubs and Roehampton respectively, before being posted to Cranwell to complete their training. During the summer of 1916, a bombing range was established at Freiston, and all pilots took a course in dropping bombs and in gunnery, using a small landing strip at Freiston as a substation of Cranwell.

Soon after its recommisioning in April 1916, HMS *Daedalus* began to expand and became the largest military aerodrome in the British Isles. In May 1916 a Wireless Telegraphy section was

55

opened, and all Royal Naval Air Service W/T Schools, repair shops and research depots were transferred to Cranwell. When the station first opened three kite balloons were on strength, with the first ascent recorded on 4th April 1916. Six spherical coal gas balloons were brought on strength in May 1916 on transfer from Wormwood Scrubs. A portable S.S. (Submarine Scout) airship shed was moved to Cranwell from Anglesey during 1916, and on 15th November the S.S.39 left Wormwood Scrubs for Cranwell, but unfortunately a valve failed in flight resulting in the airship being wrecked near Sleaford in an attempted controlled descent from 700 feet. The S.S.31 was subsequently transferred to the station and arrived during December.

On 6th January 1917 Parseval No. 6 arrived from Howden in Yorkshire following the completion of the hangar for rigid airships, followed later in the year by the R.25 which arrived at the station for ground training purposes. By the end of 1917 the aeroplane section at Cranwell had expanded into seven flights, with almost every wheeled type in service with the RNAS represented. Experimental flying was also carried out at the station with the Sage Type 2 and the Beardmore W.B.1 at that time. During 1917 the South Aerodrome was established, the original flying field having been on the site of the present College building. By 1918 the station covered some 3,000 acres.

When the Royal Flying Corps and the Royal Naval Air Service were amalgamated on 1st April 1918 to form the Royal Air Force, the flights at Cranwell

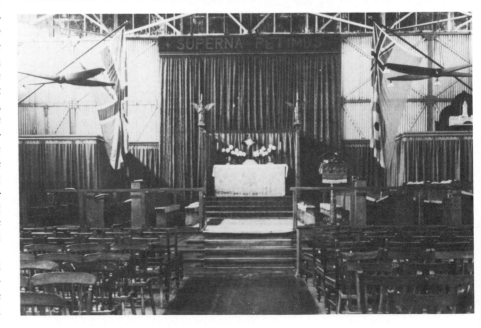

Left: **The Repair Workshop, West Camp, Cranwell.** *(LAM)*

Left centre: **A Coastal Class airship about to commence a flight from Cranwell.** *(LAM)*

Lower left: **The interior of Cranwell's church in the late 1920s. Note the use of propellers on the altar and as light fittings.** *(RAF Museum P2742)*

STATION BADGE CRANWELL

Description: An eagle wings expended and inverted perched on a rook.

Motto: ALITUM ALTRIX (Nurturer of the winged).

Authority: King George VI, September 1948.

The unit has adopted as its badge an eagle perched on a rook to suggest its function of watching over and protecting the personnel being trained at Cranwell.

Crown Copyright / RAF Photograph

were formed into three Training Depot Stations, which were originally numbered 201, 202 and 203 TDS but re-designated 56, 57 and 58 TDS in July 1918. These three units, along with the lighter than air and W/T sections, operated from Cranwell until the end of the war when the station started to run down.

For several months during 1919 the future of Cranwell hung in the balance, but the now famous Memorandum submitted during that year by Winston Churchill and Major General Sir Hugh Trenchard, Chief of the Air Staff, included proposals for the formation of a Cadet College for the peacetime Royal Air Force. Trenchard favoured the siting of this College at Cranwell because of its remoteness from large towns and the reasonably flat land surrounding the airfield. Trenchard's wishes prevailed, and on 5th February 1920 the Royal Air Force Cadet College and School of Technical Training for Boy Mechanics was opened at Cranwell. At this time the station was divided into three areas; East Camp housed the Boy's Wing and Technical Training Departments; West Camp comprised the Cadet College, flight sheds and the lighter than air sections; the third area contained two airship hangars and a number of barrack blocks which were used as an isolation hospital when the need arose.

The flying school was made up of three Flights: 'A' Flight operating de Havilland D.H.9As; 'B' Flight operating Bristol Fighters and 'C' Flight operating Avro 504s. There was sufficient room on the aerodrome to enlarge the Flying School to six flights, so Sopwith Snipes were added to the strength in 1921, and in 1922 a Vickers Vimy was allocated to the station to enable the Boy Mechanics to gain some air experience.

Because of its favourable runway length, Cranwell was chosen as the starting point for an attempt to break the long-distance record, when on 20th May 1927, at 10.38 am, fuel-laden Hawker Horsley J8607 struggled into the air. After a flight lasting 34½ hours the aircraft was forced down in the Persian Gulf by fuel problems; but a distance of 3,419 miles had been covered and this constituted a new World Record. After only a few hours this record was broken by Charles Lindbergh on his New York–Paris flight. Two more efforts to break the record were made with a second Horsley; on 6th June 1927 the aircraft took off from Cranwell for India but was forced down at Martlesham Heath in

Suffolk, with oil trouble. The third attempt ended with a forced landing in the River Danube.

At the end of February 1928, one of the station's former wartime instructors, Captain W.G.R. Hinchliffe, returned to Cranwell with his Stinson SM-1 Detroiter mono-plane *Endeavour* to prepare for an east-west crossing of the Atlantic Ocean. Hinchliffe took off at 08.35 am on 13th March 1928, and was last seen heading out over the Atlantic from the coast of Ireland. It must be supposed that Hinchliffe crashed into the Atlantic Ocean, as nothing was ever heard again of him or his passenger, the heiress Elsie Mackay.

Armstrong Whitworth Siskin IIIs were allocated to replace the ageing Snipes in early 1927, and at the same time the Avro 504K was replaced by the more modern Avro 504N. The unit was re-named the Royal Air Force College in January 1929, and the foundation stone of the new College was laid in April by Lady Maude Hoare, wife of the then Secretary for Air, Sir Samuel Hoare, Bt. The magnificent building was opened by the Prince of Wales, later King Edward VIII, in October 1934.

Cranwell again became the scene for record attempts on 24th April 1929, when J9479, the first of two Fairey Long Range Monoplanes designed and built to

Above: **Hinchliffe's disappearance in Stinson SM-1 X4183, serial no.223 (not X41831 as painted on the aircraft), caused considerable consternation, particularly in Holland where his wife and family remained.**

(via Underwood, Collinge & Associates)

Left: The Avro Tutor saw extensive service at the RAF College. *(via R.C.B. Ashworth)*

Centre left: Bristol Bulldog (TM) of the RAF College. *(N.Franklin)*

Below left: This immaculate Audax was one of many training airframes in use at Cranwell. *(Crown Copyright H233)*

Right: Shown in the full markings of the RAF College, one of a number of Fury I fighters used at Cranwell. *(via R.C.B.Ashworth)*

Centre right: Cranwell CLA4 biplane G-EBPB constructed during 1926 by the Cranwell Light Aeroplane Club. *(via R.C.B.Ashworth)*

Below right: Miles Master II DL119 after being taxied into by Master DL193 on 17th September 1942. In the background is a Master I plus a number of Oxfords. *(RAF Museum P7929)*

Foxes to its strength. The Avro 504N was replaced by the Avro Tutor on 1933, the Siskins were replaced by the Bristol Bulldog II at the end of 1933, while in 1934 Hawker Harts and Audax began to arrive. Hawker Furies and Hectors also operated from the station during the late 1930s.

On 30th August 1939, as the political situation in Europe deteriorated, the College was closed and re-named the RAF College Service Flying Training School. The station formed part of 21 Group Flying Training Command, but in July 1940 it was transferred to 26 Group at which time the station housed: The RAF College SFTS; No.1 Electrical and Wireless School; Royal Air Force Hospital; School of Clerks Accounting; School of Equipment Training; The Specialist Signals Course and the Supplies Depot. In September 1940, No.2 Flying Instructors School was formed on the station, equipped with Airspeed Oxfords and Avro Tutors and tasked with the training of flying instructors along the same lines as the Central Flying School. At the end of January 1941 the School of Clerks Accounting was transferred to Penarth in South Glamorgan, and the School of Equipment Training moved to Bridlington in Yorkshire in June. No. 2 FIS also left the station at this time and moved with its aircraft to Church Lawford in Warwickshire.

Because of its situation in a fairly remote part of the country, Cranwell was selected for the initial flight testing of Britain's first jet aircraft. At the beginning of May 1941, the Gloster E28/39, serial number W4041/G, was brought to the station by road. A Whittle jet engine, developed by Air Commodore Frank Whittle, an old Cranwellian, was installed in the aircraft and on the 14th of that month the aircraft was passed as fit to fly. At 7.00 pm on the following day the first official all-jet flight in the United Kingdom took place, and lasted for seventeen minutes. Before the aircraft finally left Cranwell at the end of the month, a further fifteen flights totalling some ten hours flying time had been made.

Early in August 1941, No.3 (Coastal) Operational Training Unit formed at Cranwell equipped with Vickers Wellington, Armstrong Whitworth Whitley and Avro Anson aircraft, to commence training crews for Coastal Command, and at the beginning of 1942 the station was earmarked as an emergency station for

capture the World Long Distance Record took off for its first attempt. Owing to bad weather conditions and fuel shortage Squadron Leader A.G. Jones-Williams and Flight Lieutenant N.H. Jenkins ended their flight at Karachi after fifty hours flying, a new England to India record. A second attempt was made in December that year on a route planned to Cape Town but misfortune overtook the flight when the aircraft encountered turbulence over North Africa and crashed into the Atlas Mountains. A second Long Range Monoplane, K1991, was prepared and took off from Cranwell in bad weather on 6th February 1933 and set course for Cape Town. Fifty-seven hours and twenty-five minutes later Squadron Leader O.R. Gayford and Flight Lieu-

tenant G.E. Nicholetts made an emergency landing at Walvis Bay, South West Africa, with only ten gallons of fuel remaining in the tanks. The flight of 5,309 miles established a new World Long Distance Record for Great Britain.

Probably still the longest, non-stop flight by a formation of four single-engined aircraft was made by four Vickers Wellesleys of the Long Range Development Flight. Taking off from Cranwell on 7th July 1938, they flew 4,300 miles in thirty-two hours, the flight ending at Ismalia on the Suez Canal.

Meanwhile, back with Cranwell's more normal activities, the Armstrong Whitworth Atlas began to replace the Bristol Fighter and D.H.9 in May 1930, and the following year the unit added Fairey

Coastal Command. In November 1942 one flight of 3 (C)OTU left Cranwell for Haverfordwest in Pembrokeshire, and its place was taken by 303 Ferry Training Unit (Coastal Command).

Experimental and test flying continued from the airfield and one hangar was taken over by General Aircraft Ltd for the assembly of gliders, which were test flown from the South Aerodrome. One hangar was also allocated to Gloster Aircraft for test work associated with the Type F9/40 jet fighters, the first of which made its maiden flight from Cranwell on 5th March 1943. The F9/40 was developed into the Meteor, Britain's first operational jet fighter.

In June 1943 the remainder of 3 (C) OTU moved to Haverfordwest and all the other flying units were concentrated on the North Aerodrome while the South Aerodrome had its grass relaid. The RAF College SFTS was renamed 17 SFTS on 20th March 1944, at around which time Cranwell took over control of Wellingore airfield as a satellite; two flights of Airspeed Oxfords were detached here in May 1944. In November Coleby Grange was taken over as a satellite in place of Caistor. On 30th April 1945 17 SFTS was moved to Spitalgate and a much reduced 19 FTS formed at Cranwell in its place; almost immediately Digby was brought into use as a satellite airfield for the de Havilland Tiger Moths of this new unit.

The Royal Air Force College re-opened in October 1946 while the station was still operating as a FTS. No.19 FTS disbanded on 12th April 1947 and on 18th April the RAF College was officially re-formed as an independent unit instead of a combined College/FTS. The flying wing of the College was again organised into three flights: 'A' Flight with North American Harvards; 'B' Flight with Tiger Moths and 'C' Flight with Ansons.

With the re-opening of the College the station expanded rapidly. During 1947 trainees destined for the Equipment and Secretarial Branches were accepted for training. The flying wing was re-organised in September 1948 and divided into two squadrons, the first with two flights of Percival Prentices and the second with three flights of Harvards. The Tiger Moth was phased out during November 1948 although six aircraft were retained for glider towing work.

Although the College had operated single examples of the de Havilland Vampire and Gloster Meteor since May 1948, it was not until 1954 that an

COAT OF ARMS ROYAL AIR FORCE COLLEGE CRANWELL

The Armorial Bearings of the
ROYAL AIR FORCE COLLEGE, CRANWELL,
in the County of Lincoln.

College of Arms.
January, 1943.

Chester Herald,
and Inspector of Royal
Air Force Badges.

(IWM 14186)

Coat of Arms Blazon: Azure on a chevron between three cranes volant argent as many torteaux each charged with a lion's face Or.

Crest: On a wreath of the colours a figure representing Daedalus proper.

Motto: SUPERNA PETIMUS (We seek things that are above).

Authority: Granted to the RAF College by letters Patent dated 19 December 1929.

The Cranwell family crest gave the main features of the present College coat 'three cranes argent'. Firstly, the colour argent had already been chosen for the College blazer. Secondly, the crane is a bird of long flight. Thirdly, when the

feature was accepted three squadrons of Flight Cadets had been at the College. The azure field of the shield typifies the sky and is overlaid by a chevron for ancient and modern signification. The motto existed some years before the grant of arms. The crest represents both Daedalus the flying man of Greek mythology and HMS *Daedalus* which was the name of Cranwell when it was a station of the Royal Naval Air Service during World War One.

In 1970, in recognition of its Fiftieth Anniversary, the RAF College was granted the right to bear Supporters on its existing armorial bearings. The Senior Illustrator of the College, Mr J B Ellingham, was approached to prepare designs for submission to the College of Arms. A number of designs were prepared and considered in consultation with the RAF Museum, the Cranwell Advisory Board and several senior Old Cranwellians. The final draft was prepared in full colour by Mr Ellingham and sent to the College of Arms in January 1971.

The design, with minor changes, was approved in August 1971 and the College of Arms agreed that Mr Ellingham should prepare the registered copy on vellum. This was a unique honour for Mr Ellingham who was probably the first artist outside the College of Arms to be granted permission to prepare such a piece of work. Letters Patent, granting authority for Supporters of the Arms of the Royal Air Force College, Cranwell, were signed and sealed by the Garter King of Arms in October 1971.

In heraldic terms the Supporters show: On either side an eagle argent with wings adorned and inverted, membered gules, gorged with astral crown Or, on the dexter side, charged on the breast a fleur-de-lys Or, fimbricated verte, on the sinister side the same fimbricated gules.

element of jet training was introduced into the formal course; in order to accommodate the use of these types on flying training courses concrete runways were built on the South Aerodrome. Training of navigators began in 1955 and a flight of Vickers Valetta aircraft were added to the strength of the College. These were later joined, and eventually replaced by the Vickers Varsity, which operated from Cranwell until navigator training ceased in February 1972. The flying training became all-jet in 1961

when the Hunting Jet Provost basic trainer began to replace the earlier piston Percival Provost and de Havilland Canada Chipmunk.

Hawker Siddeley HS.125 Dominies of the former RAF College of Air Warfare at Manby moved to Cranwell in early January 1974 when the CAW became the Department of Air Warfare of the RAF College. On 12th April 1975 the Jet Provosts of the Central Flying School arrived at Cranwell from Little Rissington in Gloucestershire. With its Headquarters

and Jet Provost squadron at Cranwell, the CFS continued to control its Folland Gnat element at Valley, Anglesey, its Scottish Aviation Bulldog element at Leeming in Yorkshire and its helicopter element at Ternhill in Shropshire, and later at Shawbury in the same county, but because of difficulties caused by the fragmentation, CFS Headquarters and the Jet Provost squadron moved to Leeming during September 1977. The Jet Provosts of the RAF College continue to operate from Cranwell today, but in early 1978 the Dominies were passed to 6 FTS at Finningley, Yorkshire.

Faced with an acute shortage of pilots by the late 1970s the RAF increased the intake of student pilots into the flying training system from 1979. The basic flying training element of the RAF

Above: **Harvards and staff of the RAF College being inspected by HRH Princess Elizabeth during a visit to Cranwell on 1st August 1951.** *(Crown Copyright PRB2958)*

Below: **For many years a number of service gliders have been operated, normally wearing the full College markings as seen on this Sedbergh TX1 WG498 in October 1975.** *(MAP)*

Bottom: **Vampire T11s on the aircraft servicing platform at Cranwell.** *(N. Franklin)*

Left: **Dominies of the RAF College wore a stylised version of the famous Cranwell blue band, as seen on XS733 in March 1976.** *(MAP)*

Below: **Jet Provost T.5A XW408 of the RAF College Basic Flying Training School, approaching Cranwell in July 1982. Note that the underwing serial appears on only the port wing.** *(W.J. Taylor)*

College became known as the Basic Flying Training School and by early 1980 had standardised its fleet on the Jet Provost T.5A, the Jet Provost T.3As going to other flying training schools. The increased flying training led to more use being made of the Relief Landing Ground at Barkston Heath and the re-opening of Swinderby as a second RLG.

A further increase in the importance of Cranwell to the RAF of the 1980s took place in early 1980 with the gradual transfer from Henlow of the Officer Cadet Training Unit. On completion of the OCTU course at Henlow in April 1980 Cranwell became the only place of initial training for all officers joining the RAF, emphasising Cranwell's position as a centre of excellence in the Royal Air Force.

Today the Cranwell complex is an active training station, covering about 2,500 acres (1,000 ha), though a substantial part has been let for agriculture. Jet training is carried out from the paved runways of the South Aerodrome, but the North Aerodrome is still in use for gliding, and a handful of civilian light aircraft are based here. Two of the latest arrivals amongst these aircraft are Robin R.1180T G-CRAN and Robin R.2112 G-RAFC, both with special registrations of local significance.

Since shortly after its opening in April 1916 Cranwell has maintained a very close association with the Royal Family. The first royal visit was made by Their Majesties King George V and Queen Mary in July 1916 and later, on 11th October 1934, the new College Hall was

opened by His Royal Highness The Prince of Wales. Following the Second World War His Majesty King George VI revisited the College on 13th June 1945 and during a further visit on 6th July 1948 His Majesty the King presented the College with his Sovereign's Colour - the first RAF unit to receive such an honour.

This close association was developed by Her Majesty Queen Elizabeth II when, on 27th May 1960, she graciously consented to become Commandant-in-Chief of the College. The Queen visited Cranwell on 25th July that year to present a new Colour and the Sovereign's Colour presented by her father was paraded for the last time before being laid up in the Church of St. Michael. The Golden Jubilee of the College was marked by a further visit of Her Majesty the Queen, in company with His Royal Highness The Duke of Edinburgh, on 12th June 1970 and the following year His Royal Highness the Prince of Wales carried out his flying training at Cranwell, receiving

his wings from Air Chief Marshal Sir Denis Spottiswoode, Chief of the Air Staff, on 20th August.

Since then Her Majesty the Queen has visited Cranwell twice: on the first occasion, on 30th May 1975, she presented a new Queen's Colour for the Royal Air Force College, the third to be presented in twenty-seven years; on the second occasion, on 24th July 1981, Her Majesty carried out the first Queen's Review of the College during which she also reviewed the graduation parade of 52 Initial Officer Training Course and presented the College annual awards.

The Royal connection has continued into 1982 with the arrival on 19th July of His Royal Highness the Prince Edward for three weeks of flying training on Bulldog aircraft from Barkston Heath. There is no doubting the affection with which Cranwell is held by the Royal Family, emphasising its long and proud tradition as the worlds's premier air academy.

Right: **The control tower and terminal building at Crowland (Postland) aerodrome in May 1979.** *(W.J.Taylor)*

Crowland/Postland

4 km NNE of Crowland Church
131/TF 255 140   10 ft (3 m) AMSL

A small civil aerodrome at Postland near Crowland was opened in 1968, on the farm of J.W.E.Banks Ltd. Aircraft based there included several Austers and gliders of the Perkins Sports Association Gliding Club. In early 1971 a number of blister hangars were erected and a little later a control tower was also built. By 1974 the aerodrome comprised two grass runways and the Peterborough and Spalding Gliding Club had taken over the gliding activities. A limited amount of flying training was undertaken from Postland, using a number of modern training aircraft. Functioning mainly at weekends, the airfield is operated today by the Peterborough and Spalding Gliding Club, is un-licensed and occupies little more than 40 acres (16 ha).

Cuxwold

1 km ESE of Cuxwold Church
113/TA 185 010   280 ft (90 m) AMSL

A class 2 night landing ground was situated about half a mile from Cuxwold Village for use by 33 (Home Defence) Squadron during the period December 1916 to June 1919. During the night of 24-25th September 1917, Zeppelin *L46,* doubtless attracted by the light of the flares marking out the landing ground, aimed most of its bomb load at the site. No damage was sustained as the bombs

fell in the surrounding fields. The two strips measured 750 yards apiece and the whole site, which today is farmed, covered 80 acres (32 ha).

Digby/Scopwick

2.5 km WSW of Scopwick Church
121/TF 045 570   120 ft (35 m) AMSL

It is probable that the site of the present Digby aerodrome was initially used by RNAS Cranwell as a Relief Landing Ground, at which time the station was named Scopwick. By mid-1917 it had been decided to enlarge the site and use it as an overflow for cadets from *HMS Daedalus* at Cranwell and work commenced at this time on aircraft sheds and domestic accomodation. Flying facilities were maintained but Scopwick aerodrome was not officially opened until March 1918. With the formation of the Royal Air Force on 1st April 1918 Scopwick became a Training Depot Station within the Midland Defence Area having a complement of Avro 504, Royal Aircraft Factory F.E.2 and Handley Page O/400 training aeroplanes.

Construction work at Scopwick was completed in October 1918 and the unit was renumbered 59 Training Depot Station. However, with the end of the war and the rundown of the RAF, Scopwick received just one Training Squadron, but a normal TDS had three squadrons, and the unit was, therefore, retitled 59 Training Squadron. Former RNAS units provided the flights for this squadron, the first two coming from 209 and 210

Description: In front of a Maple Leaf Or
            a crane rising proper.
Motto: ICARUS RENATUS
            (Icarus Reborn)
Authority: Queen Elizabeth II,
            July 1952.

The Maple Leaf is indicative of Digby having been a Royal Canadian Air Force station during World War Two. The crane is taken from the arms of Cranwell, as Digby's origins were as an offshoot of RNAS Cranwell. At that time Cranwell was known as HMS *Daedalus,* so that Icarus, son of Daedalus, may be regarded as having been brought to life in Digby station.

Crown Copyright/RAF Photograph

Left: **An Avro 504K of 2 FTS, Digby. Note the distinctive colours painted on the wheel centre and the unusual scoop under the fuselage aft of the lower wing.** *(Crown Copyright H1631)*

Below: **Maintenance work under way on Bristol Fighters of 2 FTS, Digby.** *(J.K.Fletcher)*

Below: **Aerial view of Digby circa 1928-1930.** *(Sqn Ldr Hart)*

Right: **Mishap with Avro 504N of 2 FTS at Digby.** *(RAF Museum P7317)*

Below left: **DH.9A at Digby. Note Hucks starter in foreground.** *(P.H.T.Green)*

Below right: **A Vimy of 2 FTS after crash landing at Digby in the early 1930s.** *(P.H.T.Green)*

Squadrons, which arrived in February 1919, followed in March by a flight from 213 Squadron.

In June 1919 209 and 210 Flights disbanded, but 213 Flight carried on until December 1919 when it too was disbanded and replaced by a flight from 203 Squadron which remained at Scopwick until January 1920 when 59 Training Squadron disbanded.

With the end of hostilities in November 1918 many of the squadrons on the continent were reduced to cadre strength prior to returning to Britain for disbandment. Two such squadrons, 11 and 25, were posted to Scopwick; 11 arrived on 3rd September 1919, 25 in December: 11 Squadron disbanded on 31st December after a stay of three months, 25 Squadron on 31st January 1920. The aerodrome remained inactive until April 1920 when 3 Flying Training School, a unit within 23 Group, moved onto the station. Because of a nominal confusion with the RAF Station at Shotwick in Flintshire, it was decided to change the name of

Scopwick aerodrome to that of Digby, and this was done in July 1920. No. 3 FTS continued to operate throughout the name change and served at Digby until April 1922. Also resident at this time was 2 Squadron, which moved in with Bristol F.2bs on 13th February 1922 for a short stay lasting until 2nd June 1922 when they moved on to Aldergrove in Northern Ireland.

Shortly after this Digby was placed on a Care and Maintenance basis until June 1924, when 2 Flying Training School arrived from Duxford which, flying Avro 504s, Bristol Fighters and Sopwith Snipes, trained pilots for the fighter squadrons. In 1925 Armstrong Whitworth Siskins were added to the unit and in 1926, with the further addition of the Vickers Vimy, the unit was enlarged to five flights; 'A' and 'B' Flts flew the Avro 504, 'C' Flt the Bristol Fighter, 'D' Flt the Siskin and 'E' Flt the Vimy. Later on the Armstrong Whitworth Atlas was added to the unit's strength.

In 1922 King George V created a new medal for bravery — the Empire Gallantry Medal, which was second only to the Victoria Cross. Awarded very sparingly, it was on 20th June 1928 that LAC Walter Arnold, then stationed at Digby, made history by earning this award, when as a passenger in an aircraft that crashed and caught fire, he extricated himself and the unconscious pilot from the burning wreckage.

During 1931 and 1932 the Vimy and Bristol Fighter were phased out, followed by the Avro 504 in March 1933. In December 1933 2 FTS was closed down and the station came under the control of nearby Cranwell. During October 1934 2 FTS was re-established at Digby and equipped with Avro Tutors, Hawker Harts and Hawker Furies. In 1935 and 1936 the station underwent a structural modernisation programme when the seven First World War hangars were replaced by two C Type hangars. Another was planned but with the prospect of yet another European war, priority was given

Top: **Avro 504N J8497 of 2 FTS.** (*RAF Museum P7318*)

Left: **Pou du Ciel G-AEBS. Fatal crash at Digby 21st May 1936.** (*M.Hodgson*)

Below: **A September 1942 photograph of Digby. Note the radio masts in the foreground and compare the layout and hangars with those on page 64.** (*RAF Museum W17/4/6*)

to the erection of married quarters and other domestic buildings.

In 1937 the station severed its links with flying training and on 7th September 2 FTS moved to Brize Norton, Oxfordshire. Digby then came under the control of 12 Group Fighter Command. Two fighter squadrons moved into the aerodrome in November 1937 — 46 Squadron with Gloster Gauntlets and 73 Squadron with Gloster Gladiators. During the summer of 1938, 73 Squadron was equipped with the Hawker Hurricane and by the time the Second World War commenced the squadron was operational with its new machines and was posted to France in September 1939 to join 1 Squadron as part of the Hurricane Wing of the Advanced Air Striking Force.

No.46 Squadron continued to operate the Gauntlet until March 1939 when it also converted to the Hurricane and started to fly patrol missions. On 24th October 46 Squadron spotted an enemy flight of Heinkel He 115 seaplanes attacking a convoy. A short, sharp engagement took place and three enemy aircraft

were claimed as shot down plus a further one damaged, the first enemy aircraft to fall victim of Digby-based aircraft. No.46 Squadron moved to Acklington in Northumberland during December but returned to Digby the next month.

No. 46 Squadron remained at Digby until May when it was embarked on *HMS Glorious* to take part in the attack on Norway, but, following its fall in June 1940, re-embarked on the *Glorious* to return home. However, on 8th June the ship was sunk and all the aircraft of the squadron were lost, together with some of the personnel. Those who remained returned in other vessels and by the end of the month the squadron had re-equipped with new aircraft and was again operational.

On 6th October 1939 No.229 Squadron was re-formed at Digby and a month later received its aircraft, the Bristol Blenheim Mk.1F. Declared operational during December, the squadron's first sorties were flown as night patrols for North Sea convoy protection. Exchanging the Blenheim for the Hurricane in March 1940, No.229 Squadron sent several detachments to France before moving to Wittering, near Peterborough, in June.

No.504 Squadron used Digby during September 1939 to work up with Hurricanes and in October 611 Squadron moved in with Spitfires to fly coastal patrols and to counter enemy intruders over Lincolnshire. Having moved to Ternhill in Shropshire in July 1940, 611 Squadron returned to Digby in August

and operated from the station throughout the Battle of Britain, finally leaving Digby to return to Ternhill in September when detailed for training duties. Towards the end of May 1940 three squadrons, 56, 79 and 111, were posted to Digby to recuperate after extensive operations over the Dunkirk beaches. A further unit, 222 Squadron, also arrived during May but moved south with the others to take part in the Battle of Britain. In June 1940 29 Squadron arrived at Digby with Blenheim Mk.1 aircraft to commence flying operational night fighter patrols. Successes were forthcoming when two Heinkel He 111s were destroyed by the squadron during August. In September 29 Squadron received its first Bristol Beaufighter and this machine gradually replaced the Blenheim.

On 2nd November 1940 Digby was honoured by a visit from King George VI, who awarded decorations to station personnel. One recipient was a member of 29 Squadron, Flying Officer Guy Gibson, who received the DFC on this occasion.

A group of Canadian officers arrived at Digby on 11th December 1940 to form a second Canadian fighter squadron in Britain. These officers, drawn from 110 and 112 Squadrons of the Royal Canadian Air Force, became 2 Squadron, RCAF. Hurricanes arrived and the squadron began to work up, becoming fully operational on 25th February 1941. Renumbered 402 (RCAF) Squadron on 1st March, it began East Coast patrols, but in May 1941 was moved to Wellingore, a satellite

of Digby.

The first Canadian unit to be formed in Britain, 1 Squadron, RCAF, moved to Digby in February and was renumbered 401 (RCAF) Squadron on 1st March. Flying Hurricanes, this squadron flew several sorties against enemy intruders and made fighter sweeps, usually operating from advanced landing grounds. Re-equipped with the Spitfire in September, the squadron moved to Biggin Hill in Kent the following month.

No.409 (RCAF) Squadron formed at Digby on 17th June 1941 to become the second Canadian night fighter unit in Britain. Boulton Paul Defiant aircraft were taken on charge at the beginning of July and the squadron moved to Coleby Grange to complete its work-up. The day before the formation of 409 (RCAF) Squadron, another, 411 (RCAF) Squadron was formed at Digby and issued with the Spitfire. It became operational by the middle of August and moved to Hornchurch in Essex, to spend the winter, returning to Digby in March 1942, where it continued to train until March 1943.

No.92 Squadron came up from Gravesend in Kent in October 1941 to prepare for overseas service and, when operational, was moved to Egypt in February 1942. The winter of 1941-42 also saw 609 Squadron operating from Digby, engaged mainly in the training of new pilots. No.288 Squadron formed at Digby on 18th November 1941, its personnel and equipment of four Blenheims, five Westland Lysanders and two Hurricanes having come from the 12 Group Anti-Aircraft Co-operation Flight. This squadron later received Defiants, Lockheed Hudsons and Airspeed Oxfords, and operated from Wellingore and Coleby Grange for short periods before moving to Collyweston, Northamptonshire, on 11th January 1944.

On 9th April 1942 No.421 (RCAF) Squadron was formed at Digby but remained only long enough to equip with the Spitfire before moving to Wales in

Every military airfield receives a large number of visiting aircraft and Digby was no exception. This double page spread serves to illustrate the great diversity of types making use of their facilities either by design, luck or sheer desperation. Starting upper right and continuing clockwise we have:

a) Douglas C-47A Skytrain 42-92719 '215', 1944-45. (*RAF Museum P5018*)

b) Airspeed Oxford I HN193 of 116 Sqn running up its engines against the chocks. (*RAF Museum P5011*)

c) B-17G 42-32083 of the 730th BS, 452BG which landed at Digby with flak damage to the starboard outer engine. Note the propeller is missing. (*RAF Museum P5020*)

d) P-51D 44-13630 of the 4th FG, USAAF. (*RAF Museum P5019*)

e) Piper L-4 Grasshopper carries the red and white bands of the HQ 65th Fighter Wing, US 8thAAF, Debden, around its nose together with a somewhat incongruous 'sharksmouth' marking. (*RAF Museum P5017*)

f) Wellington X MF560, KJ-O of 11 OTU in the winter 1944/45. (*RAF Museum P5013*)

g) Walrus II HD908 BA-D of 277 Sqn. (*RAF Museum P5016*)

h) Unidentified Mosquito B Mk.IV with invasion stripes covering the serial number. (*RAF Museum P5014*)

i) Fokker F.VII/3M J7986 was attached to the Royal Aircraft Establishment for evaluation. (*via M.Hodgson*)

Left: **Members of 92 Sqn at Digby, 2nd December 1941.** *(IWM CH4160)*

Below: **Tiger Moth DE454 of 19FTS seen at Digby.** *(via P.H.T.Green)*

Right: **Mustang IV KM232 of Digby Station Flight in late 1944, wearing the colourful markings of Wing Commander J.A.Storrer.** *(RAF Museum P5121)*

May. During March and June 1942 two squadrons were moved to Digby, without aircraft, to prepare for duty overseas, 54 Squadron being destined to operate from Australia and 601 Squadron from Malta. September 1942 saw 242 Squadron at Digby in a similar situation, preparing for service in North Africa.

Digby became an official Canadian airfield, known as RCAF Digby, on 16th September 1942, an event commemorated to this day by the Maple Leaf Cypher mounted in the station's armorial bearing. No.198 Squadron was re-formed at Digby on 8th December, equipped with Hurricanes. Declared fully operational on 18th December, the squadron moved to Ouston in Northumberland the following month.

In March 1943, after a detachment from 302 Squadron had spent February at Digby, 402 Squadron returned to the station. It then underwent a period of training in preparation for moving overseas, but the move was cancelled and the squadron resumed normal duties in the Digby sector. In August 402 Squadron flew south for a few weeks before returning to spend the winter at Digby. In 1944 dive bombing practice began but training was interrrupted by detachments to Ayr and the squadron finally moved out in April.

During May 1943 two squadrons spent a few weeks on the station engaged in bomber escort duties; 19 with North American Mustangs and 167 with Spitfires. The following month 416 (RCAF) Squadron brought its Spitfires to the station; it spent the autumn away from Digby but returned in October and remained on the station until February

1944. During its absence two Belgian squadrons operated from the station, namely 349 which spent a few weeks around August working up with Spitfires, and 350 which joined it from Acklington in Northumberland, also operating the Spitfire. Both squadrons flew on convoy patrols before leaving Digby in October. Formed at Bournemouth in Hampshire, by the renumbering of 118 Squadron, RCAF, 438 (RCAF) Squadron arrived at Digby on 20th November, but, newly equipped with Hurricanes, it moved to Wittering before becoming operational.

The spring of 1944 was a busy time for RCAF Digby and with pressure mounting for the forthcoming invasion, three new squadrons were formed there in early February: No.441 was formed from personnel of 125 Squadron, RCAF, and received Spitfires; 442 was formed

from 14 Squadron, RCAF, and also received Spitfires, both of which moved to Holmsley South, Hampshire in March; and 443 Squadron arrived from Bournemouth on 8th February and began to work-up with the Spitfire, also moving south during March.

No.310 Squadron, formed from Czechoslovakian refugees in June 1940, moved to the station in July 1944 and for a few weeks flew offensive sweeps along the Dutch Coast, before reverting to bomber escort duties on its return to North Weald, Essex, in August.

By the autumn of 1944 the battle zones were out of the range of aircraft operating from Digby so that following the departure of 310 Squadron, Digby was used for units employed in calibration flying for radar units, GCI stations and anti-aircraft gun emplacements. The

Squadrons involved were 116, 527 and 528, operating between them a very mixed fleet including Oxfords, Blenheims, Avro Ansons, de Havilland Dominies, Vickers Wellingtons, and de Havilland Hornet Moths. On 1st September 1944 528 Squadron was disbanded and its personnel and aircraft were absorbed into 527 Squadron, which operated from Digby until July 1945.

Nos.441 and 442 (RCAF) Squadrons returned to the station in May 1945 where they converted to the Mustang. The war ended before the two squadrons could become operational again and later in the year both moved to Molesworth in Huntingdonshire where they disbanded. In April 1945 a British Commanding Officer was appointed to command the station for the first time since 1941 and in May the station was handed back to the RAF. The station reverted to its former name of RAF Digby and was placed in Technical Training Command, thus breaking a long association with Fighter Command. During the war Digby had been a Sector Station responsible for the defence of much of north-east England; during this period the Sector Operations Room was established at nearby Blankney Hall.

In July 1945 1 Officers Advanced Training School was transferred to Digby from Cranwell, and remained there until June 1947 when it was moved to Hornchurch in Essex. Flying training recommenced at Digby in January 1946 when de Havilland Tiger Moths of 19 FTS from Cranwell started to use the airfield. The aircraft were based at Digby but the aircrew travelled from Cranwell each day. In February 1948 the Secretarial Branch

Training Establishment and the Equipment Officers School arrived, but remained for only a month before moving on to Bircham Newton in Norfolk. September of that year saw the Aircrew Educational Unit and the Aircrew Transit Unit established at Digby again, but the ATU stayed only a few weeks and was replaced by 1 Initial Training School, which gave basic training to officer cadets entering the RAF. In December 1948 the AEU moved to Driffield in Yorkshire.

No.1 ITS moved to Jurby, Isle of Man, in 1950 and 2 ITS was formed in its place at Digby, 1 Grading School being formed in June 1951 to operate Tiger Moths in conjunction with it. The Grading School gave a limited flying course to the cadets of the ITS to grade them prior to their despatch for formal flying training, the aircraft being operated by Airwork Services Ltd. Nos. 1 and 2 Wings of 2 ITS were moved to Kirton in Lindsey during September 1951, with 3 Wing continuing to operate from Digby until 31st March 1951 when all flying ceased.

Digby was then placed on Care and Maintenance until October 1954 when it was transferred to 90 Group Signals Command. The station was immediately prepared to receive 399 Signals Unit which arrived in January 1955. Soon the airfield was covered with aerials and in consequence has received no aircraft movements since that time. The new unit was operational by February and was joined in July by 591 SU. Two further units arrived in September 1959, the Wireless Operators School and the Aerial Erectors School, which both began to train their respective students. The Wireless Operators School moved to North

Luffenham in Rutland in October 1964.

In February 1959 54 SU arrived at Digby and, together with 399 and 591 Signals Units and the Aerial Erectors School, it remains at Digby today. The aerodrome, which covered some 210 acres (84 ha) in 1918 now occupies approximately 440 acres (175 ha). During the early months of 1978 one of Digby's two C Type hangars was demolished and the remaining hangar is used as a gymnasium.

Donna Nook

2.5 km NNE of N. Somercoates Church
113/TF 430 985   10 ft (3 m) AMSL

A Relief Landing Ground, part of the North Coates aerodrome and bombing/gunnery ranges complex, was in use at Donna Nook by 1936 and was probably used when North Coates airfield was waterlogged as well as during the summer months when North Coates became the temporary home of squadrons engaged in bombing and gunnery practice.

In December 1939 a flight of Hawker Demons was detached from Manby to the landing ground at Donna Nook when the parent airfield was closed due to flooding; the aircraft remained until the spring of 1940.

With the increase in German air attacks on Britain in the spring of 1940, a considerable number of which were aimed at military airfields, a system of decoy airfield sites was established in an attempt to draw hostile aircraft away from the operational bases. Donna Nook became

Left: **Donna Nook, 21st September 1946.** *(DoE, Crown Copyright)*

Dunholme Lodge

2 km SW of Welton Church
121/SK 000 785   100 ft (30 m) AMSL

Dunholme Lodge was built as a satellite of Scampton and its first unit arrived on 1st August 1942, this being 1485 Target Tow and Gunnery Flight, which moved across from Scampton. Operating a mixture of aircraft including the Fairey Battle, Westland Lysander and Vickers Wellington, the flight was joined on 27th August by its Air Bomber Training Unit which had been based at Wigsley in Nottinghamshire. At about this time the name of the unit was changed to 1485 (Bomber) Gunnery Flight and it moved to Fulbeck on 27th October.

During the stay of the Gunnery Flight, the station was by no means complete, runways having been laid between October 1942 and May 1943 and when 52 Base formed at Scampton on 10th May, Dunholme Lodge became one of its sub-stations. The first operational squadron to arrive was 44, which moved from Waddington on 31st May when that airfield was closed for runway construction and carried out its first operation from Dunholme Lodge on 11th June. Due to runway break-up at Fiskerton, 49 Squadron arrived on 13th September to remain until repairs were completed on 24th October, when it returned home. With the arrival of the second unit Dunholme Lodge was raised to station status on 17th September.

Work re-commenced on Dunholme Lodge's main runway in February 1944, This task was the construction of a 300-yard extension to the east/west strip, undertaken by 5002 Airfield Construction Unit, which was required to allow aircraft with an all-up weight of 65,000 lbs to take off in a westerly direction, previously impossible due to an adverse gradient, and was completed in time to allow the arrival of 619 Squadron from Coningsby on 17th April. The Prime Minister of Southern Rhodesia, the Rt

a decoy, designated a 'Q' site, for its parent airfield, North Coates, and a number of wood and fabric 'Bristol Blenheim' dummy aircraft were erected at strategic points around the site and airfield lighting was installed. It would appear that this ruse was successful, for the Donna Nook decoy was attacked on at least one occasion.

By 1942, with the decrease in enemy air attacks and an increase in operations from North Coates, Donna Nook was once again brought into use as a Relief Landing Ground. The North Coates 'Q' site was dismantled and Donna Nook was given a 'Q' site of its own. Although there were never units permanently stationed

at Donna Nook, it was often used by aircraft from North Coates to take off on operations, and several times aircraft used the landing ground for emergency landings when returning from operations with battle damage or mechanical failure. On occasions during heavy or wheels-up landings, the bomb loads or torpedoes exploded, sometimes with tragic results.

Donna Nook remained in use as a satellite of North Coates until 1945 when it was closed down. The 335 acre (135 ha) site has now reverted to agricultural purposes, although the perimeter track and some buildings still exist and a scrap dealer makes use of a dispersed accommodation site.

Left: Lancasters of 619 Sqn dispersed at Dunholme Lodge awaiting bombing up. *(Bill Baguley/Rod Houldsworth)*

Below left: G.A.L.56 TS510 was tested at Dunholme Lodge. *(via P.H.T.Green)*

Below right: One of Dunholme Lodge's temporary brick buildings was still in use as a school during 1979. *(Bill Baguley/Rod Houldsworth)*

Bottom: LA728 was the prototype of the Hamilcar 10 powered glider, a type operated from Dunholme Lodge in 1945. *(MAP)*

Hon Godfrey Huggin made a visit to the station during June to see the work of 44 (Rhodesia) Squadron.

The station became no stranger to tragedy. The Commanding Officer of 619 Squadron, Wing Commander J.R. Maling, DFC, was posted missing on the night of 25-26th July following a raid on Stuttgart. The crew of a 1660 Conversion Unit Avro Lancaster were killed on 10th November, when their aircraft crashed on the servants' quarters of the Officers Mess. Fortunately none of the Mess staff were killed, though several were injured.

Following the decision to transfer 52 Base to 1 Group, 619 Squadron was moved to Strubby on 28th September and 44 Squadron to Spilsby on 30th September. Dunholme Lodge remained a sub-station when 15 Base was formed at Scampton on 7th October and preparations were made for the receipt of 170 Squadron from Kelstern, which arrived on 22nd October. It was at this time that Scampton became operational again following runway construc-

tion and problems were experienced with the circuit patterns at the two airfields due to their overlap. To reduce the risk of collision it was necessary to plan a joint circuit and although the system worked satisfactorily, the landing times were so increased that it was decided to close Dunholme Lodge to operational flying. Its place in 15 Base was taken by Hemswell and 170 Squadron moved there on 29th November. Dunholme Lodge was then earmarked for use by non-operational units.

The first to arrive was a Ministry of Aircraft Production glider modification detachment. Staffed by seventeen men from General Aircraft Ltd., this unit was

allocated two hangars and workshop facilities to enable it to carry out modifications to Hamilcar gliders. One such modification to be tested at Dunholme Lodge was the Hamilcar Mk.X, a powered version of the famous glider. Tugs in use with the unit included a Handley Page Halifax and an Armstrong Whitworth Whitley. The occasional General Aircraft Hotspur training glider was also in use. The station was transferred from 15 Base to 28 Group Technical Training Command and the glider modification unit left on 28th June 1945.

Dunholme Lodge then became the home of the RAF (Polish) Record Office, which was moved from Blackpool in

Lancashire on 25th July. This unit operated in conjunction with the Polish Air Force Depot, and the combined units were known as the RAF Liaison Unit. During late 1946 the Polish Record Office was moved to Gloucester to join its RAF counterpart and the Liaison Unit disbanded on 1st December 1946, the station then being renamed 3 Polish Resettlement Corps (RAF) Station. From 3rd December work started to attest those Polish personnel who wished to join the Polish Resettlement Corps, this work continuing until late 1947 when the station was closed.

During 1958 the Air Ministry again took over part of the old airfield and a Bristol-Ferranti Bloodhound surface-to-air missile site was constructed to form part of the defences for the nearby V-bomber stations and Thor IRBM sites. No. 141 Squadron was formed in April 1959 to operate the missiles which remained in use until early 1964 when the squadron was disbanded and the airfield closed. During 1965 and 1966 the airfield's 715 acres (290 ha) were sold and today are predominantly farmland with a few acres of concrete and hutments surviving demolition.

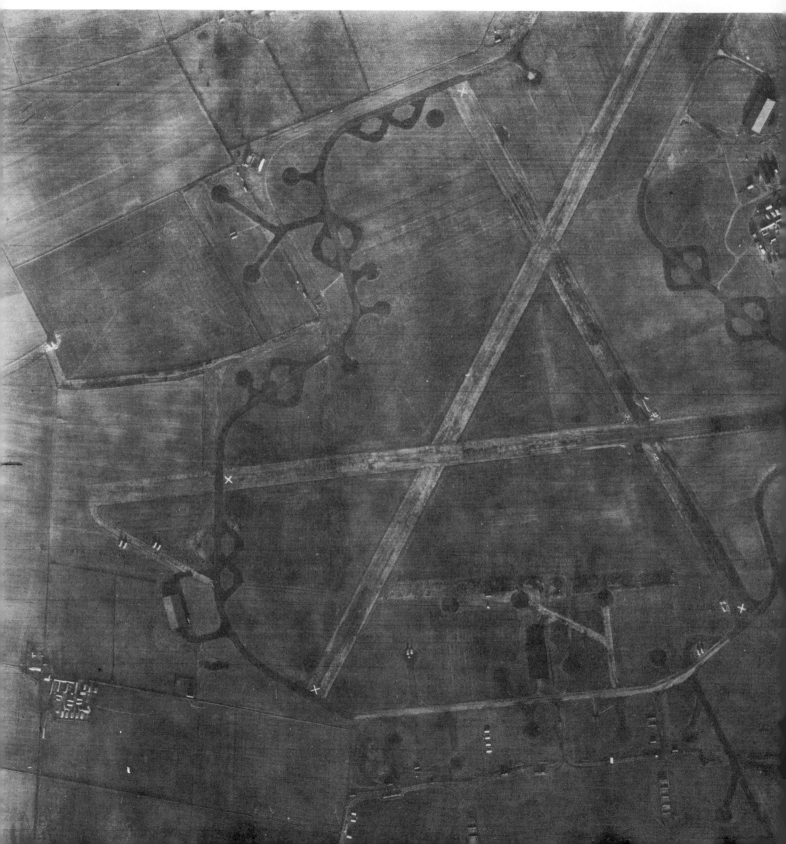

Left: **Dunholme Lodge, 6th December 1946. Note the extension to the East-West runway.** *(DoE, Crown Copyright)*

Right: **US Air Force Douglas C-47 gets airborne from East Kirkby with the aid of rockets.** *(via M.Hodgson)*

East Kirkby

1.5 km SSE of East Kirkby Church
122/TF 345 615   50 ft (15 m) AMSL

The site that was later to become East Kirkby airfield was first pressed into use during 1940 as a decoy site for Manby; as such it was supplied with several dummy Armstrong Whitworth Whitleys, and was bombed several times. Construction of the airfield proper began during 1942 and it was ready for occupation by the middle of the next year. The first operational unit to arrive was 57 Squadron which moved in with its Avro Lancasters on 20th August from Scampton, which was being closed for the construction of paved runways. The squadron flew its first operation from East Kirkby on the 27th of the month.

On 15th November 1943 'B' Flight of 57 Squadron provided the nucleus for 630 Squadron which formed at East Kirkby that day. The new squadron's first operation was carried out on the night of 18-19th November when nine Lancasters bombed Berlin. On 15th April 1944 the Headquarters of 55 Base was established at the station, controlling the satellites of Spilsby and Strubby. The last enemy raid against East Kirkby was carried out on 4th March 1944 when some casualties were sustained following a low-level machine gun attack. Unfortunately they were not the last ground casualties to be sustained at East Kirkby for on 17th April 1945 a fully bombed-up Lancaster of 57 Squadron blew up at its dispersal, killing three people and destroying four other aircraft.

With the war in Europe over 55 Base started an intensive training programme for *Tiger Force,* but as 630 Squadron was not required it disbanded on 18th July. This provided space at East Kirkby for the arrival from Binbrook of 460 (RAAF) Squadron, the main party of which arrived on 27th July, the squadron having been transferred to 5 Group for duty with *Tiger Force.*

Shortly before this 57 Squadron was selected as the unit to carry out the service trials of the Avro Lincoln, and it received its first aircraft on 23rd July. It was intended that *Tiger Force* would eventually be fully equipped with the Lincoln so training proceeded apace. However, *Tiger Force* was disbanded following the surrender of Japan. No. 460 Squadron disbanded on 10th October, having flown its last mission, to photograph the Australian War Memorial in France, a few days earlier. No. 57 Squadron was disbanded on 25th November, only to re-form the following day from the disbanded 103 Squadron at Elsham Wolds. The Squadron's Lincolns were taken to Scampton to form the Lincoln Service Trials Flight.

With the last of its home squadrons shortly due to disband, 55 Base itself was disbanded on 15th November. The station was closed to all flying on 5th December although the main runway remained open for emergency landings. On 1st January 1946 the station was placed on a self-accounting Care and Maintenance basis but after a short period was re-opened to house 139 Squadron and 231 OCU from Coningsby while reconstruction work proceeded there. When the work was completed during

February 1948, the de Havilland Mosquitos of both units returned to Coningsby and East Kirkby returned to Care and Maintenance.

As American forces built up in the United Kingdom during the years of political tension in the early 1950s East Kirkby was selected for use by the 7th Air Division of the USAF's Strategic Air Command. The station underwent major reconstruction which involved extending runway 08/26 by 3,800 feet (1160m) and consturction of a 200 yard (180m) square aircraft parking area. Other facilities were also improved and the station was reactivated on 17th April 1954 by the 3931 Air Base Group which began preparations for the arrival of operational units. The 3931 ABG had been replaced by November 1954 with the 3197 Air Base Squadron which maintained the station for use as a temporary base for units deployed from the mainland USA.

Only one aircraft, a C-47D, was permanently based at East Kirkby during this period and was used for a variety of administrative duties and for pilot proficiency flights by station pilots which took it to all of the USAF bases in the UK and many in Europe. Base personnel, including their wives and children, were accommodated in the local area, many in the Warwick Hotel in Skegness.

The units earmarked to operate from East Kirkby were the 62nd, 63rd and 64th Air Rescue Squadrons which were most unusual in that they undertook a number a special duties including the rescue of aircrews shot down behind enemy lines. The squadrons were equipped with specially modified C-47 aircraft

fitted with long range fuel tanks, three rocket assisted take off bottles and the freight hold modified for use as an air ambulance. Their aircraft were also unusual in that they carried a special navigator in addition to the normal crew and undertook many long range flights from East Kirkby, almost always operating at low level and out of radio contact. Each squadron had some twelve to fifteen aircraft and would operate from East Kirkby for up to three months at a time.

During 1958 the American units started to leave and the final unit disbanded on 1st August 1958. The station was formally returned to Air Ministry control on 31st October, becoming inactive on 31st December. After it had been largely returned to agricultural use the airfield's 855 acres (348 ha) were finally sold between 1965 and 1967.

As East Kirkby had been a Base Station during the Second World War, it housed the 55 Base aircraft major servicing unit which was responsible for the overhaul and major servicing of the aircraft from Spilsby and Strubby as well as those based at East Kirkby. This task required the construction of four more hangars in addition to the station's normal entitlement of three. The first hangars to be built were three T2s to meet the station's entitlement as a bomber unit. To these were added three more T2s and a MAP B1 for the Base major servicing unit. With the exception of one T2 hangar on the eastern boundary, all of the hangars were located within the main technical site in the north-west corner of the airfield, those within the Base maintenance area being built side-by-side.

With closure of the airfield in 1958, the hangars were quickly dismantled, but by some strange quirk of fate, the Base maintenance area was destined to become a potato storage depot in the early 1970s and the company concerned promptly erected four specially modified former T2 hangars for potato storage on the foundations of the wartime hangars.

With the building boom of the early 1970s, removal of runways and taxiways became an attractive proposition and much of East Kirkby's concrete was reclaimed. The 3,800 ft (1160m) north-eastern extension of runway 08/26 was left intact and this now serves as a seasonal base for crop-spraying aircraft working in the locality. Also left intact

Left: **Lancaster N-Nuts of 57 Sqn is refuelled at East Kirkby on 20th April 1944.** *(IWM CH12868)*

Right: **East Kirkby control tower in November 1970.** *(W.J.Taylor)*

Below left: **The pall of smoke immediately after a Lancaster of 57 Sqn blew up at dispersal on 17th April 1945 killing three people.** *(via M.Hodgson)*

Below right : **East Kirkby's hangars no longer house Lancasters, only potatoes. The aircraft mass parking area can also be seen in this May 1979 photograph.** *(W.J.Taylor)*

was the huge concrete mass-parking area built by the Americans in the 1950's and this is now used to stockpile huge wooden crates in which potatoes are moved from the fields to the storage depot.

To commemorate East Kirkby's wartime use, a memorial was erected close to the former Guardroom and dedicated in October 1979 (see Appendix K). After many years of dereliction the former watch office was converted into farm offices but these again fell into disuse. Following a recent change of ownership of that part of the airfield which contained some of the technical site, a project has been announced to restore the watch office to its 1945 condition. A number of intensive poultry units have been built on the airfield and on the site of the USAF base hospital.

From April 1980 the remaining part of the runway has been used by the East Kirkby Soaring Group. Started by former members of the Strubby club, this new group was operating three gliders in the summer of 1981: Slingsby T.21 BGA 1465, Grunau Baby BGA 1463 and EoN 460 BGA 1155. Also to be seen operating alongside the gliders was a Typhoon Tripacer microlight aircraft G-MBAI. A number of private owners have also used East Kirkby as a home for their aircraft, usually during the summer months, and those based here recently have included Cessna F-150L G-BAXV and two Cessna 172Ms, G-BBKI and G-BIHI.

Elsham

2 km ENE of Elsham Church
112/TA 055 138   210 ft (65 m) AMSL

Elsham Flight Station was situated just east of what became a Second World War airfield and the land is now used for agriculture. In December 1916 No.33 Squadron had moved to Lincolnshire and established its Headquarters at Gainsborough. In early 1917 Elsham aerodrome was opened as a Home Defence Base from which 'C' Flight operated eight Royal Aircraft Factory F.E.2b and F.E.2d aircraft. Activity by Zeppelins over this area was frequent and the flight played a defensive role in each raid, managing several times to drive the invading airships from their intended targets but never succeeding in destroying one.

During the daylight hours the flight was engaged in training and one corner

of the airfield was used as a practice bombing range. Lieutenant Leefe Robinson, VC, was stationed at Elsham for a time after he had become famous for shooting down the German Schutte Lanz airship S.L11 over Potters Bar in Hertfordshire. He was posted on to France from Elsham in 1917.

In June 1918 the detached flights of 33 Squadron were all moved to Kirton in Lindsey (Manton) and as the Zeppelin threat diminished, the Home Defence aerodrome at Elsham was closed down. Typical of its type, it covered 120 acres (48 ha).

Elsham Wolds

1 km NE of Elsham Church
112/TA 045 135   250 ft (75 m) AMSL

This station began to operate within 1 Group Bomber Command in July 1941, but it was not complete when 103 Squadron arrived from Newton in Nottinghamshire on the 11th of that month. There was however little delay before the station was declared operational and the squadron's Vickers Wellingtons undertook their first operation on 24th July. By the end of the year the station was able to record as many as seventeen aircraft airborne on a single night.

Handley Page Halifaxes began to replace Wellingtons in the summer of 1940 and the first raids using this type were undertaken in August. At the same time 103 Squadron Conversion Flight was formed to enable pilots to train on the four-engined type, but was re-

numbered 'B' Flight of 1656 Conversion Unit on 10th October and early the following month it moved to Lindholme in Yorkshire. Hardly had the station become used to the Halifax when there was another change of aircraft. This time 103 Squadron converted to the Avro Lancaster, the change being complete by the middle of December.

In November 1943 'C' Flight of 103 Squadron was detached to provide the operational nucleus for 576 Squadron which was formed at Elsham Wolds; the two squadrons operated together until October 1944. On 1st January 1944 Elsham Wolds became the Base Station of 13 Base, controlling the nearby airfields at Kirmington and North Killingholme. No. 576 Squadron left on 30th October for Fiskerton and it was not until 2nd April 1945 that 103 Squadron was joined by 100 Squadron from Grimsby. The last bombing mission flown from Elsham Wolds took place on 25th April and at the end of the war aircraft from the base dropped supplies over Holland and ferried home ex-prisoners-of-war.

Elsham Wolds was the home of probably the most famous Lancaster of the war, ED888 coded PM+M2 (Mike Squared) of 103 Squadron. It made its first operational sortie on 4th May 1943 and, after service with both 103 and 576 Squadrons, was retired in December 1944 with 140 missions to its credit — a Bomber Command record.

No. 103 Squadron was disbanded on 25th November 1945 and re-formed the following day as 57 Squadron which moved to Scampton, together with 100 Squadron, at the beginning of

Left: **Piper Pawnee crop-sprayers operating from part of the disused main runway at East Kirkby, 4th July 1978.** *(W.J.Taylor)*

Right: **Lancaster EB888 'Mike Squared' of 103 Sqn takes off from Elsham Wolds. This aircraft flew more operational missions than any other Lancaster.** *(IWM HU2352)*

Left: **103 Sqn Lancaster with all armament removed used for repatriating prisoners of war in 1945.** *(via T.Stone)*

Below: **Wellington IC R1459 of 103 Sqn after a forced landing near the main gate of Elsham Wolds, 22nd October 1941.** *(Wg Cdr K.H.Wallis)*

December. On 15th December 1945 13 Base was disbanded and control of the two sub-stations was passed to Hemswell. Elsham Wolds itself passed into the care of 23 Group Flying Training Command and an advance party of seven Airspeed Horsa gliders with Armstrong Whitworth Albemarle tug aircraft from 21 Heavy Glider Conversion Unit at Brize Norton, Oxfordshire, arrived on 13th December. By the end of December the remainder of the unit had arrived.

Due to the poor serviceability of the Albemarle, twelve Halifax Mk.3 aircraft were added to the strength of the unit in February 1946. The unit operated from Elsham Wolds until December 1946, when the dispersed nature and poor condition of the airfield forced a move to North Luffenham in Rutland. The station also housed the Flying

Training Command Instructors School which arrived during December 1945, but it had moved on by the end of 1946.

On 5th December 1946 the station was placed on Care and Maintenance but in 1948 its 750 acres (300 ha) were de-requisitioned and eventually sold. When the station was built it was provided with three hangars, one permanent J Type and two T2s, which were grouped together on the eastern edge of the airfield. On its selection as a Base Station it was necessary to contruct more hangars for the 13 Base aircraft major servicing unit and

Right: **The J-type hangar and watch office, the latter now converted to a residence. Elsham Wolds 1979.**
(P.H.T.Green)

Below: **Elsham Wolds, June 1970. Note the remains of arrester gear installations at each side of the runway ends.**
(Fairey Surveys)

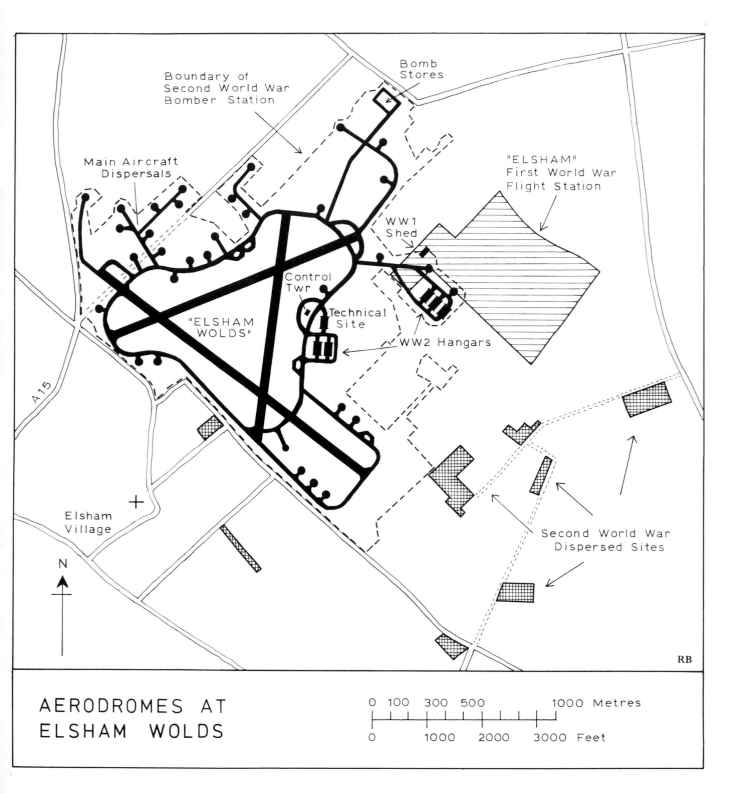

Boundary of
Second World War
Bomber Station

Bomb
Stores

Main Aircraft
Dispersals

"ELSHAM"
First World War
Flight Station

WW1
Shed

Control
Twr

"ELSHAM
WOLDS"

Technical
Site

WW2 Hangars

A15

Elsham
Village

Second World War
Dispersed Sites

N

RB

AERODROMES AT
ELSHAM WOLDS

0   100   300   500   1000 Metres

0   1000   2000   3000 Feet

three MAP B1 hangars were built side by side on an extension of the airfield to the east. Following the Second World War the hangars were used for storage but the temporary ones were soon dismantled leaving only the J Type, which remains today. The former watch office also remains, having been converted into a dwelling.

During the 1970s the shape of the air-field began to change as new construction work was started. A water treatment works was built in the western corner of the airfield and on 20th June 1975 it was opened by Air Vice-Marshal D.G. Evans CBE, the Air Officer Commanding 1 Gp. The works form part of the River An-cholme scheme to provide water for Humberside and are operated by the Lincoln Water Division of the Anglian Water Authority. Since then the airfield has been bisected by one of the approach roads for the new Humber Bridge.

At the time of the opening of the water treatment works, a memorial plaque to 103 Squadron and RAF Elsham Wolds was unveiled in the foyer. This has subsequently been expanded to include 576 Squadron and a memorial garden was added in 1981 *(see App K)*.

Above: **The relatively dense population of an RAF station usually necessited construction of a water tower, as typifed by this example at Faldingworth in April 1980.** *(W.J.Taylor)*

Faldingworth

3 km WNW of Faldingworth Church
112, 121/TF 035 855 50 ft (15 m) AMSL

The second on-site review for an airfield on the former Toft Grange decoy near Faldingworth was held on 16th June 1942, the go-ahead to start construction being given on 1st August. The initial opening phase commenced on 5th July 1943 and on 27th July Faldingworth opened as an incomplete satellite for 1 Group Heavy Conversion Base at Lindholme in Yorkshire. On 8th August the mixed Avro Lancaster and Handley Page Halifax fleet of 1667 Heavy Conversion Unit arrived from Lindholme, the move being completed in time to allow the first course to commence training on 11th August. No.1 Group HCB was renamed 11 Base on 18th September and Faldingworth remained one of its sub-stations.

With the decision to concentrate all the Lancaster training of 1 Group within one unit, the Lancaster Flight of 1667 HCU was renamed 'C' Flight of 1 Lancaster Finishing School, which formed with its Headquarters at Lindholme on 21st November 1943. The Conversion Unit at Faldingworth then became an all Halifax unit established for thirty-two aircraft. Faldingworth was re-allocated as a sub-station of 14 Base which formed on 23rd January 1944 with its Headquarters at Ludford Magna, and the following day the Lancasters left for Hemswell. The air party of 'A' Flight of 1667 HCU left for Sandtoft on 18th February, followed the next day by 'B' and 'C' Flights.

On 1st March 300 (Polish) Squadron arrived from Ingham, at which time the squadron was operating one flight of Vickers Wellingtons, and was in the process of converting to the Lancaster. No. 1546 BAT Flight formed at Faldingworth on 8th May with eight Airspeed Oxford aircraft, based there due to shortage of space at Gamston in Nottinghamshire where it was to operate with 18(P) AFU. A second flight for 300 Squadron was formed on 12th June but, owing to a lack of Polish nationals, it was manned by English personnel who were replaced as more Polish crews became available.

When 153 Squadron was formed at Kirmington on 7th October with a nucleus drawn from 166 Squadron, also at Kirmington, a replacement flight for 166 Squadron was formed at Faldingworth the same day. No. 153 Squadron moved from Kirmington to Scampton on 15th October and the new flight of 166 Squadron moved from Faldingworth to become 'C' Flight of its parent unit. The BAT Flight was disbanded on 9th January 1945, leaving 300 Squadron as the sole inhabitant of Faldingworth. No. 300 Squadron was the only Polish unit to operate the Lancaster and it participated in the post-war Operations *Dodge, Manna* and *Exodus*. No. 14 Base disbanded on 25th October 1945 and Faldingworth became an independent unit.

No.300 Squadron continued to operate the Lancaster from Faldingworth until 11th October 1946 when it to was disbanded. Later that month 305 (Polish) Squadron arrived from Germany, but shortly afterwards its de Havilland Mosquitos were relinquished and on 1st January 1947 it was disbanded. The station was then placed on Care and Maintenance, becoming an inactive unit parented from Hemswell.

In April 1949 the station was transferred from Bomber Command to 42 Group Maintenance Command for use as a sub-site for 93 MU, which controlled it until October 1957 when Faldingworth became the home of 92MU, which formed that day, tasked with the supply of munitions to other Royal Air Force units. In November 1972 92MU was disbanded following a ceremony at Scampton

The 720 acres (290 ha) of land are now under the control of Scampton, the domestic accommodation having been used to house displaced Ugandan Asians in 1972 and 1973. In recent years the former munitions storage site has been taken over by the British Manufacturing and Research Company from Grantham. During 1979 a mural located on the wall of the former operations room used by 300 Squadron was rediscovered and donated to the Lincolnshire Aviation Museum at Tattershall. The mural depicts briefing details of the last night mission flown by the squadron when fifteen aircraft attacked Potsdam on the night of 14-15th April 1945. During early 1980 much of the former domestic site constructed in 1959 was being refurbished for use as office accommodation and the Officers' Mess and officers married quarters site was placed on the market for sale.

Fiskerton

1 km N of Fiskerton Church
121/TF 045 730   70 ft (22 m) AMSL

Fiskerton aerodrome was constructed during 1942 and opened that November, but the first unit did not move in until the New Year, that being 49 Squadron which moved from Scampton. No. 52 Base was established at Scampton on 10th May 1943 and Fiskerton became one of its sub-stations. However, 49 Squadron was forced to move to Dunholme Lodge on 13th September because the Fiskerton runways started to break up. Repairs were accordingly made and the squadron returned on 24th October.

The Airspeed Oxfords of 1514 Beam Approach Training Flight arrived from Coningsby on 2nd January 1944. In October 1944 52 Base was handed over

to 1 Group Bomber Command and with effect from 7th October Fiskerton became a sub-station of 15 Base. No. 49 Squadron, however, remained with 5 Group and moved to Fulbeck on 10th October. The BAT flight was a Flying Training Command lodger unit and it remained at Fiskerton following the change of Group, as did a detachment of de Havilland Mosquitoes from 141 Squadron which had arrived on 4th September.

The first unit of 1 Group to be moved to the station was 576 Squadron which arrived from Elsham Wolds on 30th October. Two days later 150 Squadron was re-formed at Fiskerton, its Avro Lancasters all coming from within Group resources, each operational Base allocating five aircraft. The new squadron moved to Hemswell on 22nd November and the BAT Flight disbanded on 9th January 1945.

A re-organisation of units within 1

Above: **Lancaster C-Charlie of 576 Sqn landing at Fiskerton, 1945.** *(P.H.T.Green)*

Below: **The operations board at Fiskerton showing 49 Squadron's order of battle for a Berlin raid, 18/19th November 1943. Note that all aircraft returned safely although many landed at other airfields.** *(Bill Bay)*

Nº 49 SQUADRON BERLIN 18/19 Nov 1943

A/C LETTER	CAPTAIN	BOMB LOAD	CALL SIGN	FIXES ETC	ATO	ETR/ATR
O	ADAMS		NMY	LANDED WARBOYS	1657	0131
A	DAY	"	"	TANGMERE	1658	0140
G	COTTINGHAM	"	"	DUNSFOLD	1700	0115
N	EDY				1702	0112
C	HALES				1704	0135
T	BLACKMORE				1705	0121
M	JUPP				1706	0116
H	IDDERLEY				1710	0147
F	REYNOLDS				1708	0129
V	TANCRED				1707	0137
S	PALMER				1706	0138
R	FOSTER			LANDED CRANWELL	1711	0135
J	BACON			WOODHALL	1714	0159
U	WEBB			GRANSDEN	1715	0229
K	JONES				1716	0142
Q	BARNES				1719	0148
E	SIMPSON			LANDED MANSTON	1717	0100
B	GEORGE			W. MALLING	1720	0139
D	ROANTREE				1713	0115

CLOUD. BASE A/C Nº&LETTER CAPT

LOCAL WEATHER
TIME:
STATION VIS QFE WIND
SCAMPTON
FISKERTON

AERODROME STATE

FIXES QDM'S ETC
A/C Lᵗ A/C Lᵗ A/C Lᵗ
FIX TIME FIX TIME FIX TIME

OFFICER I/C G/c GRINDELL.

Right: **The watch office and crash tender shed at Fiskerton stand forlorn in 1978, shortly before their demolition.** *(Bill Baguley/Rod Houldsworth)*

Below: **Folkingham, 3rd January 1947.** *(DoE, Crown Copyright)*

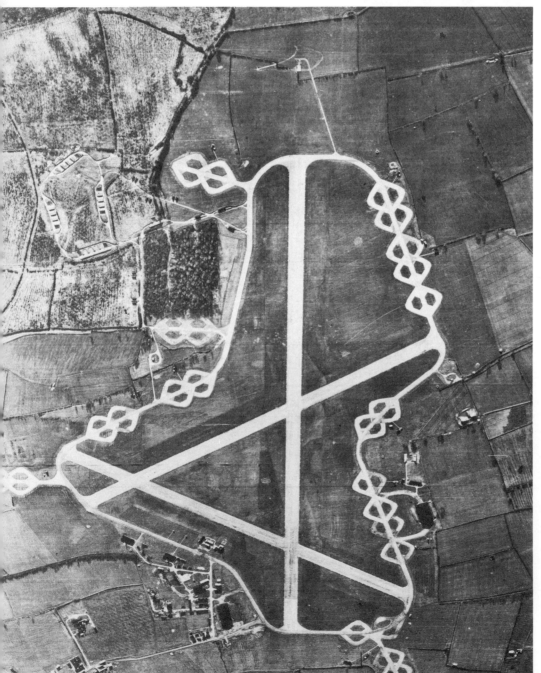

Group saw the former 'C' Flight of 625 Squadron at Kelstern move to Fiskerton on 5th April to join 576 Squadron as its 'C' Flight. Also arriving that day, but from Scampton, was the 1 Group Bombing-Up School. The Mosquitoes of the 141 Squadron detachment left on 3rd July 1945 and on 19th September 576 Squadron was disbanded. No. 15 Base disbanded on 20th October and on 20th November the station was handed over to 40 Group, Maintenance Command

As a sub-site of 16 MU at Stafford, the station was placed on Care and Maintenance with effect from 15th December. The airfield was closed to all flying, but the main runway remained open for emergency use. During 1947 the dispersed hutted accommodation sites were allocated to the Ministry of Health for use as emergency housing for homeless families. The majority of the airfield's 630 acres (256 ha) were sold to farmers during 1963 and 1964, but in one corner today stands the Headquarters building of 15 Group, Royal Observer Corps. The one remaining hangar is derelict.

Folkingham

3.5 km W of Aslackby Church
130/TF 050 305   250 ft (75 m) AMSL

The site that was subsequently to become Folkingham aerodrome was first brought into use during 1940 as a decoy site for Spitalgate, and as such it was bombed several times. The decoy site was equipped with Battle dummy air-

Left: **A derelict installation within the Thor missile site at Folkingham, November 1971.** *(W.J.Taylor)*

craft but was abandoned by August 1942 when it was decided to build a full station on the site. Construction took place during 1943 and on completion the new airfield was allocated for use by the US Ninth Army Air Force.

American personnel first occupied Folkingham during January 1944 to prepare the station to receive the 313 Troop Carrier Group, the first elements of which arrived from Sicily on 4th February 1944. The group comprised four Troop Carrier Squadrons, 29, 47, 48 and 49; the last element arrived on 5th March. Equipped with Douglas C-47 aircraft, the group formed part of the 52nd Troop Carrier Wing.

The group began an intensive training period to ready itself for its part in the coming invasion of Europe. During the D-Day operations the 313 TCG dropped parachutists and for its work that day was awarded its second Distinguished Unit Citation. Parachutists from the 1st Parachute Brigade of the British First Airborne Division were dropped on Arnhem and Nijmegen in September and gliders were released in back-up operations a few days later. As the Allied advance pressed on it was decided to move the group to France so that it would be nearer the front line. Accordingly, the 313 TCG left Folkingham on 28th February 1945, by which time it had started to receive Douglas C-53 aircraft.

The airfield was returned to the control of the Air Ministry following the departure of the Americans and handed over to 40 Group, Maintenance Command on 4th June. Although still a sub-site of 16 MU at Stafford, 3 RAF Regiment Sub-Depot was formed at

Folkingham shortly after the end of the war and many RAF Regiment Field Squadrons moved to Folkingham to disband. Apart from housing these disbanding units, the Sub-Depot also carried out the advanced training of recruits under the control of the Regimental Depot at Belton Park; but it had closed by mid-1946. Later the airfield saw service as a Civil Defence training area and as a test track for BRM racing cars.

Folkingham's connection with BRM was significant as it allowed the company to test a British contender for the new World Championship Grand Prix series only ten miles from its workshops in Bourne. Design and construction of the first BRM car began in 1947 but due to many difficulties it was not completed until December 1949. The car was formally unveiled to the press at Folkingham on 15 December 1949 when it was demonstrated by Raymond Mays and hailed by the press as a world beater. Folkingham was the scene for much of the development testing of the early cars that were beset by a series of early misfortunes which were not to be vindicated for more than twelve years.

As the 1950s drew to a close, Folkingham was selected to become a base for three Douglas Thor IRBMs which were to form part of the North Luffenham missile wing within 3 Group, of Bomber Command. The missile complex was constructed in the centre of the former airfield and the three missiles were operated by 223 Squadron which formed at Folkingham in December 1959. For three and a half years the squadron maintained its vigil but in August 1963, the Thor force was declared non-operational and the

Squadron disbanded. The missile site was closed and its installations were dismantled although the massive concrete blast walls remained for many years.

With the demise of the Thor there was no further use for Folkingham airfield and between 1965 and 1967 it was sold. Since then the airfield has almost totally reverted to agricultural uses. Almost all of the perimeter taxiway, the runways and dispersals have now been removed and almost all of the buildings have been demolished. In late 1981 part of the main runway and a few adjacent dispersals remained and were in use as storage areas for large quantities of used contractors plant and machinery.

Freiston

3.2 km SSE of Freiston Church
131/TF 388 408   10 ft (3 m) AMSL

After an aerial survey of the South Lincolnshire coastline, a suitable site for a bombing and gunnery range for the new RNAS Flying School at Cranwell was selected on the mud flats to the south of the village of Freiston. In early summer of 1916, several targets were set up, at least one of them being an old and unserviceable aircraft.

Trainee pilots flew across from Cranwell and used the range for part of their training, but with a journey time of about forty minutes each way, depending on the weather, it was not long before a 90 acre (36 ha) tract of farmland was requisitioned for a landing strip. As the flying training programme expanded, the landing ground at Freiston was enlarged and the RNAS School of Aerial Fighting and Bomb Dropping was established as a satellite unit of Cranwell from where pilots spent part of their training period at Freiston.

A complement of aeroplanes was based at the school and comprised Royal Aircraft Factory B.E.2s, Avro 504s, Sopwith Camels, and later on, Sopwith

Above: **The Frieston hangars circa 1918.** *(via LAM)*

Left: **Sopwith Snipe E6274 at Frieston.** *(via LAM)*

Below: **Gunnery training at Frieston.** *(via LAM)*

Dolphins, as well as a flight of Bristol Scouts which were used for anti-Zeppelin duties, which attempted to intercept Zeppelins in transit over Boston on several occasions. In 1918 Freiston was again enlarged and became 4 Fighting School with the task of training pilots for 'fighting scout' squadrons, an assignment undertaken until the aerodrome was finally closed in the spring of 1919.

Soon after closing, a severe gale blew down several of the aerodrome buildings, which were subsequently sold off with the rest of the surplus establishment equipment at a public auction. The only remains of the former aerodrome to be seen today are the foundations of the Headquarters building. However, in Freiston churchyard there are several graves of pilots who were killed during their flying training at Freiston.

Left: **Post-war weapon storage at Fulbeck 1945/1946.** *(D.Jones)*

Below: **The former watch office at Fulbeck derelict but still standing in April 1980.** *(W.J.Taylor)*

Fulbeck

3.5 km SSW of Brant Broughton Church
121/SK 900 510   50 ft (15 m) AMSL

Fulbeck aerodrome came into operation in late 1940 as a Relief Landing Ground for 2 Flying Instructors School at Cranwell. Later the station was allocated to 5 Group Bomber Command and was closed to all flying on 25th February 1942 for the construction of paved runways. When these were almost complete, 1485 (Bomber) Gunnery Flight moved in from Dunholme Lodge to carry out gunnery training for 5 Group, operating a mixture of aircraft including the Westland Lysander, Armstrong Whitworth Whitley, Hawker Henley and Miles Martinet.

By December the aerodrome was ready for night flying and the RAF College SFTS started to use the stations night flying facilities. In May 1943 1506 BAT Flight arrived from Waddington with Airspeed Oxfords, which were immediately allocated out to the operational squadrons within the Group who were then free to carry out their own training as they wished. The personnel of the flight were absorbed into 1485 Flight, but a Headquarters Unit did remain in operation.

On 23rd July 1485 Flight started to operate two Avro Lancasters on loan from 1660 and 1661 HCUs, but as they could not be spared from the training programme at the Conversion Units they were exchanged a week later for five Avro Manchesters. In early August another increase in strength was made when the

unit's first Vickers Wellington arrived. Both flights moved to Skellingthorpe on 23rd August and the station was closed and placed on Care and Maintenance. However, on 5th September, authority was granted for Cranwell to take over night flying facilities again following the loss of a Cranwell aircraft to suspected enemy action during night flying from Caistor.

The station was then allocated to the US Ninth Army Air Force and assigned to the 53 Troop Carrier Wing as Station 488. The first unit arrived at Fulbeck directly from the United States on 7th October 1943; this was the 434th Troop Carrier Group operating Douglas C-47 aircraft. The group commenced an intensive training programme which included dropping parachutists and the towing of Airspeed Horsa and General Aircraft

Hadrian gliders, but on 10th December it moved to Welford Park in Berkshire.

The replacement unit was the 442nd TCG which arrived at Fulbeck with C-47 and Douglas C-53 aircraft on 29th March 1944, and was assigned to 50 TCW. Training continued in preparation for the invasion and during the D-Day landings of 6th June the group dropped parachutists near the beaches, for which it was awarded a Distinguished Unit Citation. On 13th June the 442nd TCG was moved to Weston Zoyland in Somerset and from August to September Fulbeck housed the 440th TCG for two short periods. During the ill-fated Arnhem operation of September 1944 the 440th TCG was operating from the station and dropped elements of the American 101st Airborne Division 'The Screaming Eagles'. In late September the station was returned to RAF control and allocated to 5 Group.

No. 56 Base formed at Syerston in Nottinghamshire on 1st October 1944 and Fulbeck became one of its sub-stations. Ten days later 49 Squadron arrived from Fiskerton and re-commenced operations with its Lancaster aircraft on 19th October, being joined by 189 Squadron from Bardney on 2nd November. Lancaster aircraft of the Automatic Gun Laying Turret Training Flight arrived at Fulbeck from Binbrook on 1st February 1945 to continue operations with 49 Squadron, which had pioneered the use of the AGLT. No. 189 Squadron returned to Bardney on 8th April and the Bomber Command Film Unit moved to Fulbeck, a temporary measure pending the move of all Fulbeck based units to Syerston on 22nd April. No. 56 Base disbanded on 25th April and Fulbeck was placed on Care and Maintenance.

Maintenance Command took over the station on 1st June 1945 and 4 Equipment Dispersal Depot was formed, which operated as part of 55 (Maintenance) Wing and was re-numbered 255 Maintenance Unit on 15th June. The first surplus stores arrived from Gamston in Nottinghamshire four days later. The hangars were fitted out with some 750 tons of racking, and as the roofs were in poor condition, all the hangars were re-roofed. No. 255 MU became the controlling unit for several other disused airfields in the area: Saltby in Leicestershire was taken over on 12th December; Fiskerton on 14th January 1946; Leicester East on 21st January. In addition a Care and Maintenance party was sent to take over Balderton in Nottinghamshire on 17th July 1946.

Disposal of the accumulated stores started in January 1948 when the first of several sales were held. In all some 1500 tons of equipment were put up for sale in 1198 lots at the first sale, realising just over £29,000. The sixth and final sale to be held at Fulbeck took place during August when 13,000 tons of equipment realised £159,291 10s 0d. As the MU ran down the station was placed on a Care and Maintenance footing with effect from 30th November 1948.

During November 1953 Fulbeck became a sub-site of 93 MU and also housed the Air Historical Branch collection of historic aircraft which contained many of the aircraft now on display in the RAF Museum at Hendon, including Avro Lancaster R5868, the one time

proud 'gate guardian' at Scampton. Not all of the aircraft were so fortunate though, for when the collection was dispersed in the late 1950s, some of the exhibits were scrapped. It is believed that at least a Handley Page Hampden and a Dornier Do 217 were disposed of at this time.

In 1956 the 670 acre (268 ha) airfield was brought into use as a Relief Landing Ground for the RAF College at Cranwell, and continued to be used as such until the late 1960s. Since then Fulbeck has seen occasional use as a venue for various motor sport and aeromodelling events. The former grassed areas are used for agricultural purposes and the one remaining hangar is used as a store, while the runway system is intact and used on occasions for go-karting. In early 1980 local newspapers were carrying details of proposals to use Fulbeck as a military training area.

Gainsborough

1.3 km SW of Gainsborough Railway Station
112, 121/SK 812 888 20 ft (6 m) AMSL

During 1916 33 (Home Defence) Squadron was transferred to Lincolnshire for anti-Zeppelin patrol duties. Three of its flights were detached to Flight Stations at Brattleby ('A' Flight), Kirton in Lindsey ('B' Flight) and Elsham ('C' Flight). The Headquarters was established in a large house called 'The Lawns' situated in Summerhill Road, Gainsborough, and its landing ground was at 'Laynes Field' across the river in the county of Nottinghamshire.

On 3rd September 1917 a nucleus of officers was detached from the Headquarters to form 192 Training Squadron, a night fighter unit which, although formed at Gainsborough, was destined to operate from Retford in Nottinghamshire, where it arrived on 24th September. In June 1918, as the threat of Zeppelin attacks diminished, 33 Squadron began to undertake training duties and the squadron Headquarters then moved to Kirton in Lindsey, along with 'A' and 'C' Flights. With the departure of the Headquarters staff, 'The Lawns' was derequisitioned and handed back to its former owners. Shortly after the war the house itself was demolished and a more modern building was erected in its

place, still retaining the name of 'The Lawns'.

During the First World War, the well known Gainsborough engineering firm of Marshall & Co ltd., was awarded a contract to build two hundred Bristol F.2b Fighters. It is probable that these aircraft were test flown from the field situated near the Trent Bridge and known to local inhabitants as 'Laynes Field'. There was one hangar erected on this field, but at the end of hostilities it was dismantled and moved to Southolme for use as a garage. The 30 acre (12 ha) landing strip was closed down at the same time and returned to agricultural use, the purpose it fulfils today.

Gosberton

7.5 km WSW of Gosberton Church
130/TF 167 297   10 ft (3 m) AMSL

A class 2 landing ground (unlit) was established on Gosberton Fen for the use of 38 (Home Defence) Squadron during its period of operation over south Lincolnshire from October 1916 until May 1918. In the closing phase of the First World War, from August 1918 until June 1919, it came under 90 (Home Defence) Squadron based at Buckminster. The field was situated adjacent to the north side of the B1397 road half a mile east of the South Forty Foot Drain. It had strips of 400 and 640 yards, covered 55 acres (22 ha) and is today farmed. Several Zeppelin bomb craters can still be seen when the site is freshly ploughed.

Goxhill

1 km E of Goxhill Church
113/TA 115 215   20 ft (6 m) AMSL

A war office map dated 30th April 1916 shows an RFC Landing Ground at Goxhill. No subsequent references have been found regarding its use but the site surveyed may have been within the aerodrome built twenty-five years later.

Construction of Goxhill aerodrome began during early 1941 and the station opened within 1 Group Bomber Command on 26th June. The Air Ministry established a target towing flight at Bin-

Above: **Spitfire Vc W3815 of the 496th FTG at Goxhill during 1944.** *(via P.H.T.Green)*

Left: **P-38 Lightning 267199 of the 55th FG, 1944.** *(via P.H.T.Green)*

Below: **P-47B Thunderbolt 27944 'Strato Viking' during 1944 probably from 3rd Gunnery/Tow Target Flight USAAF.** *(via P.H.T.Green)*

brook for the use of 1 Group on 5th August, but due to lack of space there it was decided that the flight would form at Goxhill and move to Binbrook at a later date. The 1 Group Target Towing Flight was duly formed at Goxhill on 18th September with an establishment of nine Westland Lysanders; the first two arrived on 25th October, an exciting arrival because one aircraft ran off the runway and tipped on its nose. The flight left Goxhill on 10th November as space had become available at Binbrook.

The following month the station was transferred to 12 Group, Fighter Command and for ten days during January 1942 was used by the Spitfires of 616 Squadron from Kirton in Lindsey during a trials programme. Later in the spring the station was allocated for the use of 15 (P)AFU based at Kirmington, and

Above: **Bird Strike?** Three A-20s taking off from Goxhill in 1944. (*via P.H.T.Green*)

Left: **Ensign raising ceremony at Goxhill, 1944.** (*via P.H.T.Green*)

Below left: **The former watch office and fire tender shed still standing in July 1980.** (*W.J.Taylor*)

later still was reserved for the use of the US Eighth Army Air Force which began to arrive in England during 1942.

The first American unit to use Goxhill arrived directly from the United States on 10th June, this being the Headquarters Unit and 71st Fighter Squadron of 1st Fighter Group and its aircraft, Lockheed P-38 Lightnings, started to arrive the following month. Goxhill was established as a fighter training base to train pilots in the procedures they would need while operating in Europe; and the formal handover of the station took place in August.

The period spent at Goxhill varied but was usually in the order of one or two months. Aircraft were not confined to the P-38, for the Spitfires of the 52nd FG arrived during August and the Bell P-39 Airacobras of the 81st FG fol-

lowed during October. Lightnings returned during December and the Republic P-47 Thunderbolt appeared in early 1943. The arrival of units was normally planned so that only one was in residence at any one time.

In late 1943 it was decided to form an independent unit to train all P-38 Lightning and North American P-51 Mustang pilots for both the 8th and 9th Army Air Forces. Designated the 496th Fighter Training Group, this new unit was formed at Goxhill on 25th December 1943 and comprised two squadrons, 554 and 555 Fighter Training Squadrons, which operated the P-38 and P-51 respectively. In conjunction with the fighters the group also operated a number of Lysanders and Masters for target towing and general duties from Goxhill until it was moved to Halesworth in Suffolk on

15th February 1945.

The station had been handed back to the RAF on 20th January and when the Americans left a Care and Maintenance party was installed under the control of Kirton in Lindsey. Maintenance Command took the station over on 27th May and during 1948 the requisitioned sites containing the dispersed hutted accommodation were allocated to the Ministry of Health for emergency use. In recent years the hangars and buildings have been in use as a Home Office Supply Depot, the airfield's 500 acres (200 ha) having been sold during 1964 and 1965 and largely returned to the plough. However, compared with many disused airfields in Lincolnshire, considerable expanses of undisturbed concrete remain.

Right: **Waltham 1938. Note the new buildings and aircraft of 25 E&RFTS.** *(via P.H.T.Green)*

Greenland Top

1.5 km W of Stallingborough Church
113/TA 180 120   40 ft (12 m) AMSL

When 33 (Home Defence) Squadron was moved into Lincolnshire in December 1916 a Night Landing Ground was established at Greenland Top but, at the beginning of 1918 as increased damage was being caused to coastal convoys by enemy U-Boats, a plan was made to augment the seaplane and flying boat patrols with land-based aeroplanes. As the majority of shipping losses were sustained within ten miles of the coastline, it was reasoned that if our convoys could be patrolled at twenty-minute intervals by aircraft, the U-Boats would be deterred from making bold attacks, and so Greenland Top was accordingly up-graded to a Naval Operational Aerodrome.

Some 300 DH.6 training aeroplanes were surplus to the training requirement and these were chosen for the new coastal patrol duties. When equippped with bomb racks and flown as single-seaters the DH.6s were able to carry a 100 lb bomb into action. Two thirds of the patrol aircraft were modified to this configuration and instructions for the formation of thirty-two special duty flights were issued on 19th April 1918.

Selected as the base for one special duty flight, Greenland Top was transferred to the control of 79 Wing, 18 (Operations) Group, and 505 Flight was formed on 31st May. In August the flights were absorbed into squadrons and 505 Flight became 'B' Flight of 251 Squadron which had its Headquarters at Hornsea (Yorkshire). However, around October, the flight moved north to West Ayton (near Scarborough) where it was later fully absorbed into the squadron.

With RNAS Killingholme being used in part for the primary training of seaplane pilots, a few wheeled types were maintained there and Greenland Top was used as a Relief Landing Ground for

the pilots undergoing training at Killingholme. In December 1918 arrangements were made for all anti-submarine flights within 18 Group to be concentrated at Killingholme and by April all units were either at Killingholme, Greenland Top, North Coates or Seaton Carew in County Durham. Flights from 251, 252 and 256 Squadrons were gradually run down and all three squadrons disbanded on 30th June 1919.

With the disbandment of the anti-submarine flights, the 112 acre (45 ha) aerodrome was closed down and all the buildings, none of which were permanent, were removed.

Grimsby (Waltham)

2.5 km SE of Waltham Church
113/TA 280 025   50 ft (16 m) AMSL

After several years of negotiations a small civil airport was opened at Waltham near Grimsby on 12th June 1933 by Major R.H.S.Mealing of the Air Ministry. Originally used by the Lincolnshire Aero Club and several small air services, it was not until June 1938 that the Air Ministry took any further interest in the airport.

After inspection by officials from 5 Group, Bomber Command, 25 Elementary and Reserve Flying Training School was established at Waltham. Equipped with de Havilland Tiger Moths and Miles Magisters, the school trained members of the Royal Air Force Volunteer Reserve. The School's instructors were civilians employed by the Herts and Essex Aero

Club Ltd., the company which managed the airport at that time.

In September 1938 a local branch of the Civil Air Guard was formed at Waltham, which, administered by the Herts and Essex Aero Club, also used club aircraft which, at that time were a mixture of popular light types of the period, including the BA Swallow and Avro Avian. This Government-subsidised unit enabled its members to receive weekend flying instruction at the very low rate of 10/- per hour for standard training types (aircraft above 1,200 lb) and 5/- per hour for the lighter types. Several members of the CAG went on to achieve fame in the RAF during the war and at least one member of the Grimsby unit was awarded the DFC.

Early in 1939 25 E&RFTS was enlarged, a few Hawker Harts and Hawker Hinds being taken on charge and training expanded to include air observers, wireless operators and air gunners. However, volunteers were slow in coming forward, and by the time the school was closed on 1st September 1939 the full quota of aircrew had not been accepted. In July 1939 control of the airfield had been taken from the civil authority and for a short time the buildings were utilised by the Army — the 6th Battalion the Leicestershire Regiment.

The airfield was formally requisitioned in May 1940 and after the laying of concrete runways it became operational as a bomber station within 1 Group, Bomber Command. When it opened the station became a satellite of Binbrook and was given the official title of RAF Station Grimsby. Although known throughout the war as such, it is still

91

known locally as Waltham.

On 15th November 1941 the Vickers Wellingtons of 12 and 142 Squadrons were detached to Grimsby from Binbrook for operational purposes and, although both returned to their home base the following day, 'A' and 'B' Flights of 142 Squadron moved back to Grimsby on 26th November 1941. No.142 Squadron operated from Grimsby until December 1942 when, on the 9th, twelve of its Wellingtons left Grimsby for Blida in North Africa, the remainder of the units aircraft moving to Kirming-

ton on the 20th.

No.100 Squadron, which had ceased to exist after losing its Vickers Vilde-beests in the Far East earlier in the year, started to re-form at Grimsby on 15th December 1942. For a few days at the end of the month 'A' Flight was moved to Holme-on-Spalding-Moor in Yorkshire and 'B' Flight to Elsham Wolds while work was carried out at Grimsby. The squadron received its first Avro Lancasters on 24th January 1943 and began its work-up on the new aircraft. Bristol Beaufighters from 143 Squadron arrived

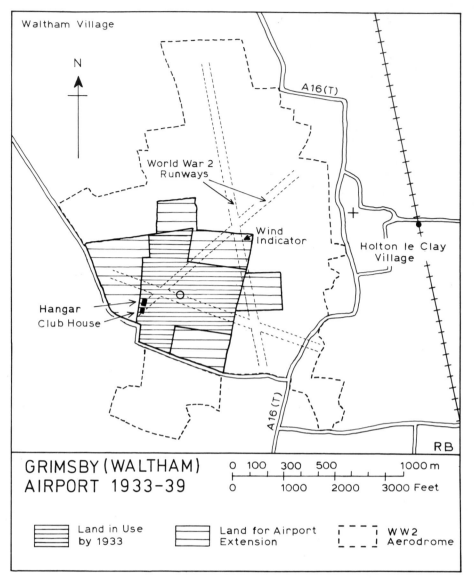

Waltham Village

N

World War 2
Runways

Wind
Indicator

A16(T)

Holton le Clay
Village

Hangar
Club House

A16(T)

RB

GRIMSBY (WALTHAM)
AIRPORT 1933-39

| 0 | 100 | 300 | 500 | | 1000 m |

| 0 | | 1000 | 2000 | 3000 Feet |

Land in Use by 1933   Land for Airport Extension   WW2 Aerodrome

the same day due to its home airfield at North Coates being unserviceable.

No.100 Squadron rapidly became operational and flew its first operation with the Lancaster on the night of 8-9th March. It was increased in strength to three flights on 9th April and on 21st October started to receive aircraft equipped with H2S radar. During the year Grimsby became a sub-station of RAF Base Binbrook, later re-numbered 12 Base.

No.550 Squadron formed at Grimsby on 25th November 1943 with a nucleus from 'C' Flight of 100 Squadron and became operational immediately, flying its first mission the following night. The squadron's permanent home was to be North Killingholme where it moved on 3rd January 1944. No.100 Squadron remained at Grimsby until 2nd April 1945

when it was moved to Elsham Wolds.

At the end of March 1945 5546 Works Flight moved to the airfield as part of the Air Ministry maintenance programme. It was planned to use the facilities of the station to store large quantities of Allied rations and two flights of the RAF Regiment were moved in at the beginning of April to carry out guarding duties but were removed one month later as the requirement no longer existed.

With the departure of 100 Squadron the airfield was placed on a Care and Maintenance footing until transferred to 40 Group Maintenance Command on 1st June 1945 for use as a storage sub-site of 35 MU at Heywood in Lancashire. Flying facilities were not maintained, and the airfield was used for storage purposes for several years, although during the summer of 1949 22 Gliding

School moved onto the airfield and operated gliders to give air experience to Air Cadets until moving to Kirton in Lindsey in June 1950.

Although much civil flying activity took place in the late 1950s, Grimsby was never restored to its pre-war status as a civil airport and despite an attempt to reform the Grimsby Flying Club, regular flying from the airfield ceased. In 1958 the land was sold and parts of the airfield have been put to a variety of industrial uses, including the bulk storage of foodstuffs in the hangars and scrap metal dealing on one of the dispersed accommodation sites.

The former airfield has now been bisected by diversion of the A16 trunk road around the adjacent village of Holton le Clay. There has been some reclamation of the paved areas, mainly aircraft

Harlaxton

2 kms E of Harlaxton Church
130/SK 905 325   420 ft (130 m) AMSL

A training aerodrome was established at Harlaxton during 1916 which became the home of 44 Training Squadron, although as the flying training programme expanded 26 and 54 Training Squadrons were posted to the aerodrome, the latter moving from nearby Spittlegate.

No.68 Squadron was formed at Harlaxton on 30th January 1917 from Australian personnel and, having received de Havilland D.H.5 aircraft, the squadron worked up as a fighter unit and moved to France in September that year. On 30th August 1917 No.98 Squadron was formed with a nucleus of officers from 4 Training Squadron. Destined to serve as a day bomber unit, it was posted to Old Sarum in Wiltshire, the same day that it was formed.

No.44 Training Squadron moved to Waddington in November 1917. Nos 26 and 54 Training Squadrons also left in 1918 but were replaced by 20 and 53 Training Squadrons, later amalgamated in July of that year to form 40 Training Depot station. No.40 TDS then became part of 24 Training Wing and the day-to-day administration of the unit came under Wing Headquarters at Spittlegate. Pilots were trained at the station in both fighter and reconnaissance roles until the end of the war but in 1919 the station was run down and closed in 1920.

The permanent buildings on the site of the aerodrome remained for several years after its closure. Indeed, some of the hangars remained until 1931 when they were sold. One hangar was taken to Boston and erected as a vehicle store for Holland Bros garage and until the mid-1970s it was a well-known landmark.

When the Royal Air Force expanded in the mid-1930s, the site of the First World War airfield at Harlaxton was reopened, this time as a Relief Landing Ground for Grantham and part of the airfield was also used as a practice bombing range by Hawker Hart trainers of 3 FTS from Grantham.

The airfield was enlarged when the Second World War started and brick buildings replaced the older wooden structures. A small control tower was also erected. With this expansion, the station became a satellite of Grantham and housed a detachment of 12 (P)AFU.

dispersals, but much of the runways still remain. In the mid-1970s efforts were made to make Grimsby the home airfield of the International Auster Pilots Club and planning permission was obtained for use of the runways, a hangar and the old clubhouse. Although several Austers and other light aircraft visited, some for maintenance by a locally based engineer, these efforts floundered and there has been no regular use of the airfield by aircraft.

In November 1978 a memorial to 100 Squadron was dedicated *(see Appendix K)* and in 1980 the disused runways were used to store hundreds of unsold imported cars. Today a number of the pre-war airport buildings still stand, including the original hangar and the former clubhouse.

Above: **A DH.4 and Crossley tender outside one of Harlaxton's aircraft sheds, 13th April 1917.** *(Crown Copyright H2385)*

Right: **Harlaxton, the home of 20 TS, 1918. Some twenty-four aircraft can be identified on the original print.** *Gerald Muir)*

Below: **RE.8 B845 crashed at Harlaxton.** *(RAF Museum P3691)*

Eight open-ended blister hangars were erected as shelter for the station's complement of Fairey Battles, Avro Ansons and Airspeed Oxfords, which were later joined by Bristol Blenheims.

The airfield was also often used as an emergency landing ground by damaged aircraft returning from operations. Crashes were frequent and for one period from Febraury 1942 to February 1943, a detachment of 58 Maintenance Unit was based at the airfield to deal with crashed aircraft and their recovery. On several occasions Vickers Wellingtons and Short Stirlings made forced landings on the airfield and in one incident an Avro Lancaster made an emergency landing, had repairs effected and then made a successful take-off from the small grass airfield.

By late 1944, the grass at Harlaxton was in such poor condition that all flying ceased and the site came under Care and Maintenance. However, in April 1945, Harlaxton became operational once again and was used as a Relief Landing Ground for 17 FTS operating from Spitalgate. This unit continued to use the airfield until 1947 when it was once more placed under Care and Maintenance before being closed down. The station was retained by the Air Ministry until 1958 when it was finally sold.

Since 1958 much of the airfield's 380 acres (150 ha) have vanished under the workings of an open cast iron ore mine. A few buildings still remain and are now used as farm stores.

Hemswell/Harpswell

1 km ESE of Hemswell Church
112/SK 940 905   230 ft (70 m) AMSL

The former First World War aerodrome at Harpswell was situated within what is now Hemswell airfield (see map). A Night Landing Ground was opened and maintained by 33 (Home Defence) Squadron at Harpswell in December 1916 and was used as such until the end of hostilities.

In the summer of 1917 it was decided to enlarge the landing ground and turn it into a proper training aerodrome and, on 26th June 1918, 199 Training Squadron, a night training unit, was moved to Harpswell from East Retford in Nottinghamshire. A second unit, 200 (Night) Training Squadron, was added to the station's strength in November 1918.

By the end of the war in 1918 a brick operations room and four hangars had been built and a further three hangars were under construction. The cessation of hostilities stopped any further expansion, although 199 and 200 Squadrons continued to undertake night training duties until disbanded in June 1919. The 150 acre (60 ha) aerodrome was closed down immediately after this, although the buildings remained until the early 1920s, when all but the brick operations room were removed. This same brick building still stands and is used today as a farm store.

Royal Air Force Station Hemswell was opened under 3 Group, Bomber Command, on 31st December 1936 with an establishment for two medium bomber squadrons. The station, which encompassed the whole of the former RFC site, was first occupied on 7th January 1937. The first personnel of 144 Squadron arrived on 9th February and 61 Squadron was formed at Hemswell on 8th March, both squadrons being fully equipped with Avro Anson and Hawker Audax aircraft by April. With effect from 1st September the station was placed under the control of 5 Group and Blenheims began to arrive, 144 Squadron being fully equipped by 17th December while 61 Squadron re-equipped during the following month.

The station was still not fully complete by 1938 but that did not deter the presentation of the Standard to 144 Squadron. The ceremony was held on 26th July and the presentation was made by Air Commodore W.A. Calloway, AFC, Air Officer Commanding 5 Group. The

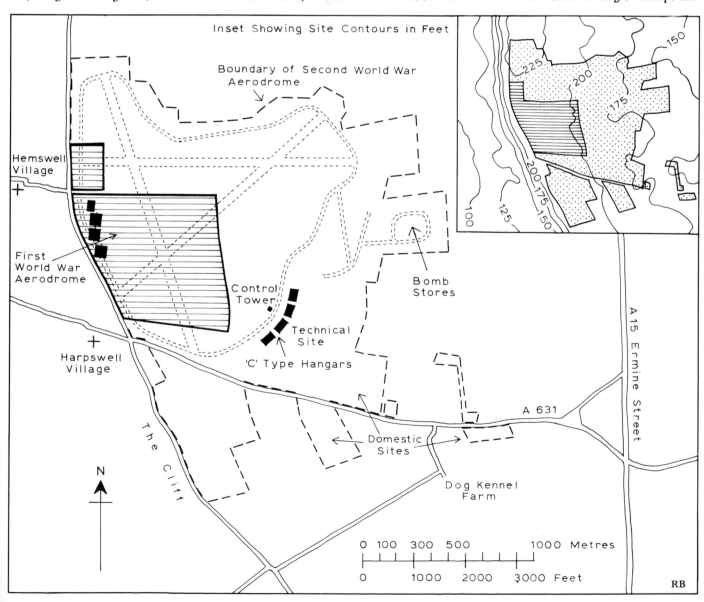

Inset Showing Site Contours in Feet

Boundary of Second World War Aerodrome

Hemswell Village

First World War Aerodrome

Harpswell Village

Control Tower

Technical Site

'C' Type Hangars

Bomb Stores

Domestic Sites

Dog Kennel Farm

The Cliff

N

A 15 Ermine Street

A 631

0 100 300 500   1000 Metres

0   1000   2000   3000 Feet

RB

STATION BADGE
HEMSWELL

Description: An Ermine Saliant.
Motto: Bold and Tenacious.
Authority: Queen Elizabeth II, October 1958.

The Ermine was chosen as the symbol of the unit's badge because of the proximity to Ermine Street, the ancient Roman road running north from Lincoln, and because this animal is pertinacious, preferring to die rather than turn away from its prey or abandon its attack - a quality considered to be appropriate for the aircraft operating from Hemswell.

first Handley Page Hampden for 61 Squadron arrived at Hemswell on 16th February 1939 and the unit was fully equipped by 9th March. It was then the turn of 144 Squadron to re-equip, and conversion to the new type was completed between 10th and 20th March. Hemswell also held an open day on 20th May 1939 to celebrate Empire Air Day, when the visitors arrived in 707 cars and 175 motor cycles. Some £300 was collected for the RAF Benevolent Fund.

When the Second World War started the first operation to be flown from Hemswell was not carried out until 26th September, when both squadrons supplied aircraft for an anti-shipping mission off Heligoland. Camouflaging of the station had commenced before mobilisation had been ordered but it was not completed until well into 1940. As an aid to camouflaging, a dummy airfield or 'K' site was constructed at Toft Grange and was opened on 10th March 1940, the same day that ten dummy Armstrong Whitworth Whitley aircraft arrived for erection. The station was visited by His Majesty King George VI on 27th May when awards for gallantry were presented.

Hemswell saw some action for itself on 29th August when at 20.30 hours a Messerschmitt Bf 110 dropped several bombs, one of which failed to explode. When it was detonated the following day a 20-foot crater was left in the middle of the Parade Ground.

Both of Hemswell's resident squadrons were moved to North Luffenham in Rutland on 17th July 1941 and the following day the station was handed over to 1 Group, Bomber Command. With

Left: **Fe2b A5574 at Harpswell.**
(J.Gladish via S.Finn)

Centre left: **61 Sqn Blenheim line-up at Hemswell, including K7176 and L1328.**
(Crown Copyright H1510)

Bottom left: **Bombing-up a Hampden of 61 Sqn at Hemswell. Note additional bombs mounted externally on racks under the wings.** *(via P.H.T.Green)*

Right: **An enemy bomb being exploded at Hemswell, 30th August 1940.** *(IWM CH1300)*

Below: **Wellingtons of Hemswell-based 300 (Polish) Squadron.** *(Bill Baguley/Rod Houldsworth)*

the change of group 300 and 301 (Polish) Squadrons arrived from Swinderby with Vickers Wellington aircraft. During March 1942 awards for gallantry were presented to Polish personnel by General Sikorski, Commander in Chief Polish Forces. On 18th May 300 Squadron was dispersed to Ingham while 301 Squadron was joined at Hemswell by 305 (Polish) Squadron from Lindholme in Yorkshire on 23rd July.

Due to a re-organisation of the Polish forces 300 Squadron returned to Hemswell on 31st January 1943 and with effect from 31st March 301 Squadron was taken off operations, enabling 300 Squadron to be brought up to full strength on 1st April. Six days later 301 Squadron was reduced to a number only basis and in June the other two squadrons were moved to the satellite at Ingham to allow runway construction to proceed at Hemswell. During this period the British Ambassador to the Polish Government visited the station on 18th and 19th April and on 23rd August the 1 Group Operational Crew Pool was formed.

The work-up following runway construction commenced on 20th January 1944 with the arrival from Lindholme of the Headquarters unit of 1 Lancaster Finishing School. 'C' Flight followed from Faldingworth on 24th January and 'B' Flight on 12th February, the latter move caused by the break-up of runways and taxiways at Blyton. The LFS was formed to give some Avro Lancaster experience to aircrew from the non-Lancaster conversion units prior to their posting to operational squadrons equipped with this type of aircraft. As the Lancaster became more plentiful in late 1944 it was possible to equip the training units with it and the need for the LFS was gone. Accordingly, the last course left Hemswell on 24th November and 1 LFS disbanded the following day.

A return to operational flying had been signalled a few days earlier with the arrival of 150 Squadron from Fiskerton on 22nd November. No. 170 Squadron arrived from Dunholme Lodge on 29th November and with effect from 1st December 1944 Hemswell became a sub-station of 15 Base at Scampton. It was at this time that 1 Group was fitting the Rose rear turret, built in nearby Gainsborough, to its Lancasters and a

'production line' was set up at Hemswell for this work to be carried out. Due to further re-organisation within Bomber Command 1687 BDT Flight was moved to Hemswell from Scampton on 2nd April 1945. Following the end of the war in Europe Hemswell took part in the operations to repatriate ex-prisoners-of-war from Holland and Belgium and also dropped food supplies to the Dutch. At very short notice the station prepared to open to the public on 15th September for the first of the annual Battle of Britain displays. Over 5,000 people attended arriving in 600 cars and 1100 cycles. The sum of £72 was raised for the RAF Benevolent Fund, an interesting comparison with that of the final Empire Air Day in 1939.

The post-war concentration of Bomber Command began to make itself felt with the disbandment of 15 Base on 20th October. No. 1687 BDT Flight disbanded on 30th October followed by 150 and 170 Squadrons on 7th and 14th November respectively. The sound of the de Havilland Mosquito could be heard in the Hemswell sky from 25th November when aircraft of 109 Squadron arrived from Wickenby. An indication of the continual movement of aircraft between units may be gauged from the aircraft of 109 Squadron which simultaneously used five different marks of aircraft powered by no less than seven different marks of engine, a situation rectified by the end of January 1946 when the squadron was brought up to its establishment of thirteen Mosquito Mk.XVI bomber and three Mk.XVI photographic reconnaissance aircraft. On 4th February 139 Squadron arrived, also operating the Mosquito.

On 25th October three specially marked Avro Lincolns, RF463 (AS:A), RF467 (AS:B) and RF468 (AS:C), left Hemswell to position at St Mawgan prior to their departure on a goodwill mission to Chile. The aircraft, manned by crews from 100, 83 and 97 Squadrons respectively, and led by Wing Commander Jim Bell, Commanding Officer of 100 Squadron, arrived in Santiago on 2nd November for a ten-day visit. Only hours before departure from St Mawgan the 'AS' codes on the aircraft were replaced by 'GB'.

Also in late 1946 Nos. 83 and 100 Squadrons arrived at Hemswell and the Mosquitoes of 109 and 139 Squadrons moved to Coningsby, changing places with 97 Squadron. Between July and December 1947 Nos. 50 and 61 Squadrons operated from Hemswell whilst Waddington underwent runway maintenance. Extremely inclement weather at Binbrook brought 12 Squadron to Hemswell between January and March 1948.

In March 1950 No. 100 Squadron moved to Waddington and 109 and 139 Squadrons returned from Coningsby on 1st April. Hemswell's four squadrons, 83 and 97 with the Lincoln, 109 and 139 with the Mosquito, formed the 1 Group flare force, continuing their role of the later war years, and aided by the Mosquitoes the Lincolns specialised in radar bombing and navigation. Also arriving at Hemswell from Coningsby, during March 1950, was 231 OCU but with the impending demise of the Mosquito light bomber force, it disbanded at Hemswell during early 1952.

On 16th April 1952 No. 199 Squadron arrived with Lincolns equipped for electronic counter-measures training of air operators and for testing the reactions of ground operators and radar stations. The squadron also provided ECM cover for the flare force and main force during exercises, making particular use of voice jamming. During August 109 Squadron started to convert to the English Electric Canberra B.2 as did 139 Squadron in November 1953.

The flare force role of the Lincoln soon ended and 83 and 97 Squadrons turned to training navigators for the new V-bombers. On 1st January 1956 the two squadrons disbanded and *Antler* and *Arrow* squadrons were formed: the names being derived from the emblems of the two disbanded squadrons which were earmarked for re-equipment with V-bombers. From March 1956 Canberras started to arrive for 199 Squadron to take over the ECM role as the Lincoln was much slower than the jet bombers and would not fly high enough.

On 1st October 1957 the Lincoln element of 199 Squadron combined with *Antler* and *Arrow* Squadrons to form

1321 Lincoln Conversion Flight. Six months later 199 Squadron moved to Honington, Suffolk, and on 2nd April 1958 No. 1321 Flight moved to Lindholme to join the Bomber Command Bombing School.

The station had been transferred to the control of 3 Group on 1st April 1957 and became the home of the Nuclear Weapons Task Force. The task force comprised 76 and 542 Squadrons which were equipped with Canberras modified for high altitude cloud sampling and both squadrons took part in the Christmas Island H-bomb trials the following month. To provide communications support for the trials, code-named Operation *Grapple*, 1439 Flight was formed at Hemswell with Varsities on 1st May and moved to the trials area the following day. The trials complete, the Flight returned to Hemswell on 7th November and disbanded on the 20th. Nos. 76 and 542 Squadrons also returned to Hemswell but departed on 17th July 1958 when the station was returned to the control of 1 Group.

In 1957 Hemswell was selected as a Douglas Thor missile site. Work commenced on the construction of the

Left: **Canberra B2 WH645 in the markings of Hemswell-based 139 Sqn, 1955.** *(MAP)*

Below left: **The 83 Sqn crew of Flt Lt H.Walls, DFC, preparing to board Lincoln RF467/AS-B at Hemswell on 25th October 1946 prior to flying to St.Mawgan before departure to Santiago, Chile.** *(Crown Copyright R342)*

Above: **Hemswell was typical of the expansion period but its hangars are now used for potato and grain storage.** *(W.J.Taylor)*

Right: **When the Thor missiles were finally withdrawn from use, they were each collected by a Douglas C-133 Cargomaster. This photograph was taken on 17th May 1963.** *(Crown Copyright T4047)*

Left: **The late '60s and early '70s saw private aircraft replace their military counterparts at Hemswell. Shown here is Luton Minor G-ATFW with unusual 3-blade prop in November 1971.** *(P.H.T.Green)*

Below left: **The former Harpswell WWI operations building still intact in early 1977.** *(W.J.Taylor)*

Below: **Hemswell's control tower is unique amongst those that remain within the County. Essential maintenance continues and the external rendering is seen under repair.** *(W.J.Taylor)*

necessary facilities and 97 Squadron reformed on 1st October 1958 to operate the three missiles allocated to Hemswell. The 672nd Technical Training Squadron of SAC arrived at the same time to assist with preparations to receive the missiles, which were flown into Hemswell from America in Douglas C-124 and C-133 Cargomaster aircraft of the USAF. Initial deliveries were made direct to the station but in late 1959 the airfield was closed and further deliveries for the Hemswell Missile Wing were made through Scampton. The Missile Wing controlled the Thor sites at Bardney, Caistor, Coleby Grange and Ludford Magna, the missiles remaining at readiness until early 1963 when they were withdrawn and returned to the United States. No. 97 Squadron disbanded on 24th May 1963 and the last American unit left during June 1964.

Hemswell was then closed and with effect from 14th November 1963 was placed on Care and Maintenance. The station was earmarked as a ground training base for personnel destined to fly and service the British Aircraft Corporation TSR.2 and preparation of the buildings and hangars commenced; but all work ceased on cancellation of the project in April 1965.

Due to an increase in recruiting in early 1965, 7 School of Recruit Training at Swinderby became overcrowded, so Hemswell was opened as 2 Wing of 7 S of RT and started to house recruits during the period of their basic training. Intakes continued until March 1967 and the last entry passed out from Hemswell on 12th May.

No. 643 Gliding School moved to Hemswell from Kirton in Lindsey on 1st November 1965, to be joined on 1st January 1968 by the Lincoln Aero Club which moved from Blyborough Hall. During 1972 accommodation at Hemswell was used to house displaced Uganda Asians. The Gliding School moved to Lindholme in Yorkshire in April 1974 and the Aero Club to Sturgate in June 1975, so at present the 750 acre (300 ha) station is largely disused, although the Army make occasional use of it as a driver training area, and the disused C Type hangars have been re-roofed and converted into grain stores for use by the EEC Intervention Board. The one remaining T2 hangar has been converted into a bulk potato store and a further purpose-built grain store of 100,000 tonnes capacity has been erected adjacent to the T2 hangar.

Hibaldstow

1.5 kms SSE of Hibaldstow Church
112/SE 985 010   30 ft (10 m) AMSL

It was estimated in September 1940 that Hibaldstow airfield would be ready to open as a second satellite for Kirton in Lindsey by early December the same year but the inevitable delays brought about by the winter and shortage of materials postponed the opening until 12th May 1941. Even then none of the station's facilities were complete but it prepared nevertheless to receive its first squadron, 255 Squadron operating Boulton Paul Defiants, which moved in from Kirton in Lindsey later that month. The station was at that time controlled by Kirton in Lindsey but became self-accounting on 7th June, the month when 255 Squadron re-equipped with the Rolls-Royce Merlin powered Bristol Beaufighter Mk.II.

Between 16th and 25th August 'B' Flight of 255 Squadron was detached to Coltishall in Norfolk, but a two aircraft detachment arrived from 29 Squadron on 20th August to carry out night operational duties and stayed until 20th September when it returned to its parent unit, the remainder of 255 Squadron moving to Coltishall on the same day.

A change of the station's role was made on 23rd September with the arrival of 253 Squadron and 1459 Flight from Hunsdon in Hertfordshire, at which time the squadron's Hawker Hurricanes were operating in conjunction with the Turbinlite equipped Douglas Havocs of the Flight. The Turbinlite was a large light fitted in the nose of the aircraft which was intended to intercept enemy night

intruders by means of radar and, when in range, turn on the light to illuminate the enemy. When the enemy was illuminated the Hurricane flying in company with the Havoc would hope to shoot the enemy down. The Commanding Officer of 1459 Flight at this time was Squadron Leader J.B. Nicholson, VC, Fighter Command's only Victoria Cross of the Second World War.

Eight Beaufighters of 409 (RCAF) Squadron were detached to Hibaldstow between 10th and 21st February 1942 because their home airfield of Coleby Grange was unserviceable due to snow. For one week during May 253 Squadron was moved to Shoreham in Sussex, to take part in Army exercises, and this was followed by the detachment of the squadron to Friston between 14th and 7th July. Further Turbinlite units arrived on 27th July when six Hurricanes of 486 Squadron and five Havocs of 1452 Flight were moved in from Wittering near Peterborough. On 31st July 253 Squadron was presented with its standard by Air Vice-Marshal Saul, Air Officer Commanding 12 Group. No. 253 Squadron

saw some offensive action the following month when it spent five days away from Hibaldstow in support of the ill-fated Dieppe landings.

The Turbinlite detachment returned to Wittering between 11th and 21st August and 1459 Flight was renumbered 538 Squadron with effect from 7th September. No. 532 Squadron arrived from Wittering on 9th September, this being the old 1453 Flight which had also

Above: **Beaufighter II R2402 of 255 Sqn, Hibaldstow, September 1941.** *(IWM MH6127)*

Below: **Havoc II AM470 of 1459 Flight at Hibaldstow in 1942. Note the 'Turbinlite' installation in the nose.** *(RAF Museum P5480)*

been allocated a squadron number in common with all the other Turbinlite units. As one can imagine, the Turbinlite concept was not too successful, although a number of kills were made. It was decided to discontinue use of the Turbinlite and so 253 Squadron set off for North Africa during November. Nos. 532 and 538 Squadrons disbanded on 25th January 1943 and the station was closed a week later.

This closure was only a temporary measure for when Kirton in Lindsey was taken over by 53 OTU on 9th May Hibaldstow was re-activated as a satellite. Training was carried out mainly on Spitfires, although the unit also operated a mixture of Miles Masters and Miles Martinets. Quite a famous incident occurred on 9th February 1945 when LACW Margeret Horton was carried into the air on the tail of a Spitfire. Fortunately the pilot was able to land safely and she was unhurt. The aircraft concerned, a Mk.Vc AB910, is still in an airworthy condition and on the strength of the Royal Air Force Battle of Britain Memorial Flight, based at Coningsby. It was nearly written-off in a ground accident at a display in Switzerland in 1978, but was restored towards the end of 1981 following a lengthy rebuild at Abingdon, Oxfordshire and Kemble, Glos.

Training was continued by 53 OTU until 15th May 1945, when it was disbanded. However, even with the war over' training continued from Hibaldstow for 5 (P)AFU arrived from Ternhill, Shropshire, operating a mixture of aircraft including the Hurricane, Spitfire, Avro Anson and North American Harvard. When 5(P)AFU disbanded on 6th August 1947 Hibaldstow was closed and finally sold during 1961 and 1962.

Following closure of the station its one Bellman and twelve Blister hangars were quickly removed and the airfield reverted to agricultural uses, its 450 acre (180 ha) site today being predominantly under the plough. For many years part of one runway has been used by the Lincolnshire Police as a skid pan for driver training. Other areas of the main runway have been used for a popular Sunday market and the former Watch Office has been converted into a very pleasant dwelling. *See map on page 296.*

Holbeach Range

11 km NE of Holbeach Church
131/TF 438 325   10 ft (3 m) AMSL

A Landing Ground for emergency and communications use was provided as part of the Holbeach Bombing and Gunnery Range which came into existence in 1928. The precise years when the ground was regularly used for flying are unclear, though it is certain that no aircraft have visited in recent years despite the range remaining active. The site, which stood between the public road and the point where the Fleet Haven approaches the coastal embankment, occupied about 100 acres (40 ha) and is today farmed.

Holbeach St Johns/ Fenland

2 km WSW of Holbeach St Johns Post Office
131/TF 333 175   10 ft (3 m) AMSL

In late 1972 the Fenland Aero Club commenced operations from the newly-constructed aerodrome at Holbeach St Johns, which at the time comprised two grass runways although early the next year a clubhouse and control tower had been built, and hangars were also under construction. In 1973 the aerodrome was also licensed.

Although the initial equipment of the club was an Auster and a Beagle Terrier, these gave way to Rollason Condors in early 1973 which in turn were replaced with modern Cessna variants by mid-1976. The first flying display to be held at Holbeach St Johns took place on 8th September 1974 and these have now become an annual event. In addition to these displays the Fenland Aero Club also organises the 'Flower Fly-In' to coincide with the Spalding Tulip Parade, as well as the 'Strawberry Fly-In' to coincide with the peak of the fenland soft fruit crop.

During 1976 electric runway lighting was installed, allowing night operations to commence, and the title of the aerodrome was changed to Fenland. Today Fenland is the home of a number of light aircraft owned by individuals or companies in the Holbeach and Wisbech area and it also has available limited aircraft engineering facilities.

The whole field covers some 40 acres (16 ha) of which the mown strips occupy about half. During 1980 rebuilding of the clubhouse and control tower was completed and a new hangar was erected to house the aircraft engineering activities.

Immingham

1 km S of Immingham Dock Railway Station
113/TA 198 155   10 ft (3 m) AMSL

Early in 1917 it became apparent that an alternative method of submarine spotting, other than the haphazard searching by destroyer, was needed. An experiment carried out in the North Sea by the destroyer *HMS Patriot* using a kite balloon attached to the superstructure resulted in the successful sinking of the enemy submarine U-69. Following this attack the Admiralty began to establish Kite Balloon Bases at ports such as Lowestoft, Sheerness and Portsmouth where destroyers and other patrol vessels were favourably based for submarine hunting.

During late November 1917 an erection party arrived at Immingham and began work preparing a site on the property of the Great Central Railway depot, which was to be named 8 Kite Balloon Base. Two balloon sheds and a dozen huts were erected.

The unit became operational within 18 (Operations) Group at the beginning of 1918 and by August had four balloons on charge — numbers AM154, AM155, AM176 and AM219. The *Peel Castle,* an armed boarding steamer, and the *Cicala,* one of the 'Insect' class of river gunboats, were used as kite balloon vessels at Immingham. Unfortunately, it is recorded that balloon number AM154 burst and fell into the sea on 2nd September 1918.

Patrols were continued from 8 KBB until the end of hostilities came but, by January 1919, all of the balloons were in store and no further patrols were carried out. The unit was disbanded in April 1919 and the 26 acre (11 ha) site was de-requisitioned and reverted back to Great Central Railway ownership. Today it lies within the extensive container port complex.

Kelstern (1)

1 km NNW of Kelstern Church
113/TF 246 909   400ft (125m) AMSL

Military flying began at Kelstern in December 1916 when a site was taken over as an unlit Class 1 landing ground for use by 33 (Home Defence) Squadron which then operated over north Lincolnshire. Later lit, it covered 90 acres (36 ha) and had strips of 700 and 650 yards. The squadron gave up its landing grounds in Lincolnshire in June 1919 and the Kelstern field soon reverted to farmland and has remained as such ever since.

Kelstern (2)

2.5 km NNE of Kelstern Church
113/TF 260 920   420ft (130m) AMSL

The first examination for a Second World War aerodrome site at Kelstern took place on 13th February 1942. The site eventually selected was about a mile north of the former RFC landing ground and very much larger. A second on-site-review was completed on 2nd June and construction commenced on 1st August. The opening phase began on 18th August 1943 and the station was ready for operational use by 20th September. The first station commander, Group Captain R. A. Donkin, arrived six days later and two days after that 625 Squadron was formed at the new station around an

experienced nucleus provided from 100 Squadron. Three more crews arrived together with their Avro Lancaster aircraft, later that month. The first Flight of the Squadron was declared operational on 9th October and carried out its first sortie on 18th October when nine aircraft bombed Hanover.

The squadron operated alongside the other units of 12 Base as a two-Flight

Below: **The watch office at Kelstern shortly before demolition.** *(D. N. Robinson)*

Bottom: **Present-day reclamation of the runways and perimeter tracks of World War 2 temporary airfields is well illustrated in this view of Kelstern in May 1979.** *(W. J. Taylor)*

unit until 16th September 1944 when 'C' Flight was formed to provide the experienced nucleus for 170 Squadron which re-formed at Kelstern one month later, on 15th October. It moved to Dunholme Lodge on the 22nd and the following day another 'C' Flight was formed for 625 Squadron.

During April 1945 a re-organisation of Bomber Command took place and 625 Squadron was ordered to reduce in strength to two flights; concurrently with the reduction in strength it commenced moving to Scampton on 5th April and the flight liberated by the squadron moved to Fiskerton to become a third Flight for 576 Squadron. Kelstern was then placed on Care and Maintenance, but full flying facilities were retained.

The airfield became inactive on 24th October and was allocated to the Ministry of Agriculture; it was formally closed on 4th August 1946. In 1956 the Ministry of Agriculture relinquished management of the land and between 1965 and 1966 sold over 900 acres (380 ha) to various farmers who had been tenants. Today the concrete is slowly being removed and the remaining land reclaimed for agricultural use.

In a fitting tribute to those members of the squadron who were lost on missions from Kelstern members of the 625 Squadron Association erected a memorial in a corner of the old airfield. Dedicated on 25th October 1964, the memorial set something of a trend and a number of similar memorials have since been

dedicated within the County. An annual commemorative service is also held at Kelstern.

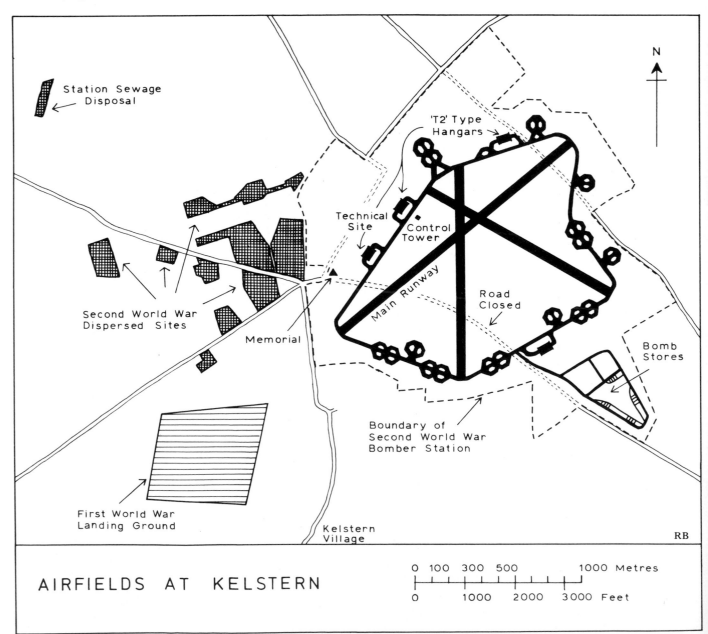

Station Sewage Disposal

'T2' Type Hangars

Technical Site

Control Tower

Second World War Dispersed Sites

Main Runway

Road Closed

Memorial

Bomb Stores

Boundary of Second World War Bomber Station

First World War Landing Ground

Kelstern Village

RB

AIRFIELDS AT KELSTERN

0 100 300 500   1000 Metres

0   1000   2000   3000 Feet

106

Killingholme

2.5 km NE of East Halton Church
113/TF 160 205   10 ft (3 m) AMSL

During October 1912 the Naval Wing of the newly-formed Royal Flying Corps was authorised to establish a chain of coastal Air Stations around the shores of Britain. Landing rights were to be obtained at North Berwick, Newcastle, Cleethorpes, Cromer, Harwich, Dover, Portsmouth, Plymouth and the Lizard, and although the Landing Ground was never commissioned at Cleethorpes, rights were gained for the strip of land adjoining the Admiralty Oil Depot at Immingham. Originally known as RNAS Immingham, the name of the landing ground was soon standardised as RNAS Killingholme.

The first aircraft to use the landing ground arrived during July 1914 and less than a month later, with hostilities with Germany imminent, the RNAS was placed on a war footing. From operational orders dated the following day, 2nd

Above: **Flt Lt F.R.Davy and his crew with Lancaster PB758 'The Green Goddess' of 625 Sqn in September 1944.** (*M.Popoff via P.H.T.Green*)

Right: **Although the hangars have long since vanished, the Admiralty brick-built oil tanks still mark the boundary of Killingholme's original landing ground.** (*RAF Museum PC 72/98/90*)

Left: **DFW biplane 154 after landing near Grimsby on 13th May 1914.** *(via P.H.T.Green)*

Below: **Sopwith Baby 8130 at Killingholme.** *(V.Everitt via C.J.Salter)*

Right: **General view of Killingholme looking NW, 1918.** *(via P.H.T.Green)*

Below right: **Avro 504 at Killingholme in 1917 displaying the extended fin used only on the naval versions of this aircraft.** *(V.Everitt via C.J.Salter)*

August, it is known that four aeroplanes were based at Killingholme under the command of Squadron Commander Courtney, RMLI. They were Bristol TB.8 No.153, Short S.38 Nos.62 and 64 and a GermanD.F.W. Biplane No. 154. Four pilots stood by and the unit was given the task of defending the nearby oil depot from hostile raiders. The armament held on the station for use by the aircrew was twelve Hales grenades.

Bristol TB.8 No.153 was a special machine built for the 1913 Paris Aero Exhibition. It was accepted for use by the RNAS and only remained in service at Killingholme for a short time, and was subsequently destroyed in a gale on Ostend racecourse during September 1914.

By the end of 1914, several Sopwith Two-Seat Scouts were added to the Killingholme establishment, a type of aeroplane which was nicknamed the 'Spinning Jenny' due to a sometimes disastrous tendency to spin. A Killingholme pilot, Lieutenant J.C.Brook, found himself in one such spin and managed to recover. He then deliberately put the aircraft into another spin and again recovered normal control and so became probably the first pilot to perform the dreaded spin intentionally and recover control. Spinning Jennys at Killingholme were equipped with Mauser rifles and were employed in an anti-Zeppelin role, at which time the only incendiary ammunition available for use was of German origin, having been purchased before the war, and it was this that necessitated the use of the Mauser rifle.

The presence of U-boats in coastal waters indicated the need for a fast single-seat seaplane for patrol duties. Sopwith Schneiders — direct descendants of the 1914 Schneider Trophy race winner, the Tabloid — began to arrive at Killingholme early in 1915 and immediately started patrol duties. These were equipped with a Lewis gun and carried incendiary ammunition for use against enemy dirigibles as well as a 60lb bomb for use against submarines.

By September 1915, the Schneider aircraft had undergone several structural changes. A larger and more powerful engine necessitated the redesigning of the engine housing and an open front cowling was fitted. This modified version was named the Sopwith Baby and was used by the RNAS and RAF until the end of hostilities, although it was phased out at Killingholme by July 1918.

By the end of 1915 the threat from Zeppelin attack caused a strategy to be devised to intercept these intruders out at sea before they were able to cross the British coastline. Two Great Northern Railway steamers were requisitioned by the Admiral, East Coast, Rear Admiral Ballard. These steamers were sent to Hull for the necessary modifications to enable two or three Sopwith Schneiders to be carried on each ship. Derricks were fitted for hoisting the seaplanes in and out of the water and small guns were added for self defence. The SS *Brocklesby* steamed away to Yarmouth and the second vessel, the SS *Killingholme*, was retained in the Humber, the plan being that the vessel should steam into the

area of the Dogger Bank, anchor after dark and wait until an enemy raid was being mounted. Then the seaplanes were to be lowered into the water, take off and intercept the enemy.

Nothing at all was sighted on the first 48-hour patrol, but the vessel smashed a paddle on the return trip to port so stronger paddles were fitted before the SS *Killingholme* undertook further patrols. During the next new moon period, while on station on the Dogger Bank, she was approached by what appeared to be two trawlers. Two torpedos were fired at the *Killingholme*, one passing underneath the hull and the other hitting amidships, damaging the paddle wheel and surrounding superstructure and wounding several of the crew. The vessel returned to port for repairs and it seems doubtful that it was ever used again in this role.

During the latter half of 1915, a few White and Thompson 'Bognor Bloaters' were added to the establishment at Killingholme and these aircraft were most probably used for training purposes. Short seaplanes began to arrive at this period and by the end of 1915 three types were being used for patrols over the North Sea — the 184, the 827 and the 830; these were joined in 1916 by examples of the Short 320 seaplane.

With the re-organisation of the RNAS training system and the commissioning of HMS *Daedalus* at Cranwell in April 1916, Killingholme was one of the seaplane stations selected for pilot training duties. After basic training at Crystal Palace in South London, pilots were posted to Killingholme for pilot training, for which purpose several of the Short 827 and 830s were fitted with dual controls. After training successful pilots were posted to Cranwell to graduate in all other subjects allied to flying. By the end of 1916, Norman Thompson N.T.4As were operating as training flying boats from the station.

At the beginning of 1917, the prototype Blackburn T.B., which had been test flown at the Isle of Grain in Kent and found to be unsuccessful, was moved to Killingholme where it was joined by five other aeroplanes of this type, but it is doubtful if these seaplanes were ever used as they were ultimately broken up at the station in August 1917.

The first hangarage erected at Killingholme in mid-1914 was a wood and canvas Bessoneau hangar which provided shelter for the frail biplanes until more substantial structures could be built. On 9 September 1914 the first of four 68 x 77 ft wooden seaplane sheds was completed within the station's technical area adjacent to the Admiralty oil tanks which the machines were to protect. The Bessoneau hangar was dismantled on 18 October and a 700 x 60 ft slipway was built to give seaplanes access to the forbidding waters of the *Humber* whilst the landplanes took off from the field in which the station was sited.

Gradually the station's complement

of machines grew and a larger 177 x 56 ft hangar was built. However, by 1916, seaplanes were becoming very large and construction of a huge hangar commenced. The new hangar, 800 ft long and 220 ft wide, was the largest ever built in the county, bigger even than Cranwell's largest airship shed and with a floor area equal to that of four expansion period 'C' type hangars (eg Scampton and Waddington). Two further hangars each 200 x 100 ft were also built during 1916, together with two new slipways each 850 ft long and 35 ft wide, one of which may be seen today. The strong tides encountered in the *Humber* made beaching seaplanes very difficult and a landing dock was dug to provide shelter for this delicate operation. Some domestic accommodation was requisitioned locally, the Officers' Mess being located in The Old Vicarage, North Killingholme.

By the middle of 1917 new and larger flying boats were entering service at various East Coast Naval Air Stations, and although Curtiss N.4 '*Small Americas*' had been in service since 1915, these were joined by a few Porte Babies at Killingholme in the spring of 1917. Curtiss '*Large Americas*' began to arrive from the United States at the beginning of the year and by June some of these aircraft were delivered and used operationally from the station. British built derivatives of the Curtiss flying boats, Felixstowe F.2As, entered service at the end of 1917 and by the end of the war had earned a reputation comparable to that of the Short Sunderland in the Second World War.

On 10th May 1918, a F.2A (N4291) from Killingholme flown by Captains T.C. Pattinson and A.H. Munday, engaged the Zeppelin L62 over the Heligoland minefields. Many hits were scored causing extensive damage to the airship, but the F.2A had to break off the offensive due to oil pipe failure and return to its base. The L62 was severely damaged and it is believed to have caught fire and exploded disappearing without trace in the North Sea.

The RNAS developed an intricate network of seaplane stations around the British Isles and Killingholme became the base station of 18 (Operations) Group, its seaplanes and flying boats undertaking many duties including coastal defence, U-boat detection, convoy escort and anti-Zeppelin patrols. On formation of the RAF this mixed collection of operational units was organised into a series of flights, those equipped with flying

boats being given numbers in the 300 series, and those primarily equipped with seaplanes being given numbers in the 400 series.

By May 1918 Killingholme's flying boats had been grouped into three flights, 320, 321 and 322. It had been intended that the flying boat flights would eventually be equipped with the Felixstowe F.2A but due to a shortage of these machines UK-built Curtiss H-12 'Large Americas' were used initially. However, when the station was handed over to the US Navy its aircraft were also handed over and Killingholm's flying boat flights ceased to exist. It had been intended to form a further flying boat flight, 324, at Killlingholme on October 31st but as a consequence of the station being handed over to the US Navy this flight never came into being.

The smaller seaplanes at Killingholme were organised into two flights, 403 and 404, which jointly operated a mixture of Short 184 and 320 aircraft. Following transfer of the station to the US Navy these two flights did not disband but moved to Hornsea Mere on 15th August.

In the summer of 1917 it was decided that the United States Naval Air Service would assist with the North Sea patrol work and that Killingholme should be one of the bases to be used by the American forces. The first American contingents arrived there early in 1918 and by May 1918 sufficient operational American pilots were available to undertake coastal patrols in Short seaplanes.

The main body of the allied force arrived at Killingholme on 1st June 1918 in the USS *Jason,* whose cargo included twenty-three crated Curtiss

110

H.16 flying boats, the first of the type to be sent to Europe. The first flight of this new type took place on 3rd July and the station was then formally transferred to the US Navy, under the command of Lieutenant Commander Kenneth Whiting; the transfer took place on 20th July 1918. The American airmen soon settled in at the station and operational patrols began over the North Sea despite the initially poor performance of the H.16s. A nucleus of RAF personnel remained on the station using Short seaplanes and F.2A and H.12 flying boats until their allies became self-sufficient.

United States Naval aircraft operating from foreign bases were not organised as squadrons but were designated as 'attached' to the air station, each station being assigned a letter to be painted on the fuselage to permit easy identification. Killingholme was allotted the letter 'K'.

During the remainder of the war the Americans flew convoy escort patrols and reconnaissance flights over the North Sea from Killingholme and on several occasions interception sorties were also flown in response to Zeppelin raid warnings. The average length of a patrol flight was just over four hours flying time and between 20th July and 11th November 1918 a total of 968 hours were flown for the loss of two crews.

The Americans stayed at Killingholme until January 1919, at which time the station was formally handed back to the Royal Air Force. Also during this month, 228 Squadron brought its Curtiss H.12 and H.16 flying boats from Yarmouth and the run-down of Killingholme began with the disbandment of the squadron in June 1919. The station was finally closed in 1920.

Apart from the preliminary training work done at Killingholme and its use as a base for North Sea patrols, the station had also been a constructional and acceptance base with reports of as many as 100 aircraft — both landplanes and seaplanes — being on the station.

After closure, the station buildings were removed and since that time the 140 acre (56 ha) site has been used for various purposes including a tar distillery and an oil refinery, whilst during the Second World War, part of the site was utilised by the Auxiliary Fire Service. Today the only recognisable remains of the seaplane base is one of the slipways, and this is fast disappearing . Violent spring tides in 1974 uncovered many relics of flying boats which had just been dumped when the station was finally closed down.

Kirmington/ Humberside

1 km SW of Kirmington Church
112/TA 095 105   80ft (25 m) AMSL

Built as a bomber base for 1 Group, Bomber Command, work was completed at Kirmington in early January 1942, and until required by 1 Group the airfield was loaned to 21 Group Flying Training Command, whose 15 (P)AFU operated its Avro Ansons and Airspeed Oxfords from there until 23rd October 1942 when the station was transferred back to Bomber Command.

Shortly after the transfer, 150 Squadron moved in from Snaith in Yorkshire with Vickers Wellingtons and operated from Kirmington until 12th December 1942 when twelve aircraft left for North Africa; a home echelon remained at Kirmington. No.142 Squadron based at Grimsby also sent twelve aircraft to North Africa and on 20th December its home echelon was moved to Kirmington and on 27th January 1943 the home echelons of the two squadrons merged to form 166 Squadron. That night seven of the new unit's Wellington aircraft successfully laid mines in enemy waters and two nights later twelve aircraft undertook the squadron's first bombing mission, a raid on Lorient.

The Wellington was operated by the squadron until September 1943 when Lancasters released from 103 Squadron were taken on charge; these new mounts were used operationally for the first time on the 22nd of that month and the squadron operated as a two-flight unit until 7th November 1943 when a third flight was formed. In January 1944 Kirmington became a sub-station of 13 Base which was formed with its headquarters at Elsham Wolds.

On 7th October 1944 'C' Flight of 166 Squadron was detached to provide the nucleus of operational crews necessary to reform 153 Squadron, which was declared operational that day and took part in its first mission that night; a week later it left for a new home at Scampton and the new 'C' Flight for 166 Squadron which had formed at Faldingworth on 7th October moved to Kirmington on the 15th.

No.166 Squadron operated from Kirmington for the remainder of the war and took part in many of Bomber Command's major raids; its last operational

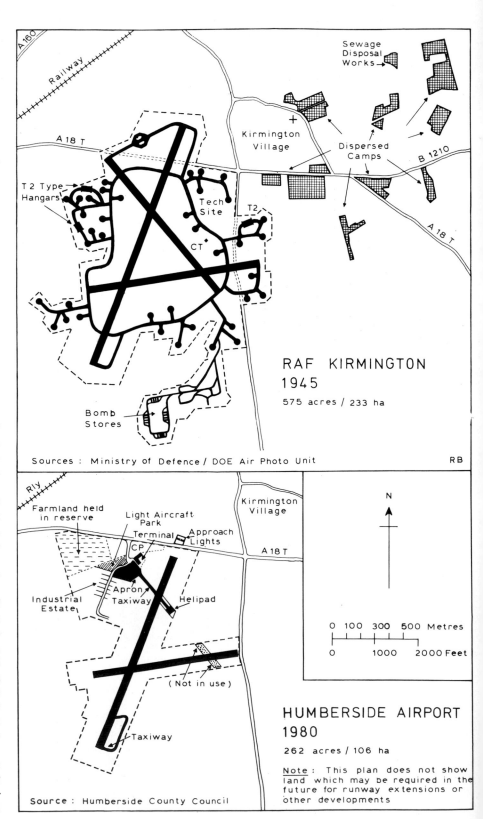

RAF KIRMINGTON
1945

575 acres / 233 ha

Sources : Ministry of Defence / DOE Air Photo Unit   RB

HUMBERSIDE AIRPORT
1980

262 acres / 106 ha

Note : This plan does not show land which may be required in the future for runway extensions or other developments

Source : Humberside County Council

Right: **Lancaster of 166 Sqn at Kirmington in 1944.** *(via P.H.T.Green)*

Below: **Aerial view of Kirmington, June 1970.** *(Fairey Surveys)*

Left: **Kirmington's derelict watch tower, since demolished.** *(via M.Hodgson)*

Below: **Sharing the apron with Air UK Fokker F-27 G-BLGW is Boeing 737 G-BGTW of Orion, which carried out short field training at Humberside Airport on 13th March 1980.** *(P.H.T.Green)*

mission was flown on 25th April 1945. After the war the squadron continued non-operational flying until it was disbanded on 18th November, which was marked by a ceremony at Elsham Wolds.

No.13 Base was disbanded on 15th December 1945 and control of Kirmington passed to Hemswell. The station was placed on Care and Maintenance and became a sub-site of 35 MU with effect from the same date. A large hutted camp was erected on one of the runways and during 1946 and 1947 several military disposal sales were held on the airfield. The whole site was transferred to the Ministry of Agriculture during 1953 and the land between the runways was returned to farming.

Apart from occasional use by various crop spraying aircraft Kirmington saw little regular use until August 1967 when Air Links Chauffeurs started to operate Cessna 172 G-AVCD from part of the disused runway. In February 1968 this company was renamed Humber Airways which gradually expanded and moved more of its operation to Kirmington. In 1970 Lindsey County Council bought the airfield and commenced repair work on the main runway and construction of terminal buildings. Kirmington Airport was formally opened on 26th March 1974 but, as a result of local government re-organisation, control of the airport passed to the new Humberside County Council the following month and the airport was renamed Humberside.

The first major user of the facilities at the new airport was Lease Air Ltd which formed in April 1972. Lease Air provided many of the ground facilities at the airport and operated a fleet of Cessna aircraft on flying training and charter work. With the arrival of a Piper Aztec in early 1973 Lease Air commenced air taxi work and in January 1975 took on many of the routes formerly flown by the Britten Norman Islanders of Humber Airways when that company ceased to operate on the 13th of the month. Gradually Lease Air's fleet began to expand and the company undertook the operation of a number of aircraft on behalf of local companies. The first Dakota for Eastern Airways, a trading company of Lease Air, arrived at Humberside on 17th July 1978. G-AMPO was joined by another two Dakotas, G-AMRA and G-AMYJ, and from July 1979 all three aircraft were engaged on

Right: Humberside Airport apron in June 1979 displays DC-6 TF-IUB of Iscargo and HS.125 G-AZVS of Eastern Airways. *(P.H.T.Green)*

Below: Eastern Airways Short SD330 G-NICE in front of their hangar in 1982. *(P.H.T.Green)*

in Yorkshire, started to use Humberside as its base for aircraft sales and for a few months a large variety of private and business aircraft passed through the airport on their way to new owners. Despite the lack of ready access to the north bank of the Humber, Humberside Airport has made a major impact on communications within the region. With the completion of the Humber Bridge, Humberside Airport should see continued growth as many more people are brought within its catchment area.

The modern airport occupies an area of 215 acres (87 ha) including about 20 acres (8 ha) let to farmers and an industrial site of similar size. It is interesting to note that the RAF station in 1945 covered some 575 acres (233 ha), over twice the area in use for aviation today.

night mail flights in various parts of the country.

In October 1982 Eastern Airways merged with two other regional airlines, Genair (based at Liverpool/Speke) and Casair (based at Carlisle). The new company began trading under the name Genair and retained its facilities at Humberside.

Flying training from Kirmington commenced in 1972 with the formation of the South Humberside Flying Club. The club's operations, initially based around a lone Auster J/1N G-ARUY, were given a much-needed boost with the formation of Lease Air when modern Cessna aircraft became available for use. As Lease Air became involved in regular operations the Cessnas passed into private ownership until the club obtained its own pair of Cessna 152s in early 1979.

A variety of other light aircraft are also operated from Humberside, many of which are in the ownership of small companies.

During February 1975 Air Anglia set up an operating base at Humberside and commenced its first scheduled service from Humberside to Amsterdam on 7th April 1975. Air Anglia Fokker F.27s became a familiar sight at Humberside as routes expanded to such destinations as Aberdeen and Jersey. Following the formation of Air UK in January 1980 former Air Anglia F.27s painted in a variety of Air UK colour schemes continued to operate the company schedules from Humberside. Some of the less popular routes are flown by the smaller, 18-seat, Embraer Bandeirante aircraft.

In early April 1980 Citation Flying Services Ltd, formerly based at Sherburn

Kirton in Lindsey/ Manton

1 km ESE of Manton Church
112/SE 945 025   200ft (60m) AMSL

The First World War aerodrome officially known as Kirton in Lindsey was not, as is often reported, on the same site as the present airfield, but was situated about three miles north of Kirton in Lindsey, on the outskirts of Manton village, and the site is still referred to as 'Manton Aerodrome' by local inhabitants.

Opened as a Flight Station in December 1916, Manton housed 'B' Flight of 33 (Home Defence) Squadron with eight Royal Aircraft Factory F.E.2b aeroplanes. This unit had its Headquarters

at Gainsborough and its aircraft were detached to three Flight Stations in the County. The flights operated against every airship raid over the area, but failed to score any victories, although the enemy was sometimes diverted from his intended target.

When the airship menace ceased, the Headquarters, together with 'A' and 'C' Flights, of the squadron was moved to Manton and the squadron assumed a training role. Bristol Fighters partly replaced the ageing F.E.2bs in June 1918 and by August both types were replaced by Avro 504NF single-seater aircraft. The squadron continued to train pilots in the night fighting role until disbandment on 13th June 1919. Soon after this the two hangars were removed and the 120 acre (50 ha) site reverted to agricultural use.

Two small wooden buildings from the original aerodrome still exist on the site and now house pigs. A small section of wall made up of rusting practice bombs is also to be seen.

See also the map on page 296.

Kirton in Lindsey

2 km SE of Kirton in Lindsey Church
112/SK 945 970   200ft (60 m) AMSL

The present airfield at Kirton in Lindsey was constructed at the beginning of the Second World War and opened on 15th May 1940, even though few buildings were complete and many more were yet to be started. The new station came under the operational control of 12 Group, Fighter Command, and soon

included in the station's establishment was a Miles Magister communications aircraft for use by the headquarters staff.

On 16th May the future arrival of 222 Squadron from Duxford was announced and the use of Coleby Grange and Hibaldstow as satellite airfields was arranged. The personnel of 222 Squadron arrived on 21st May followed three days later by the Hurricanes and personnel of 253 Squadron from Kenley. The Spitfires of 65 Squadron arrived from Hornchurch in Essex and were based here between 29th May and 14th June, its place being taken by 222 Squadron which operated from Hornchurch between 28th May and 3rd June. The distinction of making the first interception by a Kirton in Lindsey based aircraft went to Pilot Officer Morant of 222 Squadron at 00.28 hours on 26th June.

Prospects in the summer of 1940 were bleak: the British Expeditionary Force was evacuated from Dunkirk and the fear of invasion was great. Ringway, Cheshire, was allocated to Kirton in Lindsey on 28th June for use as a rearward station. Two sections of 253 Squadron were dispersed to Coleby Grange on 8th July and then to Ringway on 9th July. However, the squadron was quickly re-united at Kirton in Lindsey and then moved to Turnhouse, Edinburgh, on 21st July.

Night fighters started to arrive on 23rd July as 264 Squadron moved its nineteen Boulton Paul Defiants from Fowlmere; the main party arrived the following day. Whilst here use was made of the satellite at Coleby Grange and the rearward station at Ringway. On 11th August the squadron made its first night contact, which, although inconclusive, was the

prelude to their first night victory four days later. The Spitfires of 74 Squadron arrived on 22nd August. Four days later, 264 Squadron moved south to Hornchurch to participate in the Battle of Britain but returned only eight days later as it had suffered heavy losses during daylight combat and, thereafter, the Defiant had to be relegated to night operations. Nearby Caistor airfield was allocated for use by Kirton in Lindsey-based units from 6th September and Coleby Grange was handed back to the control of Digby.

The month of September saw considerable activity, for the Battle of Britain was at its height. No.222 Squadron had moved to Hornchurch on 29th August and on 10th September, 616 Squadron at Coltishall exchanged bases with 74 Squadron. Although 307 Squadron

officially formed at Kirton in Lindsey on 5th September the first personnel for this new squadron did not arrive until the 11th; its first nine Defiants arrived four days later and another nine on the 17th. First flights in the Defiant by the Polish crews of 307 Squadron were made on 25th September. Also in September 264 Squadron sent 'A' Flight to Caistor and 'B' Flight to Northolt. The squadron was made operational only by night and on 13th September 'A' Flight assumed full operational status at Caistor.

From mid-September 616 Squadron commenced training with Bader's famous 'Duxford Wing'. The squadron would leave Kirton in Lindsey early in the morning, returning at night after a full days flying from Duxford. The station continued to detach operational flights to Ringway with a flight of 616 Squad-

STATION BADGE KIRTON IN LINDSEY

Description: An eagle's head erased gorged with a collar of Bezants.

Motto: JE VOLE A TOUS VENTS (I fly whatever the wind)

Authority: King George VI, November 1947.

The eagle's head was adopted as indicative of the American Eagle Squadron which operated from Kirton in Lindsey 'during' the Battle of Britain (sic). The collar of Bezants is introduced to show the station's connections with the Duchy of Cornwall of which Kirton in Lindsey formed a part. The arms of the Duchy of Cornwall are 'Sable, fifteen Bezants, five, four, three, two, one'. *Crown Copyright/RAF Photograph*

ron detached there on 30th September and 'B' Flight detached between 11th and 17th November.

On 23rd October 1940, 264 Squadron moved to Martlesham Heath in Suffolk, and 85 Squadron arrived from Church Fenton with Hurricanes. No. 85 Squadron's stay was short-lived for on 7th November all but one flight moved to Debden; the other remained for training and moved to Debden two weeks later. Also on 7th November, 307 Squadron moved to Jurby, Isle of Man.

A significant chapter in the history of the station opened on 23rd November with the arrival from Church Fenton of 71 (Eagle) Squadron. Manned by American volunteers, this unit was equipped with Hurricanes and practised formation flying, convoy patrols and air combat until it was ordered to readiness for the first time on 4th January 1941.

Also on 23rd November, 255 Squadron re-formed as a night fighter unit with Defiants and, after working-up, was declared operational on 5th January 1941 and scrambled for the first time four days later. The squadron began intensive night operations but suffered from poor serviceability and a high accident rate, with the result that the Defiants had to be supplemented by Hurricanes in March. The first confirmed victory came on 5th May when the CO destroyed a Ju 88; three days later Sergeant Johnson brought down another near the airfield, and on the night of 9th May, during a heavy raid on Hull, the squadron destroyed six enemy raiders. Six days later, the squadron was moved to the adjacent satellite aerodrome at Hibaldstow.

On 26th February, No.616 Squadron went to Tangmere, exchanging places with 65 Squadron, and in April No.71 Squadron moved to Martlesham Heath. The first Australian fighter unit in the RAF, 452 Squadron, formed at Kirton in Lindsey on the 13th April, and by 10th May had twenty-two Australian aircrew on strength for its eighteen aircraft establishment, one of its flight commanders being Flight Lieutenant B.E. 'Paddy' Finucane. Defensive patrols were commenced on 22nd May and the first offensive sweeps over enemy territory were made on 11th July.

The second Eagle squadron in the RAF, No.121, formed with Hurricanes at Kirton in Lindsey on 19th May, becoming operational on 21st July. Two days earlier, 452 Squadron moved to Kenley. On 20th August, 136 Squadron was formed to undertake shipping patrols with Hurricanes and was declared operational at dawn on 28th September. On 7th October, 65 and 616 Squadrons exchanged places once more, 65 Squadron moving to Westhampnett. On 9th November 136 Squadron departed for India and 121 Squadron moved to North Weald on 16th December.

On 2nd January 1942, personnel of the third American Eagle squadron, 133, arrived after a sea and rail journey from Eglinton, Northern Ireland. At Kirton in Lindsey the squadron received some old, well-used Spitfire Mk.VAs and commenced working up to operational standard, and by April was undertaking night operations against enemy intruders. Between 1st and 17th March eight Beaufighters of 409 Squadron were detached to Kirton in Lindsey and on 3rd March,

486 (New Zealand) Squadron started to form. This proved to be New Zealand's second fighter squadron in the RAF, and was equipped with Hurricanes for night fighting, eventually moving to Wittering on 9th April to operate with Turbinlite Havocs. For two days during April, a Junkers Ju 88, Heinkel He 111 and Messerschmitt Bf 109 of the Enemy Aircraft Flight made a short stay to familiarise pilots and ground defence gunners with their shapes.

Polish personnel returned to Kirton in Lindscy on 3rd May when 133 Squadron exchanged places with the Spitfire-equipped 306 Squadron at Biggin Hill. On 1st June, 457 Squadron was retired to Kirton in Lindsey to prepare for its move to Australia a week later. Later in June, on the 16th, 306 Squadron was replaced by 303, another Polish squadron previously based at Northolt (Middlesex). The following month the air party of the 94th Fighter Squadron, 1st Fighter Group arrived at Kirton in Lindsey after a twenty two day journey which commenced on 4th July and took them from Presque Island Army Air Field, Maine, via Newfoundland, Green-

land, Iceland, Stornoway (Shetland) and Ayr. The squadron's Lockheed P-38F Lightning fighters were escorted across the Atlantic by Boeing B-17 bombers of the 97th Bombardment Group and by the end of the month twenty one aircraft had arrived. It was more usual for American units to receive their European theatre training at Goxhill but due to a lack of space there the 94th had been sent to Kirton, where it remained until moving to Ibsley, Hampshire, on 27th August 1942.

Strict security measures were in force on 15th August when 303 Squadron left for an undisclosed destination. The squadron had gone to Redhill in Surrey to take part in the ill-fated Dieppe landings, returning from Friston on 20th August. For the duration of 303's absence 316 Squadron was detached to Kirton in Lindsey from Hutton Cranswick. On 1st September 43 Squadron arrived from Tangmere and operated from here until 27th October. Another American unit, the 91st FS, part of the 81st FG, arrived on 8th October, received thirteen Bell P-39 Airacobra aircraft between 11th and 14th October, and left

for North Africa on 23rd December.

At the beginning of 1943 the station was a stronghold for Polish squadrons. On 31st January 303 Squadron was released from readiness and moved to Heston two days later, exchanging places with 302 Squadron. Eight days later the main party of 317 Squadron arrived from Woodvale, its Spitfires arriving on the 13th. Following a decision to use the station as a training base, 302 Squadron moved to Hutton Cranswick on 17th April, and on the 29th, 317 Squadron moved to Martlesham Heath.

Following the hand-over to Flying Training Command, the aircraft of 53 OTU arrived from Llandow between 6th and 10th May 1943. No.53 OTU was a vast unit, having more than eighty Spitfires, twenty Miles Masters and seven Miles Martinets on strength. Hibaldstow was used as a satellite airfield and housed 'D' Flight and No.2 Gunnery Squadron of 53 OTU. Training continued throughout the remainder of the Second World War until 15th May 1945 when the OTU was disbanded. Immediately 6 Aircrew Holding Unit was formed to assist with the dispersal of aircrew to further training or release from the Service.

Aircraft returned to Kirton in Lindsey on 4th April 1946 with the arrival from Sutton Bridge of 7 SFTS and its Airspeed Oxfords. Later, the unit re-equipped with North American Harvards and concentrated on training pilots for the Fleet Air Arm, but following a change of name to 7 FTS, it moved to Cottesmore, Rutland, during March 1948.

Remaining part of Flying Training

Above: **Harvard of No.7 FTS at Kirton in Lindsey, February 1948.** *(R.N.Lee)*

Right: **Tiger Moths of No.2 Grading School, Kirton in Lindsey in the early '50s.** *(LAM)*

Left: **Cadet T3 WT877 of No.22 GS against a background of Kirton in Lindsey's hangars, 1951.** *(P.H.T.Green)*

Below: **Seen at the time of the airfield's civil use is Links Air Touring Group's Proctor G-ANXR, 1st May 1965.** *(J.Walls)*

Command, Kirton in Lindsey then became a centre for ground training, and during August and September 1951 1 and 2 Squadrons of 2 Initial Training School arrived from Digby and in June 1952 No.2 Air Grading School was formed. The grading school, operated by Airwork Ltd, worked in conjunction with 2 ITS giving pilot and navigator cadets a short course of twelve hours flying, mainly dual instruction, in order to determine their suitability for flying training, which was usually undertaken overseas. Prior to closure of the grading school on 31st March 1953, the unit had forty-five instructors and was equipped with de Havilland Tiger Moth aircraft.

A station flight was formed to operate a small number of aircraft to keep the staff of the ITS in flying practice. Initially the flight was equipped with a Tiger Moth but that gave way to three or four de Havilland Canada Chipmunks and an Avro Anson. During September 1953, No.2 ITS was re-named 1 ITS, remaining under the control of HQ 25 Group, Manby. The ITS gave officer cadets their first insight to the RAF with a three-month course of leadership, educational and physical training. On successful completion of the course the newly fledged officers would pass to a training unit appropriate to their chosen specialisation. Pilots would go to Hullavington, Feltwell or Ternhill, navigators to Thorney Island and Air Electronics Operators to Swanton Morley. The ITS remained at Kirton in Lindsey until 22nd July 1957, when it moved to South Cerney in Gloucestershire.

In January 1959 the Adult Supply Training School formed at Kirton to train supply tradesmen for the RAF. This unit, which was re-named No.7 School of Technical Training, remained at Kirton in Lindsey until January 1962. From 1st January 1963 to December 1963 the RAF Air Movements School was located at the station to provide training in this highly specialised means of transportation.

Throughout the time of its use as a ground training station, Kirton housed an Air Training Corps Gliding School. In June 1950, No.22 Gliding School arrived from Grimsby with one Slingsby Sedbergh and four Slingsby Cadet gliders; in April 1955 it was renumbered 643 GS, indicating that it was the third gliding school under the operational control of HQ 64 Group, Home Command, at Rufforth in Yorkshire. On 1st September 1959, No.2 Gliding Centre moved in from Newton and also during 1959 Lincoln Aero Club commenced operations on the airfield.

In 1965 the Army took over the station and 643 Gliding School moved to Hemswell on 1st November 1965. Lincoln Aero Club remained until 1967 when it moved to Blyborough Hall. The Army used Kirton in Lindsey as a base for units working up with the British Aerospace Rapier surface-to-air missile system. For obvious reasons Rapier missiles have never been fired from the airfield although low flying Canberra aircraft often act as targets during training sessions. As more of the Army's light air defence regiments equipped with the Rapier, the weapon it was replacing, the ageing Bofors gun, was gradually withdrawn from Army service. To mark the final withdrawal from Army service of the Bofors a special ceremony was

held at Kirton in Lindsey on 26th March 1979, during which several salvoes were fired.

Gliding returned to the airfield during 1974 when the Trent Valley Gliding Club moved in from Sturgate. Today the gliding club continues to use the all-grass airfield and the Army continues to base Rapier units at the station. In common with other former RAF stations handed over to the Army, Kirton in Lindsey has been given a new name, Rapier Barracks. Proudly guarding the entrance to the barracks are two Rapier missiles, mounted on top of the two gateposts. The station still occupies some 422 acres (171 ha).

See also the map on page 296.

Leadenham

1.5 km ENE of Leadenham Church
121/SK970523   320ft (100m) AMSL

Leadenham aerodrome opened in September 1916 with the arrival of 'C' Flight of 38 (Home Defence) Squadron which, equipped with four Royal Aircraft Factory F.E.2b aeroplanes, operated without success against every enemy raid over the area. At the end of May 1918 the role of the squadron was changed to that of night bombing and the flight moved away

from Leadenham with the remainder of the squadron to France.

In August 1918 No.90 Squadron was re-formed at Buckminster and 'A' Flight was detached to Leadenham, but the threat from Zeppelins had diminished by this time and the flight was denied the opportunity of taking its Avro 504s into action. After the end of the war the flight remained at Leadenham until June 1919 when the squadron disbanded.

As far as can be ascertained, the 86 acre (35 ha) aerodrome closed at about the same time. The two hangars were dismantled, but two buildings within the domestic site are still in existence. Concrete searchlight bases, which were used in conjunction with the aerodrome, are still to be seen in the neighbouring woodland.

Lincoln (Handley Page Field)

2 km ESE of Lincoln Cathedral
121/SK996 702   10ft (3m) AMSL

In 1916 the Lincoln firm of Clayton and Shuttleworth built its Abbey and Tower Works, between the River Witham and the Great Central Railway Line, with a small flying field immediately east of the factory. In October 1917 a contract was placed for fifty Handley Page O/400 bombers, which were too tall for delivery by road and had to be flown out for official testing at Lincoln West Common. During 1918 Vickers Vimys were also constructed and flown from the field but it nevertheless went down into local

history as the 'Handley Page Field'. With the slump after the Great War no further aircraft were manufactured or flown from this factory field, though a little joy-riding took place around 1920. Today it is sub-divided, though still not built over despite its proximity to the city.

Lincoln (West Common)

1.5 km WNW of Lincoln Cathedral
121/SK960720   20ft (6m) AMSL

Following the award of Government contracts early in 1915 to two Lincoln engineering firms to build aeroplanes, and the prospects of further contracts to come, it was decided that a site near the city should be requisitioned for use as an Aeroplane Acceptance Park. By the time the first Lincoln-built aeroplanes were ready for testing, 4 Aeroplane Acceptance Park had been established on 129 acres (52 ha) of the West Common Race Course. One manufacturer, Robey's, built Sopwith 806 Gunbuses which were accepted in the early summer of 1915, to be followed by Royal Aircraft Factory B.E.2s built by Ruston, Proctor & Co, which also became the first contractor to build the Sopwith 1½-Strutter. By the time this type of aircraft began to reach the Acceptance Park, so urgent were requirements for aeroplanes on the Western Front that 70 Squadron collected 1½-Strutters immediately they became available at Lincoln and took them to the front. 'A' Flight began to equip in May 1916, followed by 'B' Flight the

next month. These two flights were followed by 'C' Flight which accepted its aeroplanes and joined the squadron in July 1916.

By 1917 contractors other than the local Lincoln firms were bringing aeroplanes to West Common for acceptance, but whereas Lincoln contractors had private flying fields around the City for testing their products before delivery to the Acceptance Park, outside contractors had to convey their aeroplanes to Lincoln by road and then assemble them. By the end of the war, 4 Aeroplane Acceptance Park had taken on charge many different types of aeroplane for use by the services, including Sopwith Camels and Triplanes built by Clayton and Shuttleworth, de Havilland D.H.5s built by Marsh, Jones and Crib of Leeds and Sopwith Cuckoos constructed by Pegler & Co of Doncaster. Blackburn Kangaroos and Handley Page O/400s were also a regular sight on West Common during the later stages of the war.

The maximum hangar accommodation was four permanent buildings and five canvas Bessoneau hangars. The first two hangars were erected on the present site of the tennis courts and were camouflaged so that they would not be recognised by marauding Zeppelins. Two further hangars were erected alongside Alderman's Walk and were eventually converted into one large building when the centre gap was roofed over. Of the five Bessoneau hangars, two were built extra high to house the Kangaroos and O/400s.

No.4 Aeroplane Acceptance Park was closed down soon after the end of hostilities and all the buildings were sold by public auction. Two of the hangars were destined to become garages in Lincoln, one at Gilberts in Pelham Street and the other at Stocks in Lucy Tower Street, and both these structures survived until just a few years ago. Foundations to other buildings can still be seen along the side of the Common adjoining Hewson Road.

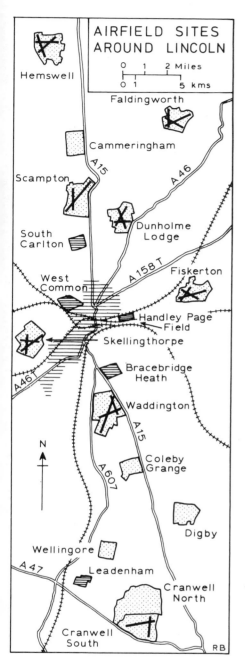

AIRFIELD SITES AROUND LINCOLN

Hemswell
Faldingworth
Cammeringham
Scampton
Dunholme Lodge
South Carlton
West Common
Fiskerton
Handley Page Field
Skellingthorpe
Bracebridge Heath
Waddington
Coleby Grange
Digby
Wellingore
Leadenham
Cranwell North
Cranwell South

N

RB

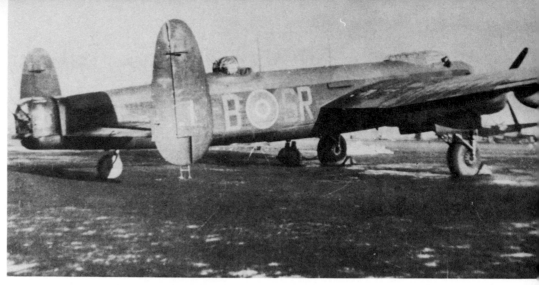

Above: **Lancaster B.III of Ludford Magna's 101 Squadron, 1944.** *(via P.H.T.Green)*

Ludborough

2 kms WNW of Ludborough Church
113/TF 280965   130ft (40m) AMSL

In 1940 all key airfields in the UK were provided with an emergency landing ground, to which aircraft could be diverted in the event of their home base being destroyed or captured by the enemy. Examples in Lincolnshire included Hykeham (for Hemswell), Sturton (for Scampton) and Normanton (for Waddington). Very little is known about these ELGs in terms of site, shape and size and it appears from the records that their function had ceased by the time the counter-offensive was underway in 1942.

One site however, appears to have had a little more substance and is recorded with a location plan in a survey of RAF airfields dated 1943 (PRO/AIR10/4038). This was at Ludborough and consisted of two strips (ENE-WSW and NNW-SSE) standing adjacent to the east side of the B1431 road in the north-west corner of the parish of the same name. In the 1943 document it is shown under the entry for Binbrook, though in the 1940 listing was originally earmarked for the use of North Coates. No evidence remains on the ground today, nor are there any firm local recollections of aircraft actually landing.

Ludford Magna

0.5 km S of Ludford Village Street
122/TF 200880   430ft (135m) AMSL

A site for an aerodrome near Ludford Magna was first examined during June 1942 and a contract for its construction was let later that month. Having taken almost a year to build, the new bomber base opened on 15th June 1943 with the arrival from Holme-on-Spalding-Moor in Yorkshire of 101 Squadron, which at that time was operating Avro Lancasters as part of 1 Group, Bomber Command. From October 1943 the squadron started to take delivery of aircraft equipped with 'Airborne Cigar' or ABC as it came to be known, which entailed carrying an extra crew member in the aircraft who would transmit on the German fighter control radio frequencies with the aid of special equipment fitted to the aircraft in an effort to confuse the night fighters. This top secret role stayed with 101 Squadron throughout the remainder of the war, ceasing in April 1945, when nearly 2,500 sorties had been flown.

During October 1943 Ludford Magna took Wickenby over as a satellite and on the 15th December became the Headquarters of 14 Base, controlling sub-stations at Wickenby and Faldingworth. To cope with the additional aircraft maintenance workload of a Base Station additional hangars were built and 14 Base Major Servicing Unit was formed on 14th April 1944. Later that year FIDO was installed and an Oxford was allocated to the station for FIDO trials work and communications duties (see Appendix E). Between April and July 1944 No.1682 Bomber Defence Training Flight operated from the station.

Because of the post-war re-organisation of Bomber Command, 101 Squadron was moved to Binbrook on 1st October 1945 and Ludford Magna became a sub-station of Binbrook. The station was placed on Care and Maintenance on 15th December and closed to all flying although the runways remained open for emergency use. Later the airfield was handed over to the Ministry of Agriculture for cultivation between the runways and buildings.

In 1958 a part of the old airfield was returned to the Air Ministry and a Douglas Thor missile site built. No.104 Squadron was formed in July 1959 to operate three missiles within the Hemswell Missile Wing, but in May 1963 the missiles were withdrawn and the squadron disbanded. The 580 acre (235 ha) airfield was finally sold during 1965 and 1966 and much of the concrete has now been torn up and the land reclaimed.

A simple but impressive memorial to

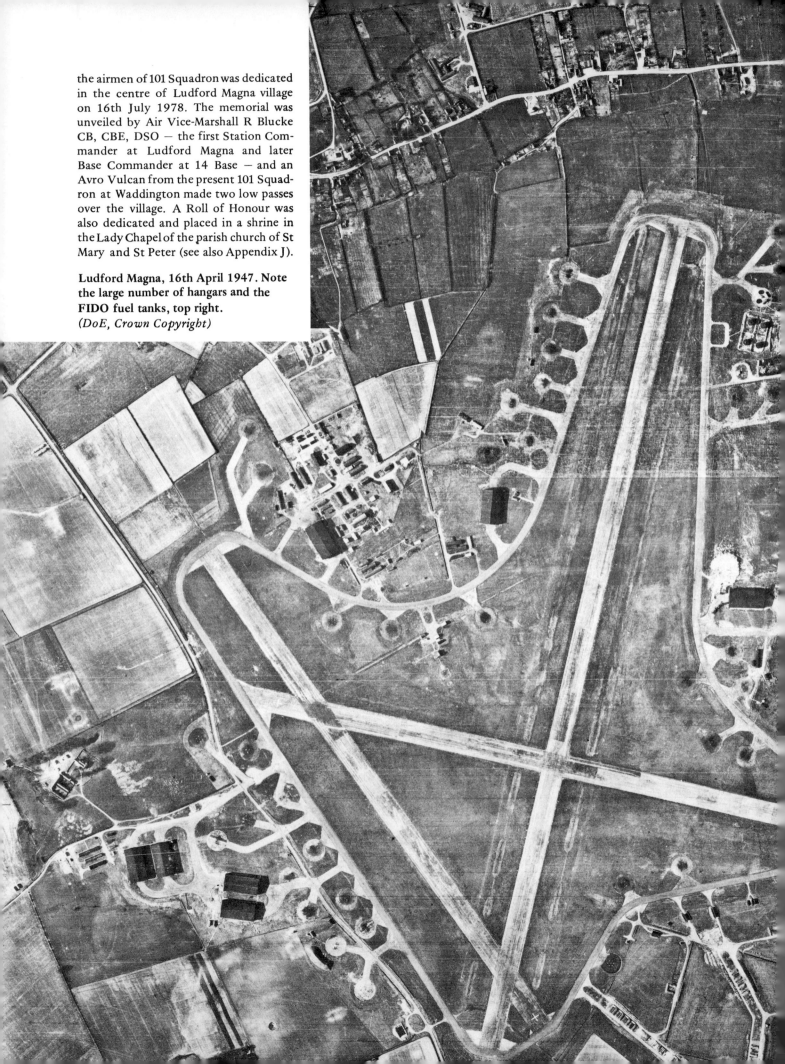

the airmen of 101 Squadron was dedicated in the centre of Ludford Magna village on 16th July 1978. The memorial was unveiled by Air Vice-Marshall R Blucke CB, CBE, DSO — the first Station Commander at Ludford Magna and later Base Commander at 14 Base — and an Avro Vulcan from the present 101 Squadron at Waddington made two low passes over the village. A Roll of Honour was also dedicated and placed in a shrine in the Lady Chapel of the parish church of St Mary and St Peter (see also Appendix J).

Ludford Magna, 16th April 1947. Note the large number of hangars and the FIDO fuel tanks, top right.
(DoE, Crown Copyright)

Right: **Manby's Boulton Paul Overstrand in the immediate pre-war period showing its newly applied camouflage scheme.** *(via P.H.T.Green)*

Below: **Hawker Henley of No.1 AAS at Manby in 1939.** *(RAF Museum P557)*

Manby

1.5 km W of Manby Church
113/TF390865   60ft (20m) AMSL

Construction of Manby aerodrome commenced during the RAF Expansion of the mid-1930s. In late 1936, when the airfield was almost complete, Manby was selected as the trials site for an experimental cross-wind landing screen, a steel framework covered with metal sheeting some 50 feet high and 500 yards long. This was erected across the airfield with the intention of protecting landing aircraft from the effects of a strong cross-wind. Flying trials were carried out during August and September 1937 with several different aircraft, including a Fairey Battle, Armstrong Whitworth

Whitley and a Bristol Blenheim, whilst later trials involved a Handley Page Harrow and a Westland Wallace. In February 1938, with the airfield due to open, the screen was dismantled and moved elsewhere (see Appendix E).

Manby prepared to receive 1 Air Armament School which arrived from Eastchurch in Kent during August 1938, The AAS was administered by 25 (Armament) Group and made extensive use of the Wash bombing and gunnery ranges in its training of Armament Officers, Air Gunners and Air Bombers. When war was declared in September 1939 the station had on strength three Hawker Harts, six Hawker Hinds, eight Hawker Furies, five Wallaces, one Boulton Paul Overstrand and thirty-three Battles. Before the month was out another eight Gloster Gauntlets and seven Hawker

Henleys had arrived.

During December 1939 the airfield was flooded and a flight of newly-arrived Hawker Demons was detached to Donna Nook. The Overstrand was relegated to use as an instructional airframe, but was damaged on 28th April 1940 when an overshooting Gauntlet (K7879) collided with it.

On 7th July 1940 the work of the AAS was supplemented by the formation of 2 Ground Armament School, which took over the ground training elements of the station that were administered by 24 Group Technical Training Command and had been granted lodger facilities at Manby. No.1 AAS continued to operate under 25 Group but took over the flying training element of the station. The station's anti-aircraft defences had a memorable day on 21st December 1940 when they shot down a Junkers Ju 88. No.2 GAS moved to Kirkham in Lancashire on 25th November 1941 leaving 1 AAS at Manby to continue its intensive courses.

Training was not limited solely to RAF personnel, as members of many Allied air arms found their way to Manby for training; for example in 1942 a party from Turkey arrived for training. The Care and Maintenance of Caistor airfield was taken over by Manby on 9th December 1942 but following a preliminary inspection on 31st March 1943 it was handed over to Technical Training Command on 1st June for use by Cranwell.

In view of the success of the Empire Central Flying School the suggestion was made that 1 AAS be raised to 'Empire' status and put under the command of an Air Commodore. The suggest-

ion was taken up and on 18th April the Empire Central Armament School was formed at Manby and the Central Gunnery School became affiliated to the new unit at the same time. The aims of the school included the formulation of a central armament policy and the setting of a standard for armament training throughout the Commonwealth, as well as advising on current training methods and preparing new instructional techniques and publications for new items of armament equipment. With the change in status the school came under the direct control of the Air Ministry but remained an active member of 25 Group. By the end of 1944 there were courses for Armament Officers, Bombing Leaders, Bombing Instructors and Armament Instructors in addition to armament refresher courses.

The ECAS operated a very mixed fleet of aircraft, the majority of which were Wellingtons. In November 1944 the name of the ECAS was changed to the Empire Air Armament School and in view of the change in status from the old 1 AAS, Air Ministry Order N170/1945 changed the old AAS motto 'Knowledge Fortifies the Kingdom' to 'Knowledge Fortifies the Empire', more in keeping with the new title.

With the end of the war aircraft numbers began to run down, but in late September 1945 Avro Lancaster PB873 arrived for preparation for the EAAS Mission to India, the aircraft being named 'Thor' by Mrs Busk, wife of the Commandant, on 15th October. However, due to the closure of facilities in India, the Mission was changed to a tour of the Middle East, Rhodesia and South Africa which began on 26th October and lasted for six weeks. This was followed in March 1946 by a tour of Australia and New Zealand.

During 1946 the original 'Thor' was replaced by Avro Lincoln RF523 appropriately named 'Thor II'. It left Manby on a tour of Canada and the USA on 2nd November 1946, and went to the Far East on 18th April 1947 and Canada and the USA again on 26th September. South Africa was toured from 2nd January 1948 and New Zealand from 10th May. The final tour of 'Thor II' was to the Far East on 18th January 1949.

The RAF Flying College was formed at Manby on 1st July 1949 operating a very mixed fleet of aircraft including the Lincoln, Vickers Valetta, Gloster Meteor, de Havilland Vampire and Avro Athena. By 1950 the Handley Page Hastings had arrived and one aircraft undertook a tour of Australia and New Zealand in October 1950, during which month a Lincoln also visited Canada, Alaska and the USA. The RAFFC inherited the 'Aries' aircraft from the Empire Air Navigation School at Shawbury; 'Aries III' being the Lincoln RE367 which was flown around the world in 130 flying hours during October 1950. 'Aries' continued to globetrot, flying to the North Pole in 18 hours during 1951 and visiting Japan in January 1952. Four months later all specialist navigation training was transferred to Manby from Shawbury.

On 20th March 1951 the Headquarters of 25 Group was re-formed at Manby to form and control all the new jet Advanced Flying Schools which were being introduced during the general expansion of the RAF at that time. During the following two months the training units at

Left: Lancaster PB873 'THOR' about to depart from Manby on 26th October 1945 for a tour of the Middle East and South Africa. *(Crown Copyright PRO AIR29/1141)*

Below left: Lincoln RF362 (FG-AH) was the first aircraft to return from a series of six long distance flights during 1950, arriving back at Manby on 16th November. Captained by Sqn Ldr Radley, DFC, this aircraft and another Lincoln RF380, had completed a 10,000 mile tour. In the background is ARIES III' RG367 (FG-AW), a Lincolnian' with extra fuel in the modified nose section, which completed a 25,000 mile round-the-world tour on Friday 17th November, captained by Sqn Ldr Downey DFC. *(Flight 25070s)*

Right: Superb in-flight study of Lincoln RF523 'THOR II' of the RAF Flying College, Manby, taken in May 1949. *(Crown Copyright R2407)*

Right: Longest of the six long distance 1950 flights was made by Hastings C1 TG617 (MFGAJ) which visited New Zealand via Malta, Habbaniya, Mauripur, Negombo and Changi, a total of almost 26,000 miles. Captained by Canadian Sqn Ldr Smith it arrived back thirty minutes after 'ARIES III'. *(Flight 25073s)*

Right: 'Lincolnian' RG367 'ARIES III' also took part in the world flights of 1952 and is seen returning from Japan via Malta, Mauripur and Sydney on 7th February captained by Sqn Ldr R.G. Oakley. *(Flight C349/30A)*

Right: The naming ceremony of 'ARIES V', Canberra B2 WT528 (on the right) was held at Manby on 14th June 1956. *(Crown Copyright PRB11841)*

Bottom: An unusual sight is presented by this formation of mixed aircraft from Manby's RAF Handling Squadron, 24th September 1953. *(Crown Copyright PRB6938)*

COAT OF ARMS
ROYAL AIR FORCE
FLYING COLLEGE
COLLEGE OF AIR WARFARE

Crown Copyright / RAF Photograph

The grant of a Patent of Armorial Bearings was approved by the King of Arms on 21 June 1951. The shield consists of a Shield of Arms surmounted by a crest. The Arms are Azure sernee of Mullets Or a cresset enflamed proper with a compass ring gold lettered sable. The crest consists of issuant from an Astral Crown Or a pelican wings elevated azure gorged with a naval crown gold mounted azure doubled Or.

The blue star-studied shield represents the sky and the stars which are aids to navigation. On to this is superimposed the badge of the Empire Air Armament School, a predecessor of this College, which was at Manby from 1938 to 1949. The gold circlet which had carried the words 'Empire Air Armament School - Royal Air Force' is now a compass ring. Within this ring is a 'cresset enflamed proper' (a metal beacon holder containing a fire). The flames symbolise knowledge; a torch is frequently a symbol of a school; beacons have been used as navigational aids since the days of ancient

Greece and their use for communication, particularly in early warning systems, is even older.

The Astral Crown symbolises aviation, while the crown around the pelican's neck represents the Royal Navy's interest in Air Warfare and in this College. The Pelican also traditionally represents a seat of learning and was previously used in the Armorial Bearings of the Empire Central Flying School.

Initially the College was formed at Manby to combine certain aspects of the work of the Empire Central Flying School, the Empire Air Armament School and the Empire Air Navigation School, with a view to integrating closely their studies and doctrines. It was originally known as the Royal Air Force Flying College but was renamed the Royal Air Force College of Air Warfare on 1 July 1962.

Driffield and Finningley in Yorkshire, Middleton St. George in County Durham, Oakington in Cambridgeshire and Valley on Anglesey were transferred to 25 Group and by the end of 1951 the Group was fully equipped with jets — Meteor Mks. F.4, T.7 and F.8. From August 1953 the Group administered a course at Weston Zoyland, Somerset to provide jet flying for Air Ministry officers which was transferred to the RAFFC at Manby in 1955 when Weston Zoyland was closed. On 1st February 1955, No.11 FTS at Swinderby was placed under the control of 25 Group, whose Headquarters remained at Manby until February 1961.

The RAF Handling Squadron also operated from Manby between 1949 and 1954. This unit usually received the second or third production model of a new aircraft entering service so that its handling qualities could be assessed and the Pilot's Notes written. The second prototype English Electric Canberra B.2 arrived at Manby on 3rd March 1951 for this purpose as did the fourth production Canberra B.6 during 1954. Other types operated by the Handling Squadron included the Vampire, Meteor, de Havilland Sea Vampire, Westland Wyvern, Grumman Avenger, Hawker Sea Hawk, Supermarine Attacker, Miles Marathon, Percival Pembroke, Scottish Aviation Pioneer and de Havilland Sea Hornet.

The successor to 'Aries III' was the Canberra B.2 WH699 which replaced the ageing Lincoln in mid-1953. In December 1953 'Aries IV' flew from London to Cape Town at an average speed of 486.6 miles per hour, setting up a new record, and this was followed on 15th October 1954 by a flight from Bardufoss in Norway to Bodo, also in Norway, during which it became the first RAF jet aircraft to fly over the North Pole.

During a reunion at the RAFFC, Canberra PR.7 WT528 was named 'Aries V' by Lady Baye, while the old 'Aries IV' stayed with the Flying College until it was destroyed in a crash at Strubby on 28th November 1959. 'Aries V' ably followed in the footsteps of its predecessors by setting up a record flight time between Tokyo and London in May 1957.

Jet refresher courses began at Strubby in June 1955 and Varsity refresher courses began at Manby in August 1960. The jet flying of the college was concentrated at Strubby because it was more suited to the aircraft then in use, the Canberra, Meteor and Hawker Hunter, while Manby operated the piston-engined part of the College fleet, the Varsities and the Percival Provosts. In June 1962 the RAFFC was renamed the RAF College of Air Warfare and the School of Refresher Flying was formed. With the formation of the CAW the Hunters left Strubby, but there were no more changes in the fleet until 1964 when Hunting Jet Provosts started to replace the piston-engined Provost. The last Meteors had left by April 1965 and the Varsities were then moved to Strubby.

Canberras continued to provide navigation training for the CAW until February 1966 when the first Hawker Siddeley Dominie twin jet trainer arrived, and the last Canberra left in December 1966. When Strubby was closed in September 1972 the Dominies moved to

Left: **Jet Provost T4 XP580 seen in the early colour scheme applied to the aircraft of 'The Macaws' aerobatic team.** *(via W.J.Taylor)*

Below: **Manby, 27th August 1978.** *(W.J.Taylor)*

Manby and the Varsities went to Oakington in Cambridgeshire.

Rumblings of Manby's closure went on for a number of years in the early 1970s. A statement from the Ministry of Defence in March 1972 stated that the aircraft would go and the RAF School of Education and the RAF Police Dog School would move to Manby. However, in September 1973, the Ministry of Defence announced that, contrary to its previous statement, the new units would not move to Manby as planned but would move to Newton instead. The announcement further stated that the School of Refresher Flying was to move to Leeming in Yorkshire by 7th December and that the CAW was to move to Cranwell to become the Department of Air Warfare within the RAF College by 7th January 1974.

Accordingly, the Macaws, the College's aerobatic team, gave their last display in November 1973 and disbanded, its aircraft moving to Leeming with the other Jet Provosts of the SoRF on 7th December. The last aircraft to leave Manby, five Dominies of the CAW, did so on 13th December, giving a low-level formation flypast before flying to Cranwell. The station then began to wind-up, closing officially on 31st March 1974. At the time it closed to flying the aerodrome had covered a total of 580 acres (235ha).

Following closure of the station the married quarter sites came under the control of Binbrook and were used to house the families of personnel stationed at Binbrook. Part of the domestic site was bought by the East Lindsey District

Council for its headquarters. The area bought by the Council included part of the parade ground, the former Station Headquarters and Tedder Hall, the former home of the CAW. In Tedder Hall the Council was able to unite all its various departments, widely fragmented since the re-organisation of local government in April 1974.

In 1978 another part of the domestic site, including the former MT section and the two machine gun ranges, was taken over by the Lincolnshire County Council as a new depot for its Highways Department. The machine gun ranges were quickly demolished and work is underway to make the new depot. Also in 1978 major renovation of the five hangars was undertaken, which included re-roofing, re-painting and conversion of

the hangars into massive grain stores for use by the EEC Intervention Board.

Further disposal of the station took place on 16th July 1980 when 280 acres (112 ha) of the airfield itself, including the two control towers, most of the runways and the taxiways, were sold by auction. A further sale to dispose of the remaining parts of the domestic and technical site, including the huge and imposing Officers' Mess, took place on 25th March 1981. Unfortunately, only one of the six lots was sold, although the Officers' Mess was subsequently sold and is expected to be converted into a retirement home for former servicemen.

Yet another sale, this time to dispose of the western edge of the airfield along with its associated aircraft dispersals and the bomb stores area took place on 29th

Above: **The original Watch Office at Manby seen in July 1980.** *(W.J.Taylor)*

Left: **Constructed during the mid-1960s, Manby's new control tower saw little service and now stands empty.** *(W.J.Taylor)*

Left: **Manby's main gate and one of the two guardrooms, whose architecture is unique in Lincolnshire.** *(W.J.Taylor)*

Below: **A microlight Eipper Quicksilver MX1 comes in to land at Manby alongside a heap of broken-up concrete, evidence of recent demolition work.** *(W.J.Taylor)*

September 1981 and a further attempt to sell the former barrack blocks and the Sergeants' Mess was made in March '82.

Having passed into private hands, Manby seems set to become a thriving centre for the growing boom in microlight aircraft. From mid-1981 the old control tower in front of the hangars has been the base of Lincs Airsports Limited which is making use of the excellent runways for microlight flying. In addition to a number of single-seat machines, the company has obtained a two-seat craft on which dual instruction is given to new owners. The microlight activity has also stimulated visits by light aircraft and is a sensible use of the excellent facilities abandoned by the Ministry of Defence.

Market Deeping

2 km NE of Deeping St James Church
142/TF 170110   10 ft (3 m) AMSL

Market Deeping was established as a class 2 landing ground for 90 (Home Defence) Squadron during the period it was based at Buckminster between August 1918 and June 1919, the site being officially listed as a 75-acre field lying 1½ miles from Deeping St James railway station (no compass directions supplied) with strips of 850 and 650 yards. Enquiries locally have established that it occupied a piece of land known to villagers as 'The 90 Acres', adjacent to the east side of the Stamford-Spalding road (A16T) between Deeping Common and Frognall.

Metheringham

3.5 km E of Metheringham Church
121/TF 105610   60 ft (20 m) AMSL

Royal Air Force Station Metheringham was opened on 20th October 1943 as a heavy bomber base within 5 Group Bomber Command. No. 106 Squadron equipped with Avro Lancasters moved in from Syerston in Nottinghamshire on 11th November 1943 and, one week later, on the night of 18-19th, carried out its first operation from the new station, a raid by thirteen aircraft on Berlin.

It was on this raid that a new Lancaster, JB663 (ZN-A) embarked on its first mission; almost a year later, on 4th November 1944, it took off for its 100th operation with the squadron and by the end of hostilities had flown 111 missions. It was eventually struck off charge and scrapped. United States aircraft were regular visitors, being chiefly employed in evacuating wounded US airmen from

the American Hospital at Nocton Hall to Prestwick in Ayr for repatriation.

It was during a raid on Schweinfurt on the night of 26-27th April 1944 that Sergeant (later Warrant Officer) Norman Jackson, a flight engineer with 106 Squadron, was awarded the Victoria Cross. After sustaining an attack by an enemy night fighter, the starboard wing of his aircraft was seen to be on fire, so Sergeant Jackson attempted to extinguish it by climbing out onto the wing, but before he could suceed he was forced to release his hold and was last seen falling with his parachute only half open. It was not until after the war when Sergeant Jackson was released from captivity that his deed was made known, his VC being gazetted on 26th October 1945.

On 1st January 1944 Metheringham became a sub-station of 54 Base and came under the control of Coningsby. Soon after this a scheme was put into operation whereby 106 Squadron would receive direct from the 5 Group Oper-

Above: **Lancaster 'Here's Howe' of 106 Sqn, Metheringham.** *(via M.Hodgson)*

Right: **Metheringham's partly demolished watch office in June 1978.** *(W.J.Taylor)*

ational Training Units crews who were destined for the Group's Pathfinder squadrons at Coningsby, Nos.83 and 97. The squadron acted as a 'nursery' and after gaining the requisite experience under the supervision of 106 Squadron's Flight Commanders, the crews were transferred to Coningsby as required.

When 52 Base was transferred to 1 Group in October 1944, 1690 Bomber Defence Training Flight was moved to Metheringham, and continued to supply its Supermarine Spitfire and Miles Martinet aircraft for fighter affiliation duties until it left the station in June 1945.

With the end of the war in Europe, it was planned to send a force of Lancasters to the Pacific for a bombing offensive against Japan, to which end 467 (RAAF) Squadron arrived from Waddington and with 106 Squadron started to form 552 Wing *Tiger Force* during July 1945. However, with the successful delivery of the first atom bombs on Japan, the Pacific War ended in August. There was no further need for *Tiger Force* and 467 Squadron was disbanded at Metheringham on 30th September, to be replaced by 189 Squadron which arrived from Bardney on 15th October equipped with Lancasters. However, 189 Squadron disbanded after only one month on the station.

No.106 Squadron remained on the station until it disbanded on 18th February 1946. To commemorate this event the personnel of the squadron erected an unofficial memorial which remained on the airfield until a few years ago, when it was moved to the Newark Air Museum.

Metheringham was one of fifteen airfields equipped with FIDO—Fog Investigation and Dispersal Operation, a sytem of pipes and nozzles laid alongside the runway, and through which petrol was pumped and ignited. The ensuing flames generated heat which dispersed the fog locally and allowed incoming aircraft to land when the airfield was fogbound (see Appendix E).

When all the aircraft had left Metheringham the 650 acre (260 ha) airfield was placed under Care and Maintenance for a short time before being returned to agricultural use. The site was retained by the Air Ministry until sold during 1961 and 1962, since when most if its runways and taxyways have been removed. It has, however, also been used as a seasonal strip for crop spraying aircraft operating in the local area. In mid-1983 a microlight training school opened on the edge of the former airfield.

Moorby

1.5 km NNE of Moorby Church
122/TF300655   250ft (75m) AMSL

This class 1 Landing Ground was established for the use of 38 (Home Defence) Squadron during its residence at Flight Stations in south Lincolnshire from December 1916 until May 1918, and although at first unlit, was later lit for night use. During 1918 it was assigned to 90 (Home Defence) Squadron and was finally given up in June 1919. It was located some way from public roads and had strips of 700 and 570 yards. Today the 82 acre (33 ha) site is farmed.

New Holland

0.5 km W of New Holland Church
112/TA078237   10ft (3m) AMSL

This class 2 Night Landing Ground was maintained for the use of 33 (Home Defence) Squadron during the period it operated over north Lincolnshire between December 1916 and June 1919, it stood between the Barton on Humber branch railway line and the road to Barrow Haven, had strips of 700 and 550 yards and covered 85 acres (34 ha). According to a map published in *Flight* magazine on 1st May 1919, New Holland was then under consideration as a civil landing ground on the proposed domestic trunk airway from Hounslow to Renfrew in Scotland, and was also one of four appointed aerodromes to deal with overseas air routes, in its case the Scandinavian link. Such proposals did not, however, come to fruition and the New Holland landing ground soon reverted to farmland, which it still is today.

North Coates

3 km NE of North Coates Church
113/TA375025   10ft (3m) AMSL

Late in 1916, as part of the Humber defence system, a Night Landing Ground was established on 22 acres (9 ha) near to the sea bank at North Coates Fitties, and was in use by 33 Squadron until the end of enemy raids in 1918. During that

Above: **North Coates Fitties, 19th July 1918 and the installation of its first bomb dump.** *(Sqn Ldr E.J.McLoughlin via P.H.T.Green)*

Right: **Heyford K3500 of 99 Sqn after a forced landing on the beach at North Coates Fitties.** *(via P.H.T.Green)*

Below: **Hyderabad J9297 of 503 Sqn under repair after striking the sea wall at North Coates Fitties due to an overloaded take-off.**
(via Sqn Ldr C.G.Jefford)

year the landing ground was enlarged into a Flight Station within 18 (Operations) Group and became the home of 404 Flight — part of 248 Squadron. Formerly a seaplane flight at Killingholme, 404 Flight was re-equipped with the de Havilland D.H.6 and began anti-submarine patrols over the coastal convoys.

When the war ended in November 1918, coastal land-plane flights in 18 Group were concentrated at Killingholme but several moved into North Coates Fitties prior to disbanding in June 1919. By the end of the year, with the aeroplanes gone, the landing ground reverted to its original owners.

In 1927 the same tract of land, which had covered 88 acres (35 ha) by the end of the First World War, was re-purchased by the Air Ministry, re-established as a landing ground, and for the next eight years was used by heavy bomber squadrons in annual summer camps, during which they spent an average of four weeks undergoing bombing and gunnery training, using Donna Nook bombing and gunnery range.

In 1935, now with permanent Station Headquarters, North Coates Fitties became 2 Armament Training Camp within 25 (Armament) Training Group.

On 1st January of the following year the first Air Observers' School was opened and squadron tradesmen selected for part-time observer duties were attached for a two month course of training in bombing and gunnery. Late in 1936, 2 ATC moved to Aldergrove in Northern Ireland, but a temporary Armament Training Camp remained behind at North Coates Fitties.

On 1st November 1937, 2 Air Armament School was formed from a merger of Station Headquarters and the Air Observer School. As the expansion of the RAF gathered momentum, 2 AOS was formed at Acklington in Northumberland and with effect from 1st March 1938 No.2 AAS at North Coates Fitties was re-designated 1 AOS.

On the outbreak of the Second World War most of the training units located on the East Coast were moved to stations on the West Coast and on 4th September 1 AOS transferred to Penrhos in North Wales. Some ten days later 2 Recruit Training Pool was formed at North Coates Fitties to give preliminary training to new recruits and at the end of November this unit was joined by the Ground

Defence Gunnery School. In January 1940, 2 RTP was re-designated 9 Recruit Centre, but it closed down only one month later. The GDGS continued to operate on the station until July 1940, when it moved to the Isle of Man.

On 26th February 1940 the aerodrome was re-named Royal Air Force Station North Coates and was transferred to 16 Group, Coastal Command, becoming the home of 235 Squadron and, in the following month, of 236 and 248 Squadrons. All three were equipped with Bristol Blenheims and began offensive patrols over the North Sea, a task which was continued until May, when the three squadrons left the station. During this period the airfield was also used as a forward landing ground by fighter squadrons operating from Digby.

No.22 Squadron moved into North Coates at the beginning of April 1940, bringing Bristol Beauforts, which were first used operationally there on the 15th of that month, when mines were successfully laid in enemy waters. Beaufort operations ceased in June when the type was grounded for modifications. In September the aircraft again became operational and the squadron dropped torpedos 'in anger' for the first time when five aircraft attacked a convoy between Calais and Ostend, and claimed one enemy merchant ship sunk.

On 11th May 1940, 812 Squadron, Fleet Air Arm, flew its Fairey Swordfish aircraft onto the airfield for minelaying and convoy escort duties. During its stay at North Coates the squadron also undertook bombing missions over enemy occupied territory. In September, 812 Squadron was detached to Thorney Island in Sussex, returning in November for further minelaying duties before leaving for Campbeltown, Mull of Kintyre, in March 1941. In the same month 816 Squadron, FAA, arrived at North Coates with its Swordfish but moved to Thorney Island in May.

In April 1941, No.42 Squadron came in with its Beauforts from Scotland to replace 22 Squadron, which was detached to St. Eval in Cornwall for attacks on the *Scharnhorst* and the *Gneisenau* in Brest Harbour. Following this operation the Victoria Cross was posthumously awarded to Flying Officer Kenneth Campbell for a valiant attack on the *Gneisenau*. 22 Squadron returned to North Coates in May, when 42 Squadron departed for Scotland, and continued operations until leaving for Thorney Island in June.

No.86 Squadron replaced 22 Squadron and began converting to Beauforts, becoming operational in November 1941 by patrolling over the Dutch Islands, mainly during the hours of darkness. Several attacks on enemy convoys had been made by the time the unit moved

135

Left: **Taken during the early days of the war, this photograph of a parade at North Coates shows in the background the station's astrodome, this example being unique within Lincolnshire.** *(LAM)*

STATION BADGE NORTH COATES

Crown Copyright / RAF Photograph

Description: In front of a ray of lightning in bend, a Balista.

Motto: Guide to Attack.

Authority: Queen Elizabeth II, October 1958.

A Balista, which is an ancient weapon for bombardment, indicates the unit's association with defensive and offensive weapons. The colour of the Balista is gules (red) as the unit has Army connections; the flash of Lightning represents the radar equipment used by the unit.

to St. Eval during January 1942.

No.407 Squadron (the second Canadian squadron within Coastal Command), formed at Thorney Island in May and after a few weeks with Blenheims, began to convert to Lockheed Hudsons, moving to complete its training at North Coates in July 1941. Declared operational in September, 407 Squadron began to carry out 'Rovers' (Anti-shipping patrols) at night along the Dutch coast.

In November 1941, the Westland Lysanders of 6 Anti-Aircraft Co-operation Unit moved onto the airfield for calibration duties with the local coastal defences. A detached flight of 278 Squadron, which had been formed at Matlask in Norfolk on 1st October, moved to North Coates for air-sea rescue duties at the end of November. Originally equipped with Lysanders, its inventory was supplemented with Supermarine Walruses and the flight began operations with 22 High Speed Launch Unit based in the docks area of Grimsby, until January 1943.

No.407 Squadron left the station for Thorney Island in January 1942 for a period of training before moving to Bircham Newton in Norfolk for front-line operations. Two further Hudson equipped Squadron were posted to the station at the beginning of 1942; in January 59 Squadron arrived, followed a month later by 53 Squadron. Both undertook anti-shipping patrols before moving on — 53 to Cornwall in May and 59 to convert to Consolidated Liberators in August.

No.217 Squadron moved into North Coates from Scotland in March 1942 and operated from the airfield for two months prior to embarking for duty in

Malta. During this period 7 Anti-Aircraft Co-operation Unit arrived and took over the duties of 6 AACU, remaining on the station until December 1943.

No.415 (RCAF) Squadron came in from Thorney Island at the beginning of June 1942. Equipped with Handley Page Hampdens, the unit continued its operational task of roving patrols with torpedos and bombs, generally at night and often accompanied by ASV radar-equipped Hudsons of 59 Squadron. No. 415 remained at North Coates for two months and moved out to Wick on 5th August.

During August 1942, 143 Squadron arrived at North Coates with Blenheims and converted to Bristol Beaufighters for the formation of the first Strike-Wing. Torpedo-dropping experiments with Beaufighters had been carried out as early as the spring of 1941 and it was due to the increasing losses of Hudsons and the obsolescence of the Beaufort and the Hampden that several strike wings of two or three Beaufighter Squadrons were planned. The idea was that two of the three squadrons would be armed with bombs and cannon to overwhelm the enemy opposition, while the third squadron, armed with torpedos, would press home attacks on the prime targets in enemy convoys. A second squadron, 254, with torpedo-equipped Beaufighters ('Torbeaus'), joined 143 at the beginning of November, and on the 20th of that month the Strike Wing mounted its initial operation. This proved to be a costly disaster; escorting Spitfires missed the rendezvous and three Beaufighters were shot down by intensive flak and fighter opposition; another four aircraft were badly damaged, and only one ship in the attacked convoy was damaged. As a result, both squadrons were withdrawn from operational duties for a period of intensive training.

No. 236 Squadron arrived with bomber Beaus during early April 1943 in time to join the Strike Wing in its first operation since the previous November, when twenty-one aircraft attacked a large

convoy off Texel. The primary target — a large motor vessel — was sunk, and three escort vessels were damaged. This time all the aircraft returned safely, thus establishing the North Coates Wing as a front-line unit.

In August 1943, 143 Squadron moved south for operations over the Bay of Biscay, returning to North Coates in February 1944. Resuming strike operations, the squadron remained on the airfield until May, when it was again moved south, this time to Manston in Kent, from where it flew patrols over the invasion forces. Returning for a few weeks in September, it departed for Banff, on the Moray Firth, in October.

Nos. 236 and 254 Squadrons contniued to operate as the North Coates Wing until the end of the war; 254 partially re-equipped with de Havilland Mosquitoes in March 1945 but 236 disbanded at North Coates on 25th May 1945 and 254 moved to Chivenor, North Devon, in June.

North Coates, reduced to a closing-down establishment by the beginning of July 1945, was then transferred from Coastal Command to Maintenance Command and almost immediately became a storage sub-site for 25 MU. In October 1945 the storage sub-site was taken over by 61 MU.

The station was transferred to Flying Training Command in December 1946 and on the 16th of that month a party of thirty-four German PoW's, together with an advance party of RAF personnel, arrived to prepare it for use as an Officer Cadet Training establishment. Permanent staff were posted in from North Luffenham and Bridgnorth, and on 1st January 1947, No.1 Initial Training School was formed. The School had to close at the beginning of February due to the severe winter weather, but re-opened the following month and remained at North Coates until May, when it moved to South Cerney in Gloucestershire.

In October 1947 North Coates was placed on a Care and Maintenance footing and remained so until re-opening in May 1948 under the control of 24 Group, Technical Training Command, when it became the home of the School of Explosives Inspection. A Bomb Disposal Wing and School were added to the strength of the station in August 1948, and in October the unit was re-named 15 School of Technical Training.

During February 1950 the Junior Armament (Foreign) Officers' Course came in from Kirkham in Lancashire. At the beginning of 1951 the Bomb Disposal Wing was re-named 5131 Bomb Disposal Squadron and the Armament Inspection Services General Course arrived from St. Athan in South Wales.

The aerodrome was flooded to a depth of four feet during the East Coast floods of January 1953 and had to be evacuated, the Foreign Officers' Course moving to Henlow in Bedfordshire on 4th February

Right: **Beaufighter X L7293 of North Coates based No.236 Squadron.** (IWM CH18539)

Below: **North Coates after the East Coast Floods of January 1953.** (Sqn Ldr S.Sills)

and 15 SoTT to Kirkham two days later. Following the cleaning-up, the station was ready to resume its normal functions by the end of the month.

Later in 1953, North Coates was transferred to 43 Group, Maintenance Command, and hosted 54 MU which dealt with the repair and salvage of aircraft.

Bristol Sycamores of 'B' Flight, 275 Squadron, flew in for air-sea rescue duties in November 1954. No. 43 Group disbanded in January 1956 and the station passed into the control of 41 Group, Maintenance Command. In July 1956, 54 MU was moved to Hucknall in Nottinghamshire and 5131 BD Squadron went to Morton Hall; the 500 acre (200 ha) station again being placed under Care and Maintenance.

North Coates re-opened in July 1957 under the control of Fighter Command as the RAF's premier surface-to-air missile base. The first Bloodhound Mk.1 missiles arrived on 3rd April 1958 and by 1st December sufficient missiles and equipment had arrived to allow formation of 264 Squadron. In May 1960 the headquarters of 148 Wing formed at North Coates to control the Bloodhound installations at North Coates, Dunholme Lodge (141 Squadron) and Woodhall Spa (222 Squadron).

The Bloodhound system was continuously developed and by 1960 the Bloodhound Mk.2 was ready for trials. During October 1960 No.17 Joint Services Trials Unit formed at North Coates to carry out operational trials on the new missile and see it brought into service. To allow development of facilities for the new missile the Bloodhound Mk.1 missiles were taken out of service and 264 Squadron disbanded in August 1962. A little over a year later, on 1st October 1963, 25 Squadron formed at North Coates and began to work up on the Bloodhound Mk.2. Also established at North Coates during October 1963 was the Surface-to-Air Missile Operational Training School, tasked with training personnel to operate the Bloodhound system.

The task of 25 Squadron was later expanded to include that of the SAMOTS and on 17th August 1964 the two units were amalgamated. Development of the Bloodhound Mk.2 complete, 17 JSTU disbanded in December 1966. The Bloodhound system was mobile and 25 Squadron often provided displays at the Farnborough and Paris air shows, deploying from Binbrook in Blackburn Beverley or Armstrong Whitworth Argosy aircraft. A further exercise in mobility was undertaken in 1969 under the code name Exercise 'Illusory'. The exercise required 25 Squadron to deploy both by road and air to Woodhall Spa between 3rd and 28th March. The airlift amounted to seven Lockheed Hercules loads which were flown between Binbrook and Coningsby. The exercise provided valuable experience for the squadron's forthcoming move to Germany.

The move of 25 Squadron to Germany commenced in April 1970 when personnel of 'C' Flight started to move to Laarbruch. The move was undertaken by road and air and was completed on 31st May and the flight was declared fully operational at Laarbruch on 15th June. Meanwhile, back at North Coates, preparation of the remaining equipment continued. Operations Flight, the training element of the squadron, moved to West Raynham in Norfolk between 20th and 27th July and the squadron headquarters was formed at Bruggen with effect from 17th August 1970. Equipment continued to be moved to Germany until the end of the year and the squadron was declared fully operational in Germany on 31st January 1971. Following the departure of 25 Squadron North Coates was formally closed on 28th February 1971.

Left: **Sycamore HR14 XJ363 of 'B' Flight, 275 Sqn at North Coates engaged in air-sea rescue training with HSL2753 out from Immingham on 7th June 1956.**
(Crown Copyright PRB11819)

However, during 1976, the Bloodhound was brought back into service in the United Kingdom to help improve the sadly depleted air defences. Logically, North Coates was re-activated and personnel of 'B' Flight of 85 Squadron arrived to operate the missiles allocated to North Coates. There are two sections of Bloodhound missiles deployed at North Coates which retains a vital role in the maintenance of our air defence.

Above: **Loading a Bloodhound Mk.I on to its launcher at North Coates 29th October 1958.**
(Crown Copyright PRB15918)

North Killingholme

1 km W of North Killingholme Church
113 / TA 135 170   30 ft (10 m) AMSL

Construction of North Killingholme aerodrome commenced on 23rd September 1942 and the new station opened within 1 Group Bomber Command on 17th November 1943. Although ready to receive its first squadron by 1st December, the first unit did not arrive there until 3rd January 1944, this being 550 Squadron, which moved in from Grimsby.

On New Year's Day 1944 the station had been absorbed as a sub-station of 13 Base which was formed that day with its headquarters at Elsham Wolds. The squadron was brought up to a three-flight strength of thirty Avro Lancasters on 12th September 1944 and three of the squadron's aircraft went on to complete more than 100 operational sorties each. No. 550 Squadron assisted in the supply of food to the Dutch and the repatriation of ex-prisoners-of-war before it was disbanded on 31st October 1945, its

Right: **Lancaster NG287/Q of 550 Sqn at North Killingholme. This aircraft was flown by F/O Franklyn and had the distinctive nose art of a kangaroo dropping a bomb with the message 'Try this for size'.** *(via G.S.Leslie)*

Below: **Lancaster ED905 'Press on Regardless' of 550 Sqn, North Killingholme takes off on its 100th mission (to Bochum) on 4th November 1944.** *(IWM CH14187)*

aircraft having flown on nearly 200 operations.

During April 1945 the 1 Group Bomb Handling School was moved to North Killingholme from Scampton and probably remained there until 13 Base was disbanded in December 1945. Administration of the station then passed to Hemswell and the station was placed on a Care and Maintenance footing until, early in 1946, 40 Group Maintenance Command took over the station as a sub-site of 35 MU for external storage purposes. Between 1946 and 1949 the Ministry of Agriculture, Fisheries and Food administered the grass areas of the airfield which was sold back to farmers in 1965.

With the expansion of industrial activity on the south bank of the Humber the 740 acre (300 ha) airfield at North Killingholme has proved to be a convenient site for industrial use. Runways have been used to store gas pipes and an intensive poultry unit has been built. The remaining hangars are used as warehouses for a number of products and a number of industrial units have already been developed with more under development. In a link with its past the approach road to the new industrial estate is aptly named 'Lancaster Approach'. In early 1981 North Killingholme was one of the sites under consideration as the location for the car assembly plant to be built in the UK by the Japanese car giant Nissan.

A memorial to 550 Squadron was dedicated on 31st July 1982 (see *Appendix J*).

North Witham

2 km ENE of North Witham Church
130/SK 945 225   380 ft (120 m) AMSL

Construction of North Witham aerodrome began in late 1942, but before completion it was allocated for use by the US Army Air Force. Given the American Station Number 479, North Witham operated as part of the Ninth Army Air Force Support Command and housed the headquarters unit of the 1st Advanced Air Depot Area, which handled the supply and maintenance for all bomber and troop carrying aircraft within the Ninth Army Air Force.

Under its control the AADA had twelve Air Depot Groups. It was usual for two of these Groups to be paired to

Right: One of six Butler hangars under construction at North Witham by the 83rd Engineer Aviation Battalion. *(USAF77877AC)*

Below: 'Shantytown', a camp made entirely of empty glider crates. The location is thought to be North Witham (note the Butler hangar in the background). *(USAF 53110AC)*

form a Tactical Air Depot; 1 TAD was housed at North Witham. The other five were deployed at other Ninth Army Air Force stations where they carried out the aircraft repair and maintenance work for a Troop Carrier or Bomber Wing. Normally all work was carried out by the TAD, but any task beyond its resources was passed to the AADA for completion.

North Witham became the base of the US Ninth Troop Carrier Command Pathfinder Group, formed from aircrew specially trained in the use of radio navigation aids by the Pathfinder School at Cottesmore. At 9.30 pm on 5th June 1944 Douglas C-47 aircraft of the Group began taking off from North Witham carrying soldiers of the American 82nd and 101st Airborne Divisions. These were the first American soldiers to land in France on D-Day and their task was to set up radio location beacons to guide the main airborne assault on to its respective dropzones.

By early 1945 the Ninth Air Force had moved to the Continent and North Witham was returned to 5 Group Bomber Command, which placed the station on Care and Maintenance. No.40 Group Maintenance Command took the station over on 1st June 1945 for use as a bomb storage sub-site of 16 MU. The domestic

area was taken over by the RAF Regiment in September 1945 and 4 RAF Regiment Sub-Depot was established as an off-shoot of the RAF Regiment Depot at Belton Park to receive RAF Regiment personnel on their return from overseas and prepare them for release from the Service. The sub-depot closed on 5th June 1946.

No.259 MU formed at North Witham on 1st July 1945 and moved to Woolfox Lodge in Rutland on 14th August; while the station remained as a sub-site of the unit until it was closed in August 1948. Today a substantial portion of its 650 acres (260 ha) lie under Forestry Commission plantations, although the derelict watch office remains, as does one sole hangar which has been converted for use as a store.

Sandtoft

3 km WNW of Belton Church
112/SE 755 080   10 ft (3 m) AMSL

The initial investigation of an airfield site near Sandtoft in January 1942 led to construction starting on 23rd October and, with the aim of being ready to receive an operational bomber unit on 10th January 1944, the nearly complete station

started to open on 12th December 1943.

The first unit did not materialise until 18th February when 'A' Flight of 1667 Heavy Conversion Unit arrived from Faldingworth, followed by 'B' and 'C' Flights the next day. Flying training commenced while at the same time Sandtoft became a sub-station of 11 Base. During July 1944 a fourth flight was formed within the unit and was named the Flying Instructors Flight, which carried out the standardisation flying for all the instructors of 11 Base.

No.11 Base was transferred to 7 Group and renumbered 71 Base on 5th November 1944, while the Handley Page Halifaxes which the unit was operating were slowly replaced by Avro Lancasters. The station remained active until October 1945 when the aircraft were finally relinquished and 1667 HCU disbanded on 10th November 1945.

Sandtoft was due to be transferred to 40 Group Maintenance Command on 27th December as a sub-site of 33 MU but was placed on Care and Maintenance and remained inactive until allocated for use by the US Air Force on 1st April 1953. The station was never occupied and returned to UK control on 8th September 1955 and sometime later its 700 acres (280 ha) were sold.

In late 1969 the Sandtoft Transport Centre opened on the former site of a T2 hangar. The centre has built up a large collection of trolley and other buses which may be seen in operation on various open days throughout the year. The former watch office is now used as a dwelling and office accommodation and a number of light industrial activities, including roof-tile manufacture and joinery, take place around the former airfield. A motorway now slices across the northern side of the old aerodrome.

A new hangar was built in 1982 and the airfield reactivated as a light aircraft training and maintenance base. By mid-1983 resident aircraft included AA-5As G-BHKV, G-BCLI and PA-28 G-BCLL.

Above: **Located on the former site of a T2 hangar, the Sandtoft Transport Centre has a large collection of trolley buses and other public transport vehicles.** *(W.J.Taylor)*

Below: **Ingenious alterations have made the watch office at Sandtoft into an excellent dwelling.** *(Bill Baguley/ Rod Houldsworth)*

Scampton / Brattleby

1.5 km E of Scampton Church
121/SK965795   200ft (60m) AMSL

The site of Brattleby aerodrome, which after the middle of 1917 became known as Scampton, occupied an area which is now in the centre of the present Scampton airfield complex. In December 1916, as part of Britain's home defence system, a searchlight unit was established on pasture belonging to Aisthorpe Farm, Brattleby; with it came 'A' Flight of 33 (Home Defence) Squadron. Using Royal Aircraft Factory F.E.2, Avro 504 and Bristol F.2b Fighter aircraft, the flight remained at Brattleby throughout the expansion into a training station and the name change to Scampton. In June 1918 33 Squadron's detached flights were transferred to Kirton in Lindsey (Manton) and 'A' Flight left Scampton to join the remainder of the squadron.

As Scampton changed its role to that of training, various training squadrons arrived: 49 from Norwich; 37 from Catterick, on 13th November 1916. No.49 TS moved to Spittlegate on 14th November 1916 and was replaced by 60 TS from Beverley in Yorkshire on 14th April 1917. In November 1917, on the 15th, 37 TS changed places with 11 TS

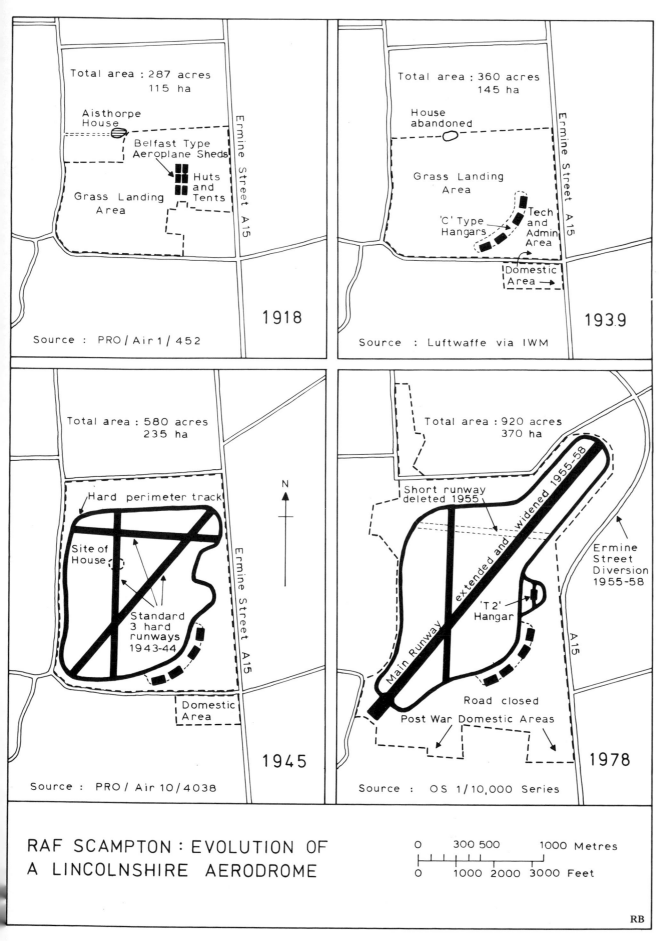

Total area : 287 acres
115 ha

Aisthorpe House

Belfast Type Aeroplane Sheds

Huts and Tents

Grass Landing Area

Ermine Street A15

1918

Source : PRO/Air 1/452

Total area : 360 acres
145 ha

House abandoned

Grass Landing Area

'C' Type Hangars

Tech and Admin Area

Domestic Area

Ermine Street A15

1939

Source : Luftwaffe via IWM

Total area : 580 acres
235 ha

Hard perimeter track

Site of House

Standard 3 hard runways 1943-44

Domestic Area

Ermine Street A15

N

1945

Source : PRO/Air 10/4038

Total area : 920 acres
370 ha

Short runway deleted 1955

extended and widened 1955-58

Main Runway

'T 2' Hangar

Ermine Street Diversion 1955-58

A15

Road closed

Post War Domestic Areas

1978

Source : OS 1/10,000 Series

RAF SCAMPTON : EVOLUTION OF
A LINCOLNSHIRE AERODROME

0   300 500   1000 Metres

0   1000 2000 3000 Feet

RB

145

at Spittlegate. Throughout this period aircraft in use at Scampton included the Avro 504, B.E.2 and R.E.8, the Armstrong Whitworth F.K.8 and various Sopwith aircraft including the Camel, Dolphin and Pup.

In August 1918 No.81 Squadron was formed at Scampton as a training unit and on 15th August 1918 it amalgamated with 11 and 60 TS to form 34 Training Depot Station. No.34 TDS, along with 46 TDS at South Carlton, formed 23 Training Wing. Wing Headquarters was established at South Carlton and was responsible for the daily administration of Scampton.

American pilots were also trained at Scampton during the closing months of the war and for a short time a USAAC detachment was established on the aerodrome. As soon as the war ended 34 TDS began the process of being run down and by April 1919, when the last few aeroplanes were moved to South Carlton, the 287 acre (112 ha) aerodrome closed down. By the year 1920 all the buildings, including the six hangars, had been removed from the site and the ground was returned to agricultural purposes.

During the early thirties, as the threat of another European conflict became evident, it was announced that Scampton would be re-opened and used as a bomber airfield, so on 27th August 1936 a Station Headquarters was set up and the airfield officially opened under 3 Group Bomber Command. In October the first flying units moved in; 9 Squadron with Handley Page Heyfords arrived from Aldergrove in Northern Ireland and 214 Squadron flying Vickers Virginias came from Andover in Hampshire. In January 1937 the latter squadron converted to the Handley Page Harrow and was fully equipped with that type of machine before being transferred to Feltwell in Norfolk during the following April. On 10th March the station came under the command of 5 Group and on 7th June 1937 one Flight from 9 Squadron was detached and became the experienced nucleus of 148 Squadron, which operated

Top: **Aerial view of Scampton taken on 8th February 1918.** *(Chaz Bowyer)*

Left: **DH6 A9644 at Scampton, 1918.** *(via M.Hodgson)*

Above: **HP Heyford III (K5190 of 9 Sqn?) at Scampton, 1936/37. Note another aircraft approaching over the roof of the partially completed C type hangar.** *(via Sqn Ldr C.G.Jefford)*

Above: **Manchester I L7427 of 83 Sqn, Scampton in March 1942 with bomb markings on the nose indicating ten operational missions.** *(MAP)*

Right: **L4039 was the first Hampden received by 49 Sqn at Scampton.** *(via Scampton Station Records)*

the Hawker Audax for a time but soon converted to the Vickers Wellesley.

In March 1938 Nos.9 and 148 Squadrons were posted to Stradishall in Suffolk and were replaced at Scampton by 49 and 83 Squadrons which brought their Hawker Hinds from Worthy Down in Hampshire and Turnhouse in Midlothian respectively. In September 1938 No.49 Squadron became the first unit to operate the Handley Page Hampden when it took delivery of its first aircraft on 20th September; 83 Squadron soon followed suit, its first aircraft arriving during November.

Both squadrons were fully operational with the new type when war broke out in September 1939. In February 1940 twelve aircraft from each squadron were detached to Morayshire, 49's aircraft to Kinloss and 83's to Lossiemouth. After carrying out several sweeps over the North Sea, the two squadrons returned to Scampton at the end of March. During their absence, 98 Squadron flew in and operated from the station and, arriving at the beginning of March, this squadron stayed at Scampton for three weeks prior to moving off to France with its Fairey Battles.

Throughout the summer of 1940 the intensity of air operations increased. On 8th June 1940 Pilot Officer Donald Parker of 49 Squadron was awarded the George Cross when, after his fully laden Hampden crashed on take-off, he rescued his unconscious wireless operator from the burning wreckage. On 1st July a Hampden of 83 Squadron, piloted by Flying Officer Guy Gibson, dropped the first 2,000 lb bomb and, on 12th August, during a raid on the Dortmund—Ems Canal Flight Lieutenant R.A.B.Learoyd of 49 Squadron was awarded the Victoria Cross when, after breaching the canal banks, Learoyd flew his badly damaged aircraft back to Scampton, where he delayed his landing until dawn, thus saving his aircraft from further damage.

The second Victoria Cross to be awarded to personnel operating from Scampton went to Sergeant John Hannah of 83 Squadron when, on 16th September 1940, Hannah successfully extinguished a fire in his badly damaged Hampden. Although he had sustained severe burns, he ably assisted the pilot in returning the aircraft safely to base.

In September 1941 the 5 Group Target Tow Flight arrived at Scampton from Coningsby, equipped with Battles, Westland Lysanders and Vickers Wellingtons to provide target towing and gunnery training facilities for the aircraft of 5 Group. The flight was re-titled 1485 Target Tow and Gunnery flight in February 1942 and it moved to Dunholme Lodge the following September. No. 83 Squadron began conversion to the Avro Manchester during December 1941, making its first operational sorties with the aircraft in January 1942. No.49 Squadron followed suit and accepted its first Manchester in April. The two squadrons operated the ill-fated type until starting conversion again in June of that year when the first Avro Lancasters arrived.

No.83 Squadron left the station in August for Wyton in Huntingdonshire, where it became one of the founder squadrons of the Pathfinder Force, and was replaced by 57 Squadron, which brought its Lancasters from Methwold. No. 467 Squadron RAAF was formed at Scampton on 7th November 1942 using some of 83 Squadron's Lancasters, including R5868, which is now housed in the RAF Museum, and commenced its work-up, but it moved to Bottesford in Leicestershire before becoming fully operational.

In May 1943 Scampton became Base Headquarters for 52 Base and assumed control of the sub-stations at Dunholme Lodge and Fiskerton which had been allocated to 52 Base. A Base Major Servicing Unit was formed at Scampton and 49 Squadron moved to Fiskerton.

One of the most famous units of the Royal Air Force was formed at Scampton on 21st March 1943 — 617 Squadron. With a special mission in mind, the breaching of the Ruhr dams, the new squadron began a period of intensive training before finnaly setting out on 16th May 1943 to attack the dams. Two of the squadron's targets, the Mohne and Eder dams, were breached with the loss of eight of the nineteen Lancasters despatched, and no less than thirty-four decorations were awarded to squadron personnel taking part in this epic raid. The leader, Wing Commander Guy Gibson, was awarded the Victoria Cross.

Scampton had been a grass airfield until the summer of 1943 when it was decided that concrete runways should be laid, so 57 Squadron moved off to East Kirkby on 29th August and 617 Squadron left for Coningsby the following day. On 31st August 1943 Scampton ceased operations and work commenced on the construction of runways, although Base Headquarters and the Base Major Servicing Unit continued to operate from the station. While the runway work was in progress several training schools were established on the station and between September and November a course was established to instruct newly commissioned aircrew on their duties and responsiblities, while the Aircrew Commando School moved in from Morton

Hall and the newly trained aircrew were taught survival and evasion techniques.

By July 1944 the airfield was fit for day flying use and 1690 Bomber Defence Training Flight arrived from Syerston in Nottinghamshire, equipped with Spitfire, Hawker Hurricane and Miles Martinet aircraft and undertook the provision of aircraft for fighter affiliation and air to air gunnery training for the whole of 5 Group. The 5 Group NCO's School was also established at the station but it remained only long enough to complete one four-week course of drill and administration before it was moved to Balderton in Nottinghamshire in October.

In October 1944 Scampton was declared operational again and was transferred to 1 Group Bomber Command, so 1690 BDT Flight moved to Metheringham to remain within 5 Group. Scampton became Base Station for 15 Base on 7th October and on the 15th 153 Squadron arrived from Kirmington, undertaking its first operation from the new station on the 20th.

No.1687 BDT Flight arrived at Scampton in December 1944 from Cammeringham and provided fighter affiliation training for 1 Group aircrews until it moved to Hemswell in April 1945. On the 5th of that month 625 Squadron arrived from Kelstern and four days later took part in a raid on Kiel. The Lancasters of both squadrons took part in their last raid of the war on 25th April.

The months of September and October 1945 saw a series of disbandments at Scampton, beginning with 153 Squadron on 21st September and followed by

148

Below left: **617 Sqn Lancaster ED817 AJ-C showing pinion wheels for the chain drive bomb spinning mechanism used on the 'Dam Buster' raid.**
(via P.H.T.Green)

Above: **A formation of six B-29 Superfortresses of the 28th BG over-flies Scampton in September 1948.**
(via Brig Gen Brian S.Gunderson USAF (Rtd))

625 Squadron on 2nd October and 15 Base on 20th October. On 26th November the Lincoln Flight of the former 57 Squadron at East Kirkby arrived to become the Lincoln Service Trials Flight, later destined to operate under the control of 57 Squadron, which itself arrived from Elsham Wolds on 3rd December. Also moving from Elsham Wolds that day was 100 Squadron, which, together with 57 Squadron, embarked on Operations *Dodge,* the repatriation of British ex-prisoners-of-war from Italy, and *Wastage,* the disposal of stock-piled bombs.

After successful trials with the Lincoln, both 57 and 100 Squadrons began to re-equip with the type. Transition was complete by May 1946 when both units moved to Lindholme in Yorkshire, exchanging places with the 1 Group Major Servicing Unit which carried out acceptance checks on all new Lincolns being issued to 1 Group units as well as the major servicing of the Group's Lancasters.

In October 1946 the MSU prepared three aircraft for a goodwill visit to Chile, one Lincoln each from 83, 97 and 100 Squadrons, which left Hemswell on 25th October and arrived safely in Chile nine days later. No.617 Squadron operated from Scampton during August and September 1946 while its own airfield at Binbrook was unserviceable.

The Bomber Command Instructors School arrived on the station in January 1947, bringing from Lindholme a collection of various types of aircraft including Lincolns, Lancasters, Vickers Wellingtons, de Havilland Mosquitoes and the odd Spitfire. This unit had the job of training and categorising all the instructors destined for Bomber Command and operated until July 1947 when its task was re-organised and it was re-named the Bomber Command Instrument Rating and Examining Flight. Making exclusive use of Lincolns, the Flight's task was the categorisation of all the aircrew within

Bomber Command, a task which entailed frequent visits to other stations.

Flying was restricted from July 1947 to April 1948 while essential maintenance and reconstruction work was carried out on the runways; 1 Group MSU was disbanded shortly after the airfield was declared fully operational again.

With worsening East-West relations and the start of the Berlin Airlift in June 1948, several RAF stations were made available for use by the United States government as heavy bomber bases and Scampton was chosen as one of these. The first American unit to arrive was the 28th Bombardment Group, which brought its Boeing B-29 Superfortresses to the station on 17th July and, after a stay of four months, was relieved by the 301st BG which remained until January 1949. By this time the European situation had eased and the Americans returned home.

Lancasters and Lincolns of 230 Operational Conversion Unit took the place of the Americans during February 1949, but the Lancasters were soon phased out leaving the unit to continue its task of training crews for the Lincoln; in May 1953 the OCU was disbanded and the aircraft were transferred to Upwood in

Left: **Salvation Army service for the ground crews of USAF B-29s at Scampton, Summer 1948.** *(via Brig Gen B.S.Gunderson USAF (Rtd))*

Below: **100 hour inspection on a B-29 at Scampton.** *(via Brig Gen Brian S.Gunderson USAF (Rtd))*

Huntingdonshire. The USAF returned to Scampton in June 1952 when the 3930 Air Base Squadron was established to look after a dump of US Equipment and a large MT park; the unit remained for a year and disbanded in July 1953.

In May 1953 the Bomber Command Instrument Rating and Examining Flight was transferred to Binbrook and the Bomber Command Bombing School, then in the process of forming at Scampton, was moved to Lindholme.

By this time Scampton had become a jet bomber station, as 10 Squadron had re-formed and equipped with the English Electric Canberra B.2 during January 1953. Three further squadrons were added to the strength of the station by the end of the year; 27 Squadron re-formed in June, 18 Squadron in August and 21 Squadron in September. All four squadrons worked up with the Canberra and operated from Scampton until May 1955 when 10 and 18 Squadrons moved to Honington in Suffolk and Upwood in Huntingdonshire respectively, and 21 and 27 Squadrons moved to Waddington.

On 1st June 1955 Scampton was closed down and placed on Care and Maintenance; the station had been earmarked for use as a V-Bomber base and so for the next three years it was extensively re-modelled. The old three runway system was scrapped and replaced by a

Below: **Line-up of 27 Squadron's Canberra B2s in front of Scampton's hangars in June 1954.** *(via P.H.T.Green)*

Crown Copyright / RAF Photograph

Description: A Hurt surmounted of an arrow bend sinisterwise and a Long Bow palewise.

Motto: ARMATUS NON LACESSITUR (An Armed Man is not Attacked)

Authority: Queen Elizabeth II, December 1958.

The topographical layout of the station is represented in the unit's badge. The bowstring represents the original Ermine Street, the bow the bend made to accommodate the runway, and the arrow the runway itself. The blue Roundel or Hurt in the background represents the sky.

single very long runway, so long in fact that the main A15 Lincoln to Brigg road had to be diverted. When the station received its own badge in 1958, the extension of the runway and diversion of the road were represented by a bow and arrow. In addition to the runway work, much new technical and domestic accommodation was erected, extending the area of the station to over 900 acres (360 ha).

Once again the station was declared fully operational and 617 Squadron re-formed with the Avro Vulcan B.1 on 1st May 1958. The 'Dambusters' were joined in October 1960 by 83 Squadron which re-formed with the Vulcan B.2; the two units were then joined by 27 Squadron which re-formed with the Vulcan B.2 during April 1961, by which time 617

Squadron had re-equipped with the Vulcan B.2 and the Scampton Wing was then up to its full strength of squadrons and aircraft.

Scampton was selected to become the station to introduce the Hawker Siddeley Dynamics Blue Steel stand-off

Above: **This simple metal plaque is set into the concrete apron in front of the hangars.** (*via M.Hodgson*)

Below: **Scampton technicians prepare to load Vulcan B2 XL318 of No.617 Squadron with a Blue Steel stand-off missile during 1963.** (*Crown Copyright PRB24614*)

Top left: **Two Vulcans overfly the RAF Ensign during the ceremony to mark the stand-down of RAF Bomber Command, held at Scampton, 29th April 1968.** (P.H.T.Green)

Above: **Some engine warm-up! Vulcan B2 XL385 of 617 Squadron burst into flames on the Scampton apron after an engine malfunction with the disastrous results seen above.** (via P.H.T.Green)

Left: **Hastings T.5 TG511, formerly of the Strike Command Bombing School, but now wearing the badge of 230 OCU on its fin.** (LAM)

bomb to the Royal Air Force, so special buildings were erected to house the weapon system and its fuel. In June 1962 No.18 Joint Service Trials Unit arrived at the station to assist with the introduction of the new missile and at the end of 1963 was absorbed into the new Missile Squadron of the station's Technical Wing; aircraft servicing became fully centralised and the squadrons drew aircraft as required from the Wing Pool.

In the late 1960s the RAF began a period of drastic reorganisation. Scampton, with its long history of distinguished service, was chosen as the venue for the ceremonial parade to mark the stand-down of Bomber Command and the formation of Strike Command. The parade was held on 29th April 1968 and Strike Command was formed by the merger of Bomber and Fighter Commands the following day. Three months later 83 Squadron was disbanded.

No.230 OCU returned to the station in late 1969 to provide both ground and flying training for all Vulcan aircrew of the new RAF Strike Command and the Near East Air Force. With the closure of Lindholme in 1972, the Strike Command Bombing School transferred to Scampton with its Handley Page Hastings aircraft to continue to provide radar training for Strike Command navigators until it was absorbed into 230 OCU on 1st January 1974. No.27 Squadron disbanded in March 1972 but re-formed again at

Above: **The last squadron to operate the Vulcan from Scampton was 27 which had the unique role of maritime radar reconnaissance and high altitude air sampling, for which XH560 was equipped on 17th February 1982.** *(W.J.Taylor)*

Scampton on 1st November 1973 with the Vulcan but in the new role of high altitude maritime radar reconnaissance. Following the upheaval in Cyprus during 1974 No. 35 Squadron was withdrawn from Akrotiri to Scampton in January 1975. Scampton became an all-Vulcan station again on 30th June 1977 when the last Hastings in use with the SCBS was withdrawn from service.

During 1979 the Ministry of Defence announced a number of plans which were to affect the long term future of the station. The first announcement, made in May, described plans for the formation of three Royal Auxiliary Air Force Regiment field squadrons in order to evaluate the use of volunteer units in the defence of home airfields. Each unit was to consist of 150 officers and men with a core of regular personnel. Scampton was selected as the base for one of the units (the others are at Honington (Suffolk) and Lossiemouth (Moray)) which, in a

link with the Royal Auxiliary Air Force prior to the Second World War, was named 2503 (County of Lincoln) Squadron Royal Auxiliary Air Force Regiment. The squadron was officially formed on 1 July 1979.

In 1981, the rundown of the RAF's Vulcan force began at Scampton, and following a gradual reduction in size 230 OCU disbanded on 1st September. The first squadron to go was 617 which held a parade to mark its disbandment on 22nd December and disbanded officially on 1st January 1982. This was followed by 35 Squadron which held its disbandment parade on 26th February and disbanded officially on 1st March, and the Vulcan era at Scampton finally came to an end a month later when 27 Squadron held its disbandment parade and disbanded officially on 31st March.

As the squadrons were disbanded some of their aircraft were allocated to Waddington but the majority were scrapped, some going to St. Athan (Glamorgan) to be broken up, others going to a variety of RAF stations for aircraft battle damage repair training or crash rescue training. A few Vulcans were scrapped at Scampton and one, XL318 of 617 Squadron, was dismantled and taken by road to the new Bomber Command Museum at Hendon.

It had been announced in 1979 that

following the Vulcan's demise Scampton would house the RAF's Victor tanker force which would move from Marham (Norfolk) as Tornado strike squadrons were formed there from 1982. However, reconsideration of the costs involved in such a move resulted in the plan being dropped at the end of 1981.

After a period of much uncertainty, particularly for the civilian work force, it became known that Scampton would transfer from Strike to RAF Support Command and become the home of the Central Flying School.

The change in Scampton's role began in March 1982 with the arrival of 643 Gliding School and the Humber Gliding Club from Lindholme (Yorkshire). On 1st October 1982 the station transferred to RAF Support Command and preparation began for the formation of the RAF Trade Management Training School using a pair of Hunter F.6A training airframes (XE653 and XF515). First of the CFS units to move to Scampton was the RAF Aerobatic Team, the Red Arrows, which arrived with its BAe Hawks on 25 March 1983 following a pre-season work-up at Akrotiri. Other units were expected to arrive from Leeming, Yorkshire, by the end of 1983. In April 1983, 50 Squadron (Vulcan K.2) spent a couple of weeks here while the runway at Waddington, its home airfield, was resurfaced.

Scunthorpe (Emmanuel)

3.5 km SE of Scunthorpe Railway Station
112/SE 921 087   60 ft (20 m) AMSL

This airfield was developed by the United Steel Companies Ltd. in 1959, was subsequently listed in the *UK Air Pilot* as a bona fide civil aerodrome and continued in use until 1969 when the land was required for the Anchor Steel Works, being finally deleted from the list of active aerodromes in 1970.

Large scale OS maps indicate that there were two hard strips. 'Emmanuel West' measured 650 yards and ran approximately WNW alongside the A18(T) road between the junction of the A1029 and the town's eastern administrative boundary. This strip now forms part of Emmanuel Road which is an internal distributor within the British Steel Corporation complex. 'Emmanuel East' measured 750 yards, running approximately N–S (20/02) just outside the municipal boundary.

The aerodrome was the base of the three small company aircraft and ground facilities (radio, ambulance and fire tender) were provided by the Steelworks police. Today the Steel Corporation uses Kirmington Airport.

Skegness (Burgh Road)

1.2 km NNW of Skegness Railway Station
122/TA 556 643   10 ft (3 m) AMSL

With the outbreak of hostilities in 1914 it was feared that the Germans would carry out mass raids over Britain with their Zeppelins so, to allay the fears of the civilian population, aeroplanes were flown to strategic points along the East Coast to conduct anti-Zeppelin patrols. It was to this end that Squadron Commander Samson lead a flight of seven aeroplanes to Skegness, arriving there two days after the declaration of war. The aeroplanes were of several different types and drawn from the Eastchurch Squadron; two of them crashed on arrival and it seems doubtful if the remaining aircraft undertook many flights. On 25th August 1914, Squadron Commander Samson was summoned to London for further orders and a few days later the aeroplanes at Skegness took off to rejoin their Squadron, from where they were subsequently posted to Ostend.

The aerodrome, which was of indeterminate size, was located on the south side of the Burgh Road opposite the water tower and is today covered by a housing development.

Skegness (Winthorpe)

1 km ENE of Winthorpe Church
122/TF 568 665   10 ft (3 m) AMSL

Skegness (Winthorpe) Aerodrome was laid out in 1930 by Mr. M. D. L. Scott, a co-director, along with Captain G. A. R. Pennington, of Eastern Air Transport Ltd. The company was equipped with de Havilland Puss Moth G-AAXL and de Havilland Gipsy Moth G-AAKM and in early April 1932 the Skegness and East Lincolnshire Aero Club was formed and based at Skegness using the aircraft of Eastern Air Transport. Captain Pennington was the club's Chief Flying Instructor and Mr. Scott was the club's secretary. At the time of its inauguration the club had fourteen flying and fifty-six non-flying members and was also affiliated to the Brooklands Aero Club. The first Skegness Air Pageant was held on 16th May 1932 and served as the opening ceremony of the Aero Club.

In addition to its work with the aero club, Eastern Air Transport operated a twice-daily service across the Wash to Hunstanton during the summers of 1931 and 1932, and it was while operating one such service that the Puss Moth made a forced landing on a sandbank in the mouth of the Wash on 26th May 1932;

Left: The Territorial Army Advance Party at camp in Skegness July 1914. When the tents were cleared, this site was used by the Eastchurch Squadron for its landing ground. *(A.Osbourne)*

Right: The Spartan 3-seater seen here was used regularly for pleasure flights from Winthorpe in the 1930s. *(via K.Wattam)*

Centre right: Visitor to the first Skegness Air Pageant, held on Whit Sunday 16th May 1932 was Puss Moth G-AAXX. *(via P.H.T.Green)*

Bottom: DH60G Gipsy Moth G-AAKM of Eastern Air Transport Ltd seen at Skegness (Winthorpe) aerodrome in the mid-1930s. *(via J.Calladine)*

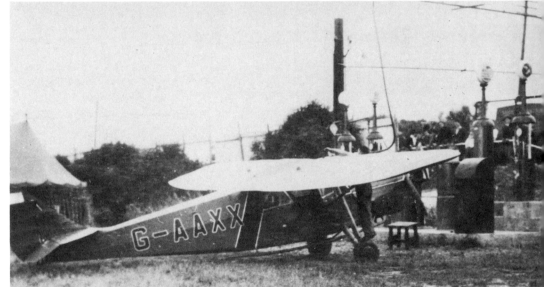

faced with a rising tide the pilot deliberately set fire to the aircraft to attract rescuers from the mainland. Captain Pennington left the resort at the end of 1932 to become the personal pilot of Mr. H. Blograve, but on 14th September the Captain, who had trained with the Royal Naval Air Service at Frieston, was killed when the de Havilland Dragon he was piloting crashed on take-off at Doncaster (Armthorpe) Aerodrome in Yorkshire.

Eastern Air Transport made good the loss of the Puss Moth in April 1933 with the acquisition of de Havilland Fox Moth G-ABVJ and continued to operate from Skegness until the end of the 1935 summer season, when it ceased operations.

The Fox Moth then went to Midland Airways Ltd., at Sywell and the Gipsy Moth, which had been sold earlier in the year, eventually served in the Indian Air Force.

Various other organisations used the aerodrome, as did a number of private owners. Notable among the latter was Alex Henshaw who learned to fly at Skegness with the Skegness and East Lincolnshire Aero Club, making his first solo flight at Skegness in April 1932. Later that year Henshaw's first aircraft, Gipsy Moth G-ABLN, was based at Skegness. However, as the European political situation deteriorated, Skegness (Winthorpe) Aerodrome was closed and the land came up for sale. Little evidence

of the old aerodrome remains today except for one of the former hangars. The 30 acre (12 ha) airfield itself is still remarkably free of caravans.

Skegness (Ingoldmells)

1.5 km SSE of Ingoldmells Church
122/TF565675   10ft (3 m) AMSL

A new civil aerodrome for Skegness was built in 1948 opposite Butlin's Holiday Camp at Ingoldmells and was titled Butlin's Skegness (Ingoldmells) Aerodrome.

Left: Despite the number of caravans in and around the town, most of the former Skegness (Winthorpe) aerodrome remains free of them, as this February 1979 view shows. *(W.J.Taylor)*

Bottom left: Much of the filming for the film 'Those Magnificent Men in Their Flying Machines' was carried out at Skegness (Ingoldmells). *(N.Franklin)*

Right: Unique resident at Skegness (Ingoldmells) between 1960 and 1962 was this Aeronca 100 G-AEXD. *(D.Stennett)*

On Sunday 13th June 1948 the official opening ceremony was held and forty aircraft were present. The ceremony was performed by Alderman J.Forester, Chairman of Lindsey County Council, and afterwards the civic party was flown over Skegness in a de Havilland Dragon Rapide of the Butlin air fleet. Further displays in Austers and Percival Proctors were given and competitions were held, including an air race, height judging and a Concours d'Elegance.

Aircraft of the Butlin fleet, painted in their distinctive light blue and yellow colour scheme, provided pleasure flying facilities for tourists at the adjacent holiday camp. However, by 1949 the fleet had been dispersed and on 9th September 1949 Skegness (Airport) Ltd was formed to continue the pleasure flights and to operate some charter flights from Skegness. The founders of the new company were Mr. F.A. Laker (now Sir Freddie Laker) and Mr. R.A. Treen, a director of Bond Air Services Ltd; the new company grew out of Bond Air Services and the two companies shared aircraft. An air display was held in 1950 at which Bond's de Havilland D.H.86 Express aircraft were used for pleasure flying, but at the end of 1951 Bond Air Services ceased operations and the aircraft were sold.

Skegness Air Taxi Service was formed in the autumn of 1951 to take over the operation of Skegness (Ingoldmells) Aerodrome and gradually built up a fleet of aircraft which carried out pleasure flying and other ad-hoc charter work.

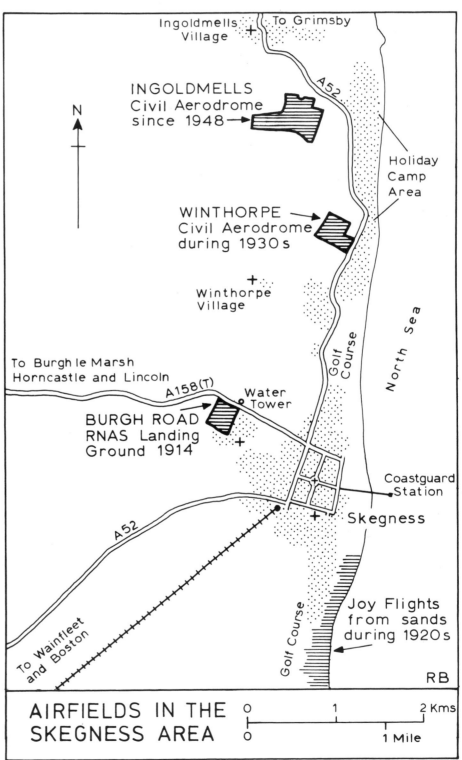

AIRFIELDS IN THE SKEGNESS AREA

Above: **Skegness (Ingoldmells), believed to have been taken during a display held in 1960.** *(via D.Stennett)*

Right: **Dart Kitten G-AMJP operated from Skegness (Ingoldmells) from mid-1963 until 5th June 1966 when it crashed near King's Lynn.** *(D.Stennett)*

Below right: **Landing at Skegness on a pleasure flight is Auster J/1N G-AHAL. In the background is Butlin's holiday camp.** *(W.J.Taylor)*

Later the company expanded into flying training work with the Skegness Aero Club and became associated with the Boston Aero Club, eventually taking over the operation of Boston Aerodrome; later, in 1956 it also took over the aircraft of Aerial Spraying Contractors Ltd.

Today Skegness Air Taxi Service continues to operate the airfield and although the Austers are no longer used for flying training, having given way in 1973 to more modern and economical Cessnas, they still operate daily, taking tourists on pleasure flights over Skegness. The airfield has two grass runways,(the longer being just over 2000 feet) and during 1966 was used as a base for the aircraft involved in the making of the film 'Those Magnificent Men In Their Flying Machines'. Its 50 acres (20 ha) make it about half as large again as its pre-war counterpart.

Skellingthorpe

2.5 km SSE of Skellingthorpe Church
121/SK 935 695   60ft (20m) AMSL

Opened late in 1941 as a satellite of Waddington in 5 Group Bomber Command, the first unit to arrive at Skellingthorpe was 50 Squadron, which moved in from Swinderby on 26th November to allow for runway construction. The following day the Handley Page Hampdens of 455 (RAAF) Squadron also arrived, but the squadron's Australian personnel remained in accommodation at Swinderby. The Australian unit moved to Wigsley in Nottinghamshire on 8th February 1942 and Skellingthorpe was passed to the direct control of Swinderby on 10th April, by which time 50 Squadron had started to equip with the Avro Manchester, its first operation with the type being made on the night of 14th April.

The squadron took part in a mass raid on Cologne on the night of 30-31st May 1942, the first '1,000 Bomber Raid'. Though Manchester L7301 was extensively damaged, its pilot, Flying

Officer L. T. Manser continued to press home his attack, but the aircraft lost height so Manser ordered his crew to bail out. He waved away a crew member who offered him a parachute and died when his aircraft plunged into the ground. For pressing home his attack in the face of strong opposition, striving against heavy odds to return his aircraft, and finally thinking only of the safety of his crew, Flying Officer Manser was awarded the Victoria Cross. Notification of the award was published in the London

Above: **A wintry scene at Skellingthorpe as a Hampden of 50 Sqn is prepared for operations.** *(Bill Baguley/Rod Houldsworth)*

Below: **Avro Manchester of 50 Sqn with the early three fin arrangement, yet displaying the C-type roundels introduced in mid-1942.** *(50 Sqn records)*

Gazette on 20th October 1942.

In June 1942 trouble was experienced with the runways which necessitated the return of 50 Squadron to Swinderby. The original estimate for repair was six weeks, but after problems with the contractor a completion date of 15th Sept-

ember was given. After the repairs had been completed the Conversion Flights of 97 and 106 Squadrons were moved to Skellingthorpe from Coningsby on 30th September and both units then exchanged places with 50 Squadron on 16th October. Waddington once more

took control of the station on 14th November. No.50 Squadron operated alone from Skellingthorpe until 23rd August 1943 when it was joined by 1485 (Bomber) Gunnery Flight from Fulbeck, which operated a mixture of Vickers Wellingtons and Miles Martinet aircraft

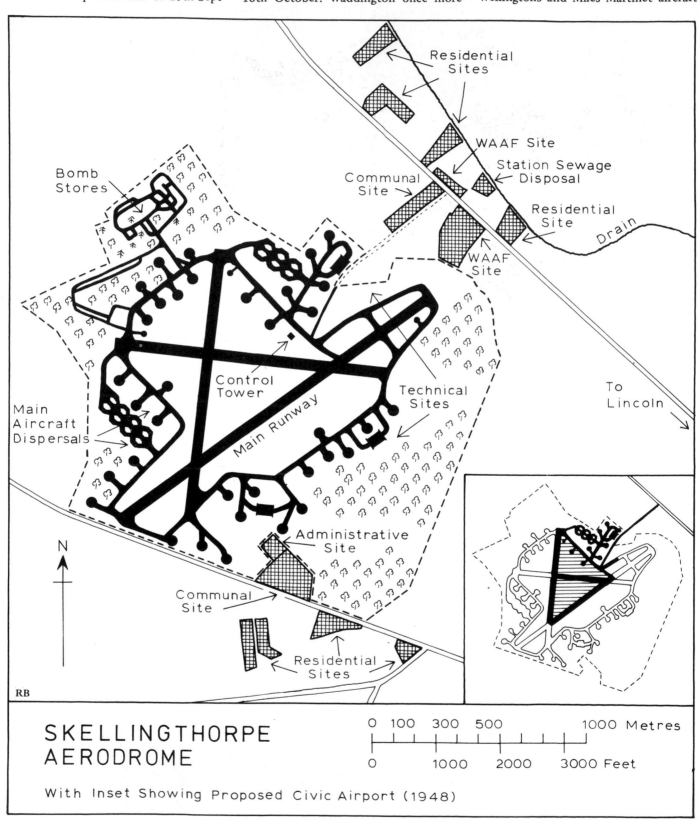

SKELLINGTHORPE
AERODROME

With Inset Showing Proposed Civic Airport (1948)

| 0 | 100 | 300 | 500 | | 1000 Metres |
| 0 | | 1000 | 2000 | | 3000 Feet |

and carried out gunnery training for 5 Group. Combined with the move of 1485 Flight was the move of the Headquarters Unit of 1506 Beam Approach Training Flight, which parented Airspeed Oxford aircraft allocated to operational units within the group for training purposes. This flight was disbanded on 2nd October and 1485 Flight moved to Syerston in Nottinghamshire on 12th November.

When No.53 Base was formed at Waddington on 15th November 1943, Skellingthorpe ceased to be a satellite and was upgraded to sub-station status for the new Base. At the same time it received another squadron, 61 flying Avro Lancasters.

The extra aircraft brought to Skellingthorpe by 61 Squadron caused the airspace around Lincoln to become heavily congested, so much so that 61 Squadron was moved to Coningsby on 12th January 1944. The move was only short-lived for it was then decided to concentrate all 5 Group Special Duty squadrons within 54 Base at Coningsby; 61 Squadron returned to Skellingthorpe on 15th April.

The whole station was shaken to its foundations on 19th May when twenty-three 1,000 lb bombs being transported to aircraft at dispersal blew up, killing two airmen and damaging many buildings although no aircraft were damaged. Yet another explosion occured the following year when Lancaster RF137(QR-E) of 61 Squadron returned from operations on 24th May 1945 with part of its bomb load hung up. The aircrew had vacated the aircraft at dispersal and the ground-crew were just assembling to deal with the problem when the aircraft blew up, killing three airmen, seriously injuring another and damaging four aircraft.

With the end of hostilities the main parties of both 50 and 61 Squadrons moved to Sturgate on 15th and 16th June respectively. No.619 Squadron arrived from Strubby on 30th June and 463 (RAAF) Squadron arrived from Waddington on 3rd July, moves brought about by the involvement of Strubby and Waddington in the preparations for *Tiger Force*. No.619 Squadron disbanded at Skellingthorpe on 18th July.

The station then became involved with the *Tiger Force* preparations itself on 7th August when, due to overcrowding at Strubby, 383 MU arrived, comprising

Above: **Lancaster ED860 of 61 Sqn being bombed up at Skellingthorpe in July 1944.** *(via P.H.T.Green)*

Right: **As long ago as 1967 modern housing developments were encroaching upon Skellingthorpe's unique watch office, now demolished.** *(Bill Baguley/ Rod Houldsworth)*

Left: **Children of the Manser School add scale to one of Skellingthorpe's dispersal pads. Note the joints radiating from the centre section.** *(via M.Hodgson)*

Below: **BE2e B3745 at South Carlton, 1918.** *(LAM)*

ground personnel for *Tiger Force* With the end of the war in the Far East *Tiger Force* was run down and 383 MU disbanded on 15th September. Four days later the disbandment parade for 463 (RAAF) Squadron took place, the salute being taken by Air Vice-Marshal Constantine, Air Officer Commanding 5 Group.

The last fifteen Lancasters were flown out to 22 MU at Silloth in Cumberland by crews from Waddington on 8th October and the last aircraft on the station, an Oxford, was flown to 12 MU at Kirkbride in Cumberland on 26th October. Skellinghtorpe closed on 31st October and was placed on Care and Maintenance with effect from 1st November, but was later allocated to 43 Group Maintenance Command for use by 58 MU which arrived from Newark in Nottinghamshire between 21st and 27th November 1945. The station was later closed and reverted to agricultural use. Plans for a Lincoln Municipal Airport, to be sited at Skellingthorpe, did not come to fruition and today most of the former 650 acre (260 ha) airfield has been taken over by residential developments.

Due to this expansion of housing, Lincolnshire County Council built a school as an annex to Birchwood Middle School. Completed during 1980 it is on the site of the former main runway and in recognition of the Royal Air Force links with Birchwood, the Education Committee decided to name the school after Flying Officer Leslie Manser, VC, the dedication and official opening taking place on 28 April 1981.

South Carlton

1.5 km ESE of South Carlton Church
121/SK 965 765   200ft (60m) AMSL

During the latter half of 1915, as the demand for front-line pilots increased, many aerodromes were established throughout England purely for training pilots and in early 1916 South Carlton was opened for this purpose. Nos.39, 45 and 61 Training Squadrons were moved into the aerodrome and, with various types of aeroplanes, began training pilots for fighter or reconnaissance duties.

No.69 Squadron, an Australian Corps unit which had been formed in Egypt in September 1916, was transferred to South Carlton in December 1916 and, re-equipped with Royal Aircraft Factory R.E.8s, worked up as a reconnaissance unit before being posted to France in September 1917. No.96 Squadron was formed at the aerodrome on 28th September 1917 and, equipped with RAF B.E.2s, operated in a training role until it was disbanded on 4th July 1918.

On this day too, South Carlton became 46 Training Depot Station, which was formed from 39 and 45 Training Squadrons. Along with 34 TDS at nearby Scampton, the station became known as the 23rd Training Wing, with the Wing Headquarters and Repair Shops situated at South Carlton. With the closure of Scampton in April 1919, the aeroplanes of 34 TDS were transferred to South Carlton and added to the strength of 46 TDS. By mid-1919, 46 TDS had run down to squadron strength and was

Above: **Aerial view of South Carlton taken on 17th March 1918.** *(via J.Walls)*

Right: **South Carlton Sopwith Dolphin D3686.** *(LAM)*

Below: **'Presentation' RE8 A3754 was used at South Carlton by 69 Squadron.** *(via W.J.Taylor)*

disbanded in April 1920.

As hostilities ended in November 1918, squadrons on the Continent were being reduced to cadre strength before returning to Britain to be disbanded. No.57 Squadron returned to South Carlton as a cadre during August 1919 and was disbanded on 31st December. Unlike 57 Squadron, 25 Squadron arrived at South Carlton complete in all respects. The squadron had left Merheim on 6th September 1919 with its de Havilland D.H.4 aircraft, and these remained with the squadron until it moved to Scopwick in December 1919.

Although the aerodrome at South Carlton was closed down in 1920, several buildings still exist, now being used as farm stores. The 200 acres (80 ha) are today farmed. In 1920 a carved pulpit was erected in South Carlton church as a memorial to the men of the RFC and RAF who had been stationed at the aerodrome and who had lost their lives on active service.

Spalding (Weston Marsh)

7.5 km NE of Spalding Railway Station
131/TF 293 285   10 ft (3 m) AMSL

A small grass aerodrome was opened near Spalding in 1947 when Mr. George Clifton formed a small air charter company named Spalding Airways Ltd. The initial equipment of the new company was Auster G-AJIU, which was supplemented over the next two years by a variety of light single and twin-engined aircraft. The work of the company included various passenger and freight charters on behalf of the local agricultural community and some charters from local business interests, particularly those in the Peterborough area.

In 1950 Spalding Airways gave up its ad-hoc charter interests and concentrated on the specialised area of business aircraft management. At the same time a lease was taken on at Peterborough (Westwood) Aerodrome and Spalding Airways started to operate aircraft owned by Mitchell Engineering, although the company retained the aerodrome at Spalding as a subsidiary flying base and maintenance centre for its aircraft fleet, which resulted in the construction of a blister hangar.

Operations continued from Spalding aerodrome until about 1954 when Spalding Airways concentrated its operations on Peterborough (Westwood) Aerodrome. The 150 acre (60 ha) site has now reverted to agricultural use and little except the hangar remains to indicate its former aeronautical connections.

Spilsby

2.5 km SSW of Candlesby Church
122/TF 450 650   30 ft (10 m) AMSL

Between 1942 and 1945 a total of 635 acres of land were requisitioned to allow construction of RAF Station Spilsby. Building began in late 1942 and the station opened as a satellite of East Kirkby on 20th September 1943, within 5 Group Bomber Command.

The first operational unit to move in was 207 Squadron with Avro Lancasters on 12th October. Thus operational, Spilsby was upgraded to sub-station status on 24th October and became a sub-station of 55 Base, which was formed with its Headquarters at East Kirkby on 15th April 1944. Exactly one month later the 5 Group Anti-Aircraft School was opened at Spilsby for the purpose of training 5 Group personnel in the use of the Hispano 20mm A-A gun, which at that time was being introduced to the group. The Wainfleet Sands bombing and gunnery ranges were used for firing, which took place on four days of the week.

On 30th September 44 (Rhodesia) Squadron with Lancasters joined 207 Squadron, moving from Dunholme Lodge when 52 Base was passed to the control of 1 Group. An intensive training programme commenced at 55 Base when the war in Europe was over in preparation for *Tiger Force*. However, it was decided that 44 Squadron was to be replaced by 75 (NZ) Squadron and a direct exchange of personnel between the two units took place on 21st July. At the same time the aircraft of 44 Squadron were passed to 75 Squadron and continued to operate from Spilsby. A short time later the *Tiger Force* was disbanded and both the Spilsby squadrons reverted to non-operational flying.

In September deliveries of the Avro Lincoln were begun to 75 Squadron, although only two aircraft were received, both of which flew over HMS *Andes* as she left port on 23rd September taking the main body of the squadron back to New Zealand. On 15th October 75 Squadron was formally disbanded and 207 Squadron left Spilsby just over two weeks later, on 30th October.

The station was taken over on 26th October by 12 Group Fighter Command, and the Armament Practice Station was installed, after a move from Bradwell Bay in Essex. Various aircraft were operated by the unit, including the Spitfire, de Havilland Mosquito, Miles Martinet and Miles Master, and several squadrons visited the APS for a three-week air firing course, including 129 Squadron with Spitfires and 264 with Mosquitos during January 1946; 65 Squadron with North American Mustangs and 29 Squadron with Mosquitoes during

Left: **Derelict control tower and hangar at Spilsby, 1971.** *(W.J.Taylor)*

Right: **44 Squadron Lancaster at Spilsby 1944/45.** *(viw M.Hodgson)*

Below: **Spilsby, 27th August 1978, looking south-west.** *(W.J.Taylor)*

February and 222 Squadron with Gloster Meteors and 219 Squadron with Mosquitoes during March. The APS moved to Acklington in Northumberland on 1st May and three months later Spilsby was transferred back to Bomber Command but inactive under the parentage of Coningsby. The requisitioned hutted accommodation was allocated to the Ministry of Health for use as emergency housing during 1947. A small Care and Maintenance party remained in residence and became self-accounting on 22nd May 1954 when Coningsby itself was placed on Care and Maintenance.

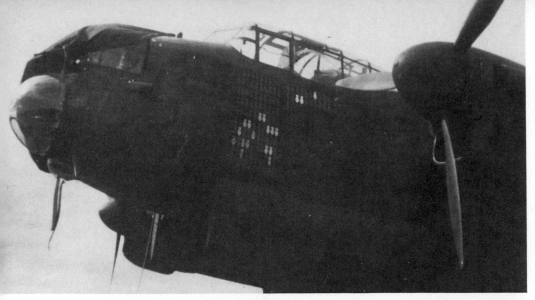

The station was allocated for use by the US Air Force on 15th June 1955 and was occupied by a detachment of the 7536th Materiel Squadron on 5th July 1956, which operated in support of the American units at East Kirkby. The Americans left on 25th May 1957, the main runway having been extended and strengthened during their period of residence, and the station was returned to Air Ministry control on 11th March 1958.

Sale of the airfield began in 1962, just two years after the final payments were made to the former landowners who owned the land on which the airfield was built. The two T2 hangars were dismantled in 1963 leaving the sole B1

Upper Left: **121 mission symbols show Lancaster KM-Y of 44 Squadron to be quite a Spilsby veteran.** *(via M.Hodgson)*

Left: **Lincoln RF389 AA-A of 75 (New Zealand) Squadron airborne from Spilsby in 1945, shortly before the unit returned to its homeland.** *(RAF Museum P421)*

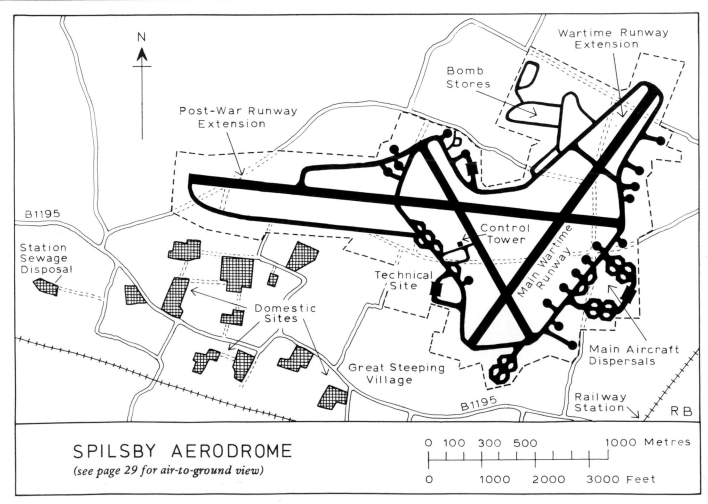

SPILSBY AERODROME
(see page 29 for air-to-ground view)

hangar which has continued in use as a store. Final disposal of the airfield was made in April 1970 and in the mid-1970s the runways and concrete areas were torn up.

A large poultry unit has now been established and, on part of the American runway extension, the Lincolnshire County Council Highways Department has located a road maintenance materials store. In recent years the former airfield has been a venue for go-kart and stock-car racing.

Spitalgate/ Grantham

2.5 km ESE of Grantham Church
130/SK 940 345   400 ft (130 m) AMSL

Early in 1917 an existing Landing Ground along the top of Spittlegate Hill was adopted as a training aerodrome for the Royal Flying Corps and became the home of 49 Training Squadron, joined by 11 Training Squadron which arrived in April 1917 but which moved to

Scampton in September. After forming at Montrose, 83 Squadron moved to Spittlegate, where it equipped with Royal Aircraft Factory F.E.2bs and worked up as a bomber unit, leaving for France in March 1918.

By 1918, Nos.15 and 37 Training Squadrons were based on the aerodrome and in July amalgamated to form 39 Training Depot Station, part of 24 Training Wing, which also comprised 48 TDS at Harlaxton and had its Headquarters at Spittlegate. Spittlegate administered both units and in addition one of the unit's six aeroplane sheds housed the 24 Wing Repair Unit.

In April 1918 the Headquarters of 3 Training Group was established at Spittlegate but, with the end of the war in November, 24 Wing was run down and the last aircraft from Harlaxton were transferred to Spittlegate in 1919. By the end of the year 39 TDS had closed down, but the Headquarters of 3 Group remained on the aerodrome until disbanded in 1921. During 1919 two squadrons, 29 and 43, returned from the Continent as cadres and disbanded at Spittlegate at the end of the year.

One other unit, 70 Squadron, moved onto the station and operated its Sopwith Pups until disbanded in January 1920.

The 200 acre (80 ha) aerodrome remained inactive until February 1922 when 100 Squadron moved in from Baldonnel in Ireland, where it had operated with Bristol F.2b Fighters against the Sinn Fein. With a change in base came a change in aircraft and the squadron soon began to convert to the de Havilland D.H.9A as well as adding a fourth flight, 'D' Flight, comprising four Vickers Vimys and one Avro 504K. These aeroplanes were supplied from the disbanded 6 TDS at Biggin Hill in Kent and operated from the aerodrome as Britain's only heavy bomber unit.

Below: **The interior of an aircraft shed at Spittlegate housing two Grahame-White Type XV aeroplanes. Note the Grahame-White emblem on the starboard rudder of A1688.** *(Crown Copyright H2378)*

The unit was posted to Bircham Newton in Norfolk to become the second flight of 7 Squadron in July 1923.

Although a cadre of 39 Squadron had existed at Spittlegate since 1921, it was not until February 1923 that the squadron was fully established as a day bomber unit operating D.H.9As. In May 1924, No.100 Squadron moved to Eastchurch in Kent where it exchanged its D.H.9As for Fairey Fawns before returning to Spittlegate in July of that year. Fawns were operated until late 1926 when the squadron began to convert to the Hawker Horsley.

In 1928 Spittlegate reverted to a training role so both resident squadrons left in January: 39 moved to Bircham Newton and 100 to Bicester in Oxfordshire. The name of the station was then changed to RAF Station Grantham and 3 Flying Training School was formed. Probably the most famous training aircraft of all time, the de Havilland D.H.82 Tiger Moth, commenced its service career at Grantham, when the first fifteen

Above: **Aerial view of Spittlegate taken during March 1918. Just visible against the hedge alongside the main road is an aircraft standing on its nose.** *(IWM Q70558)*

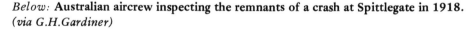

Below: **Australian aircrew inspecting the remnants of a crash at Spittlegate in 1918.** *(via G.H.Gardiner)*

Left: **Virginia III J7129 at Spitalgate.** *(via Wg Cdr Hollingsworth)*

Above: **Armstrong Whitworth Atlas trainers, Avro Tutors and other aircraft of 3 FTS at Grantham in 1932.** *(RAF Museum P2739)*

Right: **Hawker Hind L7175 of 211 Squadron at Grantham 1937. This aircraft later served with the RAF College, Cranwell.** *(via G.H.Gardiner)*

aircraft were delivered to 3 FTS between November 1931 and February 1932. Also in use at Grantham were Avro 504s, Armstrong Whitworth Siskins, Avro Tutors, Bristol Bulldogs and Hawker Hart trainers.

In 1937, No.3 FTS moved to South Cerney in Gloucestershire and the station became the home of two front-line squadrons. During July Grantham was transferred to 3 Group Bomber Command and a month later 113 Squadron arrived with Hawker Hinds from Upper Heyford in Oxfordshire, followed by 211 Squadron from Mildenhall in Suffolk, also with Hinds. In September 1937 the station was transferred to 5 Group Bomber Command and both 113 and 211 Squadrons, destined for the Middle East, left for Southampton during April 1938.

With the departure of the squadrons the airfield was placed on Care and Maintenance until it was transferred to Training Command in August 1938 and a Recruit Sub-Depot was formed. In September 1938, Nos. 106 and 185 Squadrons arrived from Thornaby in County Durham with Fairey Battles, the Recruit Sub-Depot moved to Usworth and the station was once again transferred to 5 Group. During October the two squadrons took their Battles back to Thornaby and the station was handed back to Training Command.

No.12 Service Flying Training School began to form at Grantham with effect from 1st December 1938 and in early 1939 began to take delivery of Avro Ansons and Fairey Battles. The North American Harvard — one of the first American aircraft to be ordered by the

Royal Air Force and a type that remained as standard equipment at Flying Training Schools for over sixteen years — entered service at Grantham in January 1939. The characteristic rasping note of the engine and direct drive propeller caused some consternation among the inhabitants of the surrounding area and several letters regarding the noise were printed in the local papers.

In September 1939, No.12 SFTS was transferred from 23 to 21 Group Flying Training Command. Airspeed Oxfords began to be added to the unit's strength in the Spring of 1941 and in 1942 it was re-titled 12 (Pilot) Advanced Flying Unit. From the middle of 1943 Bristol Blenheims also started to operate with the unit, by which time 12 (P) AFU had grown to such an extent that it became necessary to house some of the flights at Harlaxton, the nearby satellite airfield.

By the beginning of 1944 the grass runways had been covered with Sommerfield Tracking, a steel mesh which, in theory, provided a firmer surface for the aircraft to run on. This form of runway surfacing was in its infancy and under the weight of an aircraft it was prone to cracking, thus causing many punctures. With a unit strength of over forty aircraft it became impossible to operate at full capacity while repairs were carried out and in January a detachment of Blenheims was transferred to Woodvale in Lancashire, where flying training continued; known as the 'W' detachment, these aircraft returned during August 1944. Because there were several other military establishments in and around the Grantham area it was decided in April 1944 that the station should revert

to the name of Spitalgate.

By November 1944 the grass airfields at both Spitalgate and Harlaxton were in such poor condition that it was decided to move 12 (P) AFU to a station with concrete runways. Thus, the unit moved to Hixon in Staffordshire and Cranage in Cheshire in February 1945 and Spitalgate was placed on Care and Maintenance.

On 1 May 1945 17 FTS arrived from Cranwell and flying recommenced from the airfield. This FTS was employed training pilots of the RAF, the Dominions and the Allies and had a large variety of aircraft on strength, including the Oxford, Harvard, Anson, Spitfire, Mosquito and Beaufort, and the intensity of flying training necessitated Harlaxton being brought back into use as a RLG. However, on 18 June 1947 17 FTS was renamed 1 FTS which continued the pilot training task, training predominantly Dutch personnel, until 18 February 1948 when it was disbanded. The station was transferred to 22 Group Technical Training Command on 23 February 1948 and five days later the Officer Cadet Training Unit arrived from Cosford (Staffs). The following year, on 1 September, the RAF Mess Staff School was established at Spitalgate.

The Borough of Grantham granted the Freedom of the Borough to the station on 10 July 1952. The OCTU left Spitalgate on 24 March 1954 and the station became the HQ of 24 Group Technical Training Command. In August 1954 the RAF School of Education arrived, followed by the RAF Central Library in August 1955. HQ 24 Group and the Mess Staff School both disbanded on 1 August 1957.

Left: **Harvards of 12 FTS at Grantham during 1939.** *(via N.Franklin)*

Right: **Typical of club gliders operated from Spitalgate was Slingsby Tutor RAFGSA 161.** *(T.Hancock)*

Below: **Army lorries are now parked in front of the Spitalgate hangars. This September 1981 view shows Leyland Hippo and AEC Militant vehicles in front of a Bellman hangar.** *(W.J.Taylor)*

The School of Education moved to Bircham Newton (Norfolk) on 10 November 1958 and the following year saw the arrival of the Secretarial Officers' School and the HQ 3 Police District - later renamed HQ Provost and Security Services (Central Region). The WRAF Depot arrived in 1960 and for the first time command of the station passed to a WRAF officer, Group Officer F.B. Hill OBE WRAF. During 1964 the Secretarial Officers' School moved to Upwood (Hunts) and 2 Gliding Centre arrived from Kirton in Lindsey in October 1965. Operating alongside 2GC was 644 Gliding School but in July 1971 2 GC was renamed the RAF Central Gliding School. Other lodger units housed at Spitalgate during this period included the HQ of the Midlands Area of the Royal Observer Corps.

With the contraction of the RAF in the defence cuts of the early 1970s Spitalgate was selected for closure. The WRAF Depot moved to Hereford in March 1974 and the CGS and 644 GS had moved to Syerston (Notts) by March 1975. On 30 April 1975 Spitalgate was formally transferred from the RAF to the Army Department.

Following its take-over by the Army, Royal Assent was given for the station to be named Prince William of Gloucester Barracks. The Barracks houses a driver training unit and Territorial Army Depot of the Royal Corps of Transport, the heavy vehicles of which have become a familiar sight on the roads of Lincolnshire. The all-grass airfield sees regular use during periods of dispersed operation by the Harriers from nearby Wittering (Cambs) and at weekends it is used by the station's thriving Parascending Club. In August 1981 Spitalgate was the venue for both the Army and the British National Parascending Championships.

Footnote:
When the station was originally opened in 1917 it took the name Royal Flying Corps Station Spittlegate, a name and spelling which had been in use in the area since the year 1600. From 1928 the station was known as Royal Air Force Station Grantham, but in 1944 it was decided to revert to the original name and so an order authorising this was issued. It is thought that the typist arrived at the incorrect spelling 'Spitalgate' on the analogy of 'Spitalfields'; however the error was not discovered and the name Spitalgate was used in official documents, the station name-board and on the charter granting the Freedom of the Borough of Grantham to the station. An Air Ministry Newsletter of 1952 publicised the discovery of the error and stated that official documents and airfield maps would be amended. However, we have yet to determine why the station's name continued to be spelt Spitalgate until it closed (see Appendix L for other anomalies concerning names of airfields).

Strubby

1km WSW of Maltby le Marsh Church
122/TF450810   50ft (15m) AMSL

Construction of Strubby aerodrome began during 1943 and although allocated to 5 Group Bomber Command, the station was placed on Care and Maintenance on its completion. The first aircraft to land at Strubby was an American Republic P-47 Thunderbolt, which made a forced landing on the runway before the station had been completed.

Officially opened on 13th April 1944, Strubby became a sub-station of 55 Base on 15th April. Although a station within 5 Group, the first unit to arrive at Strubby was a unit of 16 Group, Coastal Command, 280 Squadron. Equipped with Vickers Warwick Air-Sea Rescue Mk1 aircraft, 280 Squadron was brought to Lincolnshire on 1st May 1944 to provide air-sea rescue facilities over the North Sea. In July a strike wing composed of two squadrons of Bristol Beaufighters equipped for bombing arrived; these were 144 and 404 (RCAF) Squadrons and they engaged in anti-shipping strikes over the North Sea. In common with 280 Squadron, the Beaufighters formed part of Coastal Command, but for the duration of their stay at Strubby they came under the operational control of Bomber Command. The Beaufighter squadrons departed on 3rd September, and 280 Squadron left three days later.

With the transfer of 52 Base to 1 Group, 619 Squadron was moved to Strubby from Dunholme Lodge on 28th September and commenced operations from its new base on 4th October. The squadron's first operation from Strubby involved five aircraft in a mine-laying sortie and one aircraft was lost. However, on the following two missions 619 Squadron despatched twenty aircraft on each occasion and none was lost. 7th October saw the formation of 'B' Flight 227 Squadron at Strubby; 'A' Flight formed that day at Bardney alongside 9 Squadron. 'B' Flight was attached to 619 Squadron for operations until 20th October, when both flights were united following a move to Balderton in Nottinghamshire. On the same day as 'B' Flight 227 Squadron left Strubby the 5 Group Anti-Aircraft School arrived from East Kirkby, enabling it to be nearer to the Anderby Creek gunnery range which was allocated for its use.

No.227 Squadron returned on 5th April 1945 and with the arrival of a second squadron, the monthly total of flying hours doubled in April to nearly 2000. After the end of the war both squadrons started to repatriate ex-prisoners-of-war, airlifting a total of 2112 people from Belgian and Dutch airfields. In recognition of their courage, twenty-two officers and airmen were awarded the DFC and DFM while serving at Strubby.

No.227 Squadron was moved to Graveley in Huntingdonshire on 8th June 1945 and 619 Squadron was moved to Skellingthorpe on the 18th. These movements closed Strubby so that the ground contingents of *Tiger Force* could concentrate for kitting out and, as part of this force, 381, 382, 383 and 384 MUs were formed at Strubby with effect from 9th July. Work-up commenced prior to the move to the Far East and the station strength rose to its highest ever. Two tented camps were pitched on the airfield and one hangar was converted for cooking and eating and another was converted for use as ablutions. The station became so crowded that 382 MU was moved to Syerston, Nottinghamshire on 23rd July and 383 MU was moved to Skellingthorpe on 7th August. Also in preparation for *Tiger Force*, 81 Mobile Field Hospital, 38 Field Hygiene Unit and 39 Malarial Control Unit formed at Strubby in mid-June, but with the surrender of Japan and the disbandment of *Tiger Force* the personnel started to disperse. In early September 381 and 384 MUs were disbanded.

The station was placed on Care and Maintenance and closed to all flying from 1st November. Administered by East Kirkby, 40 Group Maintenance Command took the station over as a sub-site of 35 MU from 20th November until 29th July 1949 when control was passed to the RAF Flying College at Manby.

Strubby from 1951 became a Relief Landing Ground for the many varied aircraft of the RAFFC and as this airfield was more suitable for the jet aircraft of the College than Manby, the de Havilland Vampires, Gloster Meteors and piston-engined Avro Athenas were moved here. No. 12 GCA Unit arrived from Leuchars in Fife on 15th January 1950, but was disbanded on 1st March 1951. During 1952 the Vampires were withdrawn and the following year English Electric

Above left: **Warwick ASR1 HG208 MF-Y of 208 Sqn, as operated from Strubby.** *(Air-Britain)*

Above: **Canberras of the CAW at Strubby in June 1964.** *(R.C.B.Ashworth)*

Right: **Hastings WJ327 of the RAF Flying College at Strubby with a Meteor in the background.** *(N.Jackson via P.Pountney)*

Below: **CAW Varsity T1 WF389 at Strubby, 5th February 1971.** *(W.J.Taylor)*

Canberras arrived.

The station was host to HRH The Duke of Edinburgh in February 1953 when he arrived to view for himself the devastation caused by the East Coast floods; during that autumn and the following spring the main runway was extended and an operational readiness platform built. In mid-July 1955 the Meteors of 3 All Weather Jet Refresher Unit arrived from Weston Zoyland in Somerset. The Athena was withdrawn during 1955 and by that December the first Hawker Hunters had started to arrive. Strubby was operating the Canberras and Hunters of the RAFFC and the Meteors of the AWJRU.

Until November 1961 Strubby personnel were accommodated on the station, but from then on all personnel were moved to Manby and the domestic site was closed down. In July 1962 the School of Refresher Flying was formed at Manby, undertaking all refresher flying for the RAF and operating from both Manby and Strubby, having absorbed 3 AWJRU. At the same time the RAFFC was renamed the RAF College of Air Warfare and continued to operate the Canberra for the Specialist Navigation course, but the Hunters began to leave. The Hunting Jet Provost started to replace the Meteor in March 1964, the last of this type leaving during April 1965. Eventually the Jet Provosts of the SORF were all moved to Manby, being replaced at Strubby by the Vickers Varsities of the CAW.

In February 1966 the first Hawker Siddeley Dominie twin-jet navigation trainer arrived at Strubby to replace the Canberra and, when a full complement of Dominies had arrived, the last Canberra left Strubby during December 1966. The Dominies and Varsities continued to operate from Strubby until September 1972 when the station closed. A final parade was held on 8th September when a lone Dominie and a lone Varsity made farewell flypasts. The Dominie then set

Above: **A lone Varsity flies low over Strubby during the closing ceremony, Tuesday, 5th September 1972.** *(RAF Manby)*

Left: **Long resident at Strubby, Bo 105 G-BAMF serves the Conoco gas production platforms in the southern North Sea.** *(W.J.Taylor)*

course for Manby, representing the move of the Dominies to Manby, and the Varsity set course for Oakington, representing the move of the Varsities to Oakington. The actual move of the aircraft did not take place until the end of the following week, after which the 700 acre (280 ha) station was closed.

By 1974 Strubby had been selected by Conoco as the site of a heliport for helicopters serving its gas production platforms in the southern North Sea. The company bought an area of land on the eastern side of the airfield, which included four of the spectacle type dispersals and part of the perimeter track, and constructed a new hangar and terminal buildings. Management Aviation Ltd of Bourn (Cambs) was contracted to provide the aircraft and the aircraft operating facilities and operations commenced with a number of Bolkow Bo

105 helicopters (eg G-BATC) and later Sikorsky S-58T G-BCWD.

The versatility of the helicopter has been essential to the rapid expansion of the off-shore industry and Strubby-based aircraft have undertaken many varied tasks including the movement of personnel and equipment. The Strubby-based Bo 105s are also used to carry out crew changing and other duties at Trinity House lighthouses and lightships through-

174

Left: **One of the oil rig support helicopters operated from Strubby, this Sikorsky S-58T G-BCWD was based there in October 1975.** *(W.J.Taylor)*

Below: **The former hospital site at Strubby now houses a crop-spraying company which temporarily bases helicopters there in the spring and summer. Hiller UH-12E G-ATED was seen there in July 1980.** *(W.J.Taylor)*

out the country. As the off-shore industry has expanded it has demanded newer and more reliable helicopters and, as a result, Strubby is now the base of up to four of the appealing Aerospatiale SA 365C Dauphin (Dolphin) helicopters which are often to be seen at Humberside Airport (Kirmington) collecting passengers for onward movement to the production platforms and drilling rigs.

For a period during 1979 the Lincolnshire Land Yacht Club made use of the runways, having moved to Strubby from Hibaldstow. Also, during 1978, following the closure of the Lincolnshire Gliding Club at Bardney, the Strubby Gliding Group formed. The group operates a number of gliders including Slingsby T.21 BGA 1482 and Bocian BGA 1605 formerly operated from Bardney.

Various buildings on the former technical site are used as farm stores and shortly after the station closed the hangars were renovated and repainted and then used as buffer stores for the bulk storage of food commodities. One of the former dispersed accommodation sites has been converted into a residential caravan site and the site of the former hospital is now a depot for Farmwork Services Ltd., a subsidiary of Fisons, and is used as a base for crop spraying operations. For a few months each summer a helicopter is usually based at the Farmwork Services depot and during 1979 and 1980 the helicopters using the depot were various Hiller UH.12Es of Management Aviation/Bond Helicopters.

However, in March 1980 the station was put up for sale by auction. Shortly after the sale demolition and reclamation of the runways, taxiways and dispersals commenced. The work was expected to last for two years and yield 500,000 tonnes of aggregate. The integrity of the

Conoco heliport on the northern edge of the airfield is not threatened and a portion of the perimeter track adjacent to the heliport will remain.

Sturgate

1 km NE of Upton Church
121/SK880880   60ft (20m) AMSL

Constructed during 1943, Sturgate began to open under the control of Hemswell in 1 Group Bomber Command on 1st March 1944. Aircraft from 1 Lancaster Finishing School at Hemswell were the first aircraft to use the airfield for circuits and the first touch-down was made on 22nd April. The first unit to be based at the station arrived on 18th September and was 1520 Beam Approach Training Flight, which arrived with its Airspeed Oxfords from Leconfield in Yorkshire.

No.1 Group Aircrew School was moved in from Lindholme in Yorkshire on 1st November; concurrently with the move it was transferred to 7 Group and

renamed 1 Aircrew School. One month later, on 1st December 1944, the whole station transferred to 7 Group and became a sub-station of 71 Base at Lindholme. The Aircrew School and BAT Flight remained as lodger units.

In February 1945 the BAT Flight disbanded and 1 ACS returned to the control of 1 Group on 26th May. The station was transferred three days later and on 15th June its first operational squadrons, 50 and 61, arrived from Skellingthorpe; they immediately began to fit their Avro Lancasters with the Rose No.2 Mk.1 rear turret which was allocated for the sole use of 1 Group. Having generally flown only training sorties from Sturgate the two squadrons moved to Waddington during January 1946 and on 31st March the station was placed on Care and Maintenance.

After a few idle years Sturgate was allocated for the use of the US Air Force on 30th July 1952, and in June 1953 No.3928 Air Base Group was formed. Operating within the 7th Air Division of SAC, the station housed for a short time the Republic F-84 fighters of the 508th

Right: Lt Col John Stuart Jr, Base Adjutant, in front of the Headquarters building of the 3928th ABG, Sturgate, 1954. *(Col Donald L.Wilkinson USAF)*

Below: Republic F-84F Thunderstreaks of the 508th Strategic Fighter Wing at Sturgate in the mid-1950s. *(via P.H.T.Green)*

Botton: The newly built hangars used by Eastern Air Executive at Sturgate. *(W.J.Taylor)*

Strategic Fighter Wing on rotation from Turner Air Force Base, Georgia. During 1957 the runways were rebuilt but the Americans left during August 1958 and the station was returned to RAF control on 22nd May 1959. Although back under RAF control Sturgate remained in use as an American supply depot, run by the 7513 Air Base Squadron (Det.) until 1964. The 790 acre (320 ha) station was finally sold between 1964 and 1966.

In late 1965 the Trent Valley Gliding Club formed and commenced gliding from Sturgate early the following year, operating its mixed fleet of single and two-seat gliders from Sturgate's well-kept runways. In early 1969 Eastern Air Executive Ltd formed, commencing air taxi and charter operations from Sturgate with a Piper Aztec in April 1969. With the expansion of industrial activity south of the Humber Eastern Air Executive gradually expanded. Today it operates a number of its own aircraft plus a number of others on behalf of local companies. The gliding club moved to Kirton in Lindsey during 1974 and in early June 1975 the Lincoln Aero Club moved to Sturgate from Hemswell. Today the small aerodrome continues in operation as a very active light aviation centre, although some of the more remote dispersals, taxiways and runways have been dug up.

Above: **Sutton Bridge circa 1936. The large hangar still stands.**
(via M.Hodgson)

Sutton Bridge

1 km SE of Sutton Bridge Church
131/TF 485 200   20 ft (6 m) AMSL

Sutton Bridge was established on 2nd September 1926 as a summer armament training camp when personnel of the Air Armament School first arrived from Bircham Newton to set it up. Firing started on 27th September and by the time the camp finished on 31st October, 19, 23, 29, 43 and 111 Squadrons had visited for annual firing practice. The camp was closed for the winter on 30th November and re-opened the following year on 30th March. The Air Firing Trophy was awarded for the first time in 1926 and it went to Flight Lieutenant H.C. Calvey of 23 Squadron.

In August 1928 camp personnel were moved into wooden huts and the annual firing competition for the Trophy was won by Flying Officer C.W.McK. Thompson of 43 Squadron. A Bristol Fighter equipped with Royal Aircraft Establishment sleeve target gear arrived during 1929, that year's competition for the Brooke-Popham Trophy being won by Flying Officer Thompson of 56 Squadron with a score of 88%. The Air Firing Trophy had been renamed after Air Marshal Sir Robert Brooke-Popham, Air Officer Commanding in Chief, Air Defence of Great Britain.

1932 saw one or two changes, for when the camp re-opened on 8th March it was renamed 3 Armament Training Camp. The station also received two Fairey IIIF aircraft for range work, and during that year the first units of the Fleet Air Arm, including 401, 402, 404 and 407 Flights operating Fairey Fly-catcher aircraft, arrived for air firing camps. The Brooke-Popham Trophy was won by Sergeant Williams of 3 Squadron and the following year, when the first full Fleet Air Arm squadrons visited Sutton Bridge, the Trophy again went to 3 Squadron; this time it was won by Flying Officer E.M.Donaldson, perhaps better known today as one-time holder of the World Air Speed Record and former Air Correspondent for the Daily Telegraph.

Another departure from routine was made during 1933-34 as firing exercises took place during the winter, starting on 29th January 1934. The Brooke-Popham Trophy Competition was flown on 18th and 19th October and went to Flying Officer Donaldson again, giving 3 Squadron a hat-trick of wins. During 1935 the station was visited by the Society for the Preservation of Rural England who were concerned about the effect the air firing would have on bird life of the Wash marshes. Short winter courses were started in October 1935 and on 1st March 1936 Sutton Bridge became a permanent RAF station. From 1st July 1936 the station was placed under the direct control of Training Command, with the training being under the direct control of HQ Armament Group, and the station was renamed 3 Armament Training School on 10th April 1938.

Above: **Sutton Bridge hangars and landing ground with Hawker Furies of 25 Sqn on the apron.** (via G.Patrick)

Above: **Armstrong Whitworth Atlas II G-ABIV attached to 4 Squadron for armament training at Sutton Bridge, 1933.** (R.E.Loye via P.H.T.Green)

Left: **De Havilland DH60M Moth K1222 seen at Sutton Bridge during 1933.** (R.E.Loye via P.H.T.Green)

Re-equipment of the Station Flight with Hawker Henley target-towing aircraft began in February 1939 and when General Mobilisation was ordered on 1st September 3 ATS was dispersed to the West Coast, moving to West Freugh in Wigtownshire on 2nd September. A Care and Maintenance party was left at Sutton Bridge and a Recruit Training Sub-Depot was formed to give preliminary training to recruits, this unit operating between 13th September and 21st October.

No.12 Group Fighter Command took the station over on 30th October and 264 and 266 Squadrons started to form there, but before it had received any aircraft 264 Squadron was moved to Martlesham Heath in Suffolk and was

replaced by 254 Squadron from Stradishall in Suffolk. During December 266 Squadron received Fairey Battle aircraft and early in the new year these were replaced by Spitfires, and, after 254 Squadron had been moved to Bircham Newton in Norfolk on 27th January 1940, No.266 Squadron went to Martlesham Heath on 1st March.

The advance party of 11 Group Pool arrived from St.Athan in South Wales on 4th March and the first air party followed on 6th March. Renamed 6 OTU on 9th March, this unit operated a multitude of aircraft and trained pilots for the Battle of Britain. At one stage the station housed some seventy Hurricanes, over fifteen Miles Masters, five

North American Harvards and three Henleys. The OTU was unique as it was the only unit to operate the Miles Mentor, of which it had about ten, in the training role and in addition small numbers of Battles, Battle TTs, Gloster Gladiators and a Miles Magister were also operated. Although the OTU provided most of its own target towing, the Sutton Bridge Station Flight also assisted with its Henleys as well as providing target towing facilities for other nearby units. Gunnery training was further assisted with the arrival during October of 1489 Target Tow Flight with an assortment of Henleys, Westland Lysanders and Masters. On 1st November 1941, No.6 OTU was renamed 56 OTU.

A decoy site for the airfield had been established during 1940 at Terrington Marsh and several times it proved its worth when it was bombed instead of Sutton Bridge itself. On one occasion a horse was killed and a nearby glasshouse damaged and the continued attacks resulted in a petition from the local residents to have the decoy site moved. The station did hit back on the night of 13-14th June 1941 when one of Sutton Bridge's aircraft shot down a Junkers Ju 88; the aircraft fell on the banks of the River Nene in the Wash. The body of the pilot, Unteroffizier Heinz Schultz, was recovered and buried with full military honours on the 19th. The OTU was moved to Tealing on 27th March 1942 and 1489 (B) G Flight followed on 13th April.

During March 1942 the station was transferred to 25 (Armament) Group and on 4th April the Central Gunnery School arrived and commenced flying. The functions of the CGS were numerous and included the development of gunnery techniques and tactics applicable to aircraft other than fighters, the training of gunnery leaders for the squadrons and the training of instructors for the training schools and OTUs. The CGS operated a bomber wing equipped mainly with Vickers Wellingtons and Handley Page Hampdens to which was added a fighter wing equipped mainly with Spitfires and North American Mustangs. The fighter wing was added to train gunnery leaders for fighter squadrons and both wings co-operated on joint exercises. The CGS was moved to Catfoss in East Yorkshire on 24th February 1944 and Sutton Bridge was placed on Care and Maintenance.

While still under Care and Maintenance, the station passed to the control of 7 (P) AFU at Peterborough on 23rd May and in June the (P) AFU flying commitment was transferred to Sutton Bridge due to the airfield at Sibson being unserviceable. Operating a large number of Airspeed Oxfords, the unit was training French pilots when it was renamed 7 SFTS on 21st December 1944. No. 7 SFTS moved to Kirton in Lindsey on 4th April 1946 and the 320 acre (130 ha) station was then closed down and slowly reclaimed for agricultural use.

Most significant of the agricultural activities at Sutton Bridge is the experimental station opened for the Potato Marketing Board on 15th April 1964 by Mrs. Christopher Soames MBE, JP. The station carries out research into methods of potato storage and packaging and operates a large potato pre-packing unit (which is soon to be expanded). The original 1933 hangar is used by the station for its storage research and the remaining T2 hangar is used by a local farmer as a grain store. Since 1960 there has been a small airstrip and hangar on the former airfield site which, until recently, housed Auster J/5G Autocar G-AOIY. The airstrip was ploughed up in early 1983.

Above: **Westland Wallace displaying post 1938 camouflage at Sutton Bridge.** *(M.J.F.Bowyer)*

Right: **Blenheim I L1468 at Sutton Bridge, 6th February 1939.** *(via Bill Baguley/Rod Houldsworth)*

Swinderby

2 km SE of Swinderby Church
121/SK885620   60ft (20m) AMSL

Construction of RAF Station Swinderby commenced in 1939 as part of the 'M Expansion Scheme' and the advance party arrived to open the station in early August 1940. Although the buildings were not complete a start was made on camouflaging the station by 17th August and the first unit arrived a few days later, this being 300 (Polish) Squadron from Bramcote in Warwickshire, which arrived on 22nd August with twelve operational Fairey Battles, one Battle trainer and one Avro Anson; the aircraft were immediately dispersed around the perimeter and made ready for operations. No.301 (Polish) Squadron moved in on 28th August, together with its complement of sixteen operational Battles, one Battle trainer and one Anson.

The first operation from Swinderby was flown on 14th September when three aircraft from each squadron attacked Boulogne harbour, and all the aircraft returned safely. In an effort to imitate the Junkers Ju 87 Stuka, sirens were fitted to some of the aircraft of 300 Squadron and their effectiveness was tested in a simulated attack on 1 Group Headquarters at Hucknall in Nottinghamshire. Before further progress could be made the squadron started to receive

the Vickers Wellington and the first aircraft arrived on 17th August, although one was attacked and damaged by a Hawker Hurricane during its delivery flight. The damage was not serious and the aircraft was repaired by the squadron. Conversion of 301 Squadron also commenced and both squadrons were brought up to strength on 10th and 12th November respectively. The first of the Battles was ferried out to Sealand in Cheshire on 10th November and the last aircraft left on 13th November.

The highlight of January 1941 was a visit to the station by the King and Queen on the 27th, the visit coming at a time when the station was having great difficulty meeting its task due to a large proportion of the airfield being water-logged by the winter rains and snow. Extensive use was made of the satellite at Winthorpe in Nottinghamshire and, to a lesser extent, some use was made of Waddington. A concrete perimeter track was laid and from March it was used as a runway for lightly loaded aircraft. On 18th July both Polish squadrons moved to Hemswell when the station transferred from 1 Group to 5 Group and the following day 50 Squadron arrived from Lindholme in Yorkshire with Handley Page Hampdens, flying its first operation from Swinderby on 20th July.

A start was made on the construction of runways at Swinderby during November 1941 so 50 Squadron was moved to Skellingthorpe on 26th November

and 455 (RAAF) Squadron followed a day later. This, the first Australian bomber squadron within the RAF, had started to form at Swinderby on 6th June and, operating the Hampden, it made its first operation on 29th August when a lone aircraft attacked Frankfurt. Due to a shortage of accommodation at Skellingthorpe the personnel of 455 Squadron remained in accommodation at Swinderby until the unit was moved to Wigsley in Nottinghamshire on 8th February 1942.

Runway work was complete by mid-April 1942 and preparations were made to receive 144 Squadron but the move was cancelled before it could be made. Instead, one month later, 1654 Heavy Conversion Unit was formed at Swinderby. Established for sixteen Avro Lancasters and Avro Manchesters, 1654 HCU moved to Wigsley on 16th June, having received just five Manchesters and four Airspeed Oxfords. With the Swinderby runways operational, Skellingthorpe began to experience runway trouble, and on 20th June 50 Squadron returned to Swinderby while repairs were carried out. The initial estimate of six weeks was put back until September and the squadron finally returned to Skellingthorpe on 16th October.

Training commenced at Swinderby on 22nd August 1942 with the arrival of 61 and 207 Conversion Flights, which were joined by the Conversion Flights of 97 and 106 Squadrons from Skel-

Above left: **Stirling EF146 of No.1660 HCU being salvaged at Swinderby during 1944.** *(S.Finn)*

Above: **Wellington T10 RP547 of No.17 OTU returns to Swinderby after a sortie in May 1948.** *(Crown Copyright R1506)*

Right: **The see-through Wimpey. Students of 201 AFS, Swinderby practise escape drill during 1948.** *(Crown copyright R1468)*

lingthorpe on 16th October to form 1660 Heavy Conversion Unit and, operating the Manchester, the first course started on 9th November. When the Base system was introduced within Bomber Command Swinderby became the Base Station of 51 Base which formed with effect from 15th March 1943. The Base comprised the stations at Swinderby, Winthorpe and Wigsley and carried out all the heavy conversion training within 5 Group. The Headquarters Unit of the Base was located in nearby Morton Hall, but, when it was decided to move the Headquarters of 5 Group to Morton Hall, Headquarters 51 Base moved to Swinderby; this move was made on 24th October. From 13th November Swinderby also became the home of 5 Group Communications Flight.

Lancasters started to appear with the conversion units by 1943 but, due to a shortage of aircraft for the operational squadrons, they were replaced by the Short Stirling. The change was made at Swinderby during November 1943; it gave the HCU a mixed fleet of Handley Page Halifax and Stirling aircraft. The first course to pass through the unit on the Stirling commenced training on 9th December. The following year all training within Bomber Command was centralised under 7 Group and accordingly, with effect from 3rd November 1944, No.51 Base passed to 7 Group and became 75 Base; it continued to supply crews to 5 Group.

As the Lancaster became more plentiful towards the end of 1944 it was gradually re-introduced to the conversion units. The change-over took place at Swinderby during January 1945 and by the end of February all Stirlings had been replaced. Training started to run down when the war ended and on 15th September the station was 'At Home' to over 8,000 members of the public, when aircraft on display included Lancasters,

Above: **Next stage! Dinghy drill on Swinderby's open spaces, 1948. Wellington T10 RP498 is pictured in the background.** *(Crown Copyright R1469)*

Spitfires and North American Harvards. The station became an independent unit on 26th September and 75 Base disbanded on 1st October.

Swinderby then became the home of 13 Aircraft Modification Unit which formed on 20th September, its task being the modification and conversion of Lancasters and the first aircraft arrived the following month. In December the station was transferred to 91 Group and the work of 1660 HCU started to build up again but the unit was disbanded in November.

The Vickers Wellington returned to Swinderby on 1st November 1946 when 17 OTU arrived from Silverstone in Northamptonshire to operate until September 1947 when it was renamed 201 Conversion Training Unit. Continuing to operate the Wellington, 201 CTU was later renamed 201 Advanced Flying School and replacement of the Wellington with the Vickers Varsity started on 1st October 1951 when 201 AFS received the RAF's first aircraft of the type. During 1952 there was a requirement for the training of additional navigators and so some Vickers Valettas were sent to Swinderby to assist in meeting the task; the size of the unit may be gauged by its monthly flying task of 3,000 hours. The de Havilland Mosquitoes of 204 AFS which had arrived from Brize Norton in Oxfordshire during June 1950 moved on to Bassingbourn in Cambridgeshire in 20th February 1952.

On 1st June 1954 No.201 AFS was renamed 11 FTS and in February 1955 passed from the control of 21 Group to the control of 25 Group at Manby. By now the unit's task was decreasing and its establishment was eventually reduced to one squadron of Varsities. By 1st June 1955 the aircraft had been moved to Thorney Island to join 2 Air Navigation School and 11 FTS disbanded. No. 8 FTS moved to Swinderby from Driffield in Yorkshire with its de Havil-

Top left: **Valetta T3 WJ468 was one of a number of Valettas used to supplement the Varsities of 201 AFS, Swinderby, where it was photographed in 1952.** *(Air Britain)*

Left: **Vampire FB5s of 8 FTS over Swinderby in 1956.**
(RAF Museum P1731)

land Vampire FB.9 and T.11 jets and continued to operate its large fleet of aircraft until 20th March 1964 when it was disbanded and flying training from Swinderby ceased.

The station was taken over by 22 Group Technical Training Command and 7 School of Recruit Training arrived from Bridgnorth in Shropshire. The first intake of recruits to pass out from the station did so on 21st August 1964 and by April 1965 recruiting had risen to such a level that Hemswell had to be pressed into use as an overflow station. Swinderby then became 1 Wing of 7 SoRT, and Hemswell 2 Wing, but by March 1967 recruiting had declined again and the Hemswell Wing closed. In July 1970 the 680 acres (270 ha) station became the RAF School of Recruit Training, and it continues to operate in that role today, although since the departure of 8 FTS in 1964 Swinderby

has lacked an active flying role. However, in 1979 the increased flying training task at Cranwell saw Swinderby brought into use as a second Relief Landing Ground (the other is at Barkston Heath) for the RAF College.

The high cost of pilot training (over 1½ million pounds by the time a Hawker Harrier pilot reaches his first squadron) forced the RAF to re-introduce a form of pilot grading for student pilots with little or no flying experience. This task, previously carried out at Digby and Kirton in Lindsey in the early 1950s, is essential in order to identify unsuitable students early in their training, thus releasing places for students more likely to succeed. The Flying Selection School

was formed at Swinderby on 9th July 1979 to carry out this selection task. The school uses a fleet of eleven de Havilland Canada Chipmunk aircraft and gives each student fourteen hours of flying in a course planned to last six weeks. There are ten students on each course and two courses are run simultaneously. Although the students are not taken to solo flying standard, sufficient flying is carried out to identify those students with the aptitude for basic flying training.

In a centralisation of all RAF and WRAF recruit training the WRAF School of Recruit Training was moved to Swinderby from Hereford in September 1982.

Right: **Vampire FB5 VZ109, an 8 FTS aircraft seen in Swinderby's hangar, 17th April 1959.** *(MAP)*

Below: **Chipmunks of the FSS over Swinderby in 1979.** *(P.A.Jackson)*

Swinstead

0.8 km SW of Swinstead Church
130/TF013220   250ft (75 m) AMSL

An unlit class 1 Landing Ground was established at Swinstead for the use of 38 (Home Defence) Squadron during its period of operation from aerodromes in South Lincolnshire between September 1916 and May 1918. From August 1918 to July 1919 it was used by 90 (Home Defence) Squadron which had Headquarters at Buckminster and was by then lit, suggesting night use. Records show the field to have been L-shaped with strips measuring 730 yards and 600 yards, and covering 64 acres (26 ha) overall. It adjoined the west side of the B1176 road, midway between the village and Creeton Lodge, and is today farmland.

Theddlethorpe

1 km NE of Theddlethorpe All Saints Church
113, 122/TF468890   10ft (3 m) AMSL

A small Landing Ground was established for emergency and communications use as part of the Theddlethorpe Bombing and Gunnery Range which came into existence in 1935. The precise years in which aircraft movements took place are unclear, as is the date when it was officially closed as an active airfield. According to a town planning document from the early post-war period, the site stood in the apex of the Mablethorpe branch railway line and the west side of the St Helen — All Saints road and covered approximately 140 acres (56 ha). The land has been farmed for most of the post-war period.

Below: **Almost the only sign remaining of the Theddlethorpe landing ground is this derelict brick building, photographed in July 1980.** *(W.J.Taylor)*

Tydd St Mary

1.5 km NE of Tydd St Mary Church
131/TF460195   20ft (6 m) AMSL

Tydd St Mary was opened as a class 1 Day Landing Ground for 51 (Home Defence) Squadron in the summer of 1916 and in August 1917 the squadron based its 'B' Flight at Tydd, which was then upgraded to full aerodrome status.

Primarily equipped with eight Royal Aircraft Factory F.E.2b aeroplanes, the flight was soon in operation against hostile raiders in the area. During the night of 12-13th April 1918 the German Zeppelin L62 released part of its load of bombs in a field to the east of the flare path and successfully eluded the pilots of 'B' Flight, veering off homeward, passing over Wisbech in Cambridgeshire.

By the end of hostilities the squadron had re-equipped with Avro 504NF single-seat night fighting aeroplanes which it operated until making a move to Sutton's Farm in May 1919. Immediately after the move Tydd St Mary was closed down.

The aerodrome was built into an existing farm complex and of the original farm buildings in 1917 one was used as a cinema and one as an armoury. The site covered 125 acres (50 ha) and stood adjacent to the south side of South Holland Main Drain. Of the two hangars that were erected, one remains today in use as a farm store. The Headquarters building is now inhabited by the farm foreman of the estate company which now owns the land on which the aerodrome was situated.

Below: **The former WWI hangar at Tydd St.Mary is now used as a farm store together with its adjacent contemporary buildings. However, the roof timbers with their 'TYDD AERO' stencilling still bear witness to an aeronautical past.** *(W.J.Taylor and C.H.Clover)*

Waddington

1 km E of Waddington Church
121/SK 985 645   230 ft (70m) AMSL

Waddington aerodrome opened late in 1916 as a Royal Flying Corps training station housing the Headquarters of 27 (Training) Wing, which comprised 47, 48 and 51 Training Squadrons and operated a considerable number of aircraft including the Royal Aircraft Factory B.E.2 and F.E.2b, and de Havilland D.H.4, D.H.6, and D.H.9. During the summer of 1917 the aerodrome was expanded to receive a further squadron and an Aircraft Repair Section was established.

The new squadron was 82 which came from Doncaster in Yorkshire and started to work up using a mixture of Avro 504 and Royal Aircraft Factory R.E.8 aeroplanes but when it moved to France in November 1917 the squadron had fully

re-equipped with the Armstrong Whitworth F.K.8. At about the same time 44 Training Squadron moved to Waddington from Harlaxton.

During 1918 American forces started to arrive in the United Kingdom and many came to Waddington for training, the build-up starting in July 1918 with the arrival of the 11th Aero Service Squadron. The concentration of American units reached a peak in September 1918 and in the main D.H.6, D.H.9, R.E.8 and Avro 504 aircraft were operated.

Above: **BE2e A1350 of 51 TS after losing a wing at Waddington, 6th January 1918.** *(via P.H.T.Green)*

Below: **Aerial view of Waddington looking north-east and showing the original hangar site to the south of the airfield, 18th December 1918.** *(via J.Walls)*

Left: **Refuelling a 503 Sqn Fairey Fawn in May 1928. This rare photograph clearly shows the Lincoln Coat of Arms painted on the aircraft's highly polished cowling.** (*Bill Baguley*)

under Special Reserve and Auxiliary Air Force Command, part of the Air Defence of Great Britain; it was to be called 503 (Special Reserve) (Bomber) Squadron. On its formation under Squadron Leader R.D.Oxland on 5th October, the squadron was allowed only a reduced establishment of three Avro 504N, five Fairey Fawn and two Fawn (dual) aircraft; the first six Fawns arrived on 25th October.

With effect from 11th July 1927 the Special Reserve and Auxiliary Air Force Command was renamed the Air Defence Group and 'Special Reserve' was dropped from the squadron title. A further name change occurred on 1st April 1928 when the squadron became known as 503 (County of Lincoln) (Bombing) Squadron, and later that year an open day was held which 2,000 people attended. The

No.48 Training Depot Station was established at Waddington on 4th July 1918 to encompass 47 and 48 Training Squadrons but as the war ended the training requirement dwindled and the squadrons started to disperse. No.51 Training Squadron moved to Baldonnel in Ireland on 4th October and similarly the American presence started to decline, all American units having left by early December.

The station then started to receive squadrons returning from France and 204 Squadron arrived during February 1919 followed by 23 and 203 in March. Each Squadron was in cadre, operating no aircraft, should its services be required again at short notice, but in December 1919 No.203 Squadron moved to Scopwick and on 31st December 23 and 204 Squadrons were disbanded. The 250 acre (100 ha) station was then closed.

Air Order 1647 dated 14th September 1926 gave authority for the formation of a non-regular squadron to strengthen the Home Defence Force in the event of an air attack on the British Isles. The squadron was to form at Waddington

first Handley Page Hyderabad arrived on 8th February 1929 as replacement of the Fawns commenced. The released aircraft were sent to Renfrew and re-equipment was complete by 1st June when the last Fawn left the station. Another change of equipment was made in 1933 when the Hyderabad was replaced by the Handley Page Hinaidi. The squadron operated under 1 Air Defence Group, but when Headquarters Western Area was formed at Andover on 23rd January 1934, control of the squadron was brought under the new organisation.

The unit then received the Westland Wallace and Westland Wapiti and became a light bomber squadron, so all but three of the Hinaidis were sent to Hawkinge in Kent, the last one leaving on 19th November 1935. The three remaining aircraft were somehow disposed of locally. Empire Air Day was celebrated at Waddington on 25th May 1936 by an air display and in June the Wallace was replaced by the Hawker Hind.

Work then started on the reconstruction of Waddington, which involved construction of new hangars and build-ings and progress was sufficient to allow the new Station Headquarters to open on 12th March 1937. The station was then transferred to 3 Group and control of 503 Squadron passed to 6 (Auxiliary) Group.

On 3rd and 18th May respectively, 50 and 110 Squadrons started to form at Waddington, but 110 Squadron was split on 7th June to form 88 Squadron No. 44 Squadron arrived from Andover on 16th June, while 88 Squadron moved to Andover on 10th July and No. 5 Group took over control of Waddington and its

Above: **Another rare Waddington photograph shows 44 Sqn Blenheim Is (incl L1267) with pre-war codes, B-type fuselage roundels and practice bomb carriers under the fuselage.**
(via Sqn Ldr C.G.Jefford)

Right: **Manchester I L7319 shortly after delivery to 207 Sqn at Waddington in late 1940.** *(MAP)*

squadrons on 1st September. Initial equipment of all the squadrons was the Hawker Hind, but re-equipment of 44 and 110 Squadrons with the Bristol Blenheim started on 15th and 30th December respectively, and was complete by 15th January 1938. After a long association with Waddington, No.503 (County of Lincoln) Squadron was disbanded on 31st October 1938 and the regular officers and men together with the aircraft were transferred to 616 Squadron at Doncaster in Yorkshire.

Nos.44 and 50 Squadrons re-equipped with the Handley Page Hampden during January and February 1938 and 110 Squadron moved to Wattisham in Suffolk on 11th May. At the final Empire Air Day display before the war, 7,813 people paid a total of £300 to visit the station. A ferry flight was formed at Waddington on 31st May to prepare and despatch aircraft to the Middle East and operated in conjunction with 'F' Maintenance Unit which moved to Waddington from Kenley, Surrey, 'F' MU being responsible for the custody of a reserve transport pool and the despatch of vehicles to units in the area.

General mobilisation was ordered on 1st September and war was declared on the 3rd, so at 18.35 hours on the 3rd, nine aircraft took of from Waddington to look for enemy shipping. They landed at 23.45 hours with nothing to report after Waddington's first operation of the

Second World War.

In June 1940 No.142 Squadron was withdrawn from France to Waddington where it re-equipped with the Fairey Battle before moving to Binbrook on 3rd July. No. 50 Squadron moved to Lindholme in Yorkshire during July and 207 Squadron re-formed in its place on 8th November to operate the ill-fated Avro Manchester aircraft, conducting its first operation with the new aircraft, an attack on Brest, on 24th February 1941. No.6 Beam Approach Training Flight was formed at Waddington on 6th January 1941, but its first course did not start training on the Blenheim until 12th March. The King and Queen visited the station on 27th January when they viewed the Hampden and Manchester and presented decorations.

The day after 207 Squadron had made its first operation, eight crews were hived off to form 97 Squadron, which was planned to move to Coningsby. The ground personnel travelled across by road on 10th March although the move of the aircraft was delayed until 15th due to Coningsby being unserviceable. Tragedy struck on 9th May when six high explosive bombs were dropped on the station and village by an enemy raider. The NAAFI was destroyed and eleven people were killed, including seven ladies of the NAAFI staff who died when their trench shelter suffered a direct hit. One of those killed was the NAAFI manager-

ess, Mrs Constance Raven, after whom the rebuilt NAAFI was named.

No.6 BAT Flight operated its initial equipment of four Blenheims and some Hampdens until re-equipped with the Airspeed Oxford in June, and was renumbered 1506 BAT Flight on 16th November 1941. The following day 207 Squadron moved to Bottesford in Leicestershire and 420 (RCAF) Squadron formed in its place on 19th December. Two days earlier 'F' MU had returned to Kenley and 44 Squadron began preparations to receive the first Lancaster bombers to be delivered to the RAF. Three aircraft arrived on 24th December, a further four on the 28th and three more on 9th January 1942. Seventeen Hampdens from 44 Squadron were passed to 420 Squadron on 1st January and this new squadron became operational on 21st February when six aircraft attacked Emden and one aircraft laid mines off the Frisian Islands. It moved to Skipton on Swale in Yorkshire on 6th August to convert to the Wellington.

No. 44 Squadron brought the Lancaster into operational service and Squadron Leader J.D.Nettleton was awarded the Victoria Cross for leading the daylight attack by 44 and 97 Squadrons against Augsburg on 17th April 1942. A second squadron, No.9, arrived at Waddington to equip with the Lancaster on 7th August. Conversion started with Manchesters on the 9th and the first Lancaster arrived on the 12th; the squadron's last Vickers Wellington left on 22nd August and its first operation with the Lancaster was flown on 5th September.

The Lancaster was quickly introduced into squadron service and 1661 Heavy Conversion Unit was formed at Waddington under Squadron Leader Nettleton on 9th November 1942. It comprised the Conversion Flights from 9 and 44 Squadrons which formed 'B' and 'A' Flights respectively, while 'C' Flight was formed from the Conversion Flight of 49 Squadron but remained at Scampton until the whole unit moved to Winthorpe in Nottinghamshire on 30th December. Runway construction was started at Waddington in mid-1943, so 9 Squadron took advantage of an operation to make its move to Bardney, landing there on 14th April after a raid on Spezia, while 44 Squadron moved to Dunholme Lodge during May and 1506 BAT Flight moved to Fulbeck.

When runway construction was complete, the first unit to return was 467 (RAAF) Squadron which moved from Bottesford in Leicestershire on 11th November 1943. Four days later Waddington became the Headquarters and Base Station of 53 Base, controlling the sub-stations at Bardney and Skellingthorpe, while a flight from 467 Squadron provided the experienced nucleus for

the formation of 463 (RAAF) Squadron at Waddington on 25th November.

From mid-1941 A.V.Roe and Company, manufacturers of the Manchester and Lancaster, occupied one of Waddington's hangars as a final assembly and flight test centre for aircraft that had been modified and repaired at their nearby Bracebridge Heath works, the damaged aircraft usually being taken to Bracebridge Heath by road and, following re-conditioning, moved to Waddington for final assembly and flight test before delivery back to the RAF. Aircraft modified in this way included the Manchester, Lancaster and Anson, with the Lancastrian, York and Lincoln following after the war.

With the end of the War in Europe, 53 Base started to prepare for the RAF's offensive against Japan. No.467 Squadron moved to Metheringham in June to join 553 Wing and 463 Squadron moved to Skellingthorpe on 3rd July to make room for 9 Squadron which returned to join 617 Squadron. Waddington's two squadrons comprised 551 Wing of *Tiger Force* which was created with its headquarters at Waddington although many of the ground personnel were accommodated at Woodhall Spa. When *Tiger Force* was disbanded Waddington started to run down and 53 Base was disbanded on 15th November.

On 1st January 1946, Nos.9 and 617 Squadrons set off for India and were replaced at Waddington by 50 and 61 Squadrons from Sturgate. A short time later both units started to convert to the Avro Lincoln and were joined in July by 12 Squadron from Binbrook which moved in for the same reason; conversion of the latter squadron was completed by September and it returned to Binbrook. The station complement was raised to three Squadrons during October with the arrival of 57 Squadron which was already operating the Lincoln, and when in the second half of 1947 the station underwent re-construction, the resident squadrons were detached to various stations for the duration of the work.

Below: Lancaster R5868, the famous 'S-Sugar' of 467 Squadron and now in the Bomber Command Museum at Hendon, seen embarking former prisoners of war at Frankfurt on 7th May 1945. *(IWM MH15078)*

In March 1950 No.100 Squadron arrived and later detached to Singapore for six months. No.50 Squadron disbanded on 31st January 1951 and in June of that year 57 Squadron converted to the Boeing Washington, which was the name the RAF gave to the American B-29 bomber. The type was no stranger to the base, since in late 1948 Waddington housed detachments of B-29s from the Strategic Air Command of the USAF. The first detachment was provided by the 372nd Bombardment Squadron between 18th July and 19th October 1948, while the second detachment came from the 342nd Bombardment Squadron between 2nd November 1948 and 10th February 1949. This was not the only connection the station was to have with the USAF, for the 3914th Air Base Squadron operated a few C-47 Skytrains from Waddington between 16th May 1951 and March 1955.

The Washingtons were moved to Coningsby in May 1952 and 49 Squadron arrived in July but in August 1953 all the squadrons departed and the station was placed on Care and Maintenance while contractors made Waddington ready to receive large jet aircraft.

Waddington had first operated jet aircraft in 1953 when the only two aircraft to be built by Avro at Bracebridge Heath made their first flights from Waddington. The first occasion was on 20th February when the second Avro 707A to be built, WZ736, took to the air, and this was followed on 1st July by the only Avro 707C, WZ744. Both aircraft had been assembled at Bracebridge Heath from components manufactured at other Avro factories.

The first unit to be installed after re-construction was 103 Squadron which re-formed at Waddington on 13th November 1954 to operate the English Electric Canberra B.2 and moved to Gutersloh in West Germany the following month. Further squadrons did not appear until June 1955 when 21 and 27 arrived with the Canberra. Also formed in late 1955 was 230 OCU and the first Avro Vulcans for the RAF were delivered to this unit on 20th July 1956 to carry out the Service Trials for the Vulcan; crew training began in earnest on 22nd February 1957. Sufficient crews had been trained to allow the first squadron, 83, to form at Waddington on 11th July.

The OCU was the first unit to receive

Left: **Canberra B2 WD990 of the Waddington Station Flight displays the Lincoln Coat of Arms motif on its fin.** (*A.Pearcy via P.H.T.Green*)

Below: **Vulcans (one in white finish, two in silver) of 230 OCU line up on Waddington's disused runway opposite 21 Squadron's Canberras in 1957.** (*Flight 34893*)

STATION BADGE
WADDINGTON

Description: Issuant from clouds a representation of a tower of Lincoln Cathedral.
Motto: For Faith and Freedom.
Authority: Queen Elizabeth II, June 1954.

The tower of Lincoln Cathedral was a well known landmark for pilots returning from raids; the clouds are to suggest the morning and evening mists which so often obscure all but the highest landmarks in that district.

the improved Vulcan B.2, and the first machine arrived at Waddington on 1st July 1960. On 10th August 83 Squadron was re-numbered 44 Squadron. The OCU began to operate one flight of B.1 aircraft and a second flight of B.2s, but moved as a whole to Finningley in Yorkshire in June 1961, exchanging places with 101 Squadron which was moved to Waddington. On 1st August 1961 the two squadrons were joined by a third, 50, and the station's complement of operational squadrons increased to four in January 1975 when 9 Squadron returned to Waddington from Akrotiri following the British withdrawal from Cyprus.

Rundown of the Vulcan force at Waddington began on 29th April 1982 when a ceremony was held to mark the formal disbandment of 9 Squadron on 1st May. At the parade the Squadron Standard was handed over to a Colour Party from the new 9 Squadron which, on 1st June, became the first squadron to form with the Tornado GR.1 at Honington (Suffolk). This somewhat sad

event preceded by just a few hours what was perhaps the most apposite adieu for the last of the RAF's great bombers.

Following the Argentinian invasion of the Falkland Islands on 2nd April the Ministry of Defence announced that Vulcans were to revert to the conventional bombing role and that the crews were to be trained in air-to-air refuelling. This announcement foreshadowed an attack by a lone Vulcan on the airfield at Port Stanley on 1st May. The aircraft took off from Wideawake Airfield on Ascension Island in the late evening of 30th April and, after a flight of over eight hours, during which it was refuelled in the air a number of times, it dropped twenty-one 1000lb high explosive bombs, one of which successfully cratered the

Top: **A view of Waddington typical of the many Battle of Britain air displays held there since WW2.** *(N.Franklin)*

Below: **Vulcan B2 XM657 of 101 Sqn lands at Waddington in 1979.** *(MAP)*

Port Stanley runway. The Vulcan landed safely at Ascension Island after a sortie of approx sixteen hours duration during which it had travelled some 7000 miles.

The raid was mounted over the longest distance ever in the history of the RAF and was followed two days later by a similar mission, proving beyond doubt the conventional bombing capability of this classic bomber. Between then and the Argentinian surrender a further three Vulcan raids were mounted against targets in the Falkland Islands. On one raid (3rd June) 44 Squadron Vulcan XM597 diverted into Rio de Janeiro in Brazil as a result of a refuelling probe problem.

It had been intended that Waddington's three remaining squadrons would disband together on 30th June. However, with the uncertainty of the Falklands Crisis the Vulcan was given a stay of execution. Indeed, with typical British ingenuity, a small number of Vulcans were converted into air-to-air refuelling tankers. In something of a temporary installation, a refuelling hose drum unit has been attached to the underside of the electronic countermeasures fairing at the rear of the aircraft giving the Vulcan a capability to refuel one aircraft at a time.

Despite its somewhat agricultural looks, the Vulcan tanker will usefully supplement the Victor tanker force, so hard-pressed during the Falklands campaign, pending the arrival of the VC.10 tanker. As a result, it seems likely that 50 Squadron will continue to operate the Vulcan in the tanker and other roles until late 1983. The Vulcan run-down gathered momentum following the end of the Falklands conflict, as 101 Squadron disbanded on 4th August 1982. Next to go was 44 Squadron which held a parade to mark withdrawal of the Vulcan from the bombing role on 17th September 1982 — seven Vulcans made a final scramble take-off and four went on to overfly a number of former Vulcan bases in the area. The squadron disbanded officially on 21st December 1982.

The advent of the Nimrod airborne early warning system foreshadows a role change for Waddington since it has been selected as the home of the RAF's sole squadron of Nimrod AEW.3 aircraft. The most expensive aircraft ever bought by the RAF, Nimrod AEW.3 is needed to provide low level radar coverage of the UK Air Defence Region, which extends across the North Sea from Norway out into the eastern Atlantic Ocean. With this latest change of role Waddington will become one of the most vital links in our defence from air attack. In preparation for Nimrod, Waddington's runway was resurfaced in mid-1983; 50 Squadron's tankers operating from Scampton then Coningsby whilst the airfield was closed.

Above: **Spitfire VB of 154 (Motor Industries) Squadron at Wellingore on 22nd September 1942. Note the squadron badge with 'WRM' (W.R.Morris) below. 'DY STN' clearly indicates Wellingore's status as a satellite of Digby.** *(IWM CH7282)*

Wellingore

2 km SSE of Wellingore Church
121/SK 990 545   250 ft (75 m) AMSL

A Landing Ground at Wellingore first came into use in mid-1917 when aircraft of the Royal Naval Air Service from nearby Cranwell started to use a site at Graves Farm. Aircraft types in regular use included the Avro 504, Sopwith Camel and Royal Aircraft Factory B.E.2 and its use as an RLG for Cranwell recommenced many years later in the mid-1930s. Oddly no official plans have come to light revealing the exact position.

In early 1940 a proper grass aerodrome was established as a satellite of Digby and the first aircraft to arrive were the Bristol Blenheim fighters of 29 Squadron, which moved from Digby on 8th July. The squadron then started to convert to the Bristol Beaufighter in September and carried out its first operation with the new type on 17th December. Conversion was completed in full by February 1941 and the squadron moved to West Malling in Kent at the end of April; one of 29 Squadron's pilots during this period was Flight Lieutenant Guy Gibson, later famous as the leader of the 'Dambusters' raid.

Digby was transferred to Canadian control and 402 (RCAF) Squadron arrived at Wellingore in May but was replaced in October by the Spitfires of 412 (RCAF) Squadron. Other squadrons also started to visit Wellingore in order to prepare for overseas service, the first of these to arrive being 54 on 1st June 1942 when it was not operating any aircraft, for the time at Wellingore was spent kitting out and making final preparations. No.154 and No.81 Squadron arrived later, both operating the Spitfire.

In March 1943 the Mustangs of 613 Squadron arrived, operating with Coastal Command to provide escorts for strike missions. In May the squadron departed, but from 7th June aircraft of the RAF College SFTS at Cranwell again started to use Wellingore as a Relief Landing Ground. In the meantime 349 (Belgian) Squadron arrived from Digby to work up with its Spitfires and, after becoming operational on 13th August, the squadron returned to Digby later that month. Digby required the use of the station once more and from 18th September Cranwell aircraft ceased using Wellingore as a Relief Landing Ground.

The Spitfires of 416 (RCAF) Squadron arrived later in September but moved to Digby in October. A further RCAF Squadron, No.439, arrived on 31st December 1943, having formed that day with Hurricanes as an interim measure before receiving Hawker Typhoons; in January it moved to Dyce, Aberdeen, to start re-equipment. Wellingore was then used by aircraft of 16 SFTS at Newton in Nottinghamshire, because of runway unserviceability there. The last squadron to use the station while it was under the control of Digby was 402 which operated from the station between February and March 1944; 17 SFTS at Cranwell took over on 18th April.

Cranwell aircraft returned on 25th April, but it was not until July that 'F' and 'H' Flights of Airspeed Oxfords and Miles Masters were moved to the station on a permanent basis. North American Harvards were also detached to Wellingore in September, but on 8th October the Oxfords of 'F' Flight returned to Cranwell because the aircraft were deteriorating badly in the open conditions at the station. The Oxfords were replaced by the mixed Harvard and Master fleet of 'E' Flight but on 4th May 1945 both 'E' and 'H' Flights returned to Cranwell. No.17 SFTS moved from Cranwell to Spitalgate and 19 FTS formed at Cranwell; flying continued from Wellingore with some de Havilland Tiger Moths and a few Avro Ansons.

On 28th July the Army arrived to take over some of the buildings for use by German ex-prisoners-of-war. The

Left: With 100+ mission symbols on their aircraft, the crew of Lancaster 'N-Nuts' of 12 Sqn pose for a photograph at Wickenby. Back row: W/O L.Bratby, Sqn Ldr Huggins DFC, W/O L.Laing, F/Sgt G.W.Robinson; Front Row: W/O B.Jackson, W/O S.Petchett, F/O T.Thompson.
(via G.W.Robinson)

Left: Perhaps the largest crop-spraying aircraft in use in the United Kingdom today is the turbo-prop Schweizer-Grumman Ag-Cat D, of which G-TCAT was the first of four such machines to be operated from Wickenby by Miller Aerial Spraying. It is seen here inside the new hangar constructed in 1978.
(W.J.Taylor)

Right: Aerial view of Wickenby in June 1977. The new hangar built a year later occupies the area at the bottom left, where the Ag-Cat can be seen parked.
(via P.H.T.Green)

first 700 men arrived on 11th August, followed by a further 300 on 14th September. Aircraft of 'G' and 'H' Flights arrived from Cranwell on 29th January 1946, but on 17th April 1947 all flying from Wellingore ceased and the 300 acre (120 ha) station was closed, and quickly reverted to agricultural use although the concrete perimeter track, and a number of pill-boxes and revetments still remain.

Wickenby

2km SE of Wickenby Church
121/TF 100805   80ft (25m) AMSL

Construction of Wickenby aerodrome commenced during late 1941 and the station was ready to accept its first unit by mid-1942. This was 12 Squadron which moved from Binbrook with its Vickers Wellington aircraft on 25th September 1942 although the Wellington gave way during November to the Lancaster and the squadron's first operation with the new aircraft was carried out during January 1943. By April the squadron had twenty-seven aircraft on strength and a third flight was formed on the 9th; the Wellingtons were passed to 199 Squadron which was then forming at Blyton. The last Wellington to be flown out of Wickenby by the ATA on 18th March suffered engine failure and crashed on take-off.

Wickenby then became a sub-station of Ludford Magna on 1st October and part of 14 Base on 15th December. Prior to this, on 7th November, 626 Squadron had been formed at Wickenby to operate the Avro Lancaster with an operational nucleus from 'C' Flight of 12 Squadron and carried out its first operation three days later.

The two units operated together from Wickenby until 24th July 1945 when 12 Squadron returned to Binbrook. No.626 Squadron disbanded at Wickenby on 14th October and was initially replaced by the Mosquitos of 109 Squadron from Woodhall Spa on 19th and 20th October, who moved to Hemswell on 26th November. On the previous day 14 Base had disbanded and the station was handed over to 40 Group Maintenance Command on 21st December as a sub-site of 61 MU. No.93 MU was later established at Wickenby.

The dispersed hutted accommodation was handed to the Ministry of Health during 1947 but the airfield itself remained under the control of 93 MU. In September 1952, No.92 MU was established as an independent unit at Wickenby tasked with the supply of munitions to units in north Lincolnshire and operated from Wickenby until early 1956 when it was disbanded.

Sale of the 670 acres (270 ha) of land occupied by the aerodrome was completed between 1964 and 1966. Much of the airfield has been returned to agricultural use and the two remaining hangars are used for the bulk storage of fertilisers, although a small part of the former airfield is now a very active civil aerodrome.

Civil flying from Wickenby commenced during 1963 with the formation of the Links Air Touring Group. The group commenced operations with Auster and Proctor aircraft and built new hangars during 1968. The old watch office was tastefully converted into a club house and operations room. In 1971 the group changed its name to the Wickenby Flying Club and in 1972 bought that part of the former military airfield which formed the civil aerodrome. In January 1973

the aerodrome became licensed and maintenance facilities were available from May 1973. During 1973 the old Austers and the Proctor were replaced with modern Cessnas and in early 1980 two new Cessna 152s were obtained.

A second major user of the civil aerodrome is Miller Aerial Spraying, a company formed in 1967 to carry out crop spraying operations in and around Lincolnshire. The company initially operated from Skegness but moved to Wickenby with its Piper Super Cub and Pawnee aircraft during 1968. Since then Miller Aerial Spraying has gradually expanded, operating a large fleet of Pawnees and Ag Cat aircraft. Indeed, the company is, so far, the only one in Britain to operate the turbo-prop powered Ag Cat D, having taken delivery of four such aircraft (G-TCAT, G-BHHY, G-BIVO and G-DCAT) since 1980.

Willoughby Hills

3 km ENE of Boston Church
131/TF355455   10 ft (3 m) AMSL

A Class 2 Landing Ground was established at Willoughby Hills by 38 (Home Defence) Squadron during the period it was operating over South Lincolnshire, between September 1916 and May 1918. It was upgraded from unlit to lit status, suggesting night use in its later phase. Records do not specify its acreage or dimensions, but a sketch plan on file indicates that it covered approximately 25 acres (10 ha). It stood about 200 yards clear of the north side of the A52 road, midway between the hamlet of Willoughby Hills and Round House. Today the site is farmland.

Winterton

2 km ENE of Winterton Church
112/SE 945 197   40ft (12m) AMSL

This Class 2 Landing Ground was established for the use of 33 (Home Defence) Squadron while operating over Lincolnshire between December 1916 and June 1919 and stood adjacent to the east side of Ermine Street, opposite Field Farm. It had strips of 600 and 400 yards, covered 55 acres (22 ha) and the site is today farmland.

Woodhall Spa

3 km SE of Woodhall Spa Church
122/TF 210610   40ft (12m) AMSL

When the station at Woodhall Spa opened as a satellite of Coningsby on 1st February 1942 it was prepared to receive 97 Squadron from Coningsby. The first aircraft to operate from the station did so in February 1942 but were in fact the Handley Page Hampdens of 106 Squadron for Bomber Command was required to lay mines in the Engish Channel in an attempt to stop the Channel dash by the German capital ships *Gneisenau, Prinz Eugen* and *Scharnhorst.* Coningsby's grass runways were waterlogged and so 106 Squadron had to use the concrete runways at Woodhall Spa in order that

its heavily laden aircraft could take off.

The Avro Lancasters of 97 Squadron eventually arrived on 1st March and the squadron became operational on the night of 20th March when six aircraft laid mines in the Nectarine area. Three aircraft returned safely, but one hit a rooftop in Boston and crashed on Freiston Shore and the remaining two crashed on other airfields.

When runway construction was commenced at Coningsby the Airspeed Oxfords of 1514 BAT Flight were moved to Woodhall Spa, arriving on 8th March 1943.

No.97 Squadron moved to Bourn in Cambridgeshire on 17th April but three crews remained behind as an operational nucleus for 619 Squadron which was formed at Woodhall Spa on 18th April

Above: **Sporting invasion markings, Mosquito B25 KB416 AZ-P of 'B' Flight 627 Squadron, at Woodhall Spa in early 1945.** *(via P.H.T.Green)*

Below: **A B1 (special) Lancaster of 617 Squadron seen at Woodhall Spa carrying a 22,000lb 'Grand Slam' bomb.** *(IWM MH4263)*

Right: **Woodhall Spa, 16th April 1947.** *(DoE, Crown Copyright)*

1943, its first three Lancasters arriving on 1st May; the squadron became operational on 11th June. When 54 Base was established at Coningsby on 1st January 1944 Woodhall Spa became one of the two sub-stations alongside Metheringham and in a shuffle of the squadrons within the Base 619 Squadron was moved to Coningsby in exchange for 617 Squadron.

The 'Dambusters' brought thirty-four Lancasters and two de Havilland Mosquitos to Woodhall Spa, the latter being in use as low-level target marking aircraft. The technique developed by the squadron was such a success that it was decided to establish a squadron within 5 Group to specialise in this work so 627 Squadron arrived on 15th April to train in the new role.

The first 12,000 lb 'Tallboy' bomb arrived from 233 MU on 1st June and shortly after D-Day 617 Squadron dropped one on the Saumur railway tunnel. An early fellow user of the 'Tallboy' was 9 Squadron at Bardney which operated from Woodhall Spa between 25th August and 3rd September while essential repair work was carried out at Bardney.

On the night of 19-20th September the Base Operations Officer, Wing Com-

mader Guy Gibson, VC, flew as Master Bomber on a raid to Rheydt. His mount, Mosquito KB267 'E-Easy' of 627 Squadron, unfortunately crashed in Holland on the return journey, killing both crew members.

No.617 Squadron chalked up another first on 1st March 1945 when it dropped the first 22,000 lb 'Grand Slam' bomb on enemy territory, the target on this occasion being the Bielefeld Viaduct. As the war in Europe drew to a close Bomber Command decided that the special techniques and skills developed in 617 Squadron should be spread throughout the command so 'B' Flight of the squadron was moved to Mildenhall in Suffolk to join 15 Squadron on 27th May 1945, taking with it aircraft equipped to carry the 'Tallboy'. Having reduced in strength to two flights the main body of the squadron moved to Waddington to prepare for *Tiger Force*.

Woodhall Spa became the assembly and kitting point for the ground personnel of *Tiger Force*. As six to seven thousand personnel of the contingent started to arrive, a camp of 340 bell tents was erected to house them. Hangars were swiftly converted into huge stores to contain all the equipment prior to issue and at the same time 627 Squadron started its own training programme for the part it was to play in the assault on Japan; but this was all cancelled due to Japan's defeat. On 11th September 627 Squadron was ordered to cease flying and disbanded on the 30th. The *Tiger Force* personnel started to disperse and all the accumulated equipment was returned to depots.

On the same day that 627 Squadron disbanded twenty of its aircraft, its personnel and equipment were taken over by 109 Squadron, which moved to Wickenby on 20th October. The Mosquitoes of 464 Squadron were ferried into Woodhall Spa on 24th September merely twenty-four hours before

the squadron, which had been based at 'B58' Melsbroek, was disbanded. Shortly afterwards, the Mosquitoes were ferried out, though it is something of a mystery as to where: the location quoted in the *WHS.F.540* at the PRO is *Insfield,* but this is thought to be incorrect - and possibly a mis-interpretation for the MU at Lichfield.

No. 54 Base disbanded on 15th November, and Woodhall Spa was closed and placed on Care and Maintenance on 10th December 1945. In the years following the war the site was used to store many thousands of tons of unused bombs which were slowly taken away to be stored elsewhere or dumped.

With the build-up of the V-bomber and Douglas Thor missile bases in the late 1950s Woodhall Spa was selected to become a Bristol-Ferranti Bloodhound SAM station to provide air defence for those stations nearby. Operating within 13 Group, Fighter Command the first unit formed during May 1960. This was 222 Squadron, equipped with the Bloodhound Mk.1 missile, which was replaced by 112 Squadron and the British Aircraft Corporation Bloodhound Mk.2 during 1964. The missiles were controlled by 148 Wing from North Coates until 1965 when 112 Squadron was moved to Cyprus.

Although no longer used, the former missile site remained under the control of nearby Coningsby. In March 1969 the site was reactivated when 25 Squadron deployed to Woodhall Spa from North Coates during exercise *Illusory,* an exercise designed to test the mobility of the Bloodhound missile system.

Most of the 700 acre (280 ha) airfield itself has now been returned to agricultural and forestry use. The missile site continues in use as a sub-site for Coningsby, housing a golf course and the repair shops for the Rolls-Royce Spey engines from Coningsby's Phantom aircraft.

Below: **627 Squadron aircrew find a novel use for their Mosquitoes in this June 1944 photograph taken at Woodhall Spa.** *(via P.H.T.Green)*

General Bibliography

After the Battle Magazine, *Airfields of the Eighth: Then and Now*, Battle of Britain Prints International Ltd: London, 1978, (text by R.A.Freeman; designed and edited by W.G. Ramsey).

After the Battle Magazine, *The Battle of Britain: Then and Now*, Battle of Britain Prints International Ltd: London, 1980, (various authors; edited by W.G. Ramsey).

Air Ministry (Directorate of Civil Aviation), *The Development of Civil Aviation in the United Kingdom* (The Maybury Report), Cmnd 5351, HMSO 1937.

Air Ministry (Air Historical Branch), *The Second World War 1939-1945: Works*, (restricted), 1956.

Bagley, J.A., 'A Gazetteer of Hampshire Aerodromes', *Proceedings of the Hampshire Field Club and Archæological Society*, Vol 24, 1972.

Barber, C., 'The socio-economic impact of the RAF in Lincolnshire' *Trent Geographer*, No 2, Trent Polytechnic Geography Division, 1981.

Barker, R., *The Ship Busters*, Chatto and Windus: 1957.

Barker, R., *The Thousand Plan*, Chatto: 1965.

Beamont, R.P., *Testing Years*, Ian Allan: Shepperton, 1980.

Bere, R.de la, *A History of the Royal Air Force College Cranwell*, Gale & Polden: 1934.

Billington, B. and Butler, P.H., *British Air Arms: A Review of British Military Aviation*, Merseyside Aviation Society Ltd: Liverpool Airport, 1977.

Blake, R.N.E., 'The Changing Geographical Distribution of Military Airfields in the East Midlands, 1914-80', *The East Midland Geographer*, Vol 7, No 8, Univ. of Nottingham, 1982.

Bowyer, C., *The Flying Elephants - History of 27 Squadron*, Macdonald: 1972.

Bowyer, C., *Mosquito At War*, Ian Allan: Shepperton, 1973.

Bowyer, C., *Beaufighter At War*, Ian Allan: Shepperton, 1976.

Bowyer, C., *Hampden Special*, Ian Allan: Shepperton, 1976.

Bowyer, C., *History of the Royal Air Force*, Hamlyn: 1977.

Bowyer, C., *The Air VCs*, William Kimber: London, 1978.

Bowyer, C., *Coastal Command at War*, Ian Allan Shepperton, 1979.

Bowyer, M.J.F., *Bombing Colours: RAF Bombers, their Markings and Operations 1937-1973*, Patrick Stephens Ltd: Cambridge, 1973.

Bowyer, M.J.F., *Fighting Colours 1937-1975*, Patrick Stephens Ltd: Cambridge, 1975.

Bowyer, M.J.F., *Action Stations 1: Wartime Military Airfields of East Anglia 1939-1945*, Patrick Stephens Ltd: Cambridge, 1979.

Bowyer, M.J.F., and Rawlings, J.D.R., *Squadron Codes 1937-1956*, Patrick Stephens Ltd: Cambridge, 1979.

Bowyer, M.J.F, *The Stirling Bomber*, Faber and Faber: 1980.

Bramson, A., and Birch, N., *The Tiger Moth Story*, Air Review Ltd: 1970.

Brickhill, P., *The Dam Busters*, Evans Brothers: 1977.

Bruce, J.M., *British Aeroplanes 1914-1918*, Putnam: 1969.

Butler, P.H., *British Isles Airfield Guide*, Merseyside Aviation Society Ltd: Liverpool Airport, 1962 and regular updates.

Currie, J., *Lancaster Target*, New English Library: 1977.

Ferguson, A.P., *A History of Royal Air Force Woodvale*, Merseyside Aviation Society Ltd: Liverpool Airport, 1974.

Ferguson, A.P., *A History of Royal Air Force Sealand*, Merseyside Aviation Society Ltd: Liverpool Airport, 1978.

Finn, S., *Lincolnshire Air War 1939-1945*, Aero Litho Co Ltd: Lincoln, 1973.

Flight International, *Directory of British Aviation*, (formerly entitled 'Who's Who in British Aviation' and 'The Aeroplane Directory). (Annual).

Freeman, R.A., *The Mighty Eighth*, Macdonald: 1970.

Garbett, M. and Goulding, B. *The Lancaster at War*, Ian Allan: Shepperton, 1971.

Garbett, M. and Goulding, B. *Lancaster at War - 2*, Ian Allan: Shepperton, 1979.

Gibson, M.L., *Aviation in Northamptonshire: An Illustrated History*, Northamptonshire Libraries: 1982.

Halley, J.J., *Royal Air Force Unit Histories: Volume 1 - Nos 1-200*, Air Britain Ltd :1969.

Halley, J.J., *Royal Air Force Unit Histories: Volume 2 - Nos 201-1435*, Air Britain Ltd, 1973.

Halley, J.J., *Famous Fighter Squadrons of the RAF: Volume 1*, Hylton Lacy Publishers Ltd: Windsor 1971.

Halley, J.J., *Famous Maritime Squadrons of the RAF: Volume 1*, Hylton Lacy Publishers Ltd: Windsor 1973.

Halley, J.J., *Squadrons of the Royal Air Force*, Air Britain: London, 1980.

Halpenny, B.B., *Action Stations 2: Military Airfields of Lincolnshire and the East Midlands*, Patrick Stephens: 1981.

Halpenny, B.B., *Action Stations 4: Military Airfields of Yorkshire*, Patrick Stephens, Cambridge: 1982.

Hancock, T.N., *Bomber County: A History of the Royal Air Force in Lincolnshire*, Lincolnshire Library Service: 1978.

Haslam, Gp. Capt. E. B., *The History of Royal Air Force Cranwell*, Air Historial Branch (RAF)/H.M.S.O., 1982

Hastings, M., *Bomber Command*, Michael Joseph: 1979.

Henshaw, A., *Flight of the Mew Gull*, John Murray: 1980.

Hollis, B.R., *United Kingdom Airfield Register*, Open University Faculty of Social Sciences, Occasional Paper No 2: Milton Keynes, 1978.

Hunt, L., 'RAF North Coates', *Aviation News*, Vol 1, No 2: 13-26 October 1973, p73.

Jackson, P.A., 'The Chosen Few: the Flying Selection Squadron at Swinderby', *Aviation News*, Vol 8, No 26: 23 May-5 June 1980.

James, A.G.T., *The Royal Air Force: The Past 30 Years*, Macdonald and Janes: 1976.

Jefford, Flt.Lt.C.G., *A History of RAF Scampton 1917-1968*, Delta Magazine: Scampton, Lincoln, 1968.

Jones, A.C. Merton, *British Independent Airlines since 1946*, four volumes. Merseyside Aviation Society: Liverpool Airport; LAAS International: Uxbridge, 1976-77.

Lawrence, W.J., *No.5 Bomber Group, RAF 1939-1945*, Faber: 1951.

Lewis, P., *Squadron Histories: RFC, RNAS and RAF since 1912*, Putnam: 1959, 1968.

Mason, F.K., *Battle over Britain*, MacWhirter: 1969.

Maurer Maurer (ed), *Air Force Combat Units of World War II*, Franklin Watts: 1959.

Maurer Maurer (ed), *Combat Squadrons of the Air Force in World War II*, USAF Historical Division: 1969.

Middlebrook, M., *The Nuremburg Raid*, Allen Lane: 1973.

Montgomery, Flt.Lt.B.G., *A Short History of RAF Digby 1918-1973*, RAF Digby: Lincoln.

Moyes, P.J.R., *Bomber Squadrons of the Royal Air Force and their Aircraft*, Macdonald: 1976.

Penrose, H., *British Aviation: The Pioneer Years 1903-1914*, Putnam:1964.

Penrose, H., *British Aviation: The Great War and Armistice 1915-1919*, Putnam: 1969.

Penrose, H., *British Aviation: The Adventuring Years 1920-1929*, Putnam: 1974.

Penrose, H., *British Aviation: Widening Horizons 1930-1934*, Royal Air Force Museum/HMSO: 1979.

Penrose, H., *British Aviation: Ominous Skies 1935-1939*, Royal Air Force Museum/HMSO: 1980.

Price, A., *Spitfire at War*, Ian Allan: Shepperton 1974.

Raleigh, Sir W. and Jones, H.A., *The War in the Air*, (six vols), Clarendon Press: Oxford 1923-1937; volumes 1 and 2 republished by Hamish Hamilton, 1969.

Rapier, B.J., *White Rose Base*, Aero Litho Ltd: Lincoln 1972.

Rawlings, J.D.R., *Fighter Squadrons of the RAF and their Aircraft*, (2nd edition), Macdonald: 1976.

Rawlings, J.D.R., *Coastal, Support and Special Squadrons of the RAF and their Aircraft*, Janes: 1982.

Robertson, B., *Lancaster: The Story of a Famous Bomber*, Harleyford Publications: Letchworth 1964.

Robertson, B., *Bombing Colours: British Bomber Camouflage and Markings 1914-1937*, Patrick Stephens Ltd: Cambridge.

Robertson, B., *British Military Aircraft Serials 1912-1969*, Ian Allan: Shepperton.

Robertson, B. *(ed), Epics of Aviation Archaeology*, Patrick Stephens.Ltd: Cambridge 1978.

Royal Air Force, *En Route Supplement: British Isles and North Atlantic*, 1 AIDU (RAF): Northolt; monthly.

Rust, Kenn C., *The Ninth Air Force in World War II*, Aero Publishers: California, 1970.

Sharp, C.M. and Bowyer, M.J.F., *Mosquito*, Faber: 1971.

Smith, D.J., *Action Stations 3: Military Airfields of Wales and the North-West*, Patrick Stephens Ltd: Cambridge, 1981.

Sturtivant, R., 'Flying Training in World War 1', *Aviation News*, Vol6, No10: 14-27 October 1977, p4-6, 15.

Sturtivant, R., 'RAF Operational Training in World War 2', *Aviation News*, Vol 7, No23: 13-26 April 1979, p4-7, 15.

Sturtivant, R., 'Wartime RAF Aircrew Training in the United Kingdom', *Aviation News*, Vol11, No12, 5-18 November 1982 p4-7.

Thetford, O.G., *Aircraft of the Royal Air Force since 1918*, Putnam: 1976.

Thetford, O.G., *British Naval Aircraft since 1912*, Putnam 1978.

(HQ) US Third Air Force (Office of Information), *Installations and USAAF Combat Units in the United Kingdom 1942-1945*, (date unknown); *Locations of United States Military Units in the United Kingdom, 16 July - 31 December 1967*, (date unknown).

Walls, J., *Ruston Aircraft Production*, Aero Litho Co Ltd: Lincoln 1974.

Walls, J., *Robey Aircraft Production*, Aero Litho Co Ltd: Lincoln 1974.

Walls, J., *Clayton & Shuttleworth and Marshall Aircraft Production*, Control Column Publications: Newark 1977.

Wiggins, P.R., and Reid, A.J. (eds) *Scotland Scanned: A Guide to Aviation in Scotland*, (4th edition), Central Scotland Aviation Group 1979. (First and second editions edited by A.R.Benzies, 1973 and 1975).

Willis, S., and Holliss, B., *Military Airfields in the British Isles 1939-1945: Part 1 A-E*, published by the authors: Newport Pagnell 1982.

Willis, S., and Holliss, B., *Military Airfields in the British Isles 1939-1945: Part 2 F-O*, published by the authors: Newport Pagnell 1982.

Willis, S., and Holliss, B., *Military Airfields in the British Isles 1939-1945: Part 3 P-Z*, published by the authors: Newport Pagnell 1983.

Periodicals

Aeromilitaria, Aeroplane, Aeroplane Monthly, Air-Britain Digest, Air-Britain News, Aircraft Illustrated, Air Enthusiast, Air Extra, Airfield Research Group Newsletter, Air Pictorial, Aviation News, British Military Aviation News, Control Column, Cross and Cockade, Flight, Flight International, Flypast (Merseyside Aviation Society), Humberside Aviation Review, Lincolnshire Life.

Right: **One of the earliest forms of purpose-built watch office was the 'fort' type, typified in this view of Digby's building which was demolished in 1976.** *(RAF Digby)*

PART THREE

MILITARY AIRFIELDS AND THE LINCOLNSHIRE LANDSCAPE

First World War Airfields

Lincolnshire

Second World War Airfields

Lincolnshire

RB

'Airfields have flayed it bare . . . .
Poor devastated Lincolnshire . . . . !'

(W. G. Hoskins, *The Making of the English Landscape*).

Anyone who has travelled widely in Lincolnshire will already appreciate the powerful impact which wartime airfields have made on the landscape. Until quite recently, however, this important ingredient of local scenery was almost totally ignored by historians and geographers and at the very best commanded a few dismissive lines, as the above quotation illustrates. Now that aviation archaeology has emerged as a respectable discipline, and the public are turning their attention both to the environment and events of the recent past, it seems appropriate to include a short account of how airfields have evolved agianst the backcloth of the county's natural features and in turn to assess what remains of the enormous legacy of aeronautical buildings which today add welcome variety to an otherwise essentially agricultural landscape. Airfields are undeniably part of Lincolnshire's built heritage and it is hoped that the following observations will be of some interest to conservationists, antiquarians and teachers as well as widening the horizons of the aviation enthusiast.

In all, Lincolnshire has played host to some seventy-seven military airfields, of which thirty-seven were in operation during the First World War and forty-nine during the Second World War. Nine stations saw service during both campaigns, which explains the apparent discrepancy when the two wartime totals are added together. During the First World War the county ranked only third in numerical terms, after Yorkshire (with fifty-three) and Kent (with forty-six), though it did manage to command as much as 8 per cent of all the United Kingdom's airfields (approximately 500 known sites). By contrast, at the end of the Second World War the county was clearly in top position, ahead of both Yorkshire (with forty-six) and Norfolk (with thirty-nine) but interestingly its share of the national total (over 800 by 1945) had slipped to below 6 per cent due to the much wider scatter of bases over the central and western regions of Britain (see maps pages 202, 203).

Turning to the distribution of airfields *within* the county, the most surprising feature has been its irregularity at every period and in particular during the Second World War. Although the Defence Departments have never revealed precisely how locations were chosen, one can reasonably assume that the principal deciding factors were landform, existing land uses and surface communications. To test this assumption we divided up the landscape of Lincolnshire on the basis of some three hundred 5 x 5 km grid squares in order to discern whether the airfields were in fact clustered in areas where particular geographical conditions prevailed.

Taking landform first, we discovered that the hilliest parts, notably the central Wolds, were indeed slightly under-subscribed with airfields during the Second World War, suggesting that unsuitable terrain can exist even within a county which rises no higher than 550 feet above sea level. More remarkable, though, was the RAF's obvious tendency during the Second World War to avoid the really low-lying areas, firmly dispelling the popular belief that airfields require the flattest land per se. To express this statistically, whereas about 40 per cent of Lincolnshire consists of fen and marsh, only twelve per cent of Second World War airfields stood in such terrain, most of these being the smaller grass type built close to coastal ranges. The terrain which attracted more than its fair share of airfields at that period was the slightly more elevated and gently undulating land where runways could best be drained, encampments sheltered and munitions dumps screened by more generous tree cover.

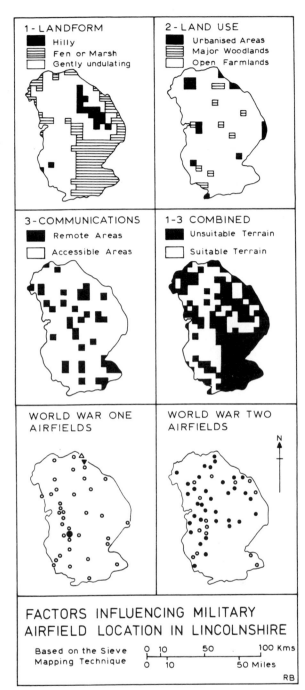

1 - LANDFORM
- Hilly
- Fen or Marsh
- Gently undulating

2 - LAND USE
- Urbanised Areas
- Major Woodlands
- Open Farmlands

3 - COMMUNICATIONS
- Remote Areas
- Accessible Areas

1 - 3 COMBINED
- Unsuitable Terrain
- Suitable Terrain

WORLD WAR ONE AIRFIELDS

WORLD WAR TWO AIRFIELDS

N

FACTORS INFLUENCING MILITARY AIRFIELD LOCATION IN LINCOLNSHIRE

Based on the Sieve Mapping Technique

0 10 50 100 Kms
0 10 50 Miles

RB

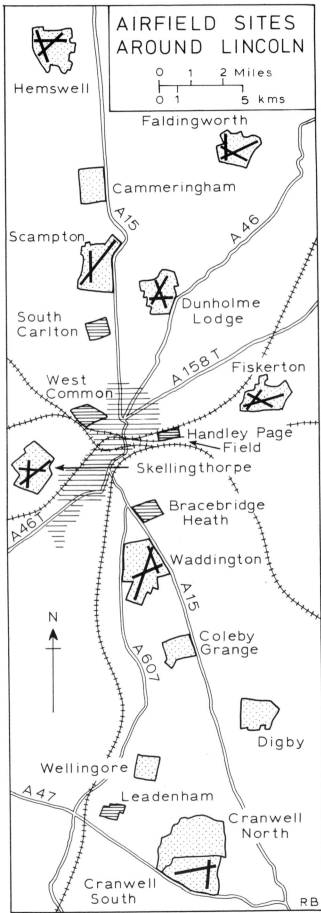

AIRFIELD SITES AROUND LINCOLN

0 1 2 Miles
0 1 5 kms

Hemswell

Faldingworth

Cammeringham

A15

A46

Scampton

Dunholme Lodge

South Carlton

A158 T

West Common

Fiskerton

Handley Page Field

Skellingthorpe

A46 T

Bracebridge Heath

N

Waddington

A15

Coleby Grange

A607

Digby

Wellingore

A47

Leadenham

Cranwell North

Cranwell South

RB

With regard to the pre-existing land use pattern, there were very few obstacles to airfield construction in Lincolnshire as some 90 per cent of the county was, and still is, open farmland. Neither woodland nor urban development was extensive enough to cause major gaps in the distribution, in fact the focal position of Lincoln does in part explain one of the principal airfield concentrations within the county. At the same time, the somewhat thinner distribution in the Scunthorpe area during the Second World War was probably a response to the unusual abundance of woodland in that distinctive corner of the county plus the heavy industry with its tall chimneys and resulting haze.

Surface communications by comparison exerted a considerable positive influence, especially with respect to bomber stations which required large quantities of sand, gravel and cement during construction and generated heavy traffic in equipment, supplies and personnel during their operational lives.

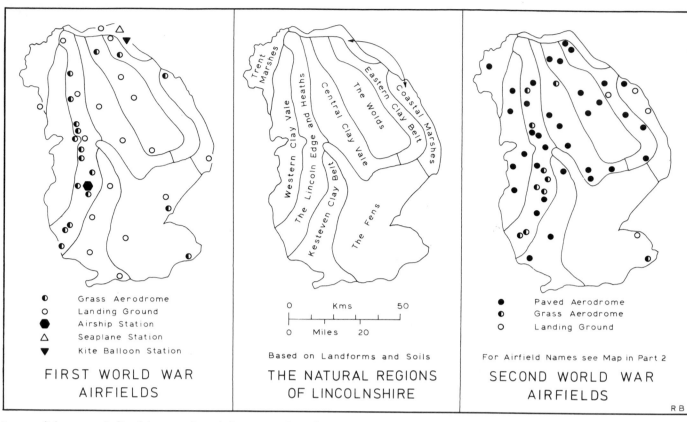

◐ Grass Aerodrome	
○ Landing Ground	
⬡ Airship Station	
△ Seaplane Station	
▼ Kite Balloon Station	

FIRST WORLD WAR
AIRFIELDS

Based on Landforms and Soils

THE NATURAL REGIONS
OF LINCOLNSHIRE

● Paved Aerodrome	
◐ Grass Aerodrome	
○ Landing Ground	

For Airfield Names see Map in Part 2

SECOND WORLD WAR
AIRFIELDS

R B

Inaccessible areas, defined here as those lying over 3 kms from both a class A road and a railway line, were confirmed by our test as having relatively few airfields during the Second World War, most of such terrain lying deep in the Wolds and Fenland sub-regions.

Overall, our analysis has proved that whereas only half the county was in theory ideal for airfield construction, i.e. gently undulating, lightly encumbered with settlements and woodlands and close to main communications, some three-quarters of all Second World War stations were actually compressed into such favourable terrain. Glancing back briefly to the First World War, the siting of airfields was then comparatively flexible, with a higher proportion of stations finding their way into both hilly and low-lying terrain and closer to main towns. Even so, there was still a positive correlation between airfields and the more favourable environments defined above.

Relating the two wartime distributions to natural sub-regions within the county, the most remarkable feature was of course the concentration on the western limestone escarpment of the Lincoln Edge. Whilst this belt of country represents only 14 per cent of the county's available land, it managed to command over 30 per cent of all airfields in each war period, clearly displaying the double advantage of well-drained plateau soils and dense communications radiating from Lincoln. At the opposite extreme, the Fens, which occupy as much as 25 per cent of the entire county, contained only 4 per cent of Second World War airfields (Holbeach Range and Sutton Bridge) and as little as 10 per cent (four landing grounds) in the First World War. Interestingly, the various clay vales, which occupy 40 per cent of the county, were markedly under-subscribed during the First World War for reasons of heavy soils, whereas by the end of the Second World War these had managed to acquire more than their fair share of airfields, thanks to the introduction of the concrete runway.

Concerning the spacing of airfields, the average distance between those in Lincolnshire in 1945 was just on 7.5 miles (12 km). Expressed as density, this was somewhat lower than elsewhere in the eastern counties due to their sparseness in the Fens. But if the former county of Holland is excluded, and fresh calculations made just for Kesteven and Lindsey, the average spacing then comes down to 7 miles which represented one of the highest wartime densities in Britain. Along the Lincoln Edge the spacing at the end of the Second World War was as little as 5 miles and even closer in the immediate vicinity of Lincoln. Dunholme Lodge, for example, stood barely one mile from Scampton, though why it was built so close is not altogether clear.

To fully understand the detailed impact of airfields on the landscape it is important to examine their individual dimensions. In the First World War all stations were grass-based and quite small by modern standards, except for the Cranwell complex which from its inception covered over 2,500 acres (1,000 ha). At the opposite end of the scale the Kite Balloon Base at Immingham measured a mere 26 acres (11 ha) and the average size for all thirty-seven airfields in the county worked out at only 167 acres (68 ha) even taking Cranwell into account. Between these extremes, the various training aerodromes averaged out at about 250 acres (100 ha) while the Aircraft Acceptance Parks, Naval Patrol Aerodromes and Home Defence Flight Stations were mostly in the order of 100 acres (40 ha) as illustrated by Buckminster and Elsham. Landing grounds had a mean size of only 56 acres (23 ha), some of them covering as little as 30 acres.

With regard to shape, all these early airfields were created by the simple device of amalgamating a few agricultural fields which resulted in more or less rectangular, or occasionally L-shaped configurations. Where numerous buildings were needed these were placed in regimented lines in one corner, or along

one side of the field, as the map of Buckminster also exemplifies. The only major discordant structure was the airship shed at Cranwell North which had to be oriented NE - SW to match the prevailing wind.

Throughout the Expansion Period, airfields remained all-grass, broadly rectangular in outline and, with the exception of Cranwell, no larger than 400 acres (160 ha). The main innovation during this phase was the construction of vastly superior technical and domestic accommodation with long-term RAF occupation in mind. Dominating the technical sites were 'C' type hangars built in crescentic lines as typified by the group which is visible from the A631 road at Hemswell. This particular group displays the 300-foot long type with twelve transverse roof sections and is repeated at Scampton and Waddington. Shorter variants with only eight sections also appeared in the landscape at Digby, Kirton in Lindsey and Manby to accommodate fighter and trainer aircraft. 'C' type hangars were stoutly constructed on steel frames in red brick and elaborate glass skylighting reminiscent of railway architecture. Further characteristics were the painting of camouflage patterns on the brickwork and the planting of trees to soften their impact on the countryside.

The layout of the new administrative, communal and residential sites was strongly influenced by the Garden City principles which were widely applied in public building at that time, being manifest in tasteful Georgian proportions, dignified approach roads, spacious lawns and generous landscaping in keeping with an expanding professional Air Force. A new style of encased water tower, exemplified at Manby, heralded a more

Above: **The stout steel framework of the 'C' type hangar is well shown at Digby in 1936.** (*B.Rear via M.Hodgson*)

Left: **Manby's encased water tower is a prominent feature of the expansion period station.** (*W.J.Taylor*)

207

Above: **Waddington's 'villa' type of watch office in 1947.** *(IWM MH4181)*

Left: **Typical of the 'austerity' watch office is this example at Wickenby, now used as a clubhouse by the resident flying club.** *(W.J.Taylor)*

Right: **Of the dispersed accommodation sites at Metheringham, the closest to the airfield were the sick quarters (bottom left) and the administration site.** *(W.J.Taylor)*

modernistic type of architecture which co-existed successfully with more traditionally designed buildings.

Mention must be made at this juncture of the first generation of control towers (or 'watch offices'). The earliest type, originating at the beginning of the expansion were of the 'double-box' or 'fort' design which have now been largely superseded (see M.J.F. Bowyer's *Action Stations 1* and B.B. Halpenny's *Action Stations 2*). By the late 1930s a much more modern style was introduced which, for want of official nomenclature, may be termed 'villa' type, in view of its external appearance. Examples can be found at Waddington, Coningsby and Kirton in Lindsey, recognisable by curved corner windows at the front, a balcony over a projecting ground floor, internal staircases and small circular windows at the side — all quite evocative of the period. An example of this design outside Lincolnshire appears in B.B. Halpenny's *Action Stations 2*, page 19. This cubist functionalism continued to characterise wartime towers but austerity caused many modifications in window shapes and superficial detailing, most notably external staircases, cantilevered balconies and sparser balcony rails.

It was during the Second World War, however, that the most fundamental changes in layout took place, namely the introduction of paved runway systems required for heavy bomber aircraft. In most cases three runways were laid out at approximately sixty degrees to one another, the longest ideally oriented NE - SW in order to minimise the likelihood of cross winds interrupting take-offs and landings. The average length of a main runway by 1945 was 2,000 yards (1.9 km), with the two subsidiaries averaging out at 1,400 yards (1.3 km) and 1,200 yards (1.1 km) respectively. In some cases the main runway had to be extended slightly to cope with increased bomb loads as the war progressed, as our plans of Elsham Wolds, Skellingthorpe and Spilsby reveal. The last named airfield also had one of its original subsidiary runways extended *after* the war for possible use by heavy jets.

Runways were of a standard width of about 150 feet (45 m) and linked one to another at their ends by a 50-foot (15 m) wide perimeter track onto which were appended the aircraft dispersal bays, loops connecting hangars and access roads leading to technical buildings, bomb stores and the local road network. As the war progressed, the 'frying pan' type of dispersal (see Elsham Wolds) was gradually superseded by the more efficient 'spectacles' design (see Kelstern). The total length of a perimeter track and its various appendages was more than three times that of the three runways combined, but because the former were smaller in width, they covered approximately the same area as the runways — a little more than 50 acres (20 ha). The total area under concrete at a typical wartime bomber station was therefore well in excess of 100 acres (40 ha), compared with that at grass-based stations where the perimeter tracks and dispersals rarely exceeded 50 acres. After the war eight Lincolnshire stations had their main runway extended to cope with jet aircraft, some up to 3,000 yards (2.8 km) as at Scampton, Waddington and East Kirkby. The combined area sterilised by concrete at Lincolnshire's thirty-five paved-runway and twelve mainly grass airfields in the Second World War can be calculated with reasonable accuracy to approximately 4,000 acres (1,600 ha).

Equally radical during the Second World War were changes in the layout of technical and residential sites. The enormous increase in operational flying and personnel made it advisable to disperse living accommodation well clear of the airfield itself in order to minimise fatalities in the event of air raids, crashes or explosions. Dispersion was normally achieved by building hutments in the corners of nearby fields where trees and hedgerows offered natural protection and, in ideal circumstances, on land sloping away from the airfield towards a local stream. Dips in the land surface helped reduce the impact of engine noise on air crews, who were often short of sleep, and also assisted the gravitation of effluents for which most stations had a

Above: **A steeply pitched roof typifies the MAP B1 hangar. This example at Coningsby now houses the Battle of Britain Memorial Flight. Note the modern office and domestic accommodation built on the side of the hangar.** (*RAF Coningsby*)

purpose-built treatment works at the lowest (and usually remotest) point in the complex. Encampments were best distributed where the density of local roads was greatest and a railway station not too far away, which in practice meant that they frequently stood on the doorsteps of a village (see plan of Spilsby). At bomber stations there were normally about a dozen dispersed sites, including not only airmen's quarters, but administrative, social, medical and WAAF accommodation too.

Hangars and technical sites at Second World War-built airfields were similarly dispersed, though the main site normally lay on the side closest to the residential accommodation for reasons of accessibility by foot and bicycle. Bomber hangars of this vintage were mostly of the transportable 'T2' type, which were distinguished by their low roof pitch, corrugated iron cladding and often black paintwork, though examples of the earlier, smaller and more steeply pitched 'B1' Type design are still to be seen at Bardney, Barkston Heath, Spilsby and Strubby. An example of the much rarer 'J/K' type with an arched roof is to be found at Goxhill. At temporary fighter stations the 'blister' hangar predominated based on an arched framework with no separable roof or walls as such.

Finally, at the bomber stations the side remotest from the camps normally contained the munitions dumps which would frequently be sited within an existing wood to provide camouflage, and also on falling land so as to further deflect blasts up and away from the populated zones of the airfield. As the plans of Elsham Wolds, Kelstern and Skellingthorpe further illustrate, the layouts were arranged so that runway approaches rarely passed over any of the residential, technical or munitions sites. The effect of dispersing the various functions during wartime was to create extremely jagged airfield boundaries.

With regard to land requirements, the average size of an airfield in Lincolnshire in 1945 was 615 acres (250 ha). Paved stations averaged out at 665 acres (270 ha), of which about 50 acres (20 ha) was under dispersed camps, while grass stations averaged out at a little less than 400 acres (160 ha) including camps which were not usually very substantial. The bomber stations chosen for illustration in this volume were by coincidence rather on the large side, e.g. Skellingthorpe which covered 788 acres (320 ha), while Caistor's 310 acres (125 ha) was a little below the average for the grass type. The largest airfield in wartime, other than Cranwell, was Kelstern (over 900 acres or 360 ha), while the smallest were the landing grounds at Theddlethorpe and Holbeach which each covered about 150 acres (60 ha).

Since the war the most strategically important stations have had their main runways and domestic areas expanded, bringing the average size of the seven current operational stations to 910 acres (364 ha). Some idea of how RAF aerodromes have evolved in layout and size can be gained from the accompanying map of Scampton's evolution. Waddington and Binbrook both exceed 1,000 acres (400 ha) today, while Scampton and Coningsby are not far short of that acreage. Taking all current stations into consideration (including pre-war 'fossils' such as Digby, Kirton in Lindsey and Spitalgate), the average size of a Lincolnshire airfield today works out at 770 acres (310 ha), almost five times that in 1918.

Added together, the 77 military airfields in the study have since 1914 occupied some 33,000 acres (13,200 ha), though not of course simultaneously. During the First World War the area taken up was as little as 6,350 acres (2,540 ha), more than a third of this being at Cranwell alone. By contrast, at the climax of the Second World War the corresponding figure was 29,000 acres (11,735 ha), some 26,000 acres having been absorbed over the ten-year period starting with the Expansion. In 1945 almost 2 per cent of Lincolnshire lay under RAF airfields, a quite remarkable figure when one considers that only 5 per cent of the county today is occupied by towns, villages and minor settlements and a similarly small proportion by rural phenomena such as woodlands, dunes, quarries, and golf courses combined.

In view of Lincolnshire's predominantly fertile soils, the construction of airfields has naturally taken a significant toll on agriculture. Some 45 per cent of the county's farmland (including acres 'borrowed' by the RAF) is classed by the Ministry of Agriculture as either Grade 1 or Grade 2 (very fertile) and almost all of the remainder falls within Grade 3 (good average quality by national standards). During the first World War the county's airfields showed a definite bias towards the high grade soils, due mainly to their concentration on the limestone escarpment and scatter along the coast and across the Fens. This association did not, however, cause serious long-term losses of production because airfields were mostly small and lacking in permanent buildings and foundations.

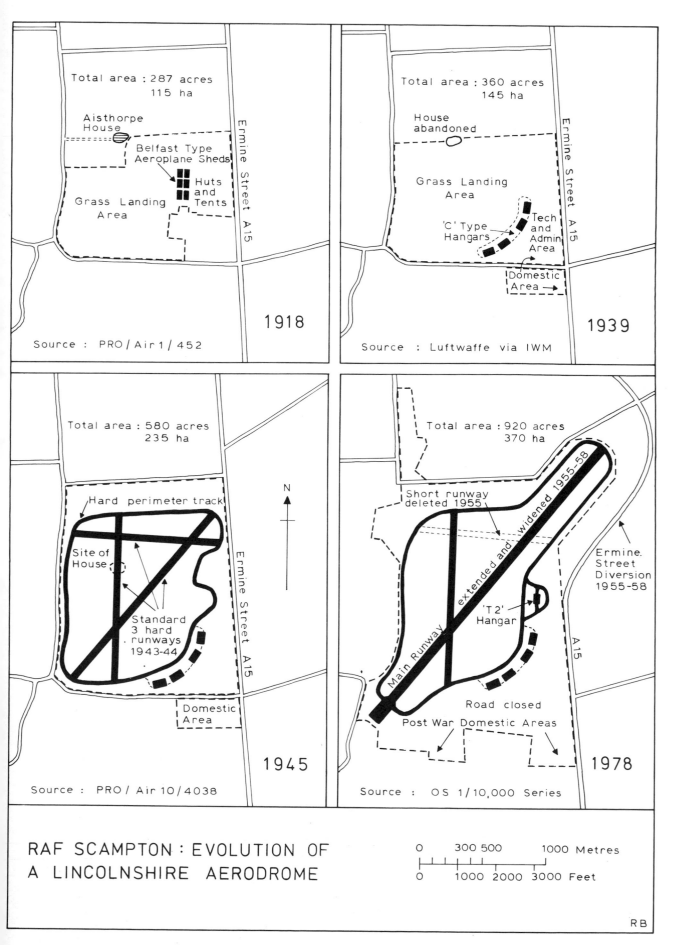

Total area : 287 acres
115 ha

Aisthorpe House

Belfast Type Aeroplane Sheds

Huts and Tents

Grass Landing Area

Ermine Street A15

1918

Source : PRO/Air1/452

Total area : 360 acres
145 ha

House abandoned

Grass Landing Area

'C' Type Hangars

Tech and Admin Area

Domestic Area

Ermine Street A15

1939

Source : Luftwaffe via IWM

Total area : 580 acres
235 ha

N

Hard perimeter track

Site of House

Standard 3 hard runways 1943-44

Ermine Street A15

Domestic Area

1945

Source : PRO/ Air 10/4038

Total area : 920 acres
370 ha

Short runway deleted 1955

extended and widened 1955-58

Ermine Street Diversion 1955-58

A15

'T 2' Hangar

Main Runway

Road closed

Post War Domestic Areas

1978

Source : OS 1/10,000 Series

RAF SCAMPTON : EVOLUTION OF A LINCOLNSHIRE AERODROME

0   300 500   1000 Metres

0   1000 2000 3000 Feet

RB

Above: The large grassed areas between the runways of a military airfield are a prolific source of forage, as exemplified by this scene at Manby in 1980. *(W.J.Taylor)*

Bottom: The massive concrete structure of a Thor missile launch pad at Bardney. Note the broiler houses built on the disused runways. *(W.J.Taylor)*

With the 1935-39 Expansion, however, the RAF began once more to consume significant tracts of high-quality farmland, e.g. at Hemswell, Kirton in Lindsey and Scampton. Although during the Second World War the majority of stations were located on the heavier (Grade 3) soils, by 1945 the 29,000 acres under all airfields were almost entirely at the expense of high-yielding grain and root crops. Since 1945 the pattern has reverted to one in which Service airfields occupy more than their fair share of the county's best soils, confirming the common suspicion that the needs of agriculture has never been an overriding consideration in defence planning. Although the avoidance of the Fens in the Second World War may appear to contradict this, the real obstacles there were practical rather than conservationist, namely the dykes and poor communications.

Although the fifteen airfields still in Crown ownership today occupy some 11,500 acres (4,600 ha), not all this land is necessarily lost to agriculture. Significant parts of the non-operational stations are grazed, or ploughed where not required for gliding, and even at operational stations some of the outermost fields are let to farmers. These savings are, however, offset to a large extent by considerable dereliction which persists at the many airfields long since relinquished. In the absence of official records, it has been estimated that something in the order of 10,000 acres (4,000 ha) of farmland still lie out of production on account of current military and semi-derelict defunct airfields in Lincolnshire.

In the opinion of farmers, the legacy of the RAF has been a mixed blessing. On the positive side it has certainly produced a system of large, hedgeless fields which conform to the post-war trend towards more efficient arable cultivation. Concrete surfaces have provided fast access roads and bases for storing produce such as hay and beet, while old water tanks have been adopted for farm purposes and certain buildings used for sheltering livestock, fertilizers and implements. Factory farming in particular has benefitted from large expanses of concrete e.g. at Bardney, East Kirkby and North Killingholme. On the negative side, natural field drainage has often been impeded by concrete and rubble and soils permanently impoverished even where the concrete has been lifted. Soil erosion has been unwittingly encouraged by the open environment and new fencing is very expensive to install. Around the peripheries the decaying hutments can be a hazard to wandering livestock and often attract vermin following the illicit dumping of domestic refuse.

Why so much land should have remained idle for so long requires lengthy explanation. To cut a long story short, up to the late 1950s the Air Ministry had retained control over virtually all Lincolnshire's airfields, even though more than half of them had no flying role after 1945. Vacant stations were wisely let to local farmers within a couple of years, but only on the understanding that concrete areas and buildings were not interfered with. In most cases the Air Ministry did not bother to maintain these installations and at a number of airfields the long-term problem of dereliction was exacerbated by the construction of short-lived missile pens in very deep concrete.

By the early 'sixties it was becoming apparent both to the Air Ministry and prospective purchasers that airfield structures had certain non-agricultural possibilities, with the result that enthusiasm for complete restoration began to wane. When surplus stations at last came onto the market in significant numbers, and were not required by other statutory bodies, they were either offered to previous owners at favourable prices in recompense for lost production, or auctioned off in such a way that market forces would decide the fate of their defunct structures. In either case the stations survived the disposal process intact and there is no airfield on record where the Crown has carried out full-scale demolition *before* relinquishing the land. In many instances the buildings were auctioned off independently for scrap metal, leaving unsightly shells, basements and rubble quite unsuitable for either arable or livestock farming. Although farmers have often successfully improvised around these obstacles, parish councils, planning authorities and amenity organisations have been less happy about the way the Service Departments have conducted land disposal.

Inevitably it has been left to private enterprise to carry out concerted programmes of demolition and restoration. During the urban construction boom of the 'sixties many farmers were able to sell off their concrete wastes to contractors who would not only carry out demolition but also pay for the material into the bargain. The normal practice of firms has been to crack up the concrete with a steel ball suspended from a crane, to scrape it up mechanically and then feed it through a crusher and grader ready for transport by lorry to construction projects elsewhere. For such exercises to be economically worthwhile it has usually been necessary for the building activity to occur within a few miles of a defunct airfield, though in 1973 material from Sturgate, near Gainsborough, was destined for a new by-pass road at Louth, some thirty miles away. In ideal circumstances up to a 100 acres (40 ha) can be lifted from one ex-bomber airfield, though in practice many bits have been left in place for continued farm use, airstrips or as replacements for pre-war highways.

In most cases the dispersal bays have been the first to go since their removal has given immediate benefits to farmers in the form of more sensibly shaped fields. Next have usually been the runways, often reduced to 15-feet (5 m) farm roads, then finally the perimeter tracks unless farmers have chosen to retain them as accesses and storage bases. The most fully cleared airfields are now at Kelstern and Metheringham, whereas at Blyton, Elsham Wolds and Wickenby substantial expanses of concrete remain intact. Two factors which have acted against comprehensive demolition have been an oscillating demand by the construction industry, especially in the recent recession, and the unwillingness of certain land owners to part with concrete at low prices while docks and motorway links promise to enhance its value in the near future. To date, something between a half and two-thirds of all the concrete on relinquished stations has been lifted in the manner described above.

Unfortunately the winning of hardcore has done little to solve the persistent problem of unsightly hutments and entangled undergrowth. Recognising this fact, the former Lindsey County Council proposed in 1969 to tackle outstanding dereliction on a selective basis by directing its limited reclamation budget to those airfields which lay either within areas of natural beauty or adjacent to busy roads. Only six airfields — Blyton, Cammeringham, Kelstern, Ludford Magna, East Kirkby and Spilsby — figured in this scheme and, although some clearances have subsequently been effected, the published programme is as yet

Below: **The broken remains of the main runway at Spilsby being collected for crushing and grading in late 1974.** *(W.J.Taylor)*

Bottom: **Tangled undergrowth and derelict huts such as this at Faldingworth have done little to prompt concerted programmes of demolition and restoration.** *(W.J.Taylor)*

not complete. At Blyton a thoughtful tree planting scheme has been carried out by the Highways Authority on dispersed camps as part of a straightening of the A159 road which passes between the sites. Finally on the subject of trees, the Forestry Commission has over the last twenty years established extensive plantations between the runways at North Witham (South Kesteven) and has also planted up peripheral sites at Bardney and Folkingham. From the visual point of view both natural regeneration and planned introductions of trees have done a great deal to hide the less pleasant remains of camps and dumps as well as providing cover for the wildlife that has been eradicated from the now hedgeless parts of airfields.

Early hopes that airfields would eventually revert wholly to their previous rural appearance have clearly not materialised in view of the radical alteration to traditional field patterns and road alignments. On top of this, a remarkable range of alternative uses have latterly established themselves, most of which would not have occurred in a rural setting had the airfields never existed. These added intrusions have often caused more controversy than the airfields themselves because they are seen as preventable and a flouting of normal planning controls. At the same time it is more sensible to encourage the re-use of land than accept persistent dereliction and many enterprises have helped to revive and diversify the rural economy. Most of the more obvious activities have been mentioned in Part Two but there are some recurrent themes which unite what might at first appear a rather random and incidental facet of airfield evolution. It is probably best to consider the main types of installation and observe which kinds of novel use have tended to colonise each one.

Taking runway systems first, the wide expanses of concrete have not only provided ideal foundations for broiler houses, but also a skid-pan for training police drivers at Hibaldstow, a test track for heavy vehicles at Elsham Wolds and temporary go-kart circuits at Blyton, Goxhill and Waltham (Grimsby) — all activities which require plenty of room for error. Some readers may also recall that in the early 'fifties the BRM racing car was tested at Folkingham. Much more recently, Blyton and Hibaldstow airfields have been used for Sunday markets, the obvious attraction being the ample display and parking facilities (one runway will accommodate well over 3,000 motor cars). L-drivers have been a familiar sight on old airfields, negotiating the pot holes, rubble and oil drums that usually litter the concrete. At Sandtoft, part of a runway is used in the cooling process of tiles and drainpipes — a rare example of open-air manufacturing use on an airfield.

The next most obvious re-usable structures are the hangars. The 'B1' and 'T2' types, many of which have now been dismantled, are used almost exclusively for storing bulky produce such as potatoes, e.g. at East Kirkby and Sutton Bridge, or seeds as at Waltham. At Goxhill and North Killingholme the government have retained hangars for storing various strategic commodities, but these buildings are increasingly being sought by, and let to, haulage firms based at Immingham Dock. The older 'C' type hangars have yet to be sold off by the Crown, though those at Hemswell and Manby have been suggested as suitable nuclei for a regional sports centre. At both these air-

fields the hangars are currently serving as grain stores under the EEC agricultural intervention scheme. In general, hangars have limited value for manufacturing industry because of partitioning and heating costs.

With regard to smaller brick buildings, many light industrial concerns have occupied these, such as a saw-mill at Metheringham, a joinery works at Waltham and crop-spray preparation at Sturgate. At Sandtoft a variety of firms comprise what now amounts to a small, scattered industrial estate. At Sturgate the old bomb stores have been used to screen a car-breaking yard. From 1973-74 Hemswell and Faldingworth provided emergency accommodation for Asian refugees from Uganda, the latter airfield also having been suggested as a possible prison site. Since the re-organisation of local government in 1974 the pre-war HQ buildings at recently-closed RAF Manby have been taken over as offices for East Lindsey District Council, the old parade

Left: **One of the remaining hangars at Grimsby (Waltham) has been converted into a treatment plant for seeds.** *(W.J.Taylor)*

Below left: **Airfields and hangars are popular with haulage contractors as they provide plenty of space for warehousing and parking; this is North Killingholme in 1980.** *(W.J.Taylor)*

Above: **The former station headquarters and Tedder Hall make excellent offices for East Lindsey District Council; the parade ground offers ample parking space.** *(R.N.E.Blake)*

Below: **Land yachting at Strubby, an unusual recreation encouraged by the spaces of a disused airfield.** *(W.J.Taylor)*

ground serving as an excellent staff car park. Lastly, several control towers have been converted for accommodation, e.g. private dwellings at Elsham Wolds, Hibaldstow and Sandtoft, offices for Eastwoods poultry farm at East Kirkby, and club houses for light aviation groups at Bardney and Wickenby.

Other significant uses have had less to do with airfield structures as such and have occurred mainly because large tracts of land have come onto the market all at once. Only one Second World War airfield, Skellingthorpe, has been substantially consumed by urban expansion (the Birchwood Estate), though Harlaxton has been disfigured by large-scale quarrying. Waltham has been sliced by the A16 Trunk Road which now by-passes the village of Holton-le-Clay, Elsham Wolds is now bisected by a new road link to the Humber Bridge, while Sandtoft is now crossed by the line of the new M180 Motorway. North Coates, should it become surplus could well interest the Central Electricity Board as a possible site for a power station. Finally, at Elsham Wolds the Water Authority has recently constructed a new reservoir and treatment plant, which presumably must be sited on elevated ground.

Having surveyed this diversity of after-uses two things are apparent. First, on the demand side, we can see that a very wide range of activities have been swift to fill the vacuum left by the RAF. All the main sectors of human endeavour, from industry and commerce to sport and recreation have been represented and the range seems to be widening. Second on the supply side, airfields offer a number of unique opportunities for activities which would be either impractical or unacceptable in urban areas. Land yachting, for example, would not have been possible in Lincolnshire had the smooth and wind-swept runways at Manby and Strubby not been available. Major local authority schemes have clearly been assisted by the acquisition of government land on favourable terms, while many under-capitalised ventures, of which the tram museum at Sandtoft is a perfect example, have benefitted from residual tracts of concrete. Vacant airfields offer expansiveness, hard surfaces for storage and parking, cheap buildings, not to mention relative remoteness from easily offended communities. They are perhaps the most flexible and versatile environmental resource we have in this crowded island of ours.

This, then, is how wartime airfields have altered over the last sixty-five years and how Lincolnshire's countryside has shaped up under their influence, particularly since 1945. It is quite obvious that they will never completely disappear from the landscape and all the trends suggest that they will come under increasing pressures from North Sea exploration, Common Market trade, modern agricultural practices and a variety of public works. Furthermore, the advent of alternative technologies, which may include solar and wind power, craft-based industries and self-sufficient farming, seems very likely to enhance their potential for positive use. These trends should be borne in mind by local authorities and amenity societies who up to now have tended to resist novel re-developments even though existing planning procedures have failed to bring about restoration. And in conclusion, the time has surely arrived when some of the buildings should be singled out for statutory protection as industrial monuments, and every airfield certainly deserves to be commemorated by at least a small plaque explaining its role, affiliation and period of service. It is hoped that this review will have done something to promote a more realistic attitude towards the planning and conservation of old airfields, which are unquestionably historic landscapes in their own right.

References

After the Battle Magazine, *Airfields of the Eighth: Then and Now,* (text by Freeman, R., designed and edited by Ramsey, W.G.,) Battle of Britain Prints International Ltd, London, 1978.

Blake, R.N.E.,'The Impact of Airfields on the British Landscape' *Geographical Journal,* Volume 135, December, 1969.

Blake, R.N.E., *Disused Airfields as a Planning Resource,* Trent Papers in Planning No 78/8, Trent Polytechnic, Nottingham, 1978.

Bowyer, M.J.F., *Action Stations 1: Wartime Military Airfields of East Anglia 1939-45,* Patrick Stephens, Cambridge, 1979.

Conolly, W.P., *British Railways Pre-Grouping Atlas and Gazetteer,* Ian Allan Ltd., 1966.

Edwards, K.C.,'Changing Geographical Patterns in Lincolnshire', *Geography,* Volume 39, 1954.

Edwards, K.C., 'Lincolnshire', Chapter 17 in Mitchell, J.B. (ed) *Great Britain: Geographical Essays,* Cambridge University Press 1962.

Halpenny, B.B., *Action Stations 2: Military Airfields of Lincolnshire and the East Midlands,* Patrick Stephens, Cambridge, 1981.

Institution of Civil Engineers, *The Civil Engineer at War: Volume 1* (collected essays, including one on airfield construction), ICE, 1948.

Kohan, C.M., *History of the Second World War: Works and Buildings,* HMSO/Longmans Green, 1952.

Lindsey County Planning Department, *Dereliction in Lindsey: A Programme for Restoration,* Lindsey County Council, 1969.

Lincolnshire County Planning Department, *Lincolnshire Structure Plan:* Papers on *Agriculture* and *Leisure, Landscape and Buildings,* Lincolnshire County Council, 1976.

Linton, D.L., 'The Landforms of Lincolnshire' *Geography,* Volume 39, 1954.

Miller, T., 'Military Airfields and Rural Planning', *Town Planning Review,* Volume 44, 1973.

Ministry of Agriculture, Fisheries and Food, *Agricultural Land Classification of England and Wales,* (series of one-inch maps, 1966 -).

Ministry of Defence, *Report of the Defence Lands Committee 1971-73,* (The Nugent Report), HMSO, 1973.

National Parks Commission, *The Coasts of Yorkshire and Lincolnshire,* HMSO, 1968.

Newton, D.E., 'Clearance of concrete from disused airfields', *Journal of the Town Planning Institute,* Vol 46, June 1960, pp 269-70.

Robertson, B., *Aviation Archaeology: A Collector's Guide to Aeronautical Relics,* Patrick Stephens, Cambridge, 1977.

Smith, D.J., 'Wartime Towers', *Aviation News,* Vol 4, No 18, 6-19 February 1976.

Smith, D.J., 'Airfields: some developments since World War I', *Aviation News,* Vol 5 No 11, 29 October - 11 November 1976, pp 10-11.

Smith, D.J., 'Island airfield: the development of airfields during World War II'. *Aviation News,* Vol 8, No 6, 17 - 30 August 1979, pp 4-5.

Smith, G.I., *The Land of Britain: Part 69 — Lincolnshire (Parts of Holland),* Geographical Publications Ltd, 1937.

Soil Survey, *1/1,000,000 Soils Map of England and Wales,* Ordnance Survey: Southampton, 1974.

Stamp, L.D., et al, *The Land of Britain: Parts 76 and 77 — Lincolnshire (Parts of Kesteven and Lindsey),* Geographical Publications Ltd., 1942.

Special Acknowledgements

Lincolnshire County Planning Department, Lincoln City Planning Department, East Lindsey District Planning Department, West Lindsey District Planning Department, North Kesteven District Planning Department, South Kesteven District Planning Department, South Holland District Planning Department, Cleethorpes Borough Planning Department, Glanford District Planning Department, Forestry Commision (Lincoln Office), Council for Small Industries in Rural Areas (Salisbury), Nature Conservancy Council (Grantham Office), W & J B Eastwood Ltd.

Right: **Cranwell-based Vampire FB(T)9s, WX221 (4), WX225 (8), WX215 (12) and WR264 (29) formate almost by tradition over the College Hall in mid-1957.** *(Flight 34974s)*

PART FOUR   APPENDICES

APPENDIX A
Location Details of Main Airfields

No.	Name(s)	Ordnance Survey Sheet Numbers:			Grid Ref:	Administrative Areas:		
		1:63 000 (One Inch)	1:50 000	1:25 000 Six-Inch & 1:10 000	Centre to nearest 100m	Old District (up to April 1974)	New District (from April 1974)	Town or Parishes
1	Anwick	113	121	TF 15 SW	110 515	East Kesteven RD	North Kesteven	Anwick
2	Bardney	113	121	TF 17 SW	140 710	Welton RD Horncastle RD	West Lindsey East Lindsey	Bardney Tupholme
3	Barkston Heath	113, 123	130	SK 94 SE	970 415	West Kesteven RD	South Kesteven	Barkston Ancaster
4	Binbrook	105	113	TA 19 NE	190 960	Caistor RD	West Lindsey	Strainton Le Vale Thorganby
5	Blyborough	104	112	SK 99 SE	953 937	Gainsborough RD	West Lindsey	Blyborough
6	Blyton	104	112	SK 89 NE	870 955	Gainsborough RD	West Lindsey	Blyton Laughton
7	Boston (Wyberton Fen)	114	131	TF 24 SE	297 437	Boston RD	Boston	Wyberton
8	Bracebridge Heath	113	121	SK 96 NE	986 673	North Kesteven RD	North Kesteven	Bracebridge Heath Canwick
9	Braceby	113, 123	130	TF 03 NW	016 358	West Kesteven RD	South Kesteven	Braceby and Sapperton
10	Buckminster	122	130	SK 82 SE	895 235	West Kesteven RD	South Kesteven	Colsterworth
11	Bucknall	113	121	TF 17 SE	170 705	Horncastle RD	East Lindsey	Waddingworth
12	Caistor	104	112	TA 00 SE	085 020	Caistor RD	West Lindsey	North Kelsey
13	Cammeringham/ Ingham	104	121	SK 98 SE	965 840	Welton RD	West Lindsey	Ingham
14	Cleethorpes Beach	105	113	TA 30 NW	320 080	Cleethorpes MB	Cleethorpes	Cleethorpes
15	Cockthorne	104	121	TF 08 NE	075 875	Caistor RD	West Lindsey	Middle Rasen
16	Coleby Grange	113	121	TF 06 SW	005 605	North Kesteven RD	North Kesteven	Coleby Boothby Graffoe Metheringham
17	Coningsby	114	122	TF 25 NW	225 565	Horncastle RD	East Lindsey	Coningsby
18	Cranwell North	113	121	TF 05 SW	010 510	East Kesteven RD	North Kesteven	Cranwell and Byards Leap North Rauceby
19	Cranwell South	113	130	TF 04 NW	015 490	East Kesteven RD	North Kesteven	Cranwell and Byards Leap North Rauceby
20	Crowland/Postland	123	131	TF 21 SE	255 140	Spalding RD	South Holland	Weston
21	Cuxwold	105	113	TA 10 SE	185 010	Caistor RD	West Lindsey	Swallow
22	Digby/Scopwick	113	121	TF 05 NW	045 570	East Kesteven RD	North Kesteven	Scopwick Ashby de la Launde and Bloxholm
23	Donna Nook	105	113	TF 49 NW	430 985	Louth RD	East Lindsey	North Somercotes
24	Dunholme Lodge	104	121	SK 97 NE TF 07 NW	000 785	Welton RD	West Lindsey	Dunholme Grange de Lings

No.	Name(s)	Ordnance Survey Sheet Numbers:			Grid Ref:	Administrative Areas:		
		1:63 000 (One Inch)	1:50 000	1:25 000 Six-Inch & 1:10 000	Centre to nearest 100m	Old District (up to April 1974)	New District (from April 1974)	Town or Parishes
25	East Kirkby	114	122	TF 36 SW	345 615	Spilsby RD	East Lindsey	East Kirkby Hagnaby West Keal
26	Elsham	104	112	TA 01 SE	055 138	Glanford Brigg RD	Glanford	Elsham
27	Elsham Wolds	104	112	TA 01 SW	045 135	Glanford Brigg RD	Glanford	Elsham
28	Faldingworth	104	112, 121	TF 08 NW	035 855	Caistor RD	West Lindsey	Toft Newton
						Welton RD	West Lindsey	Faldingworth Spridlington
29	Fiskerton	113	121	TF 07 SW TF 07 SE	045 730	Welton RD	West Lindsey	Fiskerton Reepham
30	Folkingham	113, 123	130	TF 03 SW	050 305	West Kesteven RD	South Kesteven	Lenton-Keisby and Osgodby
						South Kesteven RD	South Kesteven	Aslackby and Laughton
31	Freiston	114, 124	131	TF 34 SE	388 408	Boston RD	Boston	Freiston
32	Fulbeck	113	121	SK 85 SE SK 95 SW	900 510	North Kesteven RD	North Kesteven	Leadenham
						West Kesteven RD	South Kesteven	Fenton Fulbeck Caythorpe
33	Gainsborough	104	112, 121	SK 88 NW	812 888	East Retford RD (Notts)	Bassetlaw (Notts)	Saundby
34	Gosberton	123	130	TF 12 NE	167 297	Spalding RD	South Holland	Gosberton
35	Goxhill	99	113	TA 12 SW	115 215	Glanford Brigg RD	Glanford	Goxhill
36	Greenland Top	105	113	TA 11 SE	180 120	Grimsby RD	Cleethorpes	Stallingborough
37	Grimsby/Waltham	105	113	TA 20 SE	280 025	Grimsby RD	Cleethorpes	Waltham
						Louth RD	East Lindsey	Holton-Le-Clay
38	Harlaxton	113, 122	130	SK 93 SW SK 83 SE	905 325	West Kesteven RD	South Kesteven	Harlaxton Little Ponton and Stroxton
39	Hemswell/ Harpswell	104	112	SK 99 SW SK 99 SE SK 98 NW	940 905	Gainsborough RD	West Lindsey	Hemswell Harpswell
40	Hibaldstow	104	112	SE 90 SE	985 010	Glanford Brigg RD	Glanford	Hibaldstow Redbourne
41	Holbeach Range	124	131	TF 43 SW	438 325	East Elloe RD	South Holland	Gedney
42	Holbeach St John/ Fenland	123	131	TF 31 NW	333 175	East Elloe RD	South Holland	Crowland
43	Immingham	105	113	TA 11 NE	198 155	Grimsby RD	Cleethorpes	Immingham
44	Kelstern (1)	105	113	TF 29 SW	246 909	Louth RD	East Lindsey	Kelstern
45	Kelstern (2)	105	113	TF 29 SE	260 920	Louth RD	East Lindsey	Kelstern Binbrook North Ormesby
46	Killingholme	99	113	TA 12 SE	160 205	Glanford Brigg RD	Glanford	East Halton North Killingholme
47	Kirmington/ Humberside	104	112	TA 01 SE TA 11 SW TA 00 NE	095 105	Glanford Brigg RD	Glanford	Kirmington
48	Kirton in Lindsey (1)/Manton	104	112	SE 90 SW	945 025	Glanford Brigg RD	Glanford	Hibaldstow
49	Kirton in Lindsey (2)	104	112	SE 90 SW	945 970	Glanford Brigg RD	Glanford	Kirton in Lindsey
50	Leadenham	113	121	SK 95 SE	970 523	North Kesteven RD	North Kesteven	Leadenham Welbourn
51	Lincoln (Handley Page Field)	113	121	SK 97 SE	000 713	Lincoln CB	City of Lincoln	City of Lincoln

No.	Name(s)	Ordnance Survey Sheet Numbers:			Grid Ref:	Administrative Areas:		
		1:63000 (One Inch)	1:50000	1:25000 Six-Inch & 1:10000	Centre to nearest 100m	Old District (up to April 1974)	New District (from April 1974)	Town or Parishes
52	Lincoln (West Common)	113	121	SK 97 SE	960 720	Lincoln CB	City of Lincoln	City of Lincoln
53	Ludborough	105	113	TF 29 NE	280 965	Louth RD	East Lindsey	Ludborough
54	Ludford Magna	105	113, 122	TF 18 NE	200 880	Louth RD	East Lindsey	Ludford Burgh le Bain
55	Manby	105	113, 122	TF 38 NE	390 865	Louth RD	East Lindsey	Manby Little Carlton Grimoldby
56	Market Deeping	123	142	TF 11 SE	170 115	South Kesteven RD	South Kesteven	Deeping St James
57	Metheringham	113	121	TF 16 SW	105 610	North Kesteven RD East Kesteven RD	North Kesteven North Kesteven	Metheringham Blankney Martin
58	Moorby	114	122	TF 26 NE TF 36 NW	300 655	Horncastle RD	East Lindsey	Claxby Pluckacre
59	New Holland	99	112	TA 02 SE	078 237	Glanford Brigg RD	Glanford	Barrow upon Humber
60	North Coates	105	113	TA 30 SE	375 025	Louth RD	East Lindsey	North Coates
61	North Killingholme	104	113	TA 11 NW	135 170	Glanford Brigg RD	Glanford	North Killingholme East Halton
62	North Witham	122, 123	130	SK 92 SW SK 92 SE	945 225	West Kesteven RD	South Kesteven	Colsterworth North Witham
63	Sandtoft	104	112	SE 70 NE	755 080	Isle of Axholme RD	Boothferry	Belton Epworth
64	Scampton/ Brattleby	104	121	SK 97 NE SK 98 SE	965 795	Welton RD	West Lindsey	Scampton Aisthorpe Brattleby Hackthorne
65	Scunthorpe	104	112	SE 90 NW	921 087	Scunthorpe MB Glanford Brigg RD	Scunthorpe Glanford	Scunthorpe Broughton
66	Skegness (Burgh Road)	114	122	TF 56 SE	556 643	Skegness UD	East Lindsey	Skegness
67	Skegness (Winthorpe)	114	122	TF 56 NE	568 665	Skegness UD	East Lindsey	Skegness
68	Skegness (Ingoldmells)	114	122	TF 56 NE	565 675	Spilsby RD	East Lindsey	Ingoldmells
69	Skellingthorpe	113	121	SK 96 NW	935 695	North Kesteven RD, later in Lincoln CB	City of Lincoln	City of Lincoln
70	South Carlton	104	121	SK 97 NE	965 765	Welton RD	West Lindsey	South Carlton
71	Spalding	123	131	TF 22 NE	293 285	Spalding RD	South Holland	Weston
72	Spilsby	114	122	TF 46 NW TF 46 NE TF 46 SW TF 46 SE	450 650	Spilsby RD	East Lindsey	Great Steeping Ashby by Partney Candlesby
73	Spitalgate	113, 122	130	SK 93 SW	940 345	West Kesteven RD	South Kesteven	Londonthorpe and Harrowby Without
74	Strubby	105	122	TF 48 SW TF 48 SE	450 810	Louth RD	East Lindsey	Strubby with Woodthorpe Withern with Stain Beesby in the Marsh
75	Sturgate	104	112, 121	SK 88 NE	880 880	Gainsborough RD	West Lindsey	Heapham Upton
76	Sutton Bridge	124	131	TF 42 SE TF 41 NE	485 200	East Elloe RD	South Holland	Sutton Bridge

No.	Name(s)	Ordnance Survey Sheet Numbers:			Grid Ref:	Administrative Areas:		
		1:63 000 (One Inch)	1:50 000	1:25 000 Six-Inch & 1:10 000	Centre to nearest 100m	Old District (up to April 1974)	New District (from April 1974)	Town or Parishes
77	Swinderby	113	121	SK 86 SE	885 620	North Kesteven RD	North Kesteven	Swinderby Thurlby
78	Swinstead	123	130	TF 02 SW	013 220	South Kesteven RD	South Kesteven	Swinstead
79	Theddlethorpe	105	113, 122	TF 48 NE	468 890	Louth RD	East Lindsey	Theddlethorpe All Saints Theddlethorpe St Helen
80	Tydd St Mary	124	131	TF 41 NE	460 195	East Elloe RD	South Holland	Tydd St Mary
81	Waddington	113	121	SK 96 NE SK 95 SE	985 645	North Kesteven RD	North Kesteven	Waddington Branston and Mere Harmston
82	Wellingore	113	121	SK 95 SE	990 545	North Kesteven RD	North Kesteven	Wellingore Welbourn
83	Wickenby	104	121	TF 08 SE TF 18 SW	100 805	Welton RD	West Lindsey	Wickenby Fulnetby Holton cum Beckering Snelland
84	Willoughby Hills	114	131	TF 34 NE	355 455	Boston RD	Boston	Fishtoft
85	Winterton	104	112	SE 91 NW	945 197	Glanford Brigg RD	Glanford	Winterton
86	Woodhall Spa	114	122	TF 26 SW	210 610	Horncastle RD	East Lindsey	Tatershall Thorpe Kirkby on Bain Kirkstead

Special Note:

Two additional airfields, mainly located in Leicestershire, impinged upon Lincolnshire parishes during the Second World War. RAF Bottesford extended into Long Bennington; RAF Saltby into Skillington.

APPENDIX B
Index of Military Flying Units

The following index has been prepared as a guide to the location of aircraft operating units within the County.

A small number of units either operated flights from different fields at the same time, or visited the same airfield intermittently over a period. These units have been marked with an asterisk (*) and dates omitted, since to include the dates may have led to slight confusion. Reference to the relevant airfield history in Part Two is advised.

Unit	Airfield	From/to	Types operated
AGLT Training Flight	Fulbeck	1.2.45 to 22.4.45	Lancaster
Antler & Arrow Squadrons	Hemswell	1.1.56 to 1.10.57	Lincoln
AOS/No 1 AOS	North Coates	1.1.36 to 4.9.39	Gordon, Wallace
APS	Spilsby	26.11.45 to 1.5.46	Mosquito, Master, Spitfire, Martinet
BoBMF	Coningsby	1.3.76 to date	Spitfire, Hurricane, Lancaster, Chipmunk
RAF College	Cranwell	1.29 to 3.8.39	Atlas, Fox, Tutor, Avro 504, Bulldog, Bristol Fighter, Fury, Hector
RAF College	Cranwell	18.4.47 to date	Tiger Moth, Prentice, Harvard, Provost, Chipmunk, Anson, Vampire, Meteor, Jet Provost, Valetta, Varsity, Dominie

Boulton Paul Balliol T2 of the RAF College.
(RAF Cranwell)

RAF College	Barkston Heath	late '36 to mid '43	Master, Oxford, Tutor
RAF College	Barkston Heath	1.5.48 to date	Harvard, Tiger Moth, Vampire, Provost, Varsity, Jet Provost
RAF College SFTS	Cranwell	3.8.39 to 20.3.44	Oxford, Master, Blenheim
RAF College SFTS	Caistor	1.4.43 to 20.3.44	Master, Oxford
RAF College SFTS	Wellingore	18.4.44 to 17.4.47	Oxford, Anson, Master, Harvard, Tiger Moth
RAF CAW and S of RF	Manby	7.62 to 12.73	Canberra, Varsity, Meteor, Provost, Jet Provost, Dominie
RAF CAW	Strubby	7.62 to 8.9.72	Canberra, Dominie, Varsity

Unit	Airfield	From/to	Types operated
RAF Cadet College & S of T T	Cranwell	5.2.20 to 1.29	DH9, Siskin, Bristol Fighter
Canberra Holding Unit	Coningsby	1.58 to —	Canberra
Central Gliding School	Spitalgate	7.71 to -.75	T21B Sedbergh, T31 Cadet
CFE/AFDS	Binbrook	10.62 to 31.1.66	Hunter, Lightning

Lightning F2 XN777 of CFE, Binbrook, July 1963. *(R.C.B.Ashworth)*

Unit	Airfield	From/to	Types operated
CFS	Cranwell	12.4.76 to 9.77	Jet Provost
CGS	Sutton Bridge	4.4.42 to 24.2.44	Wellington, Hampden, Spitfire, Mustang
Civil Air Guard	Grimsby	9.38 to 1.9.39	Swallow, Avian
HMS Daedalus	Cranwell	4.16 to .18	Camel, BE 2, Avro 504, various airships/balloons
EAAS	Manby	11.44 to 1.7.49	Wellington, Lancaster, Lincoln, Meteor, Vampire
ECAS	Manby	7.44 to 11.44	Wellington, Blenheim, Hudson, Lancaster, Mosquito
Eastchurch Squadron	Skegness/Burgh Rd	6.8.14 to 27. 8.14	various
FCTU	Binbrook	1.2.66 to 30.6.67	Lightning
FSS	Swinderby	9.7.79 to date	Chipmunk
RAF Handling Squadron	Manby	7.49 to .54	Canberra, Wyvern, Avenger, Meteor, Sea Hawk, Attacker, Sea Hornet, Venom, Marathon
LTF	Binbrook	1.10.74 to date	Lightning
MAP Glider Modification Unit	Dunholme Lodge	3.12.44 to 28.6.45	Halifax, Whitley, Hamilcar, Hotspur, GAL56
RAFFC	Manby	1.7.49 to 7.62	Lincoln, Hastings, Valetta, Harvard, Athena, Canberra, Hunter, Varsity, Meteor, Provost
RAFFC	Strubby	20.7.49 to 7.62	Meteor, Vampire, Athena, Hunter, Canberra
SAMOTS	North Coates	10.63 to 17.8.64	
Radio Schools (E&WS, No1 RS, No8 RS)	Cranwell	5.16 to 1952	Wallace, Valentia, Anson, Oxford, Master, Proctor, Dominie, Harvard, Halifax

Valentia K3601 of E&WS, Cranwell 1937. *(Crown Copyright H350)*

Unit	Airfield	From/to	Types operated
RNAS Seaplane Station	Killingholme	7.14 to 7.18	various
School of Aerial Fighting and Bomb Dropping	Freiston	9.17 to .18	Avro 504, BE 2, Camel, Dolphin
STC Bombing School	Scampton	1.9.72 to 1.1.74	Hastings
TFF	Binbrook	30.6.67 to 31.12.73	Lightning
US Naval Air Station	Killingholme	7.18 to 1.19	Curtiss H16
1 AAS	Manby	8.38 to 7.44	Battle, Walrus, Fury, Hart, Hind, Henley, Gladiator, Demon, Wellington
1 Air Grading School	Digby	1.51 to 31.3.53	Tiger Moth
1 Canadian Squadron	Digby	28.2.41 to 1.3.41	Hurricane
1 FG	Goxhill	10.6.42 to 24.8.42	P-38 Lightning
1 FTS	Spitalgate	18.6.47 to 18.2.48	Oxford, Anson, Beaufort
1 GP SD Flight*	Binbrook	18.4.44 to 11.8.44	Lancaster
1 LFS 'B' Flight	Blyton	21.11.43 to 12.2.44	Lancaster
1 LFS 'C' Flight	Faldingworth	21.11.43 to 24.1.44	Lancaster
1 LFS	Hemswell	24.1.44 to 25.11.44	Lancaster
1 Group TT Flight	Goxhill	18.9.41 to 10.11.41	Lysander
(later 1481(B)'G' Flt)	Binbrook	10.11.41 to 26.9.42	Lysander, Whitley, Battle
	Binbrook	6.5.43 to 15.3.44	Wellington, Martinet
1 Squadron*	Sutton Bridge		Armament Practice Camps
2 (Army Co-Op) Squadron*	Sutton Bridge		Armament Practice Camps
2 Canadian Squadron	Digby	11.12.40 to 28.2.41	Hurricane
2 FIS	Cranwell	10.9.40 to 15.6.41	Oxford, Tutor
2 FTS	Digby	6.24 to 15.12.33	Avro 504. Snipe, Bristol Fighter, Atlas, Siskin, DH 9A

Avro 504N of 2 FTS, Digby 1929/30.
(RAF Museum P7316)

Unit	Airfield	From/to	Types operated
2 FTS	Digby	1.10.34 to 7.9.37	Tutor, Hart, Fury
2 Grading School	Kirton in Lindsey	6.52 to 31.3.53	Tiger Moth
2 Gliding Centre	Kirton in Lindsey	1.9.59 to 10.65	T21B Sedbergh, T31B Cadet, T30B Prefect
2 Gliding Centre	Spitalgate	10.65 to 7.71	T21B Sedbergh, T31B Cadet
2 Squadron	Digby	13.2.22 to 2.6.22	Bristol Fighter
3 AWJRU	Strubby	7.55 to 7.62	Meteor
3 FTS	Digby	4.20 to 4.22	Avro 504
3 FTS	Spitalgate	.28 to .37	Tiger Moth, Tutor, Bulldog
3 (C) OTU	Cranwell	6.8.41 to 23.6.43	Whitley, Wellington, Anson
3 Squadron*	Sutton Bridge		Armament Practice Camp
4 Aeroplane Acceptance Park	Lincoln (West Common)	.15 to .19	Camel, BE 2, 1½ Stutter, DH 5, Kangaroo, O/400
4 Army Co-Op Squadron*	Sutton Bridge		Armament Practice Camp
4 Fighting School	Freiston	.18 to early 1919	Avro 504, BE 2, Camel, Dolphin, Scout
5 (P) AFU	Hibaldstow	12.4.46 to 6.8.47	Hurricane, Spitfire, Anson, Harvard
5 Group Comm Flight	Spitalgate	to 13.11.43	Anson, Harvard
5 Group Comm Flight	Swinderby	13.11.43 to .45	Anson, Harvard

Unit	Airfield	From/to	Types operated
5 Group TT Flight	Coningsby	1.4.41 to 19.8.41	Battle, Lysander
5 Squadron	Binbrook	8.10.65 to date	Lightning
6 AACU	North Coates	11.41 to 22.2.42	Lysander
6 BAT Flight	Waddington	6.1.41 to 16.11.41	Blenheim, Hampden, Oxford
6 OTU	Sutton Bridge	9.3.40 to 1.11.41	Hurricane, Master, Mentor, Harvard, Battle, Henley
6 Squadron	Coningsby	7.5.69 to 1.10.74	Phantom
7 AACU	North Coates	22.2.41 to 12.43	Lysander
7 (P) AFU	Sutton Bridge	1.44 to 21.12.44	Oxford, Master
7 SFTS	Sutton Bridge	21.12.44 to 4.4.46	Oxford, Master
7 SFTS	Kirton in Lindsey	4.4.46 to 3.48	Oxford, Harvard
8 FTS	Swinderby	1.9.54 to 20.3.64	Vampire

Vampire T11 XD616 of 8FTS, Swinderby, September 1963. *(C.P.Russell-Smith via R.C.B.Ashworth)*

Unit	Airfield	From/to	Types operated
8 Kite Balloon Base	Immingham	11.17 to 4.19	Kite balloons
9 Squadron	Scampton	1.10.36 to 10.3.38	Heyford
9 Squadron	Waddington	7.8.42 to 14.4.43	Wellington, Lancaster
9 Squadron	Bardney	14.4.43 to 6.7.45	Lancaster
9 Squadron	Woodhall Spa	25.8.44 to 3.9.44	Lancaster
9 Squadron	Waddington	6.7.45 to 1.1.46	Lancaster
9 Squadron	Binbrook	19.4.46 to 7.46	Lancaster
9 Squadron	Binbrook	9.46 to 2.6.59	Lincoln, Canberra
9 Squadron	Coningsby	2.6.59 to 13.7.61	Canberra
9 Squadron	Coningsby	1.3.62 to 10.11.64	Vulcan
9 Squadron	Waddington	1.75 to 1.5.82	Vulcan
10 Squadron	Scampton	15.1.53 to 16.5.55	Canberra
11 Trg Squadron	Spitalgate	14.4.17 to 15.9.17	Avro 504, FE 2b
11 Trg Squadron	Scampton	15.9.17 to 15.7.18	BE 2, Avro 504, Elephant
11 Squadron	Digby	3.9.19 to 31.12.19	DH 4
11 Squadron	Binbrook	22.3.72 to date	Lightning

Lightning F6 XS920/F of 11 Squadron with overwing tanks, Binbrook, January 1973. *(P.H.T.Green)*

Unit	Airfield	From/to	Types operated
11 FTS	Swinderby	1.6.54 to 1.6.55	Varsity
11 Group Pool	Sutton Bridge	6.3.40 to 9.3.40	Hurricane, Master, Mentor, Harvard, Battle, Henley

Unit	Airfield	From/to	Types operated
12 (P) AFU	Spitalgate	1.4.42 to 8.2.45	Blenheim, Oxford, Anson
12 Group AAC Flight	Digby	19.6.41 to 18.11.41	Lysander
12 SFTS	Spitalgate	1.12.38 to 3.42	Harvard, Anson, Blenheim
12 Squadron	Binbrook	3.7.40 to 7.8.40	Battle
12 Squadron	Binbrook	7.9.40 to 25.9.42	Battle, Wellington
12 Squadron	Wickenby	25.9.42 to 24.9.45	Wellington, Lancaster
12 Squadron	Binbrook	24.9.45 to 26.7.46	Lancaster
12 Squadron	Waddington	26.7.46 to 18.9.46	Lincoln
12 Squadron	Hemswell	12.1.48 to 14.3.48	Lincoln
12 Squadron	Binbrook	18.9.46 to 2.7.59	Lincoln, Canberra
12 Squadron	Coningsby	2.7.59 to 13.7.61	Canberra
12 Squadron	Coningsby	1.7.62 to 17.11.64	Vulcan
13 AMU	Swinderby	20.9.45 to 1.8.46	Lancaster
13 Army Co-Op Squadron*	Sutton Bridge		Armament Practice Camp
14 BAT Flight	Coningsby	22.9.41 to 11.41	Oxford
15 (P) AFU	Kirmington	19.2.42 to 23.10.42	Anson, Oxford
15 (P) AFU	Caistor	15.5.42 to 8.12.42	Oxford
15 (P) AFU	Goxhill	15.5.42 to 4.6.42	Oxford
15 Trg Squadron	Spitalgate	15.9.17 to 15.7.18	Avro 504, FE 2D
15 Squadron	Coningsby	10.2.51 to 22.5.54	Washington, Canberra
16 Army Co-Op Squadron	Sutton Bridge		Armament Practice Camp
17 FTS	Spitalgate	1.5.45 to 18.6.47	Oxford, Blenheim, Spitfire, Beaufort, Mosquito
17 JSTU	North Coates	10.60 to 12.66	Bloodhound SAM
17 OTU	Swinderby	1.11.46 to 9.47	Wellington
17 SFTS	Cranwell	20.3.44 to 1.5.45	Master, Oxford, Harvard, Blenheim, Spitfire
17 SFTS	Caistor	20.3.44 to 16.11.44	Master, Oxford, Harvard
17 SFTS	Coleby Grange	16.11.44 to 11.11.46	Harvard, Oxford
17 Squadron*	Sutton Bridge		Armament Practice Camp
18 (Polish) OTU	Blyton	10.7.42 to 4.43	Wellington
18 Squadron	Scampton	1.8.53 to 22.5.55	Canberra
19 FTS	Cranwell	1.5.45 to 12.4.47	Oxford, Harvard, Spitfire, Beaufort, Blenheim

Harvard of 19 FTS, Cranwell, 22nd February 1946.
(RAF Museum P7404)

Unit	Airfield	From/to	Types operated
19 FTS	Digby	1.46 to 2.48	Tiger Moth
19 Squadron*	Sutton Bridge		Armament Practice Camp
19 Squadron	Digby	18.5.43 to 4.6.43	Mustang
20 Trg Squadron	Spitalgate	15.9.17 to .18	Avro 504, FE 2b
20 Trg Squadron	Harlaxton	.18 to 7.18	Avro 504, BE 2, RE 8
21 Group Comm Flight	Swinderby	1.5.47 to 11.53	Various
21 HGCU	Elsham Wolds	29.12.45 to 30.11.46	Horsa, Albemarle, Halifax
21 Squadron	Scampton	21.9.53 to 28.5.55	Canberra
21 Squadron	Waddington	28.5.55 to 30.6.57	Canberra
22 GS	Grimsby	mid 1949 to 6.50	T31 Cadet

Unit	Airfield	From/to	Types operated
22 GS	Kirton in Lindsey	6.50 to 4.55	T21B Sedbergh, T31 Cadet
22 Squadron	North Coates	8.6.40 to 25.6.41	Beaufort

Beaufort X8935 OA-T of 22 Squadron *(22 Sqn Records via P.H.T.Green)*

23 Squadron	Waddington	3.19 to 31.12.19	
23 Squadron*	Sutton Bridge		Armament Practice Camp
23 (Designate) Squadron	Coningsby	6.10.75 to 1.12.75	Phantom
23 Squadron	Coningsby	1.12.75 to 25.2.76	Phantom
25 E & RFTS	Grimsby	24.6.38 to 1.9.39	Tiger Moth, Magister, Hart, Hind
25 Squadron	South Carlton	9.19 to 12.19	DH9A/DH4
25 Squadron	Digby	12.19 to 31.1.20	DH9A/DH4
25 Squadron*	Sutton Bridge		Armament Practice Camp
25 Squadron	North Coates	1.10.63 to 17.8.70	Bloodhound SAM
25 Squadron	Woodhall Spa	3.3.69 to 28.3.69	Bloodhound SAM
26 Trg Squadron	Harlaxton	22.9.17 to 7.18	Avro 504, BE 2, DH 9
27 Squadron	Scampton	15.6.53 to 26.5.55	Canberra
27 Squadron	Waddington	26.5.55 to 31.12.56	Canberra
27 Squadron	Scampton	1.4.61 to 29.3.72	Vulcan
27 Squadron	Scampton	1.11.73 to 31.3.82	Vulcan
28 Bomb Group	Scampton	17.7.48 to 20.10.48	Superfortress

B-29 Superfortress 484114 of 28th Bomb Group, Scampton 1948. *(W.Baker)*

29 Squadron	Spitalgate	10.8.19 to 31.12.19	
29 Squadron	Digby	26.6.40 to 8.7.40	Blenheim, Beaufighter
29 Squadron	Wellingore	8.7.40 to 1.5.41	Blenheim, Beaufighter
29 Squadron	Hibaldstow	20.8.41 to 20.9.41	Beaufighter
29 Squadron	Coningsby	31.12.74 to date	Phantom
30 Squadron*	Sutton Bridge		Armament Practice Camp
32 Squadron*	Sutton Bridge		Armament Practice Camp
33 Squadron*	Blyborough	12.16 to early '18	FE 2, Bristol Fighter, Avro 504
33 Squadron*	Bucknall	12.16 to 6.19	FE 2, Bristol Fighter, Avro 504

Unit	Airfield	From/to	Types operated
33 Squadron*	Cockthorne	12.16 to 6.19	FE 2, Bristol Fighter, Avro 504
33 Squadron*	Cuxwold	12.16 to 6.19	FE 2, Bristol Fighter, Avro 504
33 Squadron* ('C' Flt)	Elsham	1.17 to 6.18	FE 2
33 Squadron* (HQ)	Gainsborough	12.16 to 6.18	FE 2, Avro 504
33 Squadron*	Greenland Top	12.16 to 12.18	BE 2, FE 2, Bristol Fighter, Avro 504
33 Squadron*	Harpswell	12.16 to 12.18	Avro 504
33 Squadron*	Kelstern	12.16 to 6.19	BE 2, FE 2, Bristol Fighter, Avro 504
33 Squadron* ('B' Flt)	Kirton in Lindsey	12.16 to 6.18	FE 2
33 Squadron*	Kirton in Lindsey	6.18 to 13.6.19	Bristol Fighter, Avro 504NF
33 Squadron	Moorby	12.16 to 6.19	FE2, Bristol Fighter
33 Squadron*	New Holland	12.16 to 6.19	FE 2, Bristol Fighter, Avro 504
33 Squadron*	Scampton	12.16 to 6.18	FE 2, Bristol Fighter, Avro 504
33 Squadron*	Winterton	12.16 to 6.19	FE 2, Bristol Fighter, Avro 504
34 TDS	Scampton	15.7.18 to 4.19	Avro 504, Pup, Camel, Dolphin
35 Squadron	Coningsby	1.12.62 to 7.11.64	Vulcan

Vulcan B2 XM604 of 35 Squadron, 1964 (*MAP*)

Unit	Airfield	From/to	Types operated
35 Squadron	Scampton	1.2.75 to 1.3.82	Vulcan
37 Trg Squadron	Scampton	13.11.16 to 15.9.17	Avro 504, RE 8
37 Trg Squadron	Spitalgate	15.9.17 to 15.7.18	Avro 504
38 Squadron* ('C' Flt)	Leadenham	9.16 to 5.18	FE 2
38 Squadron*	Anwick	9.16 to 5.18	BE 2, FE 2
38 Squadron*	Braceby	10.16 to 5.18	BE 2, FE 2
38 Squadron*	Buckminster	10.16 to 5.18	BE 2, FE 2
38 Squadron*	Gosberton	10.16 to 5.18	BE 2, FE 2
38 Squadron*	Moorby	12.16 to 6.19	Avro 504, FE 2, Bristol Fighter
38 Squadron*	Swinstead	9.16 to 5.18	BE 2, FE 2
38 Squadron*	Willoughby Hills	9.16 to 5.18	
39 TDS	Spitalgate	15.7.18 to .19	Avro 504
39 Trg Squadron	South Carlton	8.17 to 4.7.18	Avro 504, RE 8, DH 6
39 Squadron	Spitalgate	8.2.23 to 21.1.28	DH 9A

DH9A J7067 of 39 Squadron. (*Crown Copyright H1105*)

Unit	Airfield	From/to	Types operated
40 TDS	Harlaxton	7.18 to .19	Avro 504, DH 6, RE 8
40 Squadron	Coningsby	28.10.53 to 24.2.54	Canberra
41 Squadron*	Sutton Bridge		Armament Practice Camp

Unit	Airfield	From/to	Types operated
41 Squadron	Coningsby	1.4.72 to 31.3.77	Phantom
42 Squadron	North Coates	5.4.41 to 8.5.41	Beaufort
42 Squadron	North Coates	16.3.42 to 27.3.42	Beaufort
43 Squadron	Spitalgate	25.8.19 to 31.12.19	
43 Squadron	Kirton in Lindsey	1.9.42 to 27.10.42	Hurricane
43 Squadron*	Sutton Bridge		Armament Practice Camp
44 Trg Squadron	Waddington	11.17 to	DH4, DH6, DH9
44 Squadron	Harlaxton	3.11.16 to 11.17	Avro 504, DH 4, DH 6
44 Squadron	Waddington	16.6.37 to 31.5.43	Hind, Blenheim, Hampden, Lancaster
44 Squadron	Dunholme Lodge	31.5.43 to 30.9.44	Lancaster
44 Squadron	Spilsby	30.9.44 to 21.7.45	Lancaster
44 Squadron	Coningsby	9.4.51 to 20.5.54	Washington, Canberra
44 Squadron	Waddington	10.8.60 to 21.12.82	Vulcan
45 Trg Squadron	South Carlton	13.11.16 to 4.7.18	Avro 504, FB 5, DH 5
45 Squadron	Coningsby	11.57 to 12.57	Canberra
46 TDS	South Carlton	4.7.18 to .19	Avro 504, Camel, Dolphin
46 Trg Squadron	South Carlton	.19 to 4.20	Avro 504, Camel, Dolphin
46 Squadron	Digby	15.11.37 to 9.12.39	Gauntlet, Hurricane
46 Squadron	Digby	17.1.40 to 9.5.40	Hurricane
46 Squadron	Digby	12.6.40 to 1.9.40	Hurricane
46 Squadron	Digby	13.12.40 to 28.2.41	Hurricane
47 Trg Squadron	Waddington	13.11.16 to 4.7.18	Avro 504, BE 2, FE 2, RE 8, DH 6, Shorthorn
48 TDS	Waddington	4.7.18 to .19	Avro 504, Camel, Pup, DH 6
48 Trg Squadron	Waddington	13.11.16 to 4.7.18	DH6, Shorthorn
48 Trg Squadron	Waddington	.19 to .20	Avro 504, Camel, DH 9
49 Trg Squadron	Scampton	.16 to 14.11.16	BE 2, FK3
49 Trg Squadron	Spitalgate	14.11.16 to 15.9.17	Avro 504
49 Squadron	Scampton	14.3.38 to 2.1.43	Hind, Hampden, Manchester, Lancaster
49 Squadron	Fiskerton	2.1.43 to 13.9.43	Lancaster
49 Squadron	Dunholme Lodge	13.9.43 to 24.10.43	Lancaster
49 Squadron	Fiskerton	24.10.43 to 16.10.44	Lancaster
49 Squadron	Fulbeck	16.10.44 to 22.4.45	Lancaster
49 Squadron	Waddington	25.6.52 to 14.8.53	Lincoln
50 Trg Squadron	Spitalgate	.18 to .18	Avro 504
50 Squadron	Waddington	3.5.37 to 10.7.40	Hind, Hampden

Hampdens of 50 Squadron at Waddington with pre-war codes, L4076 QX-D in the foreground. *(Sqn Ldr C.G. Jefford)*

50 Squadron	Swinderby	19.7.41 to 26.11.41	Hampden
50 Squadron	Skellingthorpe	26.11.41 to 20.6.42	Hampden, Manchester
50 Squadron	Swinderby	20.6.42 to 16.10.42	Manchester
50 Squadron	Skellingthorpe	16.10.42 to 15.6.45	Lancaster
50 Squadron	Sturgate	15.6.45 to 25.1.46	Lancaster
50 Squadron	Waddington	25.1.46 to 31.1.51	Lancaster, Lincoln
50 Squadron	Hemswell	12.47 to 3.48	Lincoln
50 Squadron	Binbrook	15.8.52 to 5.1.56	Canberra
50 Squadron	Waddington	1.8.61 to date	Vulcan
51 Squadron*	Gosberton	8.17 to 5.19	FE2, Avro 504NF
51 Squadron 'B' Flt	Tydd St Mary	8.17 to 5.19	FE 2, Avro 504NF
51 Trg Squadron	Waddington	14.5.17 to 4.10.18	Avro 504, DH 4, DH 9

Unit	Airfield	From/to	Types operated
52 Fighter Group	Goxhill	26.8.42 to 29.10.42	Spitfire
53 OTU	Hibaldstow	9.5.43 to 15.5.45	Spitfire, Master, Martinet
53 OTU	Kirton in Lindsey	10.5.43 to 15.5.45	Spitfire, Master, Martinet
53 Trg Squadron	Harlaxton	.18 to 7.18	Avro 504, BE 2, DH 6
53 Squadron	North Coates	18.2.42 to 16.5.42	Hudson
54 Trg Squadron	Harlaxton	.17 to 9.18	Avro 504
54 Squadron	Coningsby	1.9.69 to 23.4.74	Phantom
56 Fighter Group	Goxhill	1.43 to 5.4.43	Thunderbolt
56 OTU	Sutton Bridge	1.11.41 to 27.3.42	Hurricane, Master, Mentor, Harvard, Battle, Henley
56 TDS	Cranwell	.18 to .19	Camel, Pup, BE 2, Avro 504
56 Squadron	Digby	1.6.40 to 3.6.40	Hurricane
56 (Designate) Squadron	Coningsby	31.3.76 to 29.6.76	Phantom
56 Squadron	Coningsby	29.6.76 to 8.7.76	Phantom
56 Squadron*	Sutton Bridge		Armament Practice Camp
57 TDS	Cranwell	.18 to .19	Camel, Pup, BE 2, Avro 504
57 Squadron	South Carlton	2.8.19 to 31.12.19	
57 Squadron	Scampton	4.9.42 to 28.8.43	Lancaster
57 Squadron	East Kirkby	28.8.43 to 25.11.45	Lancaster, Lincoln
57 Squadron	Elsham Wolds	26.11.45 to 3.12.45	Lancaster
57 Squadron	Scampton	3.12.45 to 5.46	Lancaster, Lincoln
57 Squadron	Waddington	7.10.46 to 5.6.52	Lincoln, Washington
57 Squadron	Hemswell	7.47 to 12.47	Lincoln
57 Squadron	Coningsby	5.6.51 to 22.5.54	Washington, Canberra
57 Squadron	Coningsby	15.11.56 to 9.12.57	Canberra
59 Training Squadron/59 TDS	Digby	19.9.18 to 1.20	Avro 504, FE 2, Handley Page O/400
59 Squadron	North Coates	17.1.42 to 27.8.42	Hudson
60 Trg Squadron	Scampton	14.4.17 to 15.7.18	Avro 504, Camel, Scout, SE 5, Dolphin
61 Conversion Flight	Swinderby	22.8.42 to 20.10.42	Manchester
61 TCG	Barkston Heath	18.2.44 to 13.3.45	C-47
61 Trg Squadron	South Carlton	10.5.17 to 4.7.18	Avro 504, BE 2, DH 4
61 Squadron	Hemswell	8.3.37 to 17.7.41	Anson, Audax, Blenheim, Hampden
61 Squadron	Skellingthorpe	16.11.43 to 12.1.44	Lancaster
61 Squadron	Coningsby	12.1.44 to 15.4.44	Lancaster
61 Squadron	Skellingthorpe	15.4.44 to 16.6.45	Lancaster
61 Squadron	Sturgate	16.6.45 to 25.1.46	Lancaster
61 Squadron	Waddington	25.1.46 to 8.53	Lancaster, Lincoln

Lincoln B2 of 61 Squadron at Waddington. *(V.Hawley)*

Unit	Airfield	From/to	Types operated
61 Squadron	Hemswell	7.47 to 12.47	Lincoln
62 AR Squadron	East Kirkby	Rotation	SC-47
63 AR Squadron	East Kirkby	Rotation	SC-47
64 AR Squadron	East Kirkby	Rotation	SC-47
64 Trg Squadron	Harlaxton	20.12.17 to .18	BE 2
64 Squadron	Sutton Bridge	8.39 to 8.39	Blenheim

Unit	Airfield	From/to	Types operated
64 Squadron	Binbrook	1.6.62 to 1.4.65	Javelin
65 Squadron	Kirton in Lindsey	29.5.40 to 14.6.40	Spitfire
65 Squadron	Kirton in Lindsey	26.2.41 to 7.10.41	Spitfire
68 Squadron	Harlaxton	30.1.17 to 21.9.17	DH 5
68 Squadron	Coleby Grange	5.2.44 to 3.3.44	Beaufighter
69 Squadron	South Carlton	28.12.16 to 9.9.17	RE 8
70 Squadron	Spitalgate	2.19 to 20.1.20	Camel, Snipe
71 (Eagle) Squadron	Kirton in Lindsey	23.11.40 to 9.4.41	Hurricane
73 Squadron	Digby	9.11.37 to 9.9.39	Gauntlet, Hurricane
74 Squadron	Kirton in Linsey	22.8.40 to 10.9.40	Spitfire
75 Trg Squadron	Waddington	14.11.17 to 22.12.17	DH 4, DH 9
75 Squadron	Spilsby	21.7.45 to 15.10.45	Lancaster, Lincoln
76 Squadron	Hemswell	1.4.57 to 17.7.58	Canberra
78 Fighter Group	Goxhill	1.12.42 to 1.4.43	P-38 Lightning, P-47 Thunderbolt
79 Squadron	Digby	30.5.40 to 5.6.40	Hurricane
81 Fighter Group	Goxhill	8.10.42 to 15.11.42	P-39 Airacobra
81 Squadron	Scampton	1.8.17 to 15.7.18	Avro 504, Pup, Scout, SE 5, Dolphin, Camel, 1½ Strutter
81 Squadron	Wellingore	1.9.42 to 30.10.42	Spitfire
82 Squadron	Waddington	30.3.17 to 11.17	Avro 504, RE 8, FK 8
83 Squadron	Spitalgate	1.17 to 9.17	FE 2
83 Squadron	Scampton	14.3.38 to 15.8.42	Hind, Hampden, Manchester, Lancaster
83 Squadron	Coningsby	18.4.44 to 4.11.46	Lancaster, Lincoln
83 Squadron	Hemswell	4.11.46 to 1.1.56	Lincoln
83 Squadron	Waddington	21.5.57 to 10.10.60	Vulcan
83 Squadron	Scampton	10.10.60 to 31.8.69	Vulcan
85 Squadron	Caistor	10.40 to 10.40	Hurricane
85 Squadron	Kirton in Lindsey	23.10.40 to 21.11.40	Hurricane
85 Squadron	Binbrook	25.4.63 to 28.1.72	Canberra, Meteor

Meteor F8 WL106/Y of 85 Squadron. (MAP)

85 Squadron ('B' Flt)	North Coates	1.3.76 to date	Bloodhound SAM
86 Trg Squadron	Spitalgate	1.17 to .17	
86 Squadron	North Coates	10.5.41 to 10.1.42	Blenheim, Beaufighter
88 Squadron	Waddington	7.6.37 to 10.7.37	Hind
90 Squadron ('A' Flt)	Leadenham	8.18 to 6.19	Avro 504
90 Squadron*	Anwick	8.18 to 6.19	Avro 504
90 Squadron*	Braceby	8.18 to 6.19	Avro 504
90 Squadron*	Buckminster	14.8.18 to 13.6.19	Avro 504, Camel
90 Squadron*	Gosberton	8.18 to 6.19	Avro 504
90 Squadron*	Market Deeping	8.18 to 6.19	Avro 504NF
90 Squadron*	Swinstead	8.18 to 6.19	Avro 504NF
91 Fighter Sqn/81 Fighter Grp	Kirton in Lindsey	8.10.42 to 23.12.42	P-39 Airacobra
92 Squadron	Digby	20.10.41 to 12.2.42	Spitfire
94 Fighter Sqn/1 Fighter Grp	Kirton in Lindsey	26.7.42 to 27.8.42	P-38 Lightning
96 Squadron	South Carlton	28.9.17 to 4.7.18	BE 2
97 Conversion Flight	Coningsby	2.42 to 30.9.42	Manchester, Lysander
97 Conversion Flight	Skellingthorpe	30.9.42 to 16.10.42	Lancaster

Unit	Airfield	From/to	Types operated
97 Conversion Flight	Swinderby	16.10.42 to 20.10.42	Manchester
97 Squadron	Waddington	1.12.17 to 21.1.18	DH 9
97 Squadron	Waddington	25.2.41 to 15.3.41	Manchester
97 Squadron	Coningsby	15.3.41 to 1.3.42	Manchester, Lancaster
97 Squadron	Woodhall Spa	1.3.42 to 17.4.43	Lancaster
97 Squadron	Coningsby	18.4.44 to 7.11.46	Lancaster, Lincoln
97 Squadron	Hemswell	7.11.46 to 1.1.56	Lincoln
97 Squadron	Hemswell	1.10.58 to 24.5.63	Thor IRBM
98 Squadron	Harlaxton	30.8.17 to 30.8.17	
98 Squadron	Scampton	2.3.40 to 19.3.40	Battle
100 Squadron	Spitalgate	4.2.22 to 5.24	Bristol Fighter, DH 9, Vimy, Avro 504
100 Squadron	Spitalgate	7.24 to 10.1.28	Fawn, Horsley
100 Squadron	Grimsby	15.12.42 to 2.4.45	Lancaster
100 Squadron	Elsham Wolds	2.4.45 to 3.12.45	Lancaster
100 Squadron	Scampton	3.12.45 to 5.46	Lancaster, Lincoln
100 Squadron	Hemswell	10.46 to 25.3.50	Lincoln
100 Squadron	Waddington	25.3.50 to 14.8.53	Lincoln
101 FRS/215 AFS	Blyton	9.51 to 5.54	Wellington, Meteor
101 Squadron	Ludford Magna	16.6.43 to 1.10.45	Lancaster
101 Squadron	Binbrook	1.10.45 to 1.2.57	Lancaster, Lincoln, Canberra
101 Squadron	Waddington	26.6.61 to 4.8.82	Vulcan
103 Squadron	Elsham Wolds	11.7.41 to 25.11.45	Wellington, Halifax, Lancaster
103 Squadron	Waddington	13.11.54 to 12.54	Canberra
104 Squadron	Ludford Magna	21.7.59 to 24.5.63	Thor IRBM
106 Conversion Flight	Coningsby	5.42 to 30.9.42	Manchester, Lancaster
106 Conversion Flight	Skellingthorpe	30.9.42 to 16.10.42	Lancaster
106 Conversion Flight	Swinderby	16.10.42 to 20.10.42	Manchester
106 Squadron	Spitalgate	27.9.38 to 10.10.38	Battle
106 Squadron	Coningsby	23.2.41 to 9.42	Hampden, Manchester, Lancaster
106 Squadron	Metheringham	11.11.43 to 18.2.46	Lancaster
106 Squadron	Bardney	22.7.59 to 24.5.63	Thor IRBM
107 EGS	Coleby Grange	4.45 to .47	T31 Cadet
109 Squadron	Woodhall Spa	30.9.45 to 20.10.45	Mosquito
109 Squadron	Wickenby	20.10.45 to 26.11.45	Mosquito
109 Squadron	Hemswell	26.11.45 to 4.11.46	Mosquito
109 Squadron	Coningsby	4.11.46 to 3.50	Mosquito
109 Squadron	Hemswell	1.4.50 to 1.1.56	Mosquito, Canberra
109 Squadron	Binbrook	1.1.56 to 1.2.57	Canberra

Canberra B6 WJ768 of 109 Squadron. *(E.Watts)*

Unit	Airfield	From/to	Types operated
110 Squadron	Waddington	18.5.37 to 11.5.39	Hind, Blenheim
111 Squadron	Digby	21.5.40 to 30.5.40	Hurricane
111 Squadron*	Sutton Bridge		Armament Practice Camp
111 Squadron	Coningsby	1.7.74 to 3.11.75	Phantom
111 Squadron	Coningsby	2.5.79 to 12.79	Phantom
112 Squadron	Woodhall Spa	2.11.64 to 10.65	Bloodhound SAM
113 Squadron	Spitalgate	31.8.37 to 30.4.38	Hind
116 Squadron (Detachment)	Digby	6.44 to 26.5.45	Oxford, Anson
121 Squadron	Bracebridge Heath	14.10.18 to 11.19	DH 9

Unit	Airfield	From/to	Types operated
121 (Eagle) Squadron	Kirton in Lindsey	14.5.41 to 16.12.41	Hurricane, Spitfire
123 Squadron	Waddington	1.3.18 to 1.3.18	DH 9
133 (Eagle) Squadron	Kirton in Lindsey	2.1.42 to 3.5.42	Spitfire
136 Squadron	Kirton in Lindsey	20.8.41 to 9.11.41	Hurricane
139 Squadron	Hemswell	4.2.46 to 4.11.46	Mosquito
139 Squadron	Coningsby	4.11.46 to 1.4.50	Mosquito
139 Squadron	East Kirkby	8.47 to 2.48	Mosquito
139 Squadron	Hemswell	1.4.50 to 31.1.56	Mosquito, Canberra
139 Squadron	Binbrook	31.12.55 to 31.12.59	Canberra
141 Squadron	Fiskerton	4.9.44 to 3.7.45	Mosquito
141 Squadron	Dunholme Lodge	1.4.59 to 3.64	Bloodhound SAM
142 Squadron	Waddington	15.6.40 to 3.7.40	Battle
142 Squadron	Binbrook	3.7.40 to 12.8.40	Battle
142 Squadron	Binbrook	6.9.40 to 26.11.41	Battle, Wellington
142 Squadron	Grimsby	26.11.41 to 20.12.42	Wellington
142 Squadron	Kirmington	20.12.42 to 27.1.43	Wellington
142 Squadron	Coleby Grange	22.7.59 to 24.5.63	Thor IRBM
143 Squadron	North Coates	27.8.42 to 27.8.43	Blenheim, Beaufighter
143 Squadron	North Coates	11.2.44 to 23.5.44	Beaufighter
143 Squadron	North Coates	9.9.44 to 23.10.44	Beaufighter
144 Squadron	Hemswell	9.2.37 to 17.7.41	Anson, Audax, Blenheim, Hampden

Hampdens of 144 Squadron 1939. *(via P.H.T.Green)*

Unit	Airfield	From/to	Types operated
144 Squadron	Strubby	1.7.44 to 3.9.44	Beaufighter
148 Squadron	Scampton	7.6.37 to 10.3.38	Audax, Wellesley
149 Squadron	Coningsby	17.10.50 to 22.5.54	Washington, Canberra
150 Squadron	Kirmington	10.42 to 27.1.43	Wellington
150 Squadron	Fiskerton	1.11.44 to 22.11.44	Lancaster
150 Squadron	Hemswell	22.11.44 to 7.11.45	Lancaster
151 Squadron	Digby	1.9.40 to 28.11.40	Hurricane
153 Squadron	Kirmington	7.10.44 to 14.10.44	Lancaster
153 Squadron	Scampton	15.10.44 to 28.9.45	Lancaster
154 Squadron	Wellingore	1.9.42 to 1.11.42	Spitfire
163 Squadron	Waddington	1.6.18 to 4.7.18	
166 Squadron	Kirmington	27.1.43 to 18.11.45	Wellington, Lancaster
166 Squadron ('C' Flt)	Faldingworth	7.10.44 to 15.10.44	Lancaster
167 Squadron	Digby	13.5.43 to 12.6.43	Spitfire
170 Squadron	Kelstern	15.10.44 to 22.10.44	Lancaster
170 Squadron	Dunholme Lodge	22.10.44 to 29.11.44	Lancaster
170 Squadron	Hemswell	29.11.44 to 14.11.45	Lancaster
185 Squadron	Spitalgate	27.9.38 to 10.10.38	Battle
189 Squadron	Bardney	15.10.44 to 2.11.44	Lancaster
189 Squadron	Fulbeck	2.11.44 to 8.4.45	Lancaster
189 Squadron	Bardney	8.4.45 to 15.10.45	Lancaster
189 Squadron	Metheringham	15.10.45 to 20.11.45	Lancaster
192 Training Squadron	Gainsborough	5.9.17 to 24.9.17	FE 2
198 Squadron	Digby	8.12.42 to 23.1.43	Hurricane

Unit	Airfield	From/to	Types operated
199 Squadron	Harpswell	26.6.18 to 6.19	FE 2
199 Squadron	Blyton	7.11.42 to 3.2.43	Wellington
199 Squadron	Cammeringham	3.2.43 to 20.6.43	Wellington
199 Squadron	Hemswell	16.4.52 to 1.10.57	Lincoln, Mosquito, Canberra
200 (Night) Training Squadron	Harpswell	10.11.18 to 6.19	FE 2
201 CTU	Swinderby	9.47 to	Wellington
201 AFS	**Swinderby**	**to 1.6.54**	**Wellington, Varsity, Valetta**

Varsity T1 WF380/C of 201 AFS, 1952.
(Flight 26980s)

Unit	Airfield	From/to	Types operated
203 Flight	**Waddington**	3.19 to 12.19	Camel
203 Flight	Digby	12.19 to 21.1.20	Camel
204 AFS	Swinderby	6.50 to 20.5.52	Mosquito
204 Squadron	Waddington	7.2.19 to 31.12.19	
206 Squadron	North Coates	23.6.42 to 27.6.42	
207 Conversion Flight	Swinderby	22.8.42 to 20.10.42	Manchester
207 Squadron	Waddington	8.11.40 to 17.11.41	Manchester
207 Squadron	Spilsby	12.10.43 to 30.10.45	Lancaster
209 Flight	Digby	2.19 to 24.6.19	
210 Flight	Digby	2.19 to 24.6.19	
211 Squadron	Spitalgate	30.8.37 to 30.4.38	Hind
213 Flight	Digby	3.19 to 31.12.19	
214 Squadron	Scampton	6.10.36 to 13.4.37	Virginia, Harrow
217 Squadron	North Coates	24.3.42 to 26.3.42	Beaufort
222 Squadron	Digby	10.5.40 to 23.5.40	Spitfire
222 Squadron	Kirton in Lindsey	21.5.40 to 29.8.40	Spitfire
222 Squadron	Woodhall Spa	1.5.60 to 30.6.64	Bloodhound SAM
223 Squadron	Folkingham	1.12.59 to 23.8.63	Thor IRBM
224 Squadron	North Coates	23.6.42 to 28.6.42	Hudson
227 Squadron ('A' Flt)	Bardney	7.10.44 to 21.10.44	Lancaster
227 Squadron ('B' Flt)	Strubby	7.10.44 to 20.10.44	Lancaster
227 Squadron	Strubby	5.4.45 to 8.6.45	Lancaster
228 OCU	**Coningsby**	**2.68 to date**	**Phantom**

Line up of Coningsby Phantoms with nearest FGR.2 XT902 in the markings of 228 OCU/64 Squadron. *(MAP)*

Unit	Airfield	From/to	Types operated
228 Squadron	**Killingholme**	**1.19 to 30.6.19**	**Curtiss H-12, Curtiss H-16**
229 Squadron	Digby	6.10.39 to 26.6.40	Blenheim, Hurricane

Unit	Airfield	From/to	Types operated
230 OCU	Scampton	2.49 to 15.4.52	Lancaster, Lincoln

Lincoln B2 RF562 SN-L of 230 OCU, 1950. *(MAP)*

Unit	Airfield	From/to	Types operated
230 OCU	Waddington	7.56 to 6.61	Vulcan, Canberra
230 OCU	Scampton	19.12.69 to 1.9.81	Vulcan, Hastings
231 OCU	Coningsby	15.3.47 to 3.50	Mosquito
231 OCU	East Kirkby	8.47 to 2.48	Mosquito
231 OCU	Hemswell	3.50 to early '52	Mosquito
235 Squadron	North Coates	24.2.40 to 21.4.40	Blenheim
236 Squadron	North Coates	24.2.40 to 21.4.40	Blenheim
236 Squadron	North Coates	18.9.42 to 25.5.45	Beaufighter
248 Squadron	North Coates	24.2.40 to 8.4.40	Blenheim
249 Squadron	Coningsby	8.57 to 10.57	Canberra
251 Squadron ('B' Flt)	Greenland Top	5.18 to .18	DH 6
251 Flight*	Greenland Top	12.18 to 30.6.19	DH 6
252 Flight*	Greenland Top	12.18 to 30.6.19	DH 6
253 Squadron	Kirton in Lindsey	24.5.40 to 21.7.40	Hurricane
253 Squadron	Coleby Grange	8.7.40 to 9.7.40	Hurricane
253 Squadron	Hibaldstow	21.9.41 to 24.5.42	Hurricane
253 Squadron	Hibaldstow	31.5.42 to 14.6.42	Hurricane
253 Squadron	Hibaldstow	7.7.42 to 15.8.42	Hurricane
253 Squadron	Hibaldstow	20.8.42 to 11.42	Hurricane
254 Squadron	Sutton Bridge	9.12.39 to 27.1.40	Blenheim
254 Squadron	North Coates	16.11.42 to 29.6.45	Beaufighter

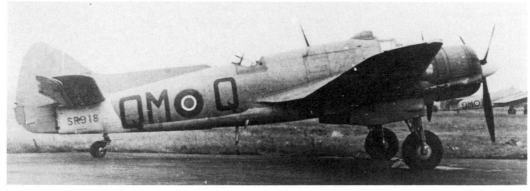

Beaufighter TFX SR918 QM-Q of 254 Squadron. *(J.D.Oughton)*

Unit	Airfield	From/to	Types operated
255 Squadron	Kirton in Lindsey	23.11.40 to 15.5.41	Defiant
255 Squadron	Hibaldstow	15.5.41 to 20.9.41	Defiant, Beaufighter
256 Flight*	Greenland Top	12.18 to 30.6.19	DH 6
264 Squadron	Sutton Bridge	3.11.39 to 4.12.39	Battle
264 Squadron	Coleby Grange	2.8.40 to 21.8.40	Defiant
264 Squadron	Kirton in Lindsey	24.7.40 to 21.8.40	Defiant
264 Squadron	Kirton in Lindsey	29.8.40 to 23.10.40	Defiant
264 Squadron	Caistor	12.9.40 to 23.10.40	Defiant
264 Squadron	Coleby Grange	17.11.43 to 18.12.43	Mosquito

Unit	Airfield	From/to	Types operated
264 Squadron	North Coates	1.12.58 to 30.11.62	Bloodhound SAM
266 Squadron	Sutton Bridge	3.11.39 to 1.3.40	Battle, Spitfire
269 Squadron	Caistor	22.7.59 to 24.5.63	Thor IRBM
275 Squadron ('B' Flt)	North Coates	11.54 to 1.9.59	Sycamore
278 Squadron	North Coates	26.11.41 to 12.1.43	Lysander
280 Squadron	Strubby	1.5.44 to 6.9.44	Warwick
288 Squadron	Digby	18.11.41 to 5.12.42	Blenheim, Spitfire, Hurricane, Hudson, Lysander, Oxford, Defiant
288 Squadron	Wellingore	5.12.42 to 18.1.43	Blenheim, Spitfire, Hurricane, Hudson, Lysander, Oxford, Defiant
288 Squadron	Digby	18.1.43 to 9.11.43	Blenheim, Spitfire, Hurricane, Hudson, Lysander, Oxford, Defiant
288 Squadron	Coleby Grange	9.11.43 to 25.11.43	Oxford, Defiant, Hudson
288 Squadron	Digby	25.11.43 to 11.1.44	Blenheim, Spitfire, Hurricane, Hudson, Lysander, Oxford, Defiant
300 (Polish) Squadron	Swinderby	22.8.40 to 18.7.41	Battle, Wellington
300 (Polish) Squadron	Hemswell	18.7.41 to 18.5.42	Wellington
300 (Polish) Squadron	Cammeringham	18.5.42 to 31.1.43	Wellington
300 (Polish) Squadron	Hemswell	31.1.43 to 22.6.43	Wellington
300 (Polish) Squadron	Cammeringham	22.6.43 to 1.3.44	Wellington
300 (Polish) Squadron	Faldingworth	1.3.44 to 11.10.46	Wellington, Lancaster
301 Bomb Group	Scampton	18.10.48 to 15.1.49	B-29 Superfortress
301 (Polish) Squadron	Swinderby	28.8.40 to 18.7.41	Battle, Wellington

Wellington Ic X9616 GR-T of 301 Squadron.
(IWM MH6253)

Unit	Airfield	From/to	Types operated
301 (Polish) Squadron	Hemswell	18.7.41 to 7.4.43	Wellington
302 (Polish) Squadron	Digby	2.43 to 2.43	Spitfire
302 (Polish) Squadron	Kirton in Lindsey	2.2.43 to 17.4.43	Spitfire
303 (Polish) Squadron	Kirton in Lindsey	16.6.42 to 2.2.43	Spitfire
305 (Polish) Squadron	Hemswell	23.7.42 to 22.6.43	Wellington
305 (Polish) Squadron	Cammeringham	22.6.43 to 5.9.43	Wellington
305 (Polish) Squadron	Faldingworth	10.46 to 6.1.47	Mosquito
306 (Polish) Squadron	Kirton in Lindsey	3.5.42 to 16.6.42	Spitfire
307 (Polish) Squadron	Kirton in Lindsey	5.9.40 to 7.11.40	Defiant
307 (Polish) Squadron	Coleby Grange	2.3.44 to 4.5.44	Mosquito
310 (Czech) Squadron	Digby	11.7.44 to 28.8.44	Spitfire
313 TCG	Folkingham	4.2.44 to 28.2.45	C-47, C-53
316 (Polish) Squadron (Det)	Kirton in Lindsey	15.8.42 to 20.8.42	Spitfire
316 (Polish) Squadron (Det)	Digby	20.12.43 to	Spitfire
317 (Polish) Squadron	Kirton in Lindsey	13.2.43 to 29.4.43	Spitfire
320 Flight	Killingholme	5.18 to 7.18	Curtiss H-12
321 Flight	Killingholme	5.18 to 7.18	Curtiss H-12
322 Flight	Killingholme	5.18 to 7.18	Curtiss H-12
342 Bomb Sqn/97 Bomb Grp	Waddington	2.11.48 to 10.2.49	B-29 Superfortress
349 TCG	Barkston Heath	3.45 to 18.4.45	C-46, C-47
349 (Belgian) Squadron	Wellingore	5.8.43 to 25.8.43	Spitfire

Unit	Airfield	From/to	Types operated
350 (Belgian) Squadron	Digby	26.8.43 to 7.9.43	Spitfire
350 (Belgian) Squadron	Digby	18.9.43 to 13.10.43	Spitfire
353 Fighter Group	Goxhill	8.1.43 to 5.8.43	P-47 Thunderbolt
356 Fighter Group	Goxhill	26.8.43 to 12.10.43	P-47 Thunderbolt
358 Fighter Group	Goxhill	20.10.43 to 3.12.43	P-47 Thunderbolt
372 Bomb Sqn/307 Bomb Grp	Waddington	18.7.48 to 19.10.48	B-29 Superfortress
401 Flight, Fleet Air Arm*	Sutton Bridge		Armament Practice Camp
401 (RCAF) Squadron	Digby	1.3.41 to 20.10.41	Hurricane, Spitfire
402 Flight, Fleet Air Arm*	Sutton Bridge		Armament Practice Camp
402 (RCAF) Squadron	Digby	1.3.41 to 22.5.41	Hurricane
402 (RCAF) Squadron	Wellingore	22.5.41 to 22.6.41	Spitfire
402 (RCAF) Squadron	Digby	21.3.43 to 7.8.43	Spitfire
402 (RCAF) Squadron	Digby	19.9.43 to 11.2.44	Spitfire
402 (RCAF) Squadron	Wellingore	12.2.44 to 29.4.44	Spitfire
403 Flight	Killingholme	5.18 to 15.8.18	Short 184, Short 320
404 Flight	Killingholme	5.18 to 15.8.18	Short 184, Short 320
404 Flight	Sutton Bridge		Armament Practice Camps
404 (RCAF) Squadron	Strubby	1.7.44 to 3.9.44	Beaufighter
407 Squadron	North Coates	9.7.41 to 17.2.42	Hudson
407 Flight, Fleet Air Arm	Sutton Bridge		Armament Practice Camp
409 (RCAF) Squadron	Digby	17.6.41 to 27.7.41	Defiant
409 (RCAF) Squadron	Hibaldstow	10.2.42 to 21.2.42	Beaufighter
409 (RCAF) Squadron	Coleby Grange	25.7.41 to 27.2.43	Defiant, Beaufighter
410 (RCAF) Squadron	Coleby Grange	21.2.43 to 21.10.43	Mosquito
411 (RCAF) Squadron	Digby	16.6.41 to 18.11.41	Spitfire
411 (RCAF) Squadron	Digby	30.3.42 to 21.3.43	Spitfire
412 (RCAF) Squadron	Digby	30.6.41 to 20.10.41	Spitfire
412 (RCAF) Squadron	Wellingore	20.10.41 to 30.4.42	Spitfire
415 (RCAF) Squadron	North Coates	5.6.42 to 30.7.42	Hudson
416 (RCAF) Squadron	Digby	7.6.43 to 8.8.43	Spitfire
416 (RCAF) Squadron	Wellingore	19.9.43 to 1.10.43	Spitfire
416 (RCAF) Squadron	Digby	2.10.43 to 11.2.44	Spitfire
420 (RCAF) Squadron	Waddington	19.12.41 to 6.8.42	Hampden
421 (RCAF) Squadron	Digby	9.4.42 to 2.5.42	Spitfire
434 TCG	Fulbeck	7.10.43 to 10.12.43	C-47
438 (RCAF) Squadron	Digby	20.11.43 to 18.12.43	Hurricane
439 (RCAF) Squadron	Wellingore	31.12.43 to 7.1.44	Hurricane
440 TCG	Fulbeck	8.44 to 9.44	C-47
441 (RCAF) Squadron	Digby	8.2.44 to 17.3.44	Spitfire
441 (RCAF) Squadron	Digby	17.5.45 to 16.7.45	P-51 Mustang
442 TCG	Fulbeck	29.3.44 to 13.6.44	C-47, C-53
442 (RCAF) Squadron	Digby	8.2.44 to 17.3.44	Spitfire
442 (RCAF) Squadron	Digby	17.5.45 to 16.7.45	P-51 Mustang
443 (RCAF) Squadron	Digby	8.2.44 to 17.3.44	Spitfire
452 (RAAF) Squadron	Kirton in Lindsey	18.4.41 to 19.7.41	Spitfire
455 (RAAF) Squadron	Swinderby	6.6.41 to 27.11.41	Hampden
455 (RAAF) Squadron	Skellingthorpe	27.11.41 to 8.2.42	Hampden

Hampden of 455 Squadron
(RAF Museum P7553)

Unit	Airfield	From/to	Types operated
457 (RAAF) Squadron	Kirton in Lindsey	1.6.42 to 8.6.42	Spitfire
460 (RAAF) Squadron	Binbrook	14.5.43 to 27.7.45	Lancaster
460 (RAAF) Squadron	East Kirkby	27.7.45 to 10.10.45	Lancaster
463 (RAAF) Squadron	Waddington	25.11.43 to 3.7.45	Lancaster
463 (RAAF) Squadron	Skellingthorpe	3.7.45 to 19.9.45	Lancaster
467 (RAAF) Squadron	Scampton	11.42 to 11.42	Lancaster
467 (RAAF) Squadron	Waddington	11.11.43 to 6.45	Lancaster
467 (RAAF) Squadron	Metheringham	6.45 to 30.9.45	Lancaster
486 (RNZAF) Squadron	Kirton in Lindsey	3.3.42 to 9.4.42	Hurricane
486 (RNZAF) Squadron	Hibaldstow	27.7.42 to 11.8.42	Hurricane
496 FTG	Goxhill	25.12.43 to 15.2.45	P-38 Lightning, P-51 Mustang, Master, Lysander
503 (County of Lincoln) Sqn	Waddington	5.10.26 to 31.10.38	Avro 504, Fawn. Tutor, Hyderabad, Hinaidi, Wallace, Hart, Hind

Westland Wallace II K5078 of 503 Squadron.
(via P.H.T.Green)

504 Squadron	Digby	26.8.39 to 7.10.39	Hurricane
504 Squadron	Digby	29.4.44 to 11.7.44	Spitfire
505 Flight	Greenland Top	.18 to 11.18	DH 6
508 SFW	Sturgate	.54 to .54	F-84
527 Squadron	Digby	28.4.44 to 8.11.45	Spitfire, Wellington, Oxford
528 Squadron	Digby	15.5.44 to 1.9.44	Blenheim
532 Squadron	Hibaldstow	9.9.42 to 25.1.43	Havoc, Hurricane
538 Squadron	Hibaldstow	2.9.42 to 25.1.43	Havoc, Hurricane
542 Squadron	Hemswell	1.4.57 to 17.7.58	Canberra
550 Squadron	Grimsby	25.11.43 to 3.1.44	Lancaster
550 Squadron	North Killingholme	3.1.44 to 31.10.45	Lancaster
576 Squadron	Elsham Wolds	25.11.43 to 30.10.44	Lancaster
576 Squadron	Fiskerton	30.10.44 to 13.9.45	Lancaster
608 Squadron	North Coates	15.9.42 to 2.11.42	Hudson
609 Squadron	Digby	21.11.41 to 30.3.42	Spitfire
611 Squadron	Digby	10.10.39 to 7.40	Spitfire
611 Squadron	Digby	8.40 to 14.12.40	Spitfire
613 Squadron	Wellingore	29.3.43 to 28.5.43	P-51 Mustang
616 Squadron	Kirton in Lindsey	10.9.40 to 26.2.41	Spitfire
616 Squadron	Kirton in Lindsey	7.10.41 to 30.1.42	Spitfire
616 Squadron (Det)	Goxhill	15.1.42 to 25.1.42	Spitfire
617 Squadron	Scampton	21.3.43 to 30.8.43	Lancaster
617 Squadron	Coningsby	30.8.43 to 9.1.44	Lancaster

Unit	Airfield	From/to	Types operated
617 Squadron	Woodhall Spa	9.1.44 to 17.6.45	Lancaster, Mosquito
617 Squadron	Waddington	17.6.45 to 1.46	Lancaster
617 Squadron	Binbrook	5.46 to 5.12.55	Lancaster, Lincoln, Canberra
617 Squadron	Scampton	1.5.58 to 1.1.82	Vulcan

Vulcan B2 XL318 of 617 Squadron, Scampton, 25th July 1981. *(MAP)*

Unit	Airfield	From/to	Types operated
619 Squadron	Woodhall Spa	18.4.43 to 9.1.44	Lancaster
619 Squadron	Coningsby	9.1.44 to 17.4.44	Lancaster
619 Squadron	Dunholme Lodge	17.4.44 to 28.9.44	Lancaster
619 Squadron	Strubby	28.9.44 to 30.6.45	Lancaster
619 Squadron	Skellingthorpe	30.6.45 to 18.7.45	Lancaster
625 Squadron	Kelstern	1.10.43 to 5.4.45	Lancaster
625 Squadron	Scampton	5.4.45 to 2.10.45	Lancaster
626 Squadron	Wickenby	7.11.43 to 14.10.45	Lancaster
627 Squadron	Woodhall Spa	15.4.44 to 30.9.45	Mosquito
630 Squadron	East Kirkby	15.11.43 to 18.7.45	Lancaster
643 Gliding School	Kirton in Lindsey	4.55 to 1.11.65	T21 Sedbergh, T30 Prefect
643 Gliding School	Hemswell	1.11.65 to 4.74	T21 Sedbergh, T8 Tutor

Slingsby T31 Cadet TX3 XE795 of 643 GS at Hemswell, 23rd March 1972. *(P.H.T.Green)*

Unit	Airfield	From/to	Types operated
643 Gliding School	Scampton	25.3.82 to date	T21 Sedbergh, T31 Cadet
644 Gliding School	Spitalgate	to .75	T21 Sedbergh, T31 Cadet
776 Squadron, Fleet Air Arm	North Coates	2.42 to 3.42	Roc
800 Squadron, Fleet Air Arm*	Sutton Bridge		Armament Practice Camp
801 Squadron, Fleet Air Arm*	Sutton Bridge		Armament Practice Camp
802 Squadron, Fleet Air Arm*	Sutton Bridge		Armament Practice Camp
812 Squadron, Fleet Air Arm	North Coates	11.5.40 to 14.3.41	Swordfish
816 Squadron, Fleet Air Arm	North Coates	15.3.41 to 2.5.41	Swordfish
1321 LC Flight	Hemswell	1.10.57 to 2.4.58	Lincoln
1439 Flight	Hemswell	1.5.57 to 20.11.57	Varsity
1453 Flight	Hibaldstow	27.7.42 to 21.8.42	Havoc
1459 Flight	Hibaldstow	23.9.41 to 2.9.42	Havoc
1481 (B) 'G' Flight	Blyton	26.9.42 to 2.11.42	Whitley, Wellington, Defiant, Lysander
1481 (B) 'G' Flight	Cammeringham	15.3.44 to 25.11.44	Wellington, Martinet
1485 (TT) Flight	Scampton	19.8.41 to 1.8.42	Wellington, Lysander
1485 (B) 'G' Flight	Dunholme Lodge	1.8.42 to 27.10.42	Lysander, Battle, Wellington
1485 (B) 'G' Flight	Fulbeck	27.10.42 to 23.8.43	Lysander, Martinet, Lancaster, Manchester, Wellington
1485 (B) 'G' Flight	Skellingthorpe	23.8.43 to 12.11.43	Wellington, Martinet
1489 Flight	Sutton Bridge	10.41 to 13.4.42	Henley, Lysander, Martinet
1506 BAT Flight	Waddington	16.11.41 to 5.43	Oxford

Unit	Airfield	From/to	Types operated
1506 BAT Flight	Fulbeck	5.43 to 23.8.43	Oxford
1506 BAT Flight (HQ Unit)	Skellingthorpe	23.8.43 to 2.10.43	Oxford
1514 BAT Flight	Coningsby	11.41 to 8.3.43	Oxford
1514 BAT Flight	Woodhall Spa	8.3.43 to .43	Oxford
1514 BAT Flight	Coningsby	3.43 to 2.1.44	Oxford
1514 BAT Flight	Fiskerton	4.1.44 to 9.1.45	Oxford
1515 BAT Flight	Coleby Grange	28.2.45 to 1.6.45	Oxford
1518 BAT Flight	Scampton	.41 to 14.6.43	Oxford
1520 BAT Flight	Sturgate	18.9.44 to 2.45	Oxford
1536 BAT Flight	Spitalgate	8.3.43 to 8.5.45	Oxford
1546 BAT Flight	Faldingworth	8.5.44 to 9.1.45	Oxford
1654 Heavy Conversion Unit	Swinderby	19.5.42 to 16.6.42	Manchester, Oxford
1656 HCU ('B' Flt)	Elsham Wolds	10.10.42 to 11.42	Halifax
1660 Heavy Conversion Unit	Swinderby	20.10.42 to 11.46	Manchester, Lancaster, Halifax, Stirling
1661 Heavy Conversion Unit	Waddington	9.11.42 to 20.12.42	Manchester, Lancaster

Lancaster I W4113 GP-J of 1661 HCU.
(via J.D.Oughton)

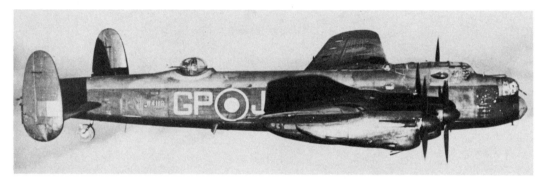

Unit	Airfield	From/to	Types operated
1662 Heavy Conversion Unit	Blyton	1.2.43 to 6.4.45	Halifax, Lancaster
1667 Heavy Conversion Unit	Faldingworth	8.8.43 to 19.2.44	Halifax, Lancaster
1667 Heavy Conversion Unit	Sandtoft	18.2.44 to 10.11.45	Halifax, Lancaster
1682 BDT Flight	Ludford Magna	4.44 to 7.44	Oxford
1687 BDT Flight	Cammeringham	1.3.44 to 3.12.44	Spitfire, Hurricane
1687 BDT Flight	Scampton	4.12.44 to 2.4.45	Spitfire, Hurricane, Martinet
1687 BDT Flight	Hemswell	2.4.45 to 30.10.46	Spitfire, Hurricane, Martinet

Hurricane II LF581 and Spitfire VB BM343 of 1687 BDT Flight.
(N.Franklin)

Unit	Airfield	From/to	Types operated
1690 BDT Flight	Scampton	13.7.44 to 27.9.44	Spitfire, Hurricane, Martinet
1690 BDT Flight	Metheringham	27.9.44 to 4.6.45	Spitfire, Hurricane, Martinet
3914 Air Base Squadron	Waddington	16.5.51 to 3.55	C-47
3917 Air Base Group	East Kirkby	c.11.54 to 1.8.58	C-47
3928 Air Base Squadron	Sturgate	6.53 to .54	C-47
3928 Air Base Group	Sturgate	.54 to 1.8.58	C-47
3931 Air Base Group	East Kirkby	17.4.54 to c.11.54	C-47

Unit	Airfield	From/to	Types operated
RAF Aerobatic Team 'The Red Arrows'	Scampton	25.3.83 to date	Hawk

A Selection of Representative Aircraft

DETAILS EXTRACTED FROM VARIOUS FORM 540 OPERATIONAL RECORD BOOKS

BARDNEY
No.9 Sqn: Lancasters known include LL845/WS-L, ME809/WS-X, PB289/WS-B. A Lancaster with the **Bomber Command Film Unit** was PD329/G7-Y).

BINBROOK
No 12 Sqn: Battle P6571. Wellington deliveries known are W5360 del 7 Dec 40, W5367 del 3 Jan 41, W5444 del 5 Jul 41, W5598 del 27 Jul 41. **No 142 Sqn:** Wellington deliveries W5363 del 4 Dec 40, W5368 del 7 Dec 40, W5383 del 17 Jan 41, W5514 del 30 Jul 41. **AFDS/CFE/FCTU:** Hunter F6 departures to 229 OCU included XE608 (11 Apr 63), XF382 (22 Feb 66), XF418 (Aug 66), XF512 (17 Feb 66), XF514 (4 Oct 63), XG197 del 13 Nov 62 (to 229 OCU 22 Feb 66). Hunter T7s XL573/L (to 229 OCU 1 Dec 63), XL591 (27 May 64), XL593 (1 Dec 63). Lightning deliveries: F1A XM137/Y on 15 Mar 66, F3 XP695/R 1 Jan 64, F6 XR752/V 26 Nov 65. **No 460 Sqn:** Lancasters known are W5005/AR-E^2, JA683/AR-D^2, LM647/AR-F^2 and ND658/AR-G2. **No 1481 'B' and 'G' Flt:** Whitley V T4176/O arr from Linton 29 Mar 42, dep to Marshall's 31 May 43; Z6469/M from Linton 29 Mar 42, Z6966/N from Linton 18 Mar 42, to 1478 Flt on 17 May 43; Z9149/P from Leeming 24 Apr 42, crashed 22 Sep 42. Wellington L7789 arrived from Lindholme 15 Mar 42, other recorded are X9815/Y, Z1150/W, Z1315/C, X3283 from 300 Sqn 24 Jul 43 then to 27 OTU 22 Aug 43, Z1686 from 166 Sqn 2 Aug 43. A Martinet of this unit was MS696 delivered from Powis Ltd 30 Aug 43.

COLEBY GRANGE
No 1515 BAT Flt: Oxford deliveries from Peplow included LX427 (27 Feb 45), V4259, HM723, HM956, LX522, PH131 all on 28 Feb 45.

CONINGSBY
No 1514 BAT Flt: Oxford deliveries from the Standard Motor Company were V4091 (29 Sep 41), V4092 (27 Sep 41), V4093 (29 Sep 41), V4094 (29 Sep 41), V4095 (29 Sep 41), V4096 (30 Sep 41), V4135 (14 Oct 41), V4136 (15 Oct 41). Also AT767 was delivered from 1506 Flt on 17 Dec 42 and DF488 on 6 Aug 42.

ELSHAM WOLDS
No 21 HGCU: Halifax serials recorded are KA375, LW651, PP376, PP378/FEP-M and RN571. Horsa serials RN516, RX777, RX817, TK869, TL187.

FALDINGWORTH
No 1546 BAT Flt: Oxford movements recorded are HM837 del May 44 to South Cerney 21 Jan 45, HM838 del May 44 to South Cerney 14 Jan 45, NJ376 del May 44 to 18(P)AFU 12 Jan 45, NJ399 del May 44 to South Cerney 20 Jan 45, NJ400 del May 44 to Church Lawford 1 Feb 45. **No 1667 HCU** operated Halifaxes serialled DG286, DG287, DG338, DG352, EB152, EB185, EB193.

FULBECK
No 49 Sqn: Lancaster PB463/EA-I crashed on tech site on 22 Apr 45, 7 crew, 8 ground staff killed, 20 to hospital of which 4 persons died later. **No 1506 BAT Flt:** This unit loaned out Oxfords to various squadrons as follows: AT760 to 9 Sqn at Bardney, AT779 to 44 Sqn Waddington, AT778 to 49 Sqn at Fiskerton, AT664 to 57 Sqn at Scampton, AT665 to 61 Sqn at Syerston, DF424 to 207 Sqn at Langar, AT653 to 467 Sqn at Bottesford and AT619 to 617 Sqn at Woodhall Spa.

GOXHILL
496 FTG: Aircraft operated included Masters W8836, DL487 and Lysander T1553.

GRIMSBY
No 100 Sqn: Lancasters LM584/HW-F^2, PB462/HW-P^2.

HEMSWELL
No 61 Sqn: Anson M9824 crashed on 12 Mar 40, N5187 crashed 17 Apr 40. Blenheims K7170/61-V and K7160/61-U. **No 144 Sqn:** Blenheim K7119 crashed on 11 Feb 38; L1321 also known. Hampden incidents recorded are L4137 which dived into the ground near Scotter on 20 Mar 40, L4143 crashed at night near Kirton in Lindsey on 22 Apr 40 and L4163 hit a house on take off on 17 Apr 40. **No 300 Sqn:** Wellingtons R1178, R1617, X9639. **No 301 Sqn:** Wellingtons T8625 and X1253/GR-B. **No 1 LFS:** Lancaster R5500/3C-K and W4965/3C-Z (crashed at Heapham on 16 May 44). **No 109 Sqn:** Mosquito B35 VR795 coded HS-B.

MANBY
No 1 AAS: Henley L3379 hit ground near North Coates on 19 Mar 41; Blenheim L1358 crashed at Great Carlton 10 Jul 40; Battle N2083 force landed at Grimoldby 8 Apr 40. Other types mentioned include Gordons K1168, K1773; Hudson T9353; Hart K2461 and Magister N3882 which arrived on 26 Sep 44. **EAAS/RAF FC:** Lancasters PB873 'Thor', NX778/FG-AD, NX779/AB; Lincoln RF523 'Thor II'; Lancastrian VM731/FG-AH, VL968/FG-AJ; Canberra B2 WH699 'Aries IV'. **RAF Handling Sqn:** Athena VR566 arrived from CFS 2 Feb 50, to RAF FC 21 Jun 50; Balliol VR595 arrived 6 Feb 50, to CFS 25 Jan 51; Marathon XA274 arrived 28 May 53, to CFS 1 Oct 53; Valetta WG256 arrived 21 Aug 51, to 5 ANS 19 Jan 52.

SANDTOFT
No 1667 HCU: Known Halifaxes on strength EB146/GG-B, EB149/GG-C, EB184/GG-C, EB190/GG-H, DG293/GG-M, DG305/GG-D, DG317/GG-J, DG345/GG-P, DG351/GG-V, DG355/GG-G, DG998/GG-E, DK182/GG-A2, LL535/GG-N. Lancasters W4154, W4891, JB306, ND855, LM509, PB565.

NORTH COATES
No 22 Sqn: Beaufort incidents recorded include L4451 which crashed on take-off at North Coates on 11 Jan 40, L4516 crashed near Marshchapel 18 Dec 40, L4518 crashed during a forced landing at North Coates. **No 143 Sqn:** Beaufighter II T3434 crashed in the sea at Tetney Haven 7 Nov 43, T3447 dived into

the ground at Aylesby 27 Jan 43, V8150 undershot on landing at North Coates on 4 Dec 42.

SCAMPTON
No 49 Sqn: Hampdens X2900/EA-S and P1251/EA-X. **No 83 Sqn**: Hampden X2978/OL-K. **No 1485 Flt**: Lysander arrivals included T1466 (on 29 Oct 41), T1687 (29 Oct 41) and later crashed 29 Feb 42, V9865 (28 Oct 41), V9866 (28 Oct 41). **No 1687 Flt**: Spitfires operated P8695, W3439, AA753, AB194, BM343/4E-U. Hurricanes PG537, LF572, PZ737. Martinets HP207, HP323, MS642, MS746. **No 230 OCU**: Had Lincolns RF350/SN-L and RF562/SN-N.

SUTTON BRIDGE
No 3 ATC: Avro 504N H2434 arrived on 25 May 28 and crashed at Henlow 1 Jul 28. **No 3 ATS**: Henleys L3262, L3270 and L3333. **No 1489 Flt**: Master III W8839 arrived 23 Mar 42, to Matlaske 12 Apr 42; W8856 arrived 23 Mar 42, to Matlaske 12 Apr 42. Henleys operated included L3247, L3267, L3310, L3320. **No 56 OTU**: Gladiator K8015 arrived from 5 OTU on 25 May 40. Hurricane L1713 crashed near Sutton Bridge on 15 Oct 40, L1851 crashed at Tydd St Mary 1 Nov 40, L2083 caught fire in mid-air and crashed near Sutton Bridge on 8 Oct 40. Other Hurricanes noted are P2558, R2680 and Z4669/F8-U. Henley L3375 crashed in a forced landing at Sutton Bridge 12 Feb 41. Battles L5714, N8011, N8021, V1204 and Harvard N7178 are also mentioned. **CGS**: Hudson N7404 crashed on take-off at Sutton Bridge on 9 Dec 42. Spitfires P7851, P8033, P8048, P8583 (crashed at Spalding 2 Jul 42), P8663. Lysander T1618 force landed at Dawsmere School 5 Jul 42, also V9496 force-landed at Holbeach 11 May 43, W6955. Master DL684 and Hampden P5343 also on strength. Mustang AM170 force-landed at Sutton Bridge 4 Mar 43 and AP230 also noted. Wellingtons used include N2876, N2909, N3019, BK277, BK632.

SWINDERBY
No 300 Sqn: Wellington R1183/BH-B. **No 301 Sqn**: Battle L5555/GR-H and Wellington R1349/GR-N noted. **No 1654 HCU**: Manchester L7419/UG-B. **No 1660 HCU**: Lancaster ED811 crashed near Lincoln 9 Dec 43 and ED812/TV-Y was written-off at Dunholme Lodge on 10 Nov 43. Stirling EF232 crashed at Carlton le Moorland 31 Jan 44 and EF246 crashed at Bardney 1 Oct 43. **No 201 AFS**: Valetta arrivals included WJ467 on 13 Mar 52, to 6 ANS on 17 Jul 53; WK474 on 6 May 52, to 2 ANS on 2 Jul 52. Earlier aircraft were Wellington T10 RP550/F-MBY and NB113/F-MBD. Varsity T1s WF423/X, WF330/D.

WADDINGTON
No 1506 BAT Flt: Blenheim movements include L1294 which arrived 2 Apr 41 to 8 BAT Flt 20 Sep 41, L1304 arr 11 Feb 41 to 8 BAT Flt 12 Oct 41, L6646 arr 24 Feb 41 to 8 BAT Flt 20 Sep 41, L6738 arr 25 Feb 41 to 8 BAT Flt 12 Oct 41. Hampden AD837 arrived 21 May 41 then to 83 Sqn on 26 Jun 41, AD859 arr 25 May 41 to 83 Sqn 25 Jun 41. Oxford movements are well documented: AS146 arr 1 Jun 41, to 16 OTU 10 Sep 41; AS147 arr 1 Jun 41, to 16 OTU 10 Sep 41; V3995 arr 11 Jul 41, to 16 OTU 3 Sep 41; V3996 arr 11 Jul 41, to 16 OTU 3 Sep 41; V4033 arr 13 Aug 41, written off 7 Oct 41; V4034 arr 12 Aug 41, written off 7 Oct 41; V4041 arr 21 Aug 41, crashed 23 Sep 41; V4042 arr 28 Aug 41; V4194 arr from 1524 Flt on 14 Dec 41. Anson N9835 was received from 44 Sqn on 2 Apr 41 and returned to 44 Sqn on 10 Jul 41.

WELLINGORE
RAF College SFTS: Master crashes at Wellingore included AZ702 on 5 May 44, DL937 on 1 May 44, DM326 on 12 May 44. Oxford crashes at Wellingore included R5952 on 15 May 44, V3858 on 12 May 44, DF950 on 7 May 44, HM946 stalled while on approach on 3 Apr 44.

WOODHALL SPA
No 617 Sqn: Lancasters recorded are ME554/KC-F, ME555/KC-C, PD114/YZ-B, PD118/YZ-M, PD139/YZ-W.

APPENDIX C
Bomber Command Base Organisation

Throughout the Second World War Bomber Command closely controlled the conduct of the bomber offensive from its Headquarters at High Wycombe (Buckinghamshire). Instructions to the stations and squadrons were issued through Group Headquarters who were responsible for ensuring that Bomber Command's requirements for the number of aircraft to be despatched, their bomb loads, departure times, route and altitude both to and from the target area were met.

The stations provided accommodation, maintenance, messing and aerodrome facilities for the squadrons which were autonomous units responsible for their own administration and aircraft servicing. To streamline this organisation in early 1943 Bomber Command began to implement its newly-devised bomber operational base system. A Base was to consist of a parent or base station plus one or more satellite or sub-stations. Usually the base station was one of the pre-war permanent stations, eg Binbrook, from which the base took its name. The sub-stations were usually wartime-built temporary airfields although, in such cases as East Kirkby and Ludford Magna some temporary airfields did become base stations.

One or two bomber squadrons were housed on each individual station and Station Headquarters assumed full administrative responsibility for the squadrons. A central maintenance facility was also provided to support the squadrons. As a result, squadron establishments were reduced to consist only of aircrew and aircraft with a small ground staff to carry out various operational duties and handle daily servicing of the aircraft.

As it had to carry out major servicings on aircraft from the sub-stations of the base in addition to its own aircraft the base station was provided with additional hangars and technical facilities. At East Kirkby three additional T2 hangars and one MAP Type B1 hangar were built side-by-side on the northwestern corner of the airfield to accommodate the base maintenance area.

Initially bases were identified geographically, eg RAF Base Binbrook, or by role, eg No.1 Group Heavy Conversion Base. However, on 16th September 1943 Bomber Command issued a directive stating that bases were to be known by number and not by geographical location.

The number was to be a two-figure combination, the first figure denoting the parent group and the second the base itself. Training or conversion bases were to be number one in each group. Thus, the No.1 Group Heavy Conversion Base became 11 Base and Binbrook became 12 Base, in each case the first digit of the base number indicating that 1 Group was the parent group. The bases in other groups were numbered in a similar manner, eg 55 Base (Operational Base within 5 Group) or 61 Base (Training Base within 6 Group). Later, groups tended to locate squadrons with similar roles within a single base as at 54

Base, Coningsby, which housed various special duty squadrons of 5 Group on its stations.

In late 1944 Bomber Command formed an additional group, No.7, to control operational training within the command. All training units were transferred from the operational groups to the new group with little disruption to the vital training task as already they were grouped into bases. As before, the training bases were identified by a two-digit number; the first, 7, indicationg the group and the second the base itself. Conveniently, 71 Base was the former 11 Base and it continued to provide crews for 1 Group squadrons, in the same manner that 75 Base (the former 51 Base) continued to supply crews for 5 Group squadrons. In this way the close liaison already developed between the training bases and the operational bases was maintained.

The table below lists those bases that contained Lincolnshire stations. Where a sub-station was part of a base throughout the existence of the base then no additional dates are shown. However, where a sub-station was part of a base for a shorter period that the existence of the base then the exact dates are shown separately.

No.1 GROUP BASES

No.11 Base.
Formed on 1st July 1943 as 1 Group Heavy Conversion Base. Renumbered 11 Base on 18th September 1943. Transferred to 7 Group and renumbered 71 Base on 5th November 1944.
Base Station: Lindholme, Yorkshire
Sub Stations: Blyton
              Faldingworth   24 Jul 1943 to 23 Jan 1944
              Sandtoft   from 18 Feb 1944

No.12 Base.
Formed on 25th March 1943 as RAF Base Binbrook, the first Base within 1 Group. Later renumbered 12 Base. Disbanded 31st March 1945.
Base Station: Binbrook
Sub Stations: Grimsby
              Kelstern

No.13 Base.
Formed 1st January 1944. Disbanded 15th December 1945.
Base Station: Elsham Wolds
Sub Stations: Kirmington
              North Killingholme

No.14 Base.
Formed 15th December 1943. Disbanded 25th October 1945.
Base Station: Ludford Magna
Sub Stations: Faldingworth   from 23 Jan 1944
             Wickenby

No.15 Base.
Formed 7th October 1944 on the handover of 52 Base to 1 Group. Disbanded 20th October 1945.
Base Station: Scampton
Sub Station: Cammeringham   1 Dec 1944 to 18 Jun 1945
           Dunholme Lodge   7 Oct 1944 to 18 Jun 1945
           Fiskerton
           Hemswell   from 1 Dec 1944

No.5 GROUP BASES

No.51 Base.
Formed 15th March 1943 as RAF (Conversion) Base Swinderby. Base Headquarters were located at Morton Hall until 24th October 1943 when they were moved into Swinderby itself. Taken over by 7 Group and renumbered 75 Base on 3rd November 1944.
Base Station: Swinderby
Sub Stations: Syerston, Notts.   21 Nov 1943 to 1 Oct 1944
            Wigsley, Notts.
            Winthorpe, Notts.

No.52 Base.
Formed 10th May 1943. Disbanded on 2nd October 1944 on handover to 1 Group.
Base Station: Scampton
Sub Stations: Dunholme Lodge
            Fiskerton

No.53 Base.
Formed 15th November 1943. Disbanded 15th November 1945.
Base Station: Waddington
Sub Stations: Bardney
            Skellingthorpe

No.54 Base.
Formed 1st January 1944. Disbanded 15th November 1945.
Base Station: Coningsby
Sub Stations: Metheringham
            Woodhall Spa

No.55 Base.
Formed 22nd April 1944. Disbanded 15th November 1945.
Base Station: East Kirkby
Sub Stations: Spilsby
            Strubby

No.56 Base.
Formed 1st October 1944. Disbanded 25th April 1945.
Base Station: Syerston, Notts
Sub Stations: Balderton, Notts
            Fulbeck

No.7 GROUP BASES

No.71 Base.
Formed 5th November 1944 on handover to 7 Group of 11 Base. Disbanded 31st October 1945.
Base Station: Lindholme, Yorkshire
Sub Stations: Blyton
            Sandtoft
            Sturgate   from 1st Dec 1944

No.75 Base.
Formed 3rd November 1944 on handover to 7 Group of 51 Base. Disbanded on 1st October 1945.
Base Station: Swinderby
Sub Stations: Wigsley, Notts
            Winthorpe, Notts

APPENDIX D

Airfield Defence and the Royal Air Force Regiment

The aerodromes which the Royal Flying Corps and later, the Royal Air Force, operated from in the 1914-18 war were defended from enemy attack by ground forces. The strength of these forces depended on the location, size and vulnerability of each station.

In the early 1930s a threat of forthcoming German aggression seemed imminent and the question of airfield defence became a matter for urgent consideration. In November 1933 the War Department agreed that the Royal Air Force would organise its own defences and in 1935 a special committee was established to examine the possible alternatives to the machine gun for defending airfields against expected enemy air attack.

In 1937 the Air Council directed that Air Officers Commanding would be responsible for . . . 'the defence of Royal Air Force stations and other Royal Air Force Establishments against air attack from low flying aircraft and for local defence against land forces'. To implement these tasks, stations were issued with up to eight Vickers machine guns or the equivalent in Lewis guns for anti-aircraft defence. The ground defence personnel were issued with light automatic weapons in place of the standard .303 rifle. It is ironical to record that the rifle had been phased out and withdrawn before a suitable replacement weapon had been decided upon. When the emergency of 1938 developed, security personnel had to be armed with whatever weapons were available at the time.

At the outbreak of hostilities 365 airfields in the British Isles were provided with machine guns manned by ground gunners trained at the Ground Defence Gunnery School at North Coates. The army provided light anti-aircraft defence for 139 airfields and up to 14,000 troops were employed on airfield defence and security tasks at 255 airfields.

With the withdrawal from France in 1940 of the British Expeditionary Force and the imminent threat of invasion, many of the Army units employed on airfield defence had to be withdrawn and redeployed. This left many RAF airfields with only lightly manned defences. The RAF was then urgently forced to develop its own defence organisation and a directive on ground defence was issued, ordering the reorganisation of existing resources to defend the airfields against enemy attack.

In April 1941 the existing station defence personnel were organised in squadrons which in December 1941 were numbered from 701 to 850. However, the squadrons were re-numbered from 2701 to 2850, when, by Royal Warrant dated 6th January 1942, all ground defence personnel became part of the RAF Regiment on 1st February 1942. Units were standardised into two types; the field squadrons, 2701 to 2850, each comprising 7 officers and 178 airmen; the Independent Anti-Aircraft Flights numbered 4001 to 4336, each comprising one officer and sixty airmen, trained to man twelve 20mm Hispano cannon.

Within a few months of having been formed the RAF Regiment was in a position to relieve most of the Army personnel engaged on airfield defence. Training for the new Regiment was provided by the Regimental Depot at Belton Park near Grantham. Four schools were set up, each dealing separately with weapons, field training, anti-aircraft gunnery and anti-tank gunnery.

At the height of the war years the RAF Regiment numbered over 85,000 officers and men formed into some 240 operational squadrons. This number was drastically cut at the end of the war, but in 1946 it was decided that the Regiment would continue to form a permanent and integral part of the Royal Air Force.

During 1980 three Royal Auxiliary Air Force Regiment units were formed to investigate the feasibility of using part-time personnel to defend airfields in the UK. One of these units, 2503 Squadron, was formed at Scampton.

Below are listed the RAF Regiment squadrons which served on the airfields of Lincolnshire during the period 1939 to 1945. Although this list is reasonably comprehensive, it is not considered by the authors to be complete and any additional information will be welcomed.

Ground Defence

| Gunnery School | North Coates | Dec 1939 – Jan 1940 |
| Regimental Depot | Belton Park | Dec 1941 – Aug 1946 |

Of the 150 defence squadrons which formed in April 1941 the following were formed in Lincolnshire:

2717	Hemswell	2749	Grantham
2724	Scampton	2782	Manby
2726	Swinderby	2793	Grantham
2729	Waddington	2806	Cranwell

Later, other squadrons were formed in Lincolnshire. These included:

2890	Waddington	Oct 1942
2953	Wellingore	1943
2956	Waddington	1943

Considerable movement of the defence squadrons took place throughout the war; some of the squadron movements within Lincolnshire were:

2702	Ludford Magna	Sep 1943 –	Apr 1944
2704	Folkingham (disbanded)	1945 –	Oct 1945
2705	North Coates	Oct 1942 –	Aug 1943
		Oct 1943 –	Jun 1944
2706	Hemswell	1943 –	Mar 1944
2709	Folkingham (disbanded)	1945 –	Oct 1945

2717	Sutton Bridge	Jun 1942 —	
2730	Belton Park (merged into Depot AA Sqn)		
		3 May 1944 —	Jun 1944
2733	Kirton in Lindsey	Dec 1943 —	
		—	Dec 1944
2735	Strubby	Nov 1944 —	
2737	Folkingham (disbanded)	29 Nov 1945 —	Dec 1945
2749	Scampton	1943 —	1944
2750	Sutton Bridge	Jun 1943 —	Jul 1943
2751	Spilsby	Feb 1944 —	
2753	Fiskerton	Dec 1944 —	
2756	Coningsby	—	Feb 1944
2778	North Coates	Jul 1944 —	Aug 1944
2790	North Coates	Sep 1943 —	Oct 1943
2791	Folkingham (disbanded)	30 Nov 1945 —	Dec 1945
2799	Dunholme Lodge	Nov 1944 —	Dec 1944
	Hemswell	Dec 1944 —	Apr 1945
	Ingham	Apr 1945 —	Jun 1945
	Fiskerton	Jun 1945 —	
2802	North Coates	Oct 1942 —	Aug 1943
2815	Digby	12 Apr 1944 —	14 Apr 1944
2830	Folkingham (disbanded)	29 Nov 1945 —	Dec 1945
2831	North Coates	Aug 1943 —	
2841	Belton Park (disbanded)	5 Jan 1945 —	Feb 1945
2842	Binbrook	Mar 1943 —	May 1943
2847	Folkingham (disbanded)	1945 —	Dec 1945
2849	Belton Park (merged into Depot AA Sqn)		
		3 May 1944 —	Jun 1944
2854	North Coates	Jun 1944 —	Aug 1944
2875	Folkingham (disbanded)	21 Nov 1945 —	Dec 1945
2882	Digby	12 Apr 1944 —	14 Apr 1944
2884	Sutton Bridge	Jun 1943 —	Oct 1943
2892	Digby	12 Apr 1944 —	14 Apr 1944
2894	Digby	12 Apr 1944 —	14 Apr 1944
2896	Digby	12 Apr 1944 —	14 Apr 1944
2899	North Coates	Aug 1943 —	Nov 1943
2949	Folkingham (disbanded)	1945 —	Dec 1945
2957	Belton Park (merged into Depot AA Sqn)		
		3 May 1944 —	Jun 1944

Independent Anti-Aircraft Flights stationed in Lincolnshire between 1939 and 1945 included:

4011	Sutton Bridge	—	Mar 1943
4074	Sutton Bridge	Mar 1943 —	Apr 1943
4182	Sutton Bridge	Apr 1943 —	
4192	Binbrook	—	Jun 1943
4212	Binbrook	—	
4214	Binbrook	May 1943 —	
4254	Hemswell	—	Jun 1943
4257	Blyton	—	Jun 1943
4307	Ludford Magna	—	Sep 1943
	Hemswell	Sep 1943 —	

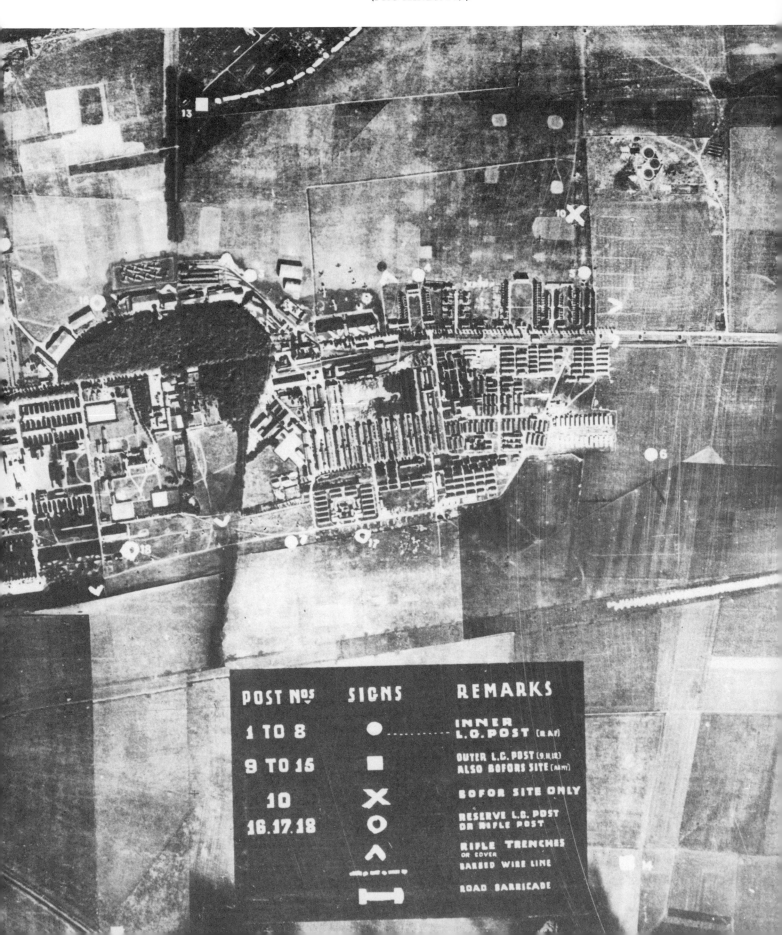

This high level aerial photograph of Cranwell taken on 13th June 1940 shows clearly the various defensive measures taken to protect this sprawling station from attack by ground forces. *(PRO AIR28/179)*

POST Nos	SIGNS	REMARKS
1 TO 8	●	INNER L.G. POST (R.A.F.)
9 TO 15	■	OUTER L.G. POST (9.11.12) ALSO BOFORS SITE (ARMY)
10	✕	BOFOR SITE ONLY
16.17.18	○	RESERVE L.G. POST OR RIFLE POST
	⋀	RIFLE TRENCHES OR COVER
	⋯⋯	BARBED WIRE LINE
	⌶	ROAD BARRICADE

APPENDIX E
Unusual and Experimental Devices

Both World Wars saw gigantic technical advances. During the latter conflict several Lincolnshire airfields had some quite interesting devices installed.

AIRCRAFT ARRESTER GEAR

When Bomber Command commenced night operations in 1940 the pilots of returning aircraft experienced great difficulty during landing in touching down near the runway threshold.. Often touch-down was not made until halfway down the runway and the remaining half was insufficient for the aircraft to be brought to a halt by use of its normal wheel brakes. In such cases the aircraft would run off the end of the runway with the consequent risk of damage to the aircraft and property and injury to the crew. The new generation of heavy bombers then in the pipeline caused this problem to be viewed with great concern.

With the object of providing protection in such cases the Royal Aircraft Establishment at Farnborough in Hampshire was instructed to investigate the provision of arresting gear and the installation of arrester hooks on bomber aircraft. The arrester unit that was developed is illustrated in the photograph. It was mounted in a pit adjacent to the runway edge and the arrester cables were laid out across the runway in a similar manner to that used on aircraft carriers.

One arrester unit was positioned at each end of each runway (a total of six for a standard bomber airfield) and they were operated manually. Prototype hook installations were made on Avro Manchester, Avro Lancaster, Handley Page Halifax and Short Stirling aircraft.

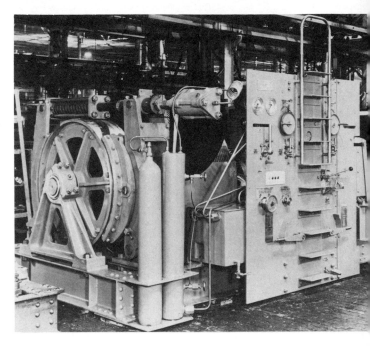

Above: **A newly produced arrester unit in the Manchester works of Mather and Platt Ltd. Easily visible are the controls and one of the two huge brake drums.** *(RAE Bedford)*

Below: **Lancaster L7529 about to engage an arrester wire during trials at the RAE.** *(RAE Bedford)*

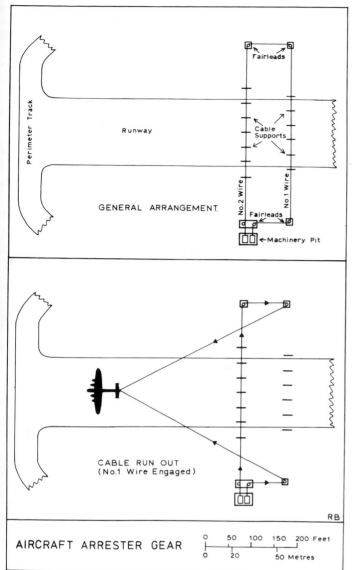

GENERAL ARRANGEMENT.

Perimeter Track

Runway

Fairleads

Cable Supports

No.2 Wire

No.1 Wire

Fairleads

←Machinery Pit

CABLE RUN OUT
(No.1 Wire Engaged)

RB

AIRCRAFT ARRESTER GEAR

0   50   100   150   200 Feet

0   20   50 Metres

Some one hundred and twenty arrester units were made. The first was installed at Farnborough and the second and third units were delivered to Woodhall Spa during August 1941. Woodhall Spa eventually had its six units installed and it became the first airfield to be fully equipped. Other Lincolnshire airfields to be equipped with arrester gear were Elsham Wolds, Grimsby and Swinderby.

The installation at Woodhall Spa was ready for testing by late 1942 and on 22nd October 1942 a Manchester aircraft of the RAE made five arrested landings. As far as can be ascertained this was the only use of the arrester units at Woodhall Spa. The arrester units at Elsham Wolds and Swinderby were installed and tested by December 1942 and testing of the units at Grimsby commenced on 28th January 1943.

In November 1942, Bomber Command decided that all its operational airfields, heavy OTU and major diversion airfields should be equipped with arrester units. However, with the bomber offensive in full swing Bomber Command began to have reservations about the weight penalty of the hook installation which noticeably reduced the fuel or bomb load of each aircraft. Moreover, aircraft piloting techniques were continually being improved and over-running of the runway became much less of a problem. In July 1943 Bomber Command finally decided

that it no longer needed any form of arrester gear and by November all the units had been 'mothballed' but were left in position pending some future requirement.

It is most probable that the majority of the installed arrester units have remained where they lay to this day. At least two at Woodhall Spa have and still evident here are the fairlead pulleys around which the arrester cable ran. It is known that those at Grimsby were dismantled in early 1945.

THE DISAPPEARING PILL BOX

In order to provide airfields with protection against landings by enemy troop carrying aircraft or parachutists, several airfields were provided with 'Disappearing Pill-Boxes'. During normal flying operations the pill-boxes were to be retracted until flush with the airfield surface and aircraft could operate without obstruction. In the event of an air attack they could be manned and raised to the operating position, giving the men inside an unobstructed view of the whole airfield.

The design was submitted by a private individual and demonstrated to the Air Staff in July 1940. The order to proceed was given and a contract was awarded to the New Kent Construction Company of Barnstaple, Devon. Termed the Hamilton-Pickett Disappearing Pill-Box, 170 were installed by June 1941.

Three pill-boxes were installed on each of the following Lincolnshire stations:

Binbrook	Hibaldstow
Caistor	Kirmington
Coningsby	Kirton in Lindsey
Digby	Manby
Elsham Wolds	North Coates
Grimsby	Sutton Bridge
Hemswell	Woodhall Spa

The raising and lowering mechanism proved unreliable and there was great difficulty in equipping the pill-boxes with automatic weapons. Many Station Commanders were concerned by the isolated situation of the pill-boxes and on some stations their effectiveness had been negated because they had been constructed on the airfield perimeter instead of in the centre of the flying field.

In view of the many objections it was decided in May 1942 not to go ahead with any further pill-boxes. By then 355 had been constructed. The three at Binbrook were demolished when runways were built in late 1942 and in November 1942 permission was given for two to be dismantled at Grimsby as they were having an adverse effect on the blind approach radio beam.

Although the majority of pill boxes were out of use by 1943 it is probable that most remained where they lay. The authors have located one at Woodhall Spa and would be interested to hear from readers who locate others on airfields within the County. The evidence likely to be seen on the surface is a concrete circle of about ten feet in diameter with a cast iron manhole cover in the centre.

THE MANBY SCREEN

By September 1936 Manby had been selected as the site for trials of a landing screen which, it was hoped, would enable aircraft to make cross-wind landings more easily. The idea originated in March 1936 and it was proposed for use on landing strips in Malaya and the Far East and at Gibraltar.

The screen, fifty feet high and five hundred yards long, was erected at Manby by April 1937. The first trials were carried out on 14th July 1937 by a Westland Wallace aircraft from the Air Observers School at North Coates. Trials continued throughout August and September using Bristol Blenheims of 114 Squadron, Armstrong Whitworth Whitleys of 10 Squadron and Fairey Battles of 63 Squadron. On the 20th September the starboard oleo of a 63 Squadron Battle collapsed and the aircraft came to rest with its nose just six yards from the screen! Further trials were carried out using a Handley Page Harrow of 215 Squadron.

The series of trials proved the feasibility of the screen but it had to be dismantled in February 1938 as Manby was shortly due to open. After a period of storage on the airfield boundary at Manby the screen was moved to a new site at Rollestone in Wiltshire.

Right: **The size of the Manby Screen can be judged from this photograph taken during its construction.** *(via P.H.T.Green)*

Below: **Although a little indistinct, this aerial view of Manby taken on 23rd September 1937 shows the cross-wind landing screen in position across the centre of the landing area.** *(PRO AIR 2/1739)*

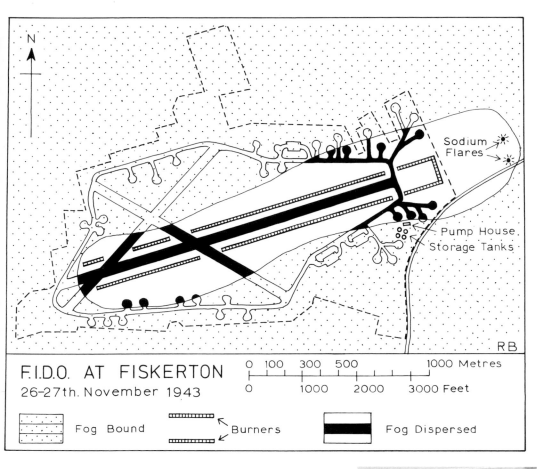

F.I.D.O. AT FISKERTON
26–27th. November 1943

Scale	0	100	300	500		1000 Metres
	0		1000	2000		3000 Feet

| ⠿ Fog Bound | ▭ Burners | ▬ Fog Dispersed |

RB

Below: **Trials of the FIDO system were initially undertaken in good weather. Note the large amount of smoke produced as the burners are lit.** *(IWM CH15274)*

Bottom: **Interior of the pump house showing installation of the five pumps used for passing the petrol mixture to the burners.** *(IWM CH15275)*

DISPERSAL OF FOG FROM AIRFIELDS

The increasing RAF bomber offensive in 1941 and 1942 suffered from considerable casualties during landings in fog in addition to the loss of potential flying hours due to fog or the threat of fog. In September 1942 the Petroleum Warfare Department was tasked with investigation of a solution to the problem and the name Fog Investigation Dispersal Operation was chosen (FIDO).

As early as 1921 the possibility of dispersing fog over airfields had been discussed. Between 1937 and 1939 some experiments were carried out by the Royal Aircraft Establishment at Farnborough in Hampshire and Martlesham Heath in Suffolk. It was discovered that a five-fold increase in heat was required to disperse the fog and the experiments were abandoned. Once the project was re-instituted in 1942 various methods of dispersing fog were considered. These included physical removal methods, e.g. 'sweeping' of the air by falling sand particles, coagulation by dropping electrically charged particles and precipitation by electro-static fields, and evaporative methods, e.g. direct heating of the air and indirect heating of the air by chemical means. In spite of the energy requirements direct heating appeared to be the most promising solution.

Construction of a FIDO installation on the Pathfinder airfield at Graveley in Huntingdonshire commenced three weeks after the FIDO project was initiated. By January 1943 the airfield was sufficiently equipped to allow experiments to commence. Petrol was found to burn with considerable smoke and clear combustion could only be obtained by burning mixtures containing 80 per cent alcohol. Considerable effort was, therefore, directed towards improvements in burner design in order to achieve clear combustion. This research effort resulted in the

'Haigill' (Hartley, Anglo-Iranian, Gill) burner illustrated in the photograph which became the standard burner for all of the FIDO installations in the United Kingdom.

The initial installation at Graveley had only 500 yards of burner along each side of the main runway. Trials indicated that burners should be laid along the whole length of the runway and across the threshold. Petrol was pumped to the burners by five pumps delivering up to 1500 gallons per minute at 75 pounds per square inch pressure. It took about twenty minutes to light the complete installation and burn off the initial smoke.

The first flight test was carried out at Graveley on 18th February 1943 by Air Vice-Marshall D. C. T. Bennett CB, CBE, DSO, then commander of No.8 (Pathfinder) Group. A second Pathfinder airfield was immediately chosen and six more installations were completed in November and December 1943. Another seven stations in the United Kingdom were equipped with FIDO during 1944, making a total of fifteen, and one in France.

FIDO was installed at Fiskerton during 1943 and it was used operationally for the first time on the night of 26-27th November 1943 when eleven Avro Lancasters of 49 Squadron landed safely back at base in conditions of poor visibility. A twelfth Lancaster crashed on approach, but this accident was unconnected with the use of FIDO. By mid-1944 the FIDO installations at Ludford Magna and Metheringham were completed and became operational. FIDO was also installed at Sturgate, but it is doubtful if this installation was ever used operationally.

The FIDO principle proved very effective and it was a useful landing aid which greatly improved the morale of returning bomber crews. During November 1943, 261 aircraft of Bomber Command were landed from operations by the aid of FIDO. On many occasions eighteen aircraft were landed at two minute intervals; at this rate the standard FIDO installation running at full power burnt 2,700 gallons of petrol per aircraft.

REFERENCE

Smith, D.J., 'FIDO: A costly wartime invention that saved lives and aircraft', *Aviation News,* Vol.18, No.12, 9-22 November 1979, pp 6-7.

Top: **The FIDO burners at the side of Fiskerton's main runway are shown lit during this 1943 demonstration.** *(Bill Baguley/ Rod Houldsworth)*

Left: **A Lancaster lands at Fiskerton with the aid of FIDO.** *(N.Franklin via P.H.T.Green)*

APPENDIX F
Decoy Airfields

'K' AND 'Q' SITES IN LINCOLNSHIRE

As early as 1938 it had been proposed by the Air Ministry that decoy airfields should be established to lure any possible enemy away from front-line airfields. Although there was some apprehension at the proposal, by 1939 a scheme was being prepared for the establishment of a line of dummy airfields complete with dummy aircraft east of a line from Perth to Southampton.

The decoy airfield was not intended as a full simulation of a front line base but as a possible representation of a typical satellite airfield. Each site would display up to ten dummy aircraft plus broken-down vehicles, buildings and runway lighting. In order to operate the dummy site the parent station would have on strength one NCO and a number of men. When an alert was sounded these men would take up positions in sandbagged enclosures and operate the lighting system by remote control.

Decoy, or to give them their proper title, Target Aircraft, were constructed by firms connected with the film industry. The first specifications, for Hurricane, Battle and Whitley aircraft, stated that the dummy must cast a realistic shadow on the ground, be resistant to weather, be capable of being folded and packed for transportation, and be cheap. Specifications were also issued for dummy Blenheims and Wellingtons. By February 1940 a total of 400 target aircraft were on order and the first deliveries were made at the beginning of March.

Below: **An aerial view of a typical decoy airfield with dummy aircraft in position.** *(via P.H.T.Green)*

In addition to spoof airfields, complete with imitation wheel rutting, and dummy aircraft, a second form of deception was introduced: night flare paths and Drem circuit lights. These were known as 'Q' Sites and were sometimes combined with dummy airfields ('K' Sites), but were often simply laid out on farm land. By mid-1940 'Q' Sites had been added to the stations protected by dummy airfields.

Both 'K' and 'Q' Sites proved their effectiveness, and confirmed deliberate attacks were made on several of them during the summer of 1940. Donna Nook (for North Coates) and Folkingham (for Spitalgate) were some of the examples in Lincolnshire which were attacked.

As the Battle of Britain drew to a close and the attacks from the Luftwaffe became less frequent, the need for decoys diminished. Thus, by 1942, all but a few had closed down and one or two sites were eventually developed into fully operational airfields.

Unfortunately for the aviation archaeologist, the exact positions of these sites are obscure today and no firm grid references can therefore be provided. However, from the place-names it should be possible to identify the fields which were probably used and some relic equipment may yet come to light.

According to a list recently published in *Aeromilitaria* (1979), 192 Second World War airfields had decoys attached to them. Some of the more important stations had up to three unshared decoys, so the number of actual sites was well over 200. Because the main function was the defence of front-line combat stations (both bomber and fighter), the overwhelming preponderance was along the east coast. Twenty-one of Lincolnshire's airfields were given one or more decoys and thirty decoy airfields (some attached to two parent stations) were established within the then county boundary. Of all the decoyed stations in the UK, Lincolnshire contained 10 per cent and of all the decoy airfields, some 15 per cent lay within the county — in both cases a concentration greater than that for airfields as a whole.

As the accompanying map shows, the decoys were predominantly located on the coastal side of their parent station, in order that enemy aircraft would be made to release their bombs and therefore have less opportunity to fly over genuine targets while retaining strike power. The distance of the decoys from their parents ranged from 3 miles (5 kms) to 12 miles (20 kms), the mean being about 6 miles (10 kms).

Official serial numbers were allocated to each decoy and can be referred to in *Aeromilitaria* (1979). On the map here the numbers refer only to the alphabetical listing of the parent station devised for this study.

PARENT AIRFIELD AND DECOY SITES SUMMARY

Barkston Heath
a) Willoughby Walks — Opened late 1941. Transferred to Cranwell 30 January 1942.

Binbrook
a) Wyham — Abandoned by January 1942.
b) Kelstern — Abandoned by August 1941.
c) Ludborough — Operational by October 1941. Probably same site as ELG (see Part Two).

Coningsby
a) Hagnaby — Opened by October 1941. Abandoned by April 1942 because adjacent to a new airfield. Whitley and Battle dummy aircraft
b) Frithville — Opened by October 1941.
c) Sibsey — Transferred from East Kirkby by October 1943.

Cottesmore
a) Swayfield — Decoy site only in Lincs. Parent airfield in Rutland.

Cranwell
a) Willoughby Walks — Transferred from Barkston Heath 30 January 1942.

Digby
a) Ruskington — Abandoned by August 1942.
b) Dorrington

Donna Nook
a) Marshchapel

East Kirkby
a) Sibsey — Opened by December 1941. Transferred to Coningsby by October 1943.

Elsham Wolds
a) Great Limber — Operational by October 1941.
b) South Ferriby

Goxhill
a) Burnham — Operational by October 1941. Abandoned by July 1942.

Hemswell
a) Caenby — Completed late April 1940. Abandoned by August 1942.
b) Toft Grange — Opened 11 March 1940, 10 Whitley dummy aircraft. Abandoned by May 1943.
c) Glentham

Hibaldstow
a) Cadney — Both open by December 1941, but
b) Thornton Le Moor — transferred to Kirton in Lindsey soon after.

Kirton in Lindsey
a) Cadney — Both transferred from Hibaldstow at
b) Thornton Le Moor — end of 1941.

Ludford Magna
a) Rand — Transferred from Wickenby.

Manby
a) Mablethorpe — Opened by January 1942.

North Coates
a) Donna Nook — Abandoned early 1941 when taken over as proper satellite. Blenheim dummy aircraft.

Scampton
a) Rand — Transferred to Wickenby by August 1942.

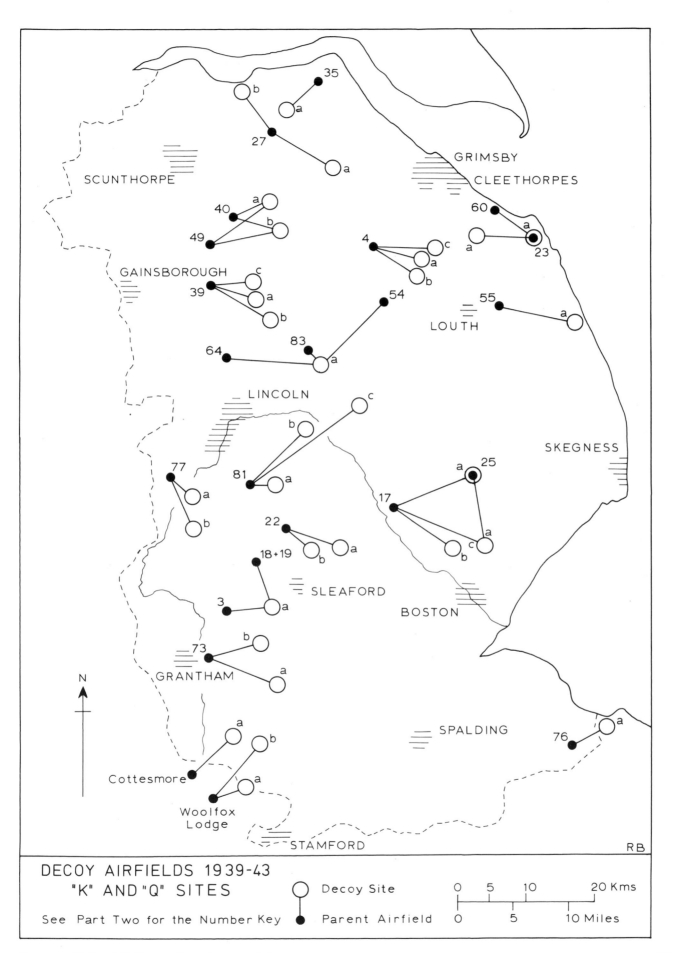

GRIMSBY
CLEETHORPES

SCUNTHORPE

35

27

40
49

a
b

60

23

a

4

c
a
b

a

GAINSBOROUGH

39

c
a
b

54

LOUTH

55

a

64

83

a

LINCOLN

c

b

77

81

a

a
b

25

a

17

22

18+19

a
b

SKEGNESS

a
c

b

3

a

SLEAFORD

BOSTON

73

b

a

GRANTHAM

a
b

SPALDING

76

a

Cottesmore

a

Woolfox
Lodge

N

STAMFORD

RB

DECOY AIRFIELDS 1939-43
"K" AND "Q" SITES

See Part Two for the Number Key

○ Decoy Site

● Parent Airfield

0   5   10   20 Kms

0   5   10 Miles

See page 30 for airfield name/number correlation.

Spitalgate

a)	Folkingham	Abandoned by August 1942. Battle dummy aircraft.
b)	Braceby	Possibly First World War LG site.

Sutton Bridge

a)	Terrington Marsh	Battle dummy aircraft (see main text).

Swinderby

a)	Bassingham	Abandoned by August 1942.
b)	Brant Broughton	Operational by October 1941.

Waddington

a)	Potter Hanworth	Abandoned by July 1943.
b)	Branston Fen	Abandoned by September 1943 (see 'starfish' sites).
c)	Gautby	Developed after August 1941 but abandoned by August 1942 as not a convincing site. Battle dummy aircraft.

Wickenby

a)	Rand	Transferred from Scampton by August 1942.

Woolfox Lodge

a)	Pickworth	Parent airfield in Rutland, but both decoys in Lincolnshire. Swinstead possibly First World War LG site.
b)	Swinstead	

REFERENCES

Anon, 'Decoy Airfields', *Aeromilitaria*, No.3, 1979, pp 77-78.

Bushby, J., *Air Defence of Britain*, Ian Allan: Shepperton, 1973, (see Chapter 9 — 'Practice and Deceive', pp 156-166).

Price, A., *Blitz on Britain: The Bomber Attacks on the United Kingdom 1939-45*, Ian Allan: Shepperton, 1977, pp 114-5.

STARFISH SITES IN LINCOLNSHIRE

Decoy fires are strictly outside the scope of this study but were still an integral part of aerial defence from the autumn of 1940. Just as 'K' and 'Q' sites were designed to lure enemy aircraft away from airfields, the 'Starfish' decoys acted as spoof towns, ports and industrial areas. They were ignited during attacks to suggest successful hits, using steel and asbestos frames decked with tarred felt. Sites were located at least a mile from genuine settlements and the last was dismantled during 1943.

Grantham

   a) Boothby Pagnell

Lincoln

a)	Branston Fen	Abandoned by June 1942.
b)	Canwick	Opened by May 1942.

Scunthorpe

a)	Risby	To protect the steel-making complex.
b)	Twigmoor	
c)	Brumby (Burringham)	

Strategic (coastal)

a)	Huttoft	Opened by March 1942. Abandoned by September 1943.

Naval Decoys, in the Humber Region

   d) Immingham Range

   e) East Halton

   f) Humberston

Right: **A Lancaster of the Empire Air Armament School, Manby, during a practice bombing sortie on the Theddlethorpe range, May 1949.** (*Crown Copyright R2420*)

APPENDIX G
Bombing and Gunnery Ranges

From the earliest days when bombs and guns were first carried on military aircraft it has always been essential for aircrew to train and practice operation of their weapons. During the First World War and up to the early years of the Second World War it was usual for bombing and gunnery ranges to be laid out on or very close to the parent aerodrome. The RNAS at Freiston used the hulk of an old aeroplane as a target and this was placed on the mud flats just over the sea wall from the aerodrome. A balloon tethered in a corner of the aerodrome was used to suspend targets for air-to-air firing practice.

In the late 1920s the RAF introduced armament practice camps which were established along the coast where the vast expanses of open sands and mud flats provided excellent facilities for bombing and gunnery. Moreover, these areas were sparsely inhabited and there was little risk of injury to civilians. The first armament training camp in Lincolnshire was established at Sutton Bridge in September 1926 and by the end of the following month five squadrons had visited for annual firing practice. The camp was closed for the winter but reopened the following spring. The targets were laid out on the mud flats of The Wash to the east of the River Nene.

A second armament training camp opened in the County during 1927 at North Coates Fitties. The targets were set up for this new camp on the foreshore off Somercotes Haven, at Donna Nook. The ranges at Donna Nook and Sutton Bridge continued in use for the remainder of the inter-war period, Donna Nook being used in the main by bomber squadrons and Sutton Bridge by fighter squadrons.

As the RAF began to expand in the mid-1930s it was apparent that the County's two ranges would be inadequate, particularly with the impending move of the Air Armament School to Manby. Accordingly, during 1935, a new range was constructed on the foreshore at Theddlethorpe. This was intended for use by the AAS and it was provided with a number of permanent buildings and its own landing ground, as was the range area at Sutton Bridge which was subsequently named Holbeach. In 1937 construction of another new range commenced on Wainfleet Sands and this was for the use of 5 Group Bomber Command.

In addition to the coastal ranges others were built at inland sites for, by the outbreak of the Second World War, runway construction prevented the use of airfields themselves for

practice bombing. Normally, only practice bombs were dropped on the inland ranges but the coastal ranges, particularly Wainfleet, saw frequent use of 500 and 1000 lb high explosive bombs. During the Second World War Donna Nook range was controlled by 1 Group; Wainfleet by 5 Group; and Holbeach and Theddlethorpe by 25 Group.

Following the Second World War, Donna Nook was closed along with the inland ranges, and those at Holbeach, Theddlethorpe and Wainfleet passed to the control of 1 Group. Theddlethorpe's main peace time user became the RAF Flying College at Manby and later the Hunter ground attack squadrons of Air Support Command. Wainfleet remained the main bombing range and saw considerable use by Mosquitoes, Lincolns, Canberras and later Vulcans and Buccaneers. Holbeach was a popular ground attack range and saw much use by Hunter and later Harrier and Jaguar squadrons.

Use of Lincolnshire's ranges has not been confined to the RAF and many NATO aircraft have been seen in their airspace. Most prolific have been aircraft of the USAF, which have included F-86 Sabre, F-100 Super Sabre, RF-101 Voodoo, F-4 Phantom, F-111 and A-10A Thunderbolt II. Other NATO air arms which have used Lincolnshire's ranges include West Germany (F-104 Starfighter) and Belgium (Mirage).

On 6 August 1976 Theddlethorpe range was closed following many complaints and a new range area was opened on the former Donna Nook site. However, the RAF retained the permanent buildings which formed the Theddlethorpe headquarters which it re-named RAF Donna Nook.

The term bombing and gunnery range was gradually replaced by Air Weapons Range and by the mid-1970s control of all ranges had passed to 38 Group, Strike Command. On 1 July 1980 all ranges became directly administered by HQ Strike Command. With the start of weapons training on the Tornado in 1981 the shape of the Tornado has become very familiar along Lincolnshire's coastline. As the RAF's Tornado squadrons build up both at home and in Germany the intensity of Tornado weapons training seems set to increase although the Buccaneer is likely to be a less-frequent user of the coastal ranges once the type is located only at Lossiemouth (Moray).

Below: **The old and the new control towers for the Wainfleet Air Weapons Range. Actually located in the parish of Friskney, the old timber and scaffolding structure was built in 1948 and served faithfully until May 1981 when it was demolished following completion of the new tower.** (*W.J.Taylor*)

Top Right: **Typical of gunnery targets used during the First World War was this example at Frieston.** *(RAF Museum P298)*

Upper centre: **Following the Second World War more durable targets became necessary. This 1971 photograph shows a tank landing craft which was used on the Wainfleet range from 1948 until the mid-1970s.** *(W.J.Taylor)*

Lower centre: **Old ships are now popular targets. This vessel is currently used as a radar bombing target at Wainfleet. Note the radar reflectors on the superstructure.** *(W.J.Taylor)*

Bottom: **The entrance to Holbeach range is adorned with two bombs, an interesting contrast to the more usual 'gate guardian' aircraft at other Royal Air Force establishments.** *(W.J.Taylor)*

There follows a brief historical and functional description appertaining to the location (OS 1:50000 and grid reference where known) of the coastal and inland bombing and gunnery ranges. To preserve the distinction between such sites and airfields, elevations above sea level are not given in this appendix.

ALKBOROUGH
112 / SK 883 236   *12 km N of Scunthorpe*
A bombing range, situated on marshland adjoining the River Humber. Controlled by Elsham Wolds and used by aircraft of 13 Base in addition to other units of 1 Group Bomber Command. Closed 19 October 1945.

ANDERBY CREEK
122 / TA 554 760   *10 km SSE of Mablethorpe*
Ground to air firing range for 1 Group. Controlled by Binbrook. The 5 Group Anti-Aircraft Gunnery School moved here from Friskney during October 1944. Also used by the RAF Regiment Depot as a Battle Training School.

BASSINGHAM FEN
121 / SK 927 587   *14 km SSW of Lincoln*
Inland bombing range controlled by Waddington. Used by all units of 5 Group, 75 and 76 Bases.

DONNA NOOK
113 / TA 431 997   *15 km SE of Cleethorpes*
Bombing and gunnery range used by squadrons during summer camp at North Coates Fitties from 1927. The range was used by units of 1 Group and Manby during the Second World War. A secondary user was the Bombing Development Unit, Newmarket. The range was closed down post-war, but was reopened in August 1976.

FENTON
121 / SK 848 776   *15 km WNW of Lincoln*
Inland bombing range controlled by Skellingthorpe. Used by units of 5 Group, Scampton, 75 and 76 Bases.

FRISKNEY
122 / TA 493 545   *12 km SW of Skegness*
Part of the Wainfleet Bombing and Gunnery Range. The 5 Group Anti-Aircraft School was based here from May 1944 until 13 October 1944.

GRIMSTHORPE PARK
130 / TF 027 190   *7 km W of Bourne*
Inland bombing range used by units of 75 Base.

HAMILTON HILL
113 / TA 123 901   *2 km NE of Market Rasen*
Gunnery range, opened in June 1941.

HOLBEACH
131 / TF 440 340   *15 km SE of Boston*
Bombing and gunnery range opened in the late 1920s for use by the Armament Training Camp at Sutton Bridge. Used by units of 3 and 8 Group during the Second World War. In use today.

INGOLDMELLS
122 / TF 5.. 6..   *About 6 km N of Skegness*
                               (precise site unknown)
Bombing and gunnery range used by Mosquitoes of 5 Group. Opened in 1940 and closed in 1945.

LEA MARSH
112 / SK 810 870   *3 km S of Gainsborough*
Inland bombing ranges on banks of River Trent completed in August 1941 and controlled by Hemswell. Used by Scampton and units of 71 Base.

LEVERTON
131 / TF 450 480   *13 km ENE of Boston*
Small bombing range used by 1 Group Bomber Command units, located on the mud flats near Sailor's Home.

MANTON COMMON
112 / SE 929 029   *9 km SSE of Scunthorpe*
Inland bombing range.

NORTH FRODINGHAM
112 / SE 8.. 1..   *About 3 km N of Scunthorpe*
Type of range and precise site not known. Used by units of 43 Base.

ROMAN HOLE
113 / TF 154 961   *8 km NNE of Market Rasen*
Turret and musketry range near the village of Thoresway. Controlled by Hemswell.

SUTTON BRIDGE
131 / TF 440 340   *15 km SE of Boston*
Bombing and gunnery range, opened in the late 1920s for use by the Armament Training Camp. Permanent buildings added in mid-1930s and thereafter known as 'Holbeach' (which see).

THEDDLETHORPE
113 / TF 470 905   *15 km ENE of Louth*
Bombing and gunnery range with its own landing strip constructed in 1935 for use by Manby. In December 1939 some of the early firing trials of the Hispano 20mm cannon were carried out here. The range was controlled by 25 Group during the Second World War but passed to 1 Group post-war. More recent users were the RAFFC at Manby and Air Support Command Hunters. Although closed down in August 1976 and the range area moved to Donna Nook, the buildings which comprised RAF station Theddlethorpe were retained and subsequently re-named RAF Donna Nook.

WAINFLEET SANDS
122 / TF 522 570   *10 km SSW of Skegness*
Bombing and gunnery range constructed in 1937 and opened in August 1938 within 5 Group. Transferred to 1 Group in October 1945. Used by units of Bomber Command and Manby. In use today, parented by Coningsby.

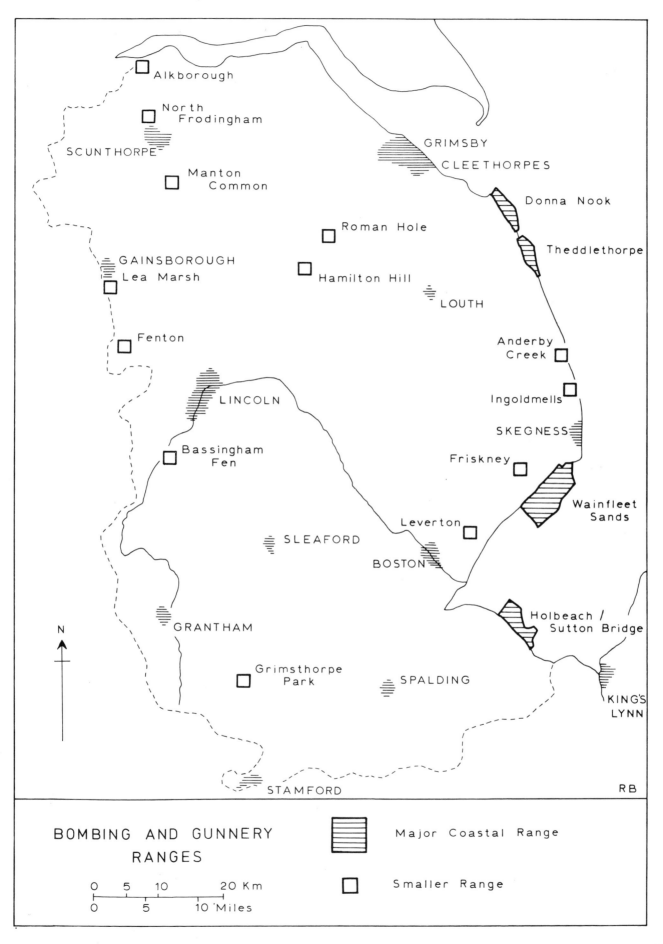

Alkborough

North
Frodingham

SCUNTHORPE

Manton
Common

GRIMSBY

CLEETHORPES

Donna Nook

Theddlethorpe

Roman Hole

GAINSBOROUGH
Lea Marsh

Hamilton Hill

LOUTH

Fenton

Anderby
Creek

Ingoldmells

SKEGNESS

LINCOLN

Bassingham
Fen

Friskney

Wainfleet
Sands

Leverton

SLEAFORD

BOSTON

N

Holbeach /
Sutton Bridge

GRANTHAM

Grimsthorpe
Park

SPALDING

KING'S
LYNN

STAMFORD

RB

BOMBING AND GUNNERY
RANGES

Major Coastal Range

0 5 10   20 Km

0   5   10 Miles

Smaller Range

261

APPENDIX H
Sundry Air Force Sites

In addition to aerodromes, bombing and gunnery ranges, landing grounds and decoys, many other small but essential sites were brought into use in Lincolnshire to support the RAF presence. Some of these are listed below with their locations (OS 1 : 50000 sheet and grid reference) and a brief historical and functional description. To preserve a distinction between sundry sites and airfields, elevations above sea level are not given in this appendix.

BELTON PARK
130 / SK 930 385   *4 km NNE of Grantham*
RAF Regiment Depot (see Appendix D).

BLANKNEY HALL
121 / TF 071 599   *15 km SE of Lincoln*
Opened in 1940 as the Sector Operations Room for the Digby Sector of 12 Group Fighter Command. On 15 July 1945 the main hall was gutted by fire. Digby Sector became an independent unit at Blankney Hall with effect from 23 July 1945 and controlled the airfield at Molesworth in Huntingdonshire. Closed in April 1946.

BOSTON DOCKS
131 / TF 333 432
The Dock area at Boston housed 1109 Marine Craft Unit from the Second World War to the mid-1950s. The unit was parented by Coningsby and its high speed launches were berthed on the River Witham close to the lock at the entrance to the dock. Domestic accommodation for the unit was located in a park to the south-west of St John's Road.

BRIGG (BROUGHTON WOOD)
112 / SE 955 097   *6 km ESE of Scunthorpe*
209 MU, an air stores park for units of 1 Group, was located here. Parented by Elsham Wolds, it closed in February 1946.

CARLTON SCROOP
Air Ministry Works Department Depot. (See Honington).

CHAPEL ST LEONARDS
122 / TF .. 7 ..   *10 km N of Skegness*
A proposal to build a Ground Defence Gunnery Practice Camp here was approved in December 1941. Precise site unknown.

CROWLAND
131 / TF 263 116   *11 km S of Spalding*
Radio relay station manned by a detachment of 2166 Communications Squadron USAF from 1961. The unit closed in 1979 and the tower was due for demolition during 1981.

GIBRALTAR POINT
122 / TA 556 583   *5 km S of Skegness*
RAF Regiment Field Firing Range. First course commenced 16 June 1944. (See Appendix D).

GRANTHAM (MILL HOUSE)
130 / SK 937 358   *2 km ENE of Grantham*
HQ 24 (Training) Wing, RFC/RAF, from late 1917 until late 1919.

GRANTHAM (MOSTYN LODGE)
130 / SK 914 365   *0.5 km N of St Wulfrum's Church*
Headquarters Midland Area, Royal Observer Corps, moved in from RAF Grantham on 5 June 1940 and out to Watnall (Notts) on 16 October 1942. Now a private house.

Mostyn Lodge photographed in 1979. (*Roy Pickworth*)

GRANTHAM (ST VINCENT'S)
130 / SK 926 350   *1 km SE of Grantham*

In 1923 the Air Ministry bought 'St Vincents', the large house located at the foot of Spittlegate Hill in Grantham. It was not used until 14 August 1926, when HQ 23 Group moved in from the nearby station at Spittlegate. The group controlled the RAF's various flying training establishments and it remained at 'St Vincents' until August 1937 when it moved temporarily back to RAF Grantham before a final move to South Cerney (Gloucestershire) in October 1939. 'St Vincents' was then taken over by the HQ of 5 Group, Bomber Command, which arrived from Mildenhall (Suffolk) on 30 September 1937. This group controlled many of Lincolnshire's bomber stations and it remained until October 1943 at which time it moved to Morton Hall near Swinderby.

'St Vincents' was then transferred to the USAAF and the advance party of the 9th Air Force Air Support Division Substitution Unit arrived from Cottesmore (Rutland) on 14 November 1943 to prepare the house for the arrival of the HQ 9th Troop Carrier Command which arrived, also from Cottesmore, on 2 December 1943. The latter unit left in mid-1945 but from November 1944 'St Vincents' also housed the HQ 7 Group, Bomber Command, which had formed on 3 November to control all training units within that Command. HQ 7 Group was disbanded on 21 December 1945 and 'St Vincents' was placed on Care and maintenance which is how it remained until its sale in 1978. It is now used as office accommodation for the local authority.

Staff of the 9th Troop Carrier Command relax in front of the American Red Cross Club, St. Vincents, on 26th August 1944.
(USAF 82510AC)

GRIMSBY DOCKS
113 / TA 280 115

No. 22 High Speed Launch Unit formed here in July 1942. It was re-named 22 Air-Sea Rescue Marine Craft Unit in January 1943. Launches had been based in the dock area since August 1941. On 16 December 1945 it ceased to function as an operational unit and was disbanded on 8 February 1946.

GRIMSBY (ORWELL STREET)
113 / TA 277 105   *In the older part of the town*

The present premises of Eskimo Foods Ltd, housed a detachment of the 59th Veterinary Inspection Flight, USAF, from 1959 to February 1962.

HABROUGH
113 / TA 147 138   *13 km WNW of Grimsby*

HQ 18 (Operations) Group, 1917 to late 1919. Moved in from RNAS Killingholme where it is thought to have been housed in North Killingholme Rectory.

The variety of forces represented on the staff of HQ 18 (Operations) Group is well illustrated in this photograph taken while it was housed in North Killingholme Rectory.
(Lincolnshire Library Service via P.H.T. Green)

HOLTON-LE-MOOR
112 / TF 090 980   *12 km SE of Brigg*
Air Ministry Works Depot.

HONINGTON
130 / SK 943 437   *9 km NNE of Grantham*
Air Ministry Works Department Depot. (Probably same site as Carlton Scroop).

'KILLINGHOLME'
Based about 16 km NW of Grimsby

A paddlesteamer of the Great Central Railway used as a sea-plane carrier by RNAS Killingholme. (See entry for Killingholme in Part Two). During the Second World War it was used by the RAF as a depot ship for Balloon Command. Scrapped in 1945.

KIRTON IN LINDSEY
112 / SK 952 980   *14 km SSE of Scunthorpe*
Radio relay station manned by a detachment of the 2166 Communications Squadron, USAF, 1961 to 1967.

LANGTOFT

130 / TF 125 125   *8 km SSE of Bourne*

GCI station, part of Digby Sector. Operational by March 1943 and used for both fighter and searchlight control. Closed in late 1950.

LINCOLN (LONGDALE ROAD)

121 / SK 980 730   *In northern suburbs of the city*

No. 6 Stores Distributing Park RFC/RAF. Opened late 1917. Placed on care and maintenance, April 1920.

MARKET STAINTON

122 / TF 228 801   *12 km SW of Louth*

233 MU munitions storage unit. Opened 19 January 1943. Closed 1948. Storage sub-site at Orby.

Although the roadside woods near Market Stainton have now been felled, the many ramps across the ditch may still be seen. Bombs were taken across the ramps for storage by 233 MU in the woods. *(W.J.Taylor)*

MORTON HALL

121 / SK 878 644   *13 km SW of Lincoln*

The Aircrew Commando School arrived from Barkston Heath in March 1943 and moved to Scampton on 25 October 1943. From 15 March 1943, HQ 51 Base also occupied Morton Hall, until moving to Swinderby on 24 October. HQ 5 Group then arrived from St Vincent's in Grantham and remained until the group disbanded in December 1945. Between 1947 and 1955, HQ 21 Group used Morton Hall and in July 1956 No.5131

Bomb Disposal Squadron arrived from North Coates. Closed as an RAF unit in the late 1950s though was later used as a remand centre and more recently has been used to house Vietnamese 'boat people' refugees.

NOCTON HALL

121 / TF 062 643   *11 km SE of Lincoln*

Nocton Hall was taken into Air Ministry ownership at the outbreak of the Second World War as a possible extension of the RAF Hospital at Cranwell. However, the Hall's size and layout precluded its satisfactory use as a hospital and the RAF took over the mental hospital at Rauceby instead. The Army used the Hall as a casualty clearing station until 1943 and the following year it was taken over by the Americans who commenced construction of the US Army Seventh General Hospital. In November 1947 the hospital was taken over by the RAF and after extensive reconstruction in 1955 its facilities were gradually expanded, until by 1969, Nocton Hall was able to offer all the routine facilities of a modern General Hospital. Unfortunately, as part of a rationalisation of RAF medical facilities Nocton Hall was closed on 31st March 1983.

STATION BADGE NOCTON HALL

Description: In front of a rod of Aesculapius in bend a Lincoln Imp.

Motto: SICUT QUI MINISTRANT
                 ([We are] As they who serve)

Authority: King George VI,
                 November 1951.

The Lincoln Imp is introduced to indicate the unit's proximity to Lincoln Cathedral, and the rod of Aesculapius has reference to its function.   *Crown Copyright / RAF Photograph*

NORTON DISNEY (FOX COVERT)

121 / SK 862 605   16 km SW of Lincoln

Satellite site for 93 MU Bomb Storage Unit as described above.

NORTON DISNEY (SWINDERBY)

121 / SK 863 645   15 km SW of Lincoln

93 MU munitions storage unit (for 5 Group units) opened 23 August 1939, adjacent to Swinderby railway station. Initially named Swinderby but changed to Norton Disney when airfield opened. Storage sub-sites at Fox Covert and Tumby Woodside.

ORBY

122 / TF 526 679   6 km NW of Skegness

GCI station within Digby Sector. Operational by March 1943 and used for both fighter and searchlight control. Closed August 1945. Now 'Skegness Stadium'.

ORBY (GOWTHAMS)

122 / TF 480 673   10 km WNW of Skegness

Satellite of 233 MU Bomb Storage Unit, located in the railway yard and nearby country lanes.

RAUCEBY

130 / TF 042 441   3 km WSW of Sleaford

RAF Hospital 1940 to 1947.

SKEGNESS

122 / TF 565 617   At the south end of the town

11. Recruit Centre and Hospital opened in February 1941 at Seacroft School. Closed in October 1944.

SKENDLEBY

122 / TF 438 708   15 km WNW of Skegness

Chain Home Low station.

SOUTH WITHAM

130 / SK 950 185   17 km S of Grantham

100 MU munitions storage unit. Opened 27 March 1942. Roadside storage sites at Stretton, Stretton Road and Moor Lane. Closed early 1950s.

SPITALGATE

130 / SK 937 345   3 km ESE of Grantham

Radio relay station. Allocated to the USAF on 16 November 1961 and manned by a detachment of the 2166 Communications Squadron.

STENIGOT

122 / TF 257 825   9 km SW of Louth

The site for a Chain Home station at Stenigot was examined by Dr R A Watson-Watt in October 1937 and the station was constructed during 1938. It was named RDF Station No. 34. Later the station was used as a GCI and 'Gee' station. It was the first of three 'Gee' ground stations to be completed in June 1941 and it was used in the first Service trial of 'Gee' on 11/12 August 1941. The Gee Chain remained operational until 26 March 1970 although the wooden receiver masts were sold for £300 each and demolished in the late 1950s. Subsequently, two of the three steel transmitter towers were demolished and the remaining tower is used for training by the Aerial Erectors School at Digby. The domestic site, about 1 km north east of the station, remains remarkably intact, its buildings now being used as farm stores.

Typical of the many buildings that still remain on the former domestic site at Stenigot is the guardroom, seen here in May 1979. *(W.J. Taylor)*

SWAYFIELD

130 / SK 995 225   16 km SSE of Grantham

RAF Regiment field training area. (See Appendix D).

TATTERSHALL THORPE

122 / TF 226 591   5 km SE of Woodhall Spa

Wartime radio station for Coningsby. From February 1966 the home of 705 Mobile Radar Bomb Scoring Signals Unit which arrived from Kenley. The unit provided electronic bomb scoring facilities for the RAF's V-bombers and various American aircraft. With the imminent demise of the Vulcan the unit ceased operations on 8 May 1981.

TUMBY WOODSIDE

122 / TF 272 578   9 km SE of Woodhall Spa

Satellite site of 93 MU Bomb Storage Unit within 5 Group, Bomber Command, located in the railway yard and nearby country lanes.

WRAGBY

121 / TF 133 781   17 km ENE of Lincoln

Munitions storage sub-site of 233 MU, Market Stainton.

APPENDIX I
Principal Civil Operators

Contrary to its popular image as a county whose aviation is almost exclusively military, Lincolnshire has in fact played host to at least sixty civil flying organisations over the survey period. These exclude many privately operated aircraft and their airstrips and comprise only commercial and recreational organisations with recognisable names. For dubious status or lack of precise information, many of the lesser outfits known to have been based in the county are not detailed in this appendix, but this still leaves forty-eight significant operators about which interesting facts can be tabulated. The latter have been grouped into four main sub-sections — airlines, general aviation operaters, flying clubs and gliding clubs and within each sub-section the organisations are listed chronologically in order to emphasis their respective historical origins and seniority. This tabulation is only the first step towards a full story of civil flying in Lincolnshire which would certainly include many organisations of necessity overlooked here.

Commercial Airlines

NORTH SEA AERIAL AND GENERAL TRANSPORT
Dates at bases: *New Holland (?)*   *1919 - 1933*
                      Grimsby (Waltham)   *1933 - 1936*
Formed 1919 as North Sea Aerial Navigation Ltd at Brough (Yorks). Probably used New Holland LG. Operated regular service from Hull (Hedon) to Waltham during 1933. Absorbed 1939 by Blackburn Aircraft Ltd.

EASTERN AIR TRANSPORT LTD
Dates at base: *Skegness (Winthorpe)*   *1930 - 1936*
Formed in 1930, the activities of this small airline are described more fully in Part 2.

W AND M FLYING SERVICES
Dates at base: *Louth (Kenwick Road)*   *1934 (May-Jul)*
Formed in May 1934 with one Avro 504K (G-ACRE) by Messrs F G Wright and H B G Michelmore. Partnership dissolved July 1934 when Michelmore withdrew whereupon Wright formed Lincolnshire Flying Services with a Mr Craig in August 1934 (see next entry).

LINCOLNSHIRE FLYING SERVICES
Date at base: *Louth (Kenwick Road)*   *1934 - 1939*
Formed 1934 at Louth. Provided joy-riding, banner towing and air taxi services. Ceased trading at outbreak of the Second World War.

Mr & Mrs F.Wright in front of Lincolnshire Flying Service's Avro 504N G-ADFW at Louth in 1935. *(F.Wright via P.H.T.Green)*

SPALDING AIRWAYS LTD
Date at base: Spalding (Weston Marsh)   1947 - 1951
Formed 1947 for charter work. Aircraft moved 1951 to Peterborough (Westwood) Aerodrome and after various changes of name and base ceased trading in 1966.

BOSTON AIR TRANSPORT LTD
Date at base: Boston (Wyberton Fen)   1948 - 1954
Formed 1948 at Wyberton Fen. Operated aircraft for Boston Aero Club until ceasing in late Summer 1954.

SKEGNESS (AIRPORT) LTD
Date at base: Skegness (Ingoldmells)   1949 - 1951
Formed 1949 at Ingoldmells. Operated charter and pleasure flights. Ceased trading 1951 when taken over.

SKEGNESS AIR TAXI SERVICE LTD
Dates at bases: Skegness (Ingoldmells)
                    and   1951 - current
                    Boston (Wyberton Fen)
Formed 1951, absorbing Skegness (Airport) Ltd later that year. Now a susidiary company of Lincs Aerial Spraying. Operates Skegness (Ingoldmells) Aerodrome and aircraft on behalf of Skegness Aero Club.

HUMBER AIRWAYS LTD
Dates at bases: Kirmington/Humberside
                    and Wickenby   1967 - 1975
Formed 1967 as Air Links Chauffeurs providing charter services to Brough and Hull (Paull). Changed name to Humber Airways in 1968, was absorbed in 1969 by Ellerman Wilson Shipping Line and ceased operating 1975.

EASTERN AIR EXECUTIVE LTD
Date at base: Sturgate   1969 - current
Formed 1969 at Sturgate to provide industrialists with charter and taxi services. Also provides operating facilities for corporate aircraft.

LEASE-AIR LTD/EASTERN AIRWAYS LTD
Date at base: Kirmington/Humberside   1972 - 1982
Formed 1972 at Kirmington to provide aircraft for instruction and charter services for local businessmen. Expanded to provide scheduled services from Humberside and Norwich airports with Douglas DC-3 and Shorts SD330 aircraft. In October 1982 amalgamated with Genair and Casair.

Top: Holidaymakers queue at Ingoldmells for a pleasure flight in an Auster of Skegness Air Taxi Service in 1971. *(W.J.Taylor)*

Upper Centre: Dakota G-AMPO in Eastern Airways' red, white and blue colour scheme at Kirmington in 1981. *(P.H.T.Green)*

Above: Islander G-AXRN, one of two operated by Humber Airways at Kirmington on 2nd June 1974. *(W.J.Taylor)*

Left: Eastern Air Executive Piper Aztec G-BBCW seen at Sturgate in October 1979. *(W.J.Taylor)*

AIR ANGLIA LTD/AIR UK

Date at base: *Kirmington/Humberside*   *1975 - current*
Formed 1970 at Norwich Airport as amalgamation of Rig-Air, Norfolk Airways and Anglian Air Charter. Out-station at Kirmington established in 1975. In January 1980 Air Anglia became the Anglia Division of Air UK which continued to operate from Humberside Airport.

GENAIR

Date at base: *Kirmington/Humberside*   *1982 - current*
A Liverpool-based operator of Embraer Bandeirante aircraft merged with Eastern Airways in late 1982. Some services are operated under the British Caledonian Commuter service using suitably repainted aircraft. The fleet now consists of Shorts SD330, Shorts SD360 and Bandeirante.

Top: **Seen in June 1982 pulling up after a spray run over a field of onions is Pawnee G-BSFZ of Lincs Aerial Spraying.** *(W.J.Taylor)*

Below: **Miller Aerial Spraying of Wickenby has been the only Lincolnshire company to operate the Ag-Cat. This example, G-BFJO, is powered by a piston engine but later aircraft have turbines.** *(W.J.Taylor)*

General Aviation Operators

AERIAL SPRAYING CONTRACTORS

Date at base: *Boston (Wyberton Fen)*   *1951 - 1956*
Formed 1951 as subsidiary of Skegness Air Taxi Service Ltd. Ceased trading 1956.

LINCS AERIAL SPRAYING CO LTD

Date at base: *Boston (Wyberton Fen)*   *1956 - current*
Formed 1956 as subsidiary of Skegness Air Taxi Service Ltd. Operates Boston Aerodrome and has become parent company for Skegness Air Taxi Service Ltd and Skegness Aero Club.

BLYBOROUGH AVIATION

Date at base: *Blyborough Hall*   *1963 - 1975*
Formed 1963 for selling and servicing light aircraft. Ceased trading 1975.

JOHN SUTCLIFFE AND SON (GRIMSBY) LTD (AERO DIVISION)

Date at base: *Louth (Crowtree)*   *1964 - 1975*
Private helicopter for executive use and air survey contract work. Firm sold its helicopter in 1975 and ceased operating an air division altogether.

BRISTOW HELICOPTERS

Date at base: *Tetney Heliport*   *1965 - 1968*
Site in Lincs used temporarily during North Sea gas explorations. Bristow still operate from bases elsewhere on the east coast.

MILLER AERIAL SPRAYING LTD

Dates at bases: *Skegness (Ingoldmells)*
                and Wickenby   *1967 - current*
Formed 1967. Operates fixed-wing crop-sprayers, also from Driffield aerodrome, Yorks. UK distributor for Schweizer Ag-Cat and dealer for Piper agricultural aircraft.

ARABLE AND BULB CHEMICALS LTD

Date at base: *Butterwick (farm strip)*   *1971 - 1975*

Formed in the late 1960s and initially used various contractors for its aerial spraying operations in the east of the county. In late 1971 an IMCO Callair A9 (G-AVZA) was obtained which was operated from a very narrow strip of grass to the rear of the company premises, adjacent to the A52. The aircraft was damaged on 4th August 1973 and not replaced. The strip had been ploughed up by 1975.

MANAGEMENT AVIATION LTD

Date at base: *Strubby*   *1972 - current*

Formed 1960 as separate company originally under Fisons Fertilizers. Crop spraying helicopters also operate from company H.Q. at Bourn, Cambs. Main work from Strubby is charter to North Sea gas and oil rigs.

SPRAYFIELDS (SCOTHERN) LTD

Date at base: *Bardney*   *1978 - current*

Until 1978 the company used various contractors for its aerial spraying operations in the north of the county. From 1978 it began to operate its own two Pawnee aircraft, G-AXED and G-BDCT. During 1980 G-AXED was replaced by G-BGPP.

G AND S G NEAL (HELICOPTERS) LTD

Date at base: *Holbeach (Northons Lane)*   *1979 - current*

For many years the company used contractors for its aerial spraying operations in east and south Lincolnshire. In 1979 obtained its own Hiller UH-12E, G-BDRY, and in 1980 added G-HILR to its fleet.

BRIDGE HELICOPTERS LTD

Date at base: *Sutton Bridge*   *1980 - current*

Subsidiary company of Sidney Garner agricultural merchants. Obtained Hiller UH-12E G-BDOH in early 1980 for crop spraying and charter work. Helicopter based at airstrip on former RAF airfield.

LINCS AIRSPORTS LTD

Date at base: *Manby*   *1981 - current*

Formed 1981 to provide training on microlight aircraft using a variety of single and two-seat machines. Also microlight aircraft sales.

AEROLIGHT AVIATION CO

Date at base: *Manby*   *1981 - current*

Formed in 1981 to become sole UK distributor for the Eipper Formance Inc. Quicksilver range of microlight aircraft. Newly imported machines assembled at Manby before delivery to customers.

CROP AVIATION (UK) LTD

Date at base: *Bicker Fen (farm strip)*   *1982 - current*

Launched on 1st January 1982 with one Pawnee (G-BETL) to provide a crop spraying service in Lincolnshire and East Anglia. Also providing consultancy service to the African distributor of the NDN Fieldmaster purpose-built crop spraying aircraft.

EASTERN MICROLIGHT AIRCRAFT CENTRE LTD

Date at base: *Fenland*   *1982 - current*

Formed early 1982 to provide training on microlight aircraft. The first of a number of different machines arrived for evaluation and instructor training in February 1982.

Flying Clubs

SKEGNESS AND EAST LINCS AERO CLUB

Date at base: *Skegness (Winthorpe)*   *1932 - 1939*

Formed 1932 at Winthorpe. Disbanded at outbreak of Second World War.

LINCOLNSHIRE AERO CLUB

Date at base: *Grimsby (Waltham)*   *1933 - 1939*

Formed 1933 at Waltham. Disbanded at outbreak of Second World War.

SKEGNESS AERO CLUB

Date at base: *Skegness (Ingoldmells)*   *1948 - current*

Formed 1948. Operated since 1951 by Skegness Air Taxi Service Ltd.

BOSTON AERO CLUB

Date at base: *Boston (Wyberton Fen)*   *1948 - 1954*

Formed 1948 at Wyberton Fen. Aircraft operated on behalf of club by Boston Air Transport Co. Ceased trading in 1954.

Below left: **Typical of the microlight aircraft distributed by the Aerolight Aviation Co. is the Eipper Quicksilver MXII. G-MBZR is seen here being rigged in front of the former Supply Squadron buildings at Manby in July 1982.**
(W.J.Taylor)

Below: **Blackburn Bluebird IV G-ABPN of the Lincolnshire Aero Club at Grimsby (Waltham) in September 1934.**
(via P.H.T.Green)

ROYAL AIR FORCE COLLEGE FLYING CLUB

| *Date at base:* | *Cranwell* | *1950 - current* |

Formed in 1950 to provide flying club for RAF College personnel. Some civilian members. Operates from the clubhouse on Cranwell North aerodrome. Equipped with appropriately registered Robin R.2112 Alpha G-RAFC and Robin R.1180TD Aiglon G-CRAN plus venerable Tiger Moth G-ANEF which flies in its former military markings T5493.

LINCOLN AERO CLUB

Dates at bases:	*Bardney*	*1956 - 1958*
	Branston Island	*1958 (Jun-Sep)*
	Kirton in Lindsey	*1958 - 1967*
	Blyborough Hall	*1967 - 1968*
	Hemswell	*1968 - 1975*
	Sturgate	*1975 - current*

Formed 1956 at Bardney. Frequent moves were necessitated by RAF re-deployments and landowners' changing attitudes.

GRIMSBY FLYING CLUB

| *Date at base:* | *Grimsby (Waltham)* | *1958 - 1959* |

Short lived attempt to revive the pre-war Lincolnshire Aero Club.

FOUR COUNTIES FLYING SYNDICATE

| *Dates at bases:* | *Ancaster (Sudbrook House)* | *1962 - 1976* |
| | *Skegness (Ingoldmells)* | *1976 - current* |

Formed 1962 to provide low-cost flying of home built and later vintage aircraft for members. Most flying done in Luton Minor (G-ASAA) and Tipsy Trainer (G-AFVN). Aircraft moved to Skegness when arrangements for Ancaster strip proved unsatisfactory. The syndicate is still registered with CAA and PFA and work continues on building its original Luton Minor, G-ASXJ.

LINKS AIR TOURING GROUP/WICKENBY FLYING CLUB

| *Date at base:* | *Wickenby* | *1963 - current* |

Formed 1963 at Wickenby. Changed name in 1971. Aircraft now operated on behalf of the club by Wickenby Aviation Ltd.

FENLAND AERO CLUB

| *Date at base:* | *Holbeach St John/Fenland* | *1972 - current* |

Formed 1971 at Holbeach St John. Flying commenced the following year.

SOUTH HUMBERSIDE FLYING CLUB

| *Date at base:* | *Kirmington/Humberside* | *1972 - current* |

Formed 1972 at Kirmington.

RAF POWERED FLYING ASSOCIATION AEROBATIC CLUB

| *Date at base:* | *Cranwell/Barkston Heath* | *1981 - current* |

Formed in late 1981 around Avions Mudry/CAARP CAP-10B G-SLEA. The club provides the impetus for RAF personnel to enter national aerobatic competitions and give displays of aerobatics at air shows.

Below: **Tipsy Trainer G-AFVN of the Four Counties Flying Syndicate undergoing maintenance (note the lack of starboard undercarriage leg) at Ancaster in October 1968.** *(J.Walls)*

Bottom: **Starting the engine of the RAF College Flying Club's Tiger Moth G-AVPJ at Cranwell in October 1967.** *(via R.C.B.Ashworth)*

Gliding Clubs

EAST MIDLANDS GLIDING CLUB

Dates at bases: *Scampton*   *1951 - 1955*
                            Kirton in Lindsey   *1955 - 1956*
                            Swinderby   *1956 - 1976*

Formed 1951 as part of the RAF Gliding and Soaring Association (RAFGSA). Amalgamated 1976 with Four Counties Gliding Club at RAF Syerston, Notts.

CRANWELL GLIDING CLUB

Date at base: *Cranwell North*   *early 50s - current*

Gliding for cadets of the RAF College started following the Second World War using RAF Tiger Moth aircraft as tugs. Later affiliated to the RAFGSA.

LINCOLNSHIRE GLIDING CLUB

Dates at bases: *Bardney/Swinderby*   *1964 - 1966*
                            Bardney   *1966 - 1978*

Formed at Bardney in October 1964 but quickly moved to Swinderby where it operated alongside the East Midlands Gliding Club. Evicted from Bardney 1978 and ceased operating. (see Strubby Gliding Club).

TRENT VALLEY GLIDING CLUB

Dates at bases: *Sturgate*   *1965 - 1974*
                            Kirton in Lindsey   *1974 - current*

Formed in 1965 following a split in the Lincolnshire Gliding Club at Swinderby.

PETERBOROUGH AND SPALDING GLIDING CLUB

Date at base: *Crowland (Postland)*   *1969 - current*

Formed 1969 at Crowland. Virgin site needed as no ex-RAF aerodrome available in the Fens.

Top: **Capstan BGA 1132 of the Peterborough and Spalding Gliding Club at Crowland (Postland) in May 1979.** *(W.J.Taylor)*

Above: **T31 glider RAFGSA 132 of the East Midlands Gliding Club at Swinderby in July 1956.** *(Tony Hancock)*

WELLAND SOARING GROUP

Date at base: *Careby (Marshalls Farm)*   *1971 - 1980*

Formed 1971 as offshoot of Perkins Diesel Sports and Gliding Club, then based at Crowland. Future uncertain due to recent change of ownership of Marshalls Farm. *(see page 274)*

STRUBBY GLIDING CLUB

Date at base: *Strubby*   *1978 - current*

Formed 1978 as remnant of the defunct Lincolnshire Gliding Club. Initially called 'Strubby Soaring Group' but re-titled in March 1979. Future uncertain with sale and demolition of Strubby aerodrome.

EAST KIRKBY SOARING GROUP
Date at base: *East Kirkby*   *1980 - current*
Offshoot of Strubby group. Began operations in April 1980.

HUMBER GLIDING CLUB
Date at base: *Scampton*   *1982 - current*
RAFGSA club. Arrived from Lindholme in Spring 1982.

Above: **One of a number of gliders operated by the East Kirkby Soaring Group is Grunau Baby BGA 1463.** *(W.J.Taylor)*

SPECIAL ACKNOWLEDGEMENTS
J.Aitken (Strubby Soaring Group), Captain M.Bond (Management Aviation Ltd), W.Callow (Four Counties Flying Syndicate), P.Clayton (Trent Valley Gliding Club), P.Coulten (Fenland Flying Club), P.Dickinson (Blyborough), D.Gittens (Welland Gliding Club), Peter Green, T.Hayes (Lincoln Aero Club), D.Hopper (Fenland Flight Centre), Flt.Lt.A.Johnson (Four Counties Gliding Club), D.Lingard (Four Counties Flying Syndicate), B.Rolfe and W.Scull (British Gliding Association), D.Stennett (Skegness Aerodrome), M.Stillingfleet (Peterborough and Spalding Gliding Club), John Walls, J.West (Lincoln Aero Club).

REFERENCES
Flight International, *Directory of British Aviation,* (Annual).
Pilot magazine.
Sailplane and Gliding magazine.

APPENDIX J
Notable Airstrips

In addition to its eighty-six military air bases and bona fide civil aerodromes, Lincolnshire has supported dozens of private airstrips since about 1930. Many have long since disappeared, leaving no flying records or physical remains, but several of recent date have facilities and landing regulations which are already itemised in aviation directories but nevertheless merit repetition here. Such publications do not, however, include any historical background, OS grid reference or indications of aircraft type and airstrip function. As these latter details are of direct relevance to the present study, an attempt is made below to give a reasonably full description of each strip so it can be fitted in with the general history of civil flying in the county.

Strips located on former RAF aerodromes are not included in this appendix since they will have been mentioned in Part Two. The sixteen additional strips selected for inclusion here have had to meet at least one of three criteria. They have either been active for an extended period, contributed something distinctive to the county's aviation or have left some clear physical evidence in the landscape. In several current cases they qualify on all three counts, but others are included because they have served as the base for some memorable flying organisation. One or two potential entries were excluded because the owners were concerned to keep their aircraft free from snoopers. Readers are reminded that before visiting any strip they should seek the owner's permission.

All sixteen sites are precisely known and are recorded in the same manner as main airfields. Unless otherwise stated, the parish in which each lies is the same as the listed name. From the various dimensions given it can be seen that the minimum length for an airstrip used by powered, fixed-wing aircraft is usually about 400 metres. Widths are normally upwards of 20 metres and in many cases there are two strips disposed at right angles to one another. The impact on land is normally minimal, however, involving just a few acres in joint use with agriculture.

ANCASTER (SUDBROOK HOUSE)
130 / SK 987463   *250 ft AMSL*
2 km N of Ancaster Railway Station
Flying began at Sudbrook House in 1954 when Mr Robin Simpson opened up a strip on his land. The exact position has shifted over the years due to crop rotations but recent listings have specified a 25-acre field accommodating two strips each of 463 metres length. From 1962 until 1976 a strip was used by the Four Counties Flying Syndicate who operated a Tiger Moth, Luton Minor and a Tipsy Trainer (see Appendix I). A strip remains active today.

BLYBOROUGH HALL
112 / SK 934950   *75 ft AMSL*
1.5 km SSW of Grayingham Church
The first of two intersecting strips at this location was laid out in 1963 for the use of the owner, Mr P H Dickinson, and friends. In 1966 a firm was formed (see Appendix I) for selling and servicing light aircraft, the original E-W strip being extended to 600 metres and a second laid out N-S. In 1975 the latter was ploughed up, the reduced site being used today mainly by a Cessna Skymaster (G-BFJR) and crop spraying aircraft. In October 1978 the airstrip achieved some notoriety when a drug smuggling gang were apprehended by customs officials while trying to land a consignment of cannabis from Luxembourg in a Piper Aztec (G-BBSR).

BRANSTON ISLAND
121 / TF 096710   *10 ft AMSL*
3 km WNW of Bardney Church
In the summer of 1958 the Lincoln Aero Club was obliged to vacate Bardney Aerodrome which was needed for a missile site. While an alternative strip was being sought, the club used a 150-acre island lying about two miles (4 kms) west of the aforementioned aerodrome. The island, bounded by the bend of the old *River Witham* and the Lincoln-Spalding railway line, was accessible from the Bardney-Fiskerton road.

Below: **Seen under construction at Ancaster in October 1969, Luton Minor G-ASXJ was moved to Boston (Wyberton) in mid-1982.** (*John Walls*)

CAREBY (MARSHALL'S FARM)

130/TF038165   *205 ft AMSL*

2 km W of Witham on the Hill Church

The formation of the Welland Soaring Group in 1971, due to the congestion at Crowland and lack of suitable aerodromes, brought into existence Lincolnshire's only 'hillside' gliding site (see Appendix I). Located on land belonging to a founder member, the site consists of two strips of about 700 metres length, orientated N-S and E-W, and occupying some 12 acres (5 ha) midway between Careby Wood and the Little Bytham to Witham on the Hill road. Although there is limited ridge lift, thermal conditions in south Lincolnshire are good and the site is deemed successful after nearly ten years' use. All launching is by winch and every one of the current 28 members flies. The club owns two 2-seat training gliders, a Primary Trainer Ka 4 and a Bergfalke 2B, both of which are German built. The site has no permanent buildings and the small blister hangar was being dismantled during October 1980 in anticipation of the club's move elsewhere.

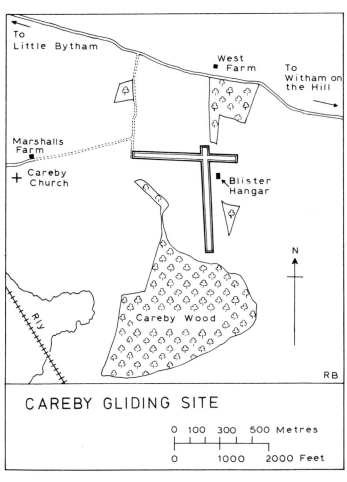

CAREBY GLIDING SITE

CUXWOLD HALL

113/TA182004   *270 ft AMSL*

1.5 km SE of Cuxwold Church

A strip to the north of the village was opened in 1960 by Mr J R Walgate to house a Jodel aircraft. This has been superceded by the present strip adjacent to the First World War landing ground which has housed a number of aircraft used for communications between the owner's farms in Lincolnshire and Scotland and for crop spraying. Notable among those aircraft was Provost T.1 G-AWVF, maintained in excellent condition and flown in its former military markings as XF877. The L-shaped landing ground area has two 50 metre wide strips, extending 280 metres N-S and 450 metres E-W. There is a hangar and lighting.

IRBY ON HUMBER

113/TA209040   *150 ft AMSL*

2 km SE of Irby on Humber Church

In 1958 an airstrip was laid out at Walk Farm, about one mile ESE of Irby village, on the land of Mr N Lockwood. Initially it was the home of an ex-RAF Auster since when several other Austers have used the strip. Some 427 metres in length, the strip runs ENE-WSW and had a hangar at the east end. It remains active today.

Below: **The Welland Soaring Group's blister hangar at Marshall's Farm, Careby, in the process of being dismantled following the club's eviction in October 1980.** *(R.N.E.Blake)*

Bottom: **Typical scene at the Cuxwold airstrip in June 1976. The aircraft are the owners Cessna U206 G-AXJY (equipped for crop-spraying), Aztec and Provost XF877/G-AWVF.** *(P.H.T.Green)*

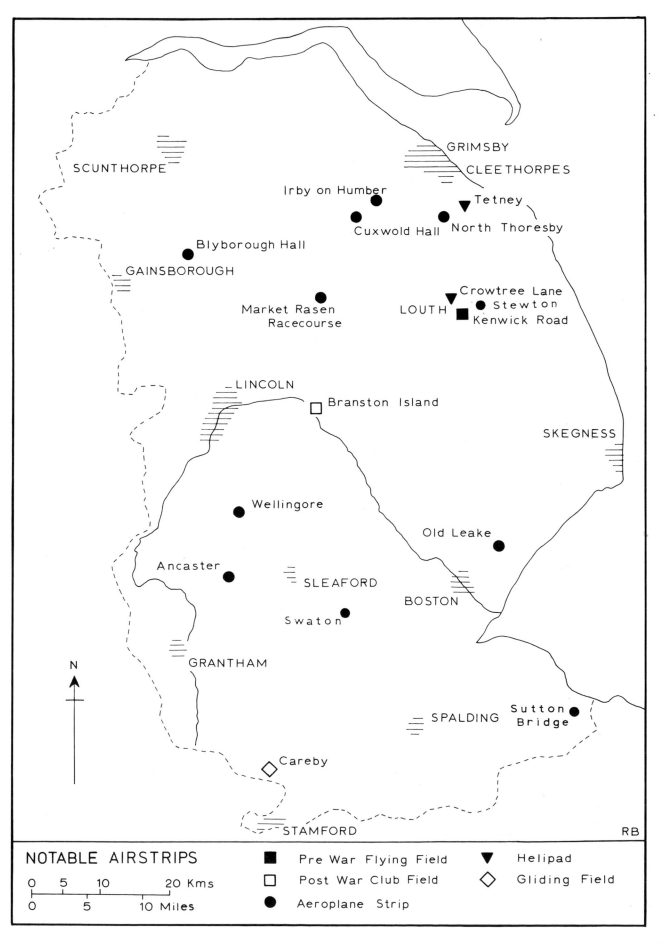

SCUNTHORPE

GRIMSBY

CLEETHORPES

Irby on Humber

Tetney

Cuxwold Hall

North Thoresby

Blyborough Hall

GAINSBOROUGH

Crowtree Lane

Market Rasen
Racecourse

LOUTH

Stewton

Kenwick Road

LINCOLN

Branston Island

SKEGNESS

Wellingore

Old Leake

Ancaster

SLEAFORD

BOSTON

Swaton

GRANTHAM

N

SPALDING

Sutton
Bridge

Careby

STAMFORD

RB

NOTABLE AIRSTRIPS

■	Pre War Flying Field	▼ Helipad
□	Post War Club Field	◇ Gliding Field
●	Aeroplane Strip	

0   5   10   20 Kms

0   5   10 Miles

LOUTH (CROWTREE)

113, 122/TF319869   100 ft AMSL
2 km SW of Louth Railway Station

A private 1-acre helipad was established in 1964 at the home of Mr Peter Sutcliffe to provide speedy communications up and down the country in connection with his shipping and forwarding business at Grimsby (see Appendix I). From 1964 until 1969 an Aero Division of Mr Sutcliffe's firm also undertook survey work along powerlines for the Yorkshire Electricity Board using a Brantly 2-seater helicopter. The helipad at Louth eventually became inactive in 1975 when the owner dispensed with his Brantly, decided against acquiring a more modern machine and began using fixed-wing services at Sturgate. The hangar in Crowtree Lane survives and is used as office storage space.

LOUTH (KENWICK ROAD)

122/TF340853   200 ft AMSL
3.5 km S of Louth Railway Station

One of the few pre-war airstrips to have a history of sustained activity was a large field behind *Southfield,* a house on the west side of Kenwick Road. This was used mainly in season by Lincolnshire Flying Services from 1934 until the outbreak of World War II for joy riding and banner towing with Avro 504's. There are no official records of the site ever being considered as a permanent aerodrome for the town.

LOUTH (STEWTON)

113/TF364868   60 ft AMSL
3.5 km E of Louth Parish Church

Situated immediately to the north of the disused Louth to Mablethorpe railway line, this grass strip is operated by Douglas Electronic Industries Ltd. The strip was opened in 1971 and has since housed Piel Emeraude G-ARRS and Scintex Super Emeraude G-ASNI. Unusually shaped, the strip tapers from 60 to 12 m in width, is orientated E-W and is 508 metres long. There is a small hangar.

MARKET RASEN

113, 121/TF125885   95 ft AMSL
2 km E of Market Rasen Railway Station

To allow horse owners, jockeys and race-goers to arrive in their own aircraft, an airstrip was established by Market Rasen Racecourse Ltd in 1969. Running E-W, it measures approximately 550 x 20 metres and occupies just under 3 acres (2.2 ha) within the racecourse site.

NORTH THORESBY

113/TF311988   25 ft AMSL
2.5 km E of North Thoresby Church

Situated about one kilometre east of the former railway line, on the north side of the road, this grass strip was opened in 1966 by Mr Michael Popoff, farmer of *Eastfield House.* It runs due E-W and extends to just over 400 metres. The main user has been the owner's Zlin Trener (G-ATDZ), plus a number of crop spraying aircraft. The strip remains active today, although the Zlin was sold in early 1982.

OLD LEAKE

122/TF407517   20 ft AMSL
1.5 km N of Old Leake Church

An airstrip was established at Fold Hill in 1968 by Mr W E Grant for agricultural and private flying purposes and remains active today. A Cessna is the current resident. There are two grass strips, 640 metres running N-S and 440 metres E-W. A distinctive feature is airstrip lighting.

SUTTON BRIDGE

131/TF466220   4 ft AMSL
2 km NW of Sutton Bridge Church

Possibly the most notable airstrip in Lincolnshire is that operated on the outskirts of Sutton Bridge by Lindsey Walton. Opened in the late 1960s this strip has housed a number of aircraft including Piper Comanche G-ARFH and Nord 1002 Pingouin G-ATBG. The latter aircraft arrived in 1968 and from

A rare view of Bristow's Tetney heliport in the mid-1960s. It is just possible to discern the outline of the North Coates hangars in the left background. *(Capt R.C.Balls)*

September 1973 has appeared regularly at air displays. For the 1981 season Lindsey Walton operated two 'new' aircraft, Morane Saulnier MS733 Alcyon G-SHOW, titled *The Cambodian Gunship*, and Boeing Stearman E.75 G-THEA. During 1982 there were persistent rumours that many of the aircraft would be sold to allow the purchase of a Chance Vought Corsair 'warbird' in the USA. The aircraft, which arrived in the UK on 12 August, was NX13371, painted in French Navy markings of the Suez era, and is normally kept at Duxford (Cambs).

SWATON
130/TF143377   *8 ft AMSL*
1 km E of Swaton Church
Operated by T G Cannon, this grass airstrip was opened in 1979. The strip is orientated N-S and is 650m long and 20m wide. There are no permanent buildings and the resident aircraft, which have included Jodel D.117 G-BFGK and Cessna F.150L G-BGOJ, have been parked in the open.

TETNEY
113/TA332009   *10 ft AMSL*
2 km E of Tetney Church
In June 1965 Bristow Helicopters established a helipad at New Delights, Tetney. The purpose was to ferry personnel of the BP and Burma Oil companies to the West Sole gas rigs in the North Sea. The initial residents were two Series 3 Whirlwinds but later three Wessexes were based there. In 1968 Captain Robert Balls, Chief Pilot based at Tetney, was awarded the OBE for rescuing 45 people from the sinking 'Ocean Prince' rig. The Tetney pad was closed at the end of 1968 when Great Yarmouth proved to be a better base for off-shore operations. The hangars survive and are used today for the storage of straw.

WELLINGORE (FOUR WINDS FARM)
121/TF002558   *200 ft AMSL*
2 km ESE of Wellingore Church
This airstrip was laid out in 1962 by Mr A W Troop for use by a group of friends with an active interest in flying. A hangar was erected and one member built an aeroplane in it and carried out repairs on other machines. The two constituent strips, each measuring 420m x 20m and together covering about 4 acres (1.7 ha), were ploughed up in 1972 when Mr Troop sold his land.

REFERENCES
Pooley, R., *Air Touring Flight Guide: United Kingdom and Ireland*, Air Touring Flight Services: Elstree Aerodrome, Herts, (annual since 1964).
Successive numbers of *Air Britain News, Air-Strip* (Midland Counties Aviation Society) and *Humberside Air Review*.

SPECIAL ACKNOWLEDGEMENTS
Mrs L E Chadwick (Tetney Parish Council), P.H.Dickinson, D.W.Gittens (Welland Soaring Group), W.E.Grant, T.Hayes (Lincoln Aero Club), N.Lockwood, Captains Robert Balls and Gordon Lucas (Bristow Helicopters), John Lucas (Market Rasen Racecourse Ltd), M.Popoff, R.G.Simpson, P.S.Sutcliffe, A.W.Troop, J.R.Walgate.

APPENDIX K
Air Memorials

A lasting reminder of the part played by the Royal Air Force during two World Wars are the various memorials to be found in the county. Over subsequent years several squadron associations have erected memorials on the site of their former wartime base or in the neighbouring village, while other memorials have been established by next of kin or grateful locals in the memory of aircrew who gave their lives in the fight for freedom.

The great majority date from the Second World War but some go back as far as the Zeppelin raids of 1916. The following details reveal a remarkable variety of site selection, ranging from individual graves and church windows to tablets on commercial premises. As to the geographical pattern of memorials, the map clearly shows that almost half of them are clustered in the north part of the Wolds and neighbouring Humberside while almost all the remainder lie in two distinct clusters, around Lincoln and on the northern edge of the Fens. The erection of memorials has rightly been an essentially unplanned process but the distribution is nevertheless a fair reflection of the density of aerial activity over the county and offers an interesting variation on the location of actual airfields.

The majority of the twenty nine memorials listed here are easily accessible, but it must be remembered that some are on private or Crown property and prior permission must always be sought by prospective visitors. It goes without saying that all memorials should be treated with due reverence and spared unnecessary wear and tear.

The 9 Squadron Memorial at Bardney. Inset in the centre of the supporting wall is a piece of rock from Kaa Fjord, the anchorage of the *Tirpitz* which was sunk during combined operations by 9 and 617 Squadrons. *(W.J.Taylor)*

BARDNEY
121/TF120696   *In the village centre*
Legend: *IX Squadron RAF. In memory of all ranks killed or missing 1939-1945. The Squadron flew from Honington, Suffolk, 1939-1942, Waddington 1942-1943 and from Bardney 1943-1945.* Dedicated 19 October 1980, a Lancaster propeller is supported on a brick base in which is incorporated a stone from that part of Norway where the mission to bomb and sink the German Battleship *Tirpitz* was executed. The memorial stands in grounds of the village Museum which also contains an excellent display of the Squadron's history.

BINBROOK
113/TA210940   *In the village centre*
Legend: *460 Squadron, Royal Australian Air Force. To those who served at Breighton (Yorks) and Binbrook (Lincs). From 15th November 1941 to 2nd October 1945. 'Strike and Return'.* Dedicated 9 September 1973.

BRATTLEBY
121/SK947808   *In the parish church cemetery*
Individual grave. Legend: *Flying Officer C.A. Connor DFC. Pilot Royal Air Force. 4 November 1940. Age 26.* Note: This lone RAF grave is that of the pilot of the aircraft in which Sgt John Hannah was awarded the Victoria Cross on the night of 15/16 September 1940, while flying from Scampton.

278

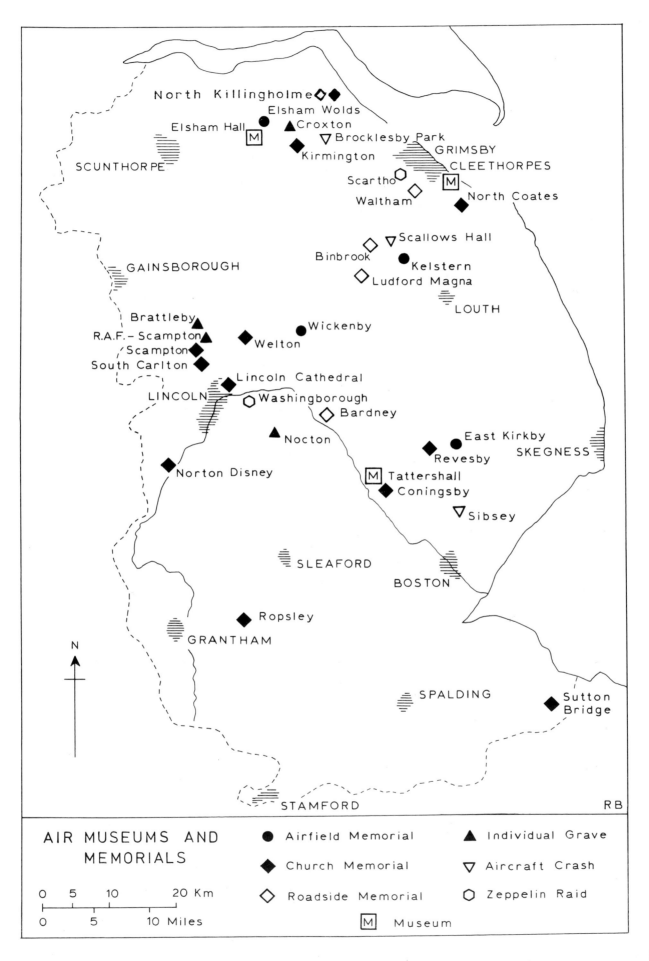

North Killingholme ◇◆

Elsham Wolds ●

Elsham Hall [M]　Croxton ▲

SCUNTHORPE　　Brocklesby Park ▽

Kirmington ◆　　　　　GRIMSBY
　　　　　　　　　　　　　　CLEETHORPES
　　　　Scartho ⬡　[M]
　　Waltham ◇　　◆ North Coates

　　　　　　▽ Scallows Hall
　Binbrook ◇
GAINSBOROUGH　　● Kelstern
　　　　◇ Ludford Magna
　　　　　　　　　　LOUTH

Brattleby ▲
R.A.F.–Scampton ▲　　● Wickenby
Scampton ◆　◆ Welton
South Carlton ◆

　　Lincoln Cathedral
LINCOLN　⬡ Washingborough
　　　　　◇ Bardney
　　　▲ Nocton
　　　　　　　　　　● East Kirkby
　　　　　　◆　　　SKEGNESS
◆ Norton Disney　Revesby
　　　　　[M] Tattershall
　　　　　◆ Coningsby
　　　　　　▽ Sibsey

≡ SLEAFORD
　　　　　　BOSTON

◆ Ropsley
GRANTHAM

≡ SPALDING　　◆ Sutton
　　　　　　　　　Bridge

STAMFORD　　　　　　R B

N ↑

AIR MUSEUMS AND
MEMORIALS

0　5　10　　20 Km
0　5　　10 Miles

● Airfield Memorial　　▲ Individual Grave

◆ Church Memorial　　▽ Aircraft Crash

◇ Roadside Memorial　　⬡ Zeppelin Raid

[M] Museum

BROCKLESBY PARK

113 / TA 133 113   *In parkland*

Legend: *Wellington Gigantea. This tree was struck by Lancaster III 442V (sic) of Bomber Command, RAF. Shot down in flames by a Ju 188 on the night of 3rd/4th March 1945. The entire crew of the Lancaster perished. The crew comprised:*

P/O J J Ryan	*Pilot Australia*	*RC*	*Age 33*
Sgt T H Jarman	*F/Engineer*	*C of E*	*Age 19*
F/Sgt R R Russell	*Navigator*	*C of E*	*Age 21*
F/Sgt H J Terry	*Air Bomber*	*C of E*	*Age 21*
Sgt H Birch	*WOP/Air*	*C of E*	*Age 21*
Sgt H Payne	*Air Gunner*	*C of E*	*Age 27*
Sgt W H Rogan	*Air Gunner*	*C of E*	*Age 19*

'May they Rest in Peace'.

Note: The aircraft was Lancaster III ME442/KM–V of 44 Squadron which was being held-off from landing at its home base of Spilsby due to enemy intruder activity.

CONINGSBY

122 / TF 223 580

Memorial plaque to 83 Sqn.
In the parish church

CROXTON

112 / TA 095 124   *In the parish church cemetery*

Individual grave. Legend (below an engraving of a Lancaster and a navigators' brevet): *Per Ardva Ad Astra. To the Glory of God in loving memory of Timothy Ianson Dee aged 20 years. Sergeant navigator R.A.F.V.R. who was killed in a plane crash near to Linton on Ouse in Yorkshire when returning from operations over Berlin on December 18th 1943. He gave his life that we might live. Also erected to his memory, the east window of this church.*

EAST KIRKBY

122 / TF 337 624   *At old airfield gates*

Legend: *In memory of those who gave their lives with 57 and 630 Squadrons, 1939-45.* Dedicated 6 October 1979.

ELSHAM WOLDS

112 / TA 041 132

At entrance to modern water treatment works

Legend: *RAF Elsham Wolds. Opened in Summer 1941 as a bomber station on No.1 Group. It was the home of No.103 Squadron and from Elsham Wolds until 1945 Wellington, Halifax and Lancaster aircraft of No.103 and other squadrons flew on bombing missions against targets in Germany and Occupied Europe.* Dedicated 20 June 1975. Subsequently the Squadron Badges of 103 and 576 Squadrons were added on either side of the plaque, together with a May 1945 photograph of 103 Squadron personnel and display boards giving details of Commanding Officers, locations, aircraft and Honours and Awards won by the personnel of 103 Squadron.

On 30 August 1981 a memorial garden and plaque was dedicated. Legend: *RAF Elsham Wolds 1941-1946. No 1 Group Bomber Command. 103 Squadron. 576 Squadron. This Memorial and Garden is in memory of all aircrews of 103 and 576 Squadrons who gave their lives operating from this airfield and to members of the RAF and WRAF who died whilst serving on this base.* Centre-piece of the Memorial Garden is the pitch-change mechanism and two blades of a propeller recovered from a crashed Lancaster.

KELSTERN

113 / TF 254 920

At roadside within site of Second World War airfield

For many years the only squadron memorial located on an airfield, the 625 Squadron example at Kelstern has been the prototype for a number of other squadron memorials erected in recent years. *(Bill Baguley/Rod Houldsworth)*

Legend: *625 Squadron Royal Air Force October 1943- April 1945. 'We Avenge'.* Dedicated 25 October 1964.

KIRMINGTON

113 / TA 106 113   *In the parish church*

Legend: *In proud and undying memory of members of 166 Squadron, RAF, who flew from Kirmington airfield and did not return from their last sortie 1943-1945. This tablet was placed here by their comrades.* Dedicated 7 April 1956.

LINCOLN

121 / SK 978 718   *In the Cathedral*

Among its many memorials to the RAF, the Cathedral notably contains the Airmen's Chapel of St Michael, in which there are plaques to Training Command, the New Zealand Air Force and the Rhodesian Air Force. The Cathedral also contains a Roll of Honour to the 21,000 aircrew of 1 and 5 Groups, Bomber Command, who lost their lives during the Second World War. The Roll of Honour was placed in the care of the Dean and Chapter of Lincoln on 8 November 1949.

LUDFORD

113 / TF 196 890   *In the village centre*

Legend: *This memorial is dedicated to the Airmen of 101 Squadron Bomber Command who failed to return from operational sorties in the First and Second World Wars. From 1943-1945 the squadron was based at Ludford Magna where they made many friends. A role of honour is kept in the village church. Under the 101 Squadron Badge: To serve was their highest aim.* The Roll of Honour is located in the Lady Chapel of the nearby parish church. Dedicated 16 July 1978.

NOCTON

121 / TF 061 641   *In the parish church cemetery*

Individual grave. Legend: *In memory of Group Captain Gilbert Stuart Martin Insall, VC, MC. Passed away on 17th February 1972 aged 77 years.*

NORTH COATES

113 / TA 350006   *In the parish church*

Memorial window. Legend (under the Station Badge in stained glass): *Presented by Royal Air Force North Coates, January 1971.*

NORTH KILLINGHOLME

113 / TA 142175   *Side of 'Lancaster Approach, on former airfield access road.*

Legend: *550 Bomber Squadron. Royal Air Force. 3 January 1944 - 31 October 1945. Through fire we conquer.*

Around the base of the memorial plinth: *Donated by the North Killingholme Fittie Lands Charity.* Dedicated: 31 July 1982.

NORTH KILLINGHOLME

113 / TA 144174   *In the parish church*

Squadron Badge and plaque. Legend: *Presented to the people of North Killingholme by Wing Commander J J Bennett DFC and Bar, Founder and first Commander of 550 (Bomber) Squadron. A token of esteem and reciprocation for the kindness and co-operation shown by your people to the squadron January 1944 - October 1945.*

NORTON DISNEY

121 / SK 890590   *In the parish church*

Two wooden plaques. Legend 1 (under badges): *To No's 300 and 301 (Polish) Squadrons, Royal Air Force, operating from Swinderby who gave their lives for freedom 1939-45. 'Za Nasza I Wasza Wolnosc'.*

Legend 2: *Sacred to the memory and in honour of F/O Michael Liniewski of 301 (Polish) Squadron, RAF, born 19th December 1911, killed on operations over Hamburg 9th August 1941. Erected by the patron of the living in recognition of a very gallant officer. 'Pray for Him'.*

REVESBY

122 / TF 298614   *In the parish church*

On the parish memorial plaque to the Second World War, under the list of the parish fallen. Legend: *Also of F/O W B Jardine*

   F/O G H Wright   *F/S A Dunae*   *W/O R C W G Baker*
   Sgt J P Olive   *Sgt J J Phillips*   *F/O Paige*

who were killed on operational duties when their aeroplane crashed in the parish.

Below: **A memorial to 550 Squadron was dedicated at North Killingholme on 31st July 1982.** *(W.J. Taylor)*

ROPSLEY

130 / SK 993343   *In the parish church*

An impressive stained glass window of three lights depicts the badge of the Royal Air Force and pilots' wings. In the centre light is a Sgt Pilot wearing Mae West and parachute harness and carrying a flying helmet. Legend: *To the Glory of God and in the memory of a beloved younger son, William Philip Dale, of Little Humby who did not return from an operational flight over Ostend, 5th November 1941. Aged 22.*

SCALLOWS HALL

113 / TA 247 948   *In woodland*

Memorial in the shape of a cross with dedication on the base. Legend: *Pray for the souls of*

F Oliver	W Reid
R Spierling	I W Anderson
S G Burton	R S Bradbury
A D Wells	

Air Crash, 5th December 1943 'Jesu Mercy'. Note: The aircraft was Lancaster MkIII DV270 of 101 Squadron.

SCAMPTON AIRFIELD

121 / SK 967 792   *On the airfield*

Individual grave near No.2 hangar. Legend: *Nigger - the grave of a black Labrador dog, Mascot of 617 Squadron, owned by Wing Commander Guy Gibson, VC, DSO, DFC. Nigger was killed by a car on the 15th May 1943. Buried at midnight as his owner was leading his Squadron on the attack against the Mohne and Eder Dams.* Note: RAF Scampton is still an operational base and this grave cannot normally be visited.

SCAMPTON VILLAGE

121 / SK 948 795   *In the parish church*

Memorial tablet. Legend (under the RAF Scampton Station Badge): *To mark the Diamond Jubilee of the Royal Air Force and the close association between Royal Air Force Scampton and this church during the years 1917-1919 and 1936-1978.*

SCARTHO

113 / TA 265 063   *In the village street*

Plaque on the wall of Lloyds Bank. Legend: *A German Zeppelin bomb was dropped on this spot. Midnight September 23rd 1916. Our God mercifully preserved the inhabitants of this village from death or injury. 'Observe Psalm 91'.*

A GERMAN ZEPPELIN BOMB WAS DROPPED ON THIS SPOT MIDNIGHT SEPT. 23RD 1916.

OUR GOD MERCIFULLY PRESERVED THE INHABITANTS OF THIS VILLAGE FROM DEATH OR INJURY.

OBSERVE PSALM 91.

SIBSEY

122 / TF 355 515   *On farmland north of the village*

Legend: *Here lies the crew of a Lancaster bomber which crashed on 20th January 1943. This memorial is their families' tribute of love and remembrance. Ronald A Brown, Charles W H Cocks, John Doran, Thomas S Henry, Bobby F Lind.* Note: the aircraft was Lancaster III ED503 of No.9 Squadron.

SOUTH CARLTON

121 / SK 951 766   *In the parish church*

A carved pulpit, erected in 1920, in memory of the Royal Flying Corps and Royal Air Force stationed at South Carlton aerodrome.

SUTTON BRIDGE

131 / TF 478 212   *In the parish church*

A memorial chapel was dedicated in the parish church on 29 March 1957. Called St Michael's Chapel, it commemorates those RAF personnel which served at Sutton Bridge and lost their lives during the Second World War.

WALTHAM

113 / TA 283 030   *At a roadside on the Holton le Clay by-pass*

Legend: *'Do not attack the hornet's nest'. 100 Squadron Royal Air Force, December 1942-April 1945. 'Honour the Brave'.* Dedicated 7 November 1978.

WASHINGBOROUGH

121 / TF 019 707   *In the parish church*

Eight stained glass windows in the Clerestory in memory of a Zeppelin raid on the village in September 1916.

WELTON

121 / TF 012 798   *In the parish church*

Stained glass window of three lights, erected in 1921, depicting First World War aircraft flying over Lincoln Cathedral. Legend: *To the Glory of God and in the memory of the officers and men of the Royal Air Force who died in the service of their country. 'Their Name Liveth for Evermore'.*

WICKENBY

121 / TF 104 810   *At the entrance to the civil aerodrome*

Memorial with representation of *Icarus* falling from the sky. Legend: *Royal Air Force Wickenby. No1 Group Bomber Command 1942-1945. In the memory of the one thousand and eighty men of 12 and 626 Squadrons who gave their lives on operations from this airfield in the offensive against Germany and the liberation of occupied Europe. Per Ardua Ad Astra.* Dedicated 6 September 1981.

REFERENCES

Smith, D.J., 'Aviation Memorials', *Aviation News*, Vol.2, No.23, 12-25 April 1974.

Smith, D.J., 'USAF Memorials and Others' *Aviation News*, Vol.5, No.3, 9-22 July 1976.

APPENDIX L
Aviation Museums

Over the past twenty years active interest in aircraft preservation has increased quite phenomenally. The Royal Air Force has founded its own Museum at Hendon and also support a number of regional collections, while the Imperial War Museum is at the centre of the impressive collection at Duxford. Such major and well publicised activities have tended to overshadow the work of numerous small organisations which, although lacking the facilities and resources of the major institutions, nonetheless make a valuable contribution to the preservation of our aeronautical heritage.

Lincolnshire has a long and varied aviation history which is being faithfully recorded by the combined efforts of two museums within the historic county boundary — the Lincolnshire Aviation Museum and the Humberside Aviation Museum. Whilst it is invariably the aircraft themselves which attract most of the attention, both museums have emphasised the part played by ordinary people, without whom the aircraft would be inanimate objects only. In a strange way these museums have more to offer in the way of aircraft than do most of the county's airfields today. For this reason they are included in a special appendix as if they were airfields.

LINCOLNSHIRE AVIATION MUSEUM
122 / TF 203570
In the Old Station Yard, Tattershall on the A153 road between Sleaford and Horncastle.
The history of LAM goes back to the formation of the Lincolnshire Aircraft Preservation Society in Grimsby by a small band of enthusiasts during 1965. Over the next few years the LAPS obtained a number of aircraft and other items and started what was to become, a few years later, the nucleus of the Museum's collection. One of the early activities of the LAPS was the recovery of exhibits from the wrecks of crashed wartime aircraft. In one such excavation the engines of a Heinkel He 111 shot down onto the beach at Chapel St Leonards on 2nd October 1940 by a Hurricane of 151 Squadron, Digby, were recovered.

The demise of the LAPS followed but, in April 1969, former members of the LAPS founded the Lincolnshire Aviation Enthusiasts Society based in Boston. The new society took over the LAPS collection of aircraft plus some other items and obtained a lease on the former goods shed in the Old Station Yard, Tattershall. The building was completely derelict but society members repainted and reglazed it and fenced the site off. With preparations complete, the Lincolnshire Aviation Museum was opened to the public on 19th July 1970 by Alderman George Whitehead, a former Mayor of Boston and a RAF pilot during the Second World War. With its opening the Museum became the first voluntarily organised aviation museum in the country to open to the public.

The main aircraft exhibits when the museum opened were Miles Gemini G-AKER and Percival Proctor NP294. Both air-

Below: **Proctor IV NP294, showing the original condition in which it was received at Grainsby in 1966.** *(LAM)*

Above: **DH Dove G-AHRI.**
(W.J.Taylor)

Left: **Gnome G-AXEI seen just after restoration during the winter of 1979/1980.** *(W.J.Taylor)*

Below: **Vampire T11 XD447 at Tattershall in the colours of the Royal Air Force College with pale blue band around the tail booms.** *(W.J.Taylor)*

craft were formerly members of the LAPS collection and had been moved to Tattershall in October 1969. Many years in the open air and damage by gales caused considerable deterioration in the Gemini's structure and it was dismantled and placed under cover during 1972, eventually moving to Goxhill to join the collection of the Humberside Aircraft Preservation Society.

The Proctor was built in 1944 and delivered to the RAF on 25th July that year. After several years of service at RAF Swanton Morley the Proctor was placed in storage and, on 22nd March 1955, was sold to the Westcol Construction Co Ltd. The aircraft was never converted for civil use and, after a number of moves, arrived at Tattershall with the Gemini. Once again, being another wooden aircraft, the Proctor did not fare well in its exposure to the elements over the years and in February 1974 it was removed from display for restoration to static display condition.

In addition to its small collection of aircraft the LAM also contained at its opening many more smaller exhibits, including one of the two Junkers Jumo 211B engines recovered on 23rd September 1967 from the He111. Another exhibit was a Supermarine Swift cockpit section which had been used as a cockpit procedures trainer and also displayed was a Merlin engine recovered the week before the Museum opened from the wreck of a Lancaster on the Black Buoy Sand in The Wash. Many small items were on display, as were a large number of models and various engines and propellors.

As the Museum became established more exhibits were obtained. On 19th December 1970 de Havilland Vampire T11 WZ549 was flown into Coningsby from the Central Air Traffic Control School at Shawbury. Intended for instructional use, WZ549 was allocated the instructional serial number 8118M. However, a short time after its arrival at Coningsby the aircraft was most generously loaned to the Museum and it was dismantled and moved to Tattershall on 20th February 1971, where it was re-erected on the loading ramp inside the goods shed. Another new arrival was Ward Gnome G-AXEI. The Gnome, built during 1966 by Mr M Ward, a former rear gunner on Stirlings, was a small low-winged monoplane powered by a converted Douglas motorcycle engine which flew for the first time at Wigsley, Nottinghamshire, on 4th August 1967. Later sold to the pilot of its first flight, Mr R Fixter, the Gnome was registered as G-AXEI on 25th April 1969 but after a brief flying career it came to the museum during 1971.

During 1973 two major exhibits were obtained; the first was de Havilland Dove G-AHRI. Initially registered on 11th August 1946, G-AHRI saw service in Iraq and Israel until October 1965 when it was placed in storage at Little Staughton in Bedfordshire. When moved to the Museum in February 1973 the aircraft was devoid of paint, engines and cowlings. However, cowlings have since been obtained and the aircraft has been painted in a blue, white and grey colour scheme.

The second arrival of 1973 was another Vampire T11, XD447. This aircraft was obtained as a direct result of the Museum's long-standing membership of the British Aircraft Preservation Council, the controlling body for aircraft preservation in Britain, and it arrived from the Hawker Siddeley factory at Woodford, near Manchester, during May 1973. Initially displayed in the colours of 8 FTS, Swinderby, XD447 has since been restored in the colours of the RAF College, Cranwell, where it served from August 1958 to January 1962.

More aircraft were loaned to the Museum during February 1974. Auster AOP9 XK417 had seen service with the British

Army both at home and in Germany. Somewhat tatty when it arrived, the Auster was repaired and repainted but, in May 1977, it was returned to its owner for restoration to flying condition. The second arrival that month was the museum's first helicopter exhibit, Westland Dragonfly WH991. First flown in 1953, WH991 had seen service with the Royal Navy ashore and at sea, including a period of service in Trinidad.

The North American Harvard entered RAF service at Spitalgate near Grantham and later saw extensive service at Cranwell. A Harvard cockpit section is displayed in the Museum to commemorate the aircraft's association with the county, although this particular aircraft, EZ259, actually served in South Africa and with the Royal Navy. The RAF's first jet bomber, the Canberra, entered service with 101 Squadron at Binbrook in May 1951. One of the early Canberra aircraft, WD954, later had its cockpit section removed and the old cockpit section may be seen in the Museum, painted in the Canberra's original Bomber Command colours of black and grey. The parent aircraft eventually went to Australia where it too was placed on display in a museum.

The first Flying Flea exhibited in the Museum was BAPC 22/'G-AEOF' loaned from the Newark Air Museum from 1970 to 1973. Further examples of the aircraft for the Museum's own collection were obtained during 1974 and 1975. The first was loaned by Mr Alan Troop of Wellingore and is the aircraft which he built himself and completed in 1938. Mr Troop's Flea was flown a couple of times and placed in storage, arriving at the Museum in October 1974. Subsequently the aircraft was restored to its original blue and silver colour scheme. The remains of the Museum's other Flea were found in Sleaford during 1975 and, although very weathered and damaged by fire, are thought to be the remains of the aircraft started by Bobby Earle at the Church Lane works of Carlight Trailers.

Unlike many other aviation museums the LAM is not located on an airfield which is a major drawback as all aircraft exhibits must in consequence be brought in by road. For this reason the Museum's collection is not large and consists of smaller, easily dismantled aircraft. However, the small collection of aircraft is supplemented by a comprehensive collection of aviation related items and ephemera.

On view to the public are such items as instruments, radio sets, engines, propellers, wheels and tyres, undercarriages and many parts recovered from the wreckage of crashed aircraft. Additionally, there are some specific components such as a complete Lancaster bomb door, the combustion chamber from a V2 rocket and a fuel filter from a Curtiss flying boat of the type operated from the Naval Air Station at Killingholme during the First World War. Although primarily an aviation museum the collection caters also for the general military enthusiast. One of the exhibits, obtained from the Butlin's holiday camp at Skegness (itself a former Naval shore station, HMS Royal Arthur), is a Second World War searchlight. There is also a bomb trolley and a reconstruction of a wartime observation post as used by the Royal Observer Corps. More modern vehicles on display include a fire tender and radar van from Stansted airport and a Nissen hut obtained early in 1980.

The modest aircraft collection was supplemented in 1980 by the arrival during April of Percival Provost T1 WW421 from the Motive Power Museum at Lytham St Annes. Although WW421 never operated in Lincolnshire it serves to commemorate an aircraft type which was in extensive use in the

County, both at the RAF College, Cranwell, and the RAF Flying College, Manby. Another aircraft on display for the first time during 1980 was the partially completed fuselage of Druine Turbulent PFA 1654. Started in 1962, the Turbulent was never completed and following a number of changes of ownership it arrived at the Museum on 28th December 1979.

A new building, presented to the Museum by the Panton family of Stickford, was opened to the public in April 1980. The building, named the Panton Wing in memory of Flight Sergeant Chris Panton, a flight engineer with 433 Squadron who was killed during the infamous Nuremburg raid of 30/31st March 1944, has enabled the museum to expand and stage several new displays including a tribute to the airborne forces of the Second World War. Centre piece of the new display is a one-fifths scale model of the 1910 Lee-Richards annular biplane built for the film 'Those Magnificent Men in Their Flying Machines', filmed partially in Lincolnshire.

Below: **An unusual but exciting exhibit at Tattershall is this reconstruction of a Second World War observation post as used by the Royal Observer Corps.** *(W.J.Taylor)*

After a period of consolidation, 1982 saw a number of important advances at the LAM. In April the fuselage of Hunter F.51 E-424 arrived from the Aerospace Museum at RAF Cosford (Staffs). Formerly used by the Royal Danish Air Force the Hunter was brought into the UK by Hawker Siddeley and was allocated the B-Conditions serial number G-9-445 pending a possible sale which did not materialise.

Also during April a new exhibition building was opened at Tattershall. Actually a genuine Nissen hut, the new building was opened by Mrs Edna Bianchi, wife of the late Doug Bianchi, founder of Personnal Plane Services and famous for the construction of many replica aircraft. The Nissen hut was quickly filled by the Proctor IV NP294, newly restored in the markings of RAF Swanton Morley.

The summer of 1982 saw the acquisition of two cockpit sections. First to arrive was that of Blackburn B.2 G-ADFV, obtained on loan from the Aeroplane Collection, Manchester. Built in 1935, G-ADFV served with Flying Training Ltd at Hanworth Aerodrome (Middlesex), and moved to 4 EFTS at Brough (Yorkshire) in October 1939. Later the B.2 served as an instructional airframe with 574 ATC Squadron at Caterham School, Surrey.

The nose of a Comet 4 airliner was the second cockpit section to arrive, in September 1982. Formerly part of the Dan-Air fleet, the nose of G-AZIY was obtained from the

British Aerospace aerodrome at Woodford (Cheshire) where the airframe had been used for ground testing since early 1977.

New exhibits in 1983 were Skeeter helicopter and Victor Cockpit.

List of Aircraft Exhibits

de Havilland DH-104 Dove Mk 1B	G-AHRI
de Havilland DH-115 Vampire T11	WZ549/8118M
de Havilland DH-115 Vampire T11	XD447
Fairchild F-24W-41A Argus II	FK338/G-AJOZ
Focke Achgellis Fa 330A-1 Bachstelze	100502
Hawker Hunter F51	G-9-445/E-424
Mignet HM-14 Pou du Ciel	BAPC 43
Mignet HM-14 Pou du Ciel	BAPC 101
Percival Proctor IV	NP294
Percival P-56 Provost T1	WW421/7688M
Piel CP.301A Emeraude	G-BLHL
Rollason D-31 Turbulent	PFA 1654
Saunders-Roe Skeeter AOP.12	XM561/7980M
Rollason D-31 Turbulent	PFA 1654
Saunders-Roe Skeeter AOP.12	XM561
Slingsby T8 Tutor	BGA 794
Stewart Ornithopter	BAPC 61
Ward Gnome	G-AXEI
Westland WS-51 Dragonfly HR3	WH991
Blackburn B.2 (cockpit only)	G-ADFV
de Havilland DH-106 Comet (cockpit only)	G-AZIY
English Electric Canberra (cockpit only)	WD954
Handley Page Victor B.2 (cockpit only)	XH670
North American Harvard (cockpit only)	EZ259
Supermarine Swift (cockpit trainer)	

-Reported as VV119, the Type 535 prototype

Top: **Dragonfly HR3 WP503 at Elsham Hall in 1979 prior to its transfer to Bomber County Aviation Museum's new premises at Cleethorpes.** (*W.J. Taylor*)

BOMBER COUNTY AVIATION MUSEUM
(Formerly the Humberside Aviation Museum)
113/TA 323 067
In the Leisure Centre complex on Cleethorpes sea front.

The County's second aviation museum is run by the Humberside Aircraft Preservation Society which formed in Immingham during 1974. The society initially obtained storage space at Goxhill where various elements of its collection were assembled. The collection centered around Miles Messenger G-AKBM, obtained from a scrapyard near Grimsby during 1973. Quite a famous aircraft, G-AKBM was placed second in the 1954 Siddeley Challenge Cup race at an average speed of 129 mph.

The store at Goxhill also absorbed a number of engines and a huge trailing edge flap from a Short Stirling bomber. In early 1976 a second Messenger, G-AHUI, was obtained and moved into store at Goxhill. Later in 1976 facilities for a museum were obtained in the grounds of Elsham Hall near Brigg and when Westland Dragonfly WP503 was collected from the Stansted fire school on 16th June 1976 it was delivered direct to the new site. During its service career WP503 did at one time serve at North Coates.

A number of Auster airframes were also obtained, including Auster 5 G-AKWT, which was stored for many years at Stroxton Lodge, near Grantham, and Auster J/1N G-AIJI which was overturned during heavy gales at Kirmington on 12th January 1975. Unfortunately the Museum's premises at Elsham Hall are in the open and the wooden aircraft, including the Messengers and a number of Miles Gemini parts began to deteriorate. Most of these exhibits were disposed of in favour of more durable metal aircraft. New exhibits to arrive were de Havilland Vampire T11 XD375 which was obtained from Duxford in mid-1979. This was joined by the centre and rear fuselage sections of Hawker Hunter T7 ET-273/G9-431 which arrived from Hawker Siddeley at Hatfield. The latter exhibit has since been fitted with the cockpit section of a former Royal Navy Hunter GA11 but still lacks wing, undercarriage and tailplane. In addition to the main aircraft exhibits the Museum has a large display of other items including a number of parts recovered in the nets of Grimsby fishing vessels.

In early 1981 the Museum announced plans to move its exhibition from Elsham Hall to the former reptile house of the defunct Cleethorpes Zoo. The new site, which the local council is converting to a leisure complex, provides the Museum with considerable covered accommodation and extensive grounds. By mid-1981 Pou du Ciel BAPC 76 'G-AFFI', and Mr. Alan Stewart's third man-powered ornithopter had been installed at the new site.

In addition to the acquisition of new civil exhibits during 1981 a number of military exhibits were also obtained by the HAPS. These aircraft included a second Vampire T11 for the collection, XD445, which arrived on 30 August from Huddersfield (West Yorkshire) where it had been used by the local Combined Cadet Force unit. A further new arrival on 19 September was Dassault Mystere IVA No.101 which formerly served with the L'Armee de l'Air and moved to Cleethorpes from open storage at Sculthorpe (Norfolk).

With the end of 1981 the HAPS was able to to concentrate on setting up its new museum and make it ready for the 1982 season. As part of this expansion the new site was named the Bomber County Aviation Museum. Gradually, the exhibits were moved over from Elsham Hall although some were placed in store pending restorartion.

With such a busy time establishing its new museum the HAPS has had little time to acquire new exhibits during 1982. However, in July a second Pou du Ciel original, G-AEJZ, was obtained from 1324 ATC Squadron at Brough (Yorkshire). 24 July 1983 saw the delivery of Canberra T.19 WJ975 which had been generously donated by Marshalls of Cambridge. This aircraft's last unit was 100 Squadron where it was 'S' before being delivered to Cambridge on 21 May 1980. It was due to be reassembled in August 1983.

Aircraft Exhibits

Auster J/1N	G-AIJI
Auster 5	G-AKWT
Bristol Babe replica	BAPC 87/'G-EASQ'
Dassault Mystere IVA	101
de Havilland DH-115 Vampire T11	XD375/7887M
de Havilland DH-115 Vampire T11	XD445
English Electric Canberra T19	WJ975
Hawker Hunter T7 hybrid	ET-273/G-9-431
Mignet HM-14 Pou du Ciel	G-AEJZ/BAPC 120
Mignet HM-14 Pou du Ciel replica	BAPC 76/'G-AFFI'
Stewart Ornithopter	BAPC 161
Westland WS-51 Dragonfly HR3	WP503
Westland WS-58 Wessex HAS1	—

REFERENCES

Ellis, K., *British Museum Aircraft*, Merseyside Aviation Society Ltd., Liverpool Airport 1977.

Ellis, K., *Wrecks and Relics*, Merseyside Aviation Society Ltd., Liverpool Airport, 1980 (revised periodically since 1961)

Ogden, B., *Aviation Museums (Worldwide excluding USA)*, Airline Publications: Hounslow, 1979.

Riley, G., *Aircraft Museum Directory (British Edition)*, Battle of Britain Prints International Ltd., 1976.

APPENDIX M

Airfield Names

One effect of airfields has been to cast a spotlight on places which might otherwise have remained unknown beyond the immediate locality. The two best examples in Lincolnshire are Cranwell and Scampton which books and films have made more famous than many of the county's ancient towns. As well as reviving memories for thousands of ex-servicemen, a study of airfield names is of practical interest to the both local and aero historians and for that reason the following notes have been compiled.

Of the eighty-six airfields in the main survey, as many as fifty-two (60 per cent) have adopted the name of the parish in which they largely lie. Of the remainder no less than twenty-four (28 per cent) relate to the nearest town or village beyond the parish boundary and only ten (12 per cent) bear names of hamlets, farmsteads or other landmarks. This statistical balance has not varied greatly over time and it does seem from the evidence that the original airfield planners did try to be consistent, notwithstanding several interesting anomalies which will now be examined.

Second World War aerodromes named after villages outside the host parish, such as Binbrook, Folkingham and Woodhall Spa, almost certainly took those names because their parish contained no substantial settlement. Caistor aerodrome on the other hand could easily have been named after the parish in which it lies, North Kelsey, which contains a large and compact village with the added facility of a railway station. It is difficult therefore to find an obvious explanation, especially as there is a well known place on the Norfolk coast with a very similar name which might have caused confusion. Likewise, North Witham aerodrome could easily have been named after Colsterworth, which is both its host parish and the nearest main settlement, and some mystery still hangs over its name.

During the Second World War the only Lincolnshire aerodromes bearing the names of tiny hamlets were Sandtoft and Sturgate, the former probably being as a memorable contrast to the rather average-sounding Belton. In Sturgate's case it was almost certainly decided not permanently to adopt the name of the nearby village of Upton (the original choice) for fear of confusion with the established RAF station at Upwood in Huntingdonshire, furthermore the host parish, Heapham, had no recognisable village to complicate the decision. The only Second World War airfield to bear the name of a natural feature was Donna Nook, which could not sensibly be named after the host parish, North Somercotes, for risk of confusion with the existing aerodrome called North Coates.

The most memorable airfields named after minor features date from the First World War. Cockthorne Farm (near Market Rasen) and Greenland Top (in the parish of Stallingborough) are especially evocative of that period and were probably so named in order to pinpoint their locations since they consisted of little more than farmer's fields. The difficulty for pilots and administrators was to know where these farmsteads actually stood in the patrol network. So a system was implemented whereby the nearest town or large village was bracketed after each name, e.g. Cockthorne (Market Rasen). This was not always done, however, for in the case of West Common Race Course the aerodrome was officially listed as 'Lincoln' with no indication in documents as to its precise location. Spitalgate (or Spittlegate) had a problem of a somewhat different nature, being named after a non-recognisable feature and alternating in name with the simple 'Grantham' throughout its history. Lastly, there were two short-lived airfields in the First World War — Skegness (Burgh Road) and Lincoln (Handley Page Field) — which had no official names and have been given identitites in retrospect for the purposes of this study.

So far as civil airfields are concerned, their economic and administrative association with particular towns has led in most cases to their adopting the names of places more distant than was the practice with military stations. Grimsby aerodrome, in the parish of Waltham, certainly acquired its official RAF name from its pre-war status as a municipal airport, though the choice may have been reinforced by potential confusion with White Waltham in Berkshire. Of the nine civil airfields with no military history at all, six (67 per cent) have been named after the town they serve rather than the local parishes or rural settlements. It is, however, customary in flying circles to suffix the official name with a more localised name, as for example Boston (Wyberton Fen). This practice not only assists in flight planning but has an added significance in writing regional aviation history where particular towns have had more than one civil airfield at different periods, as in the case of Skegness (Winthorpe) and Skegness (Ingoldmells).

Where civil airfields have a more regional function there has been a tendency in recent years to create new names altogether which more accurately define their catchment areas. These are usually linked with the original e.g. Holbeach St John/Fenland Flight Centre. In the case of Kirmington, the former RAF bomber station has been so transformed by modernisation that the Civil Aviation Authority now lists it as 'Humberside Airport', though in an historical survey such as this it is rendered as 'Kirmington/Humberside' to eliminate any possible misconception that they were on separate sites.

The distinction between brackets and oblique strokes is not an absolutely consistent one but does have a logical basis. Broadly, the oblique stroke is used either when an airfield has two alternative names of equal status, such as Holbeach St John/Fenland, or in a historical context where there has been a change of name as with Brattleby/Scampton or Ingham/Cammeringham. In the second type of relationship it is important to preserve a paired nomenclature, otherwise readers could again fall into the trap of assuming that the two names in question represented separate airfield sites. In this study it was consciously decided to place the more recent, and normally the best known name in front position, e.g Scampton/Brattleby or Spitalgate/ Grantham.

As for the use of brackets, these were first introduced in 1916 to provide RFC officers with an indication of the nearest town to their landing grounds, (as noted above), but in more recent times the function has completely changed to that of specifying the local position of a civil airfield bearing a regional or civic name. Where in rare cases two geographically separate airfields have existed within a single parish and have borne identical official names, as with Kelstern, the name has been specially suffixed in this survey with a (1) and (2) to denote the war period in which each originated. In the case of Kirton in Lindsey (1) the alternative local name of 'Manton' is also inserted behind an oblique stroke in view of its established local usage.

In the past, and particularly during wartime, airfield names have imposed a number of administrative difficulties. The anecdote about equipment destined for Scopwick, but ending up at Shotwick in Cheshire, is now legend and led to a sensible decision to re-name the Lincolnshire station 'Digby'. It is less clear though why Brattleby was re-named 'Scampton' at a similar period and the only explanation which can be hazarded today is that there were rather a lot of stations beginning with BRA, plus the fact that the station was being transformed from a Home Defence base to a more elaborate Training Depot Station. Harpswell aerodrome for its part was probably so named in preference to Hemswell, an equally close-by village, because there was already an RFC station called 'Elmswell' in Suffolk by 1917. But why the Harpswell field was later named 'Hemswell' when re-activated in 1937 remains something of a mystery. Without access to official papers, and many of these decisions may never have been justified in writing, it is impossible at this distance in time to offer any categorical explanation of the various anomalies which exist in airfield naming.

Perhaps the most serious problem for the aero-historian has been the use of identical names for quite distinct airfields at different periods. Without cartographic evidence one might reasonably conclude that the Second World War bomber station at Elsham Wolds occupied the same ground as the earlier Flight Station. Research has in fact shown that the successive sites stood side by side, with so little overlap as to make them historically distinct airfields. It is highly probable that officers looking for a site for a bomber station were able to narrow their search with the aid of First World War plans, nevertheless the precise ground selected was different.

A similar relationship existed at Kelstern where the two airfields, with identical names, stood on widely separated sites at their respective periods. A third case relates to airfields known officially as 'Kirton in Lindsey'. The early Flight Station actually lay in the parish of Hibaldstow and was known locally as Manton, whereas the fighter aerodrome constructed at the outbreak of the Second World War lay some 3 miles (5 kms) to the south, this time in the correct parish. Since there is no trace of the Manton site on modern OS Maps, historians could easily be forgiven for assuming the two establishments occupied common ground. There is certainly nothing published to clarify this point and the anomaly was only discovered while referring to First World War airfield plans at the Public Record Office.

To clarify the geographical relationship between these various pairs, maps have been specially drawn for inclusion at appropriate points in Part Two. It is suggested that as a standard practice any citation or listing of airfields should include alternative names where applicable, and grid references in every case. Otherwise the twin problems of double-counting and under-enumeration will continue to distort calculations and historians may be lured into fruitless searches.

Below and bottom: **Large name boards are now a feature at most RAF establishments, leaving visitors in no doubt as to the station's name.** *(W.J.Taylor)*

APPENDIX N

Essendine : The Airfield That Never Was

ESSENDINE

130 / TF 065 130　　　　　　　　　　　　*100 feet AMSL*
1.5 km W of Braceborough Church

During both war periods many dozens of sites were reconnoitred as potential airfields, but for various reasons a proportion were not finally developed. A comprehensive record of their locations is almost impossible to compile in retrospect, while the stage reached in the planning of each individual station usually remains obscure. There are, however, several about which sufficient is known to repay investigation and these already represent a specialised and most interesting aspect of aviation archaeology. A few such sites occurred in Lincolnshire.

A good example from the First World War was Goxhill which in 1915 was earmarked as a military landing ground, though almost certainly not proceeded with at that stage. During the great aerodrome expansion between 1935 and 1944 many major stations were located either directly on, or adjacent to, the sites of First World War airfields and there can be little doubt that old Home Defence files were consulted by Air Ministry engineers in order to speed up the search for suitable terrain during the expansion years.

But clearly it was not automatic that First World War sites would prove feasible, for comparatively few were actually adopted for enlargement after 1935. Most of the Second World War bases occupied entirely fresh sites and many more would have been constructed on virgin farmland had the war in Europe taken more strike power to win. The names of several projected aerodromes have recently come to light from released documents, three of which are cited by D.J. Smith in his informative article "Island Airfield" (*Aviation News*, Vol. 8, No. 6, 17-30 August 1979, pages 4-5). These would have been built at Appleton Wiske, near Darlington (possibly on the defunct Home Defence field of that name), at Strensall, just north of York, and near Essendine, in Lincolnshire. All three sites were apparently found defective before ground was broken, but in the last case there is a partial record of the proposed layout which merits serious attention, not only as a valuable entry in Lincolnshire's rich airfield history but as a good example of the phenomenon of RAF stations which were never to be.

The village of Essendine stands six kilometres (four miles) north of Stamford, Lincolnshire's most southerly town. But historically it lies within the County of Rutland, now relegated to a district within the new Leicestershire, and never in Lincolnshire. The projected airfield, however, did lie predominantly in the adjacent Lincolnshire parish of Braceborough, with a small portion in neighbouring Carlby and only the western most perimeter straddling the county boundary and falling within the parish of Essendine. A similar relationship has been noted at Buckminster (see Part Two), where a settlement outside Lincolnshire also gave its name to an airfield firmly within the county, while a good number of fully developed aerodromes have been observed to overlap the western boundary in settings not too dissimilar from that of the Essendine scheme.

More detailed evidence about the site has come to light from a plan recently acquired by the RAF Museum, Hendon. Covering about a square mile of countryside on the northern flank, the plan bears the title *Essendine - Layout of Bomb Stores, Scale 1 : 2500* and is dated November 1942. This title confirms the official name intended for the station and the plan contains a wealth of historically relevant information, despite the fact that it is incomplete in geographical terms. The maximum area covered by the plan is indicated in the accompanying map but has been added to by extrapolation in order to suggest more about the whole project.

The first detail of interest is the fact that the bomb stores were apparently a second-phase proposal, the 'existing AM

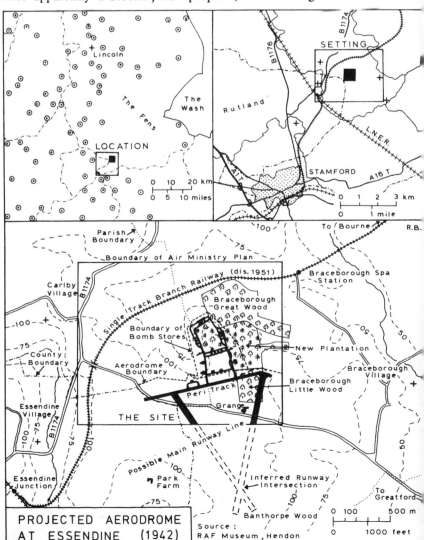

PROJECTED AERODROME AT ESSENDINE (1942)

boundary' (of the aerodrome proper) being differentiated from the 'proposed AM boundary' which demarcated only the bomb stores. This has a number of historical implications, including the possibility that the 'existing' aerodrome might have been originally intended for fighters or transporters, or even have had an earlier existence as an ELG or a decoy. Alternatively it may simply have been the practice to plan an operational landing area first and then work out the siting of the various appendages at a later stage. That an exacting plan was being drawn up for bomb storage strongly suggests that the station as a whole was at an advanced planning stage by November 1942.

The proposed extension lay on the northernmost side of the aerodrome and occupied some 14 hectares (35 acres), a fairly typical land allocation for that purpose. Also characteristic of the period was the choice of existing woodlands to provide camouflage and blast screening for the bombs. The site overlapped a group of small woodlands which today are named collectively on the 1 : 50 000 Ordnance Survey map as Braceborough Great Wood, though the main stores were to be located in a section of mixed deciduous and coniferous trees called New Plantation. Instructions on the margin of the plan stressed the importance of concealing work during construction and after completion, and stipulated that "stores and roads situated in wooded areas are to be adjusted to avoid felling of trees and reduce extent of screens. Roads adjoining hedges and trees to be constructed as close as practicable". It is interesting from this to observe that the stores were to be positioned to the west of the woods, presumably where they would be less detectable by enemy raiders coming in from across the east coast.

A one-way, clockwise track system was to be installed, the northbound run following the field divides which mark out the mutual parish boundary of Carlby and Braceborough. This track was to curve east to follow the northern edge of New Plantation, then run south to rejoin the aerodrome's perimeter track having utilised a farm track that cuts through New Plantation and finally skirts the western edge of Braceborough Little Wood. The marginal notes specify that access roads to the bombs should be 12 feet (4 metres) wide, on gradients no steeper than 1 in 25 and curved to minimum radii of 100 feet for bomb trolleys and 30 feet for lorries. As for the configuration of the land surface, the bomb stores were positioned on land falling slightly away from the 100 foot contour, characteristically below the general surface of the aircraft operating zone.

About the aerodrome itself much less is known, as the plan shows only a small part of the layout. Clearly it was to have been a bomber station, equipped with paved runways of standard width which would have been needed on the mainly clay soils of the locality. The plan reveals the ends of two runways, running roughly NW-SE and almost N-S respectively which, if projected to lengths of 1,400 yards (1,280 metres) would have intersected just north of Banthorpe Wood. As neither follows the optimal NE-SW orientation, it is assumed that the main runway was to be located south of the Carlby-Greatford road, possibly crossing it in the vicinity of Braceborough Grange. From the evidence of contours the terrain here was eminently suitable, being fairly level, just over 100 feet AMSL and affording ample room to accommodate a 2,000 yard (1828 metre) runway which avoided aircraft overflying either Braceborough or Essendine. However, the available plan does suggest that Braceborough Grange was to be demolished and the same probably applied to Park Farm, though the latter falls outside the area we know in detail. A further point of general principle is the way in which the bomb stores were positioned at least

500 metres clear of the aircraft approach lines, in the angle of the two known runways.

The positioning of the main technical site and hangars is not indicated but one can hazard a guess that they were to be adjacent to either Essendine or Greatsford, both villages having reasonable road communications and safely distant from the bomb stores. On the analogy of bomber stations which were built, the domestic accommodation was probably planned to be located on the opposite side to the bomb stores, namely to the south, in the Shillingthorpe Park area. Falling land here would have afforded good natural drainage which was no less important than the safety factor of building camps below the plateau on which the aerodrome stood.

All in all the landscape between Essendine and Braceborough looks highly plausible as a site for a Second World War bomber aerodrome. It was gently undulating, with a moderate tree cover and stood less than a mile from the B 1174 (now the A 6121) Bourne to Stamford road and close to a number of villages. The presence of a single-track railway line (Essendine Junction to Bourne) must surely have been a decisive factor in the proposed siting of the bomb stores, the link into the main London and North Eastern line being an especial advantage. Given its generally rural setting, its accessibility could hardly have been better.

So why did RAF Essendine (or was it intended for the Americans) never materialise? The answer to this has to be attempted at several levels. First, by November 1942 the peak of aerodrome construction was already past and with accumulated experience the Air Ministry engineers were no doubt becoming much more selective. With larger bomb-carrying capacity, aircraft required larger, but fewer, aerodromes and most of those established in Lincolnshire late on in the war were located north of the Fens. Second, Essendine was peripheral to the main aerodrome belt and quite close to the Fens across which enemy raiders could attack with relative impunity. It is interesting to recall that south-east Kesteven was not a particularly densely developed area and the defensibility hypothesis deserves further examination by the aero historian. Third, the proposed aerodrome, as described in the available plan, would have entailed the felling of Braceborough Little Wood (about 6 hectares or 15 acres in extent) plus the demolition of Braceborough Grange and possibly also of Park Farm. Although not without precedent, this kind of disruption was avoided wherever possible and may have been a contributory factor to the abandonment of the whole project.

The site today is crossed by high-voltage transmission lines and the passer-by would certainly remain oblivious of any past aeronautical potential. The single-track railway has been closed and dismantled and the only remote connection with aviation is the occasional low-flying aircraft from Wittering or the sight of gliders from Careby until those ceased in October 1980. But the people of Essendine and neighbouring villages may well reflect on how close they came to hosting an air force base, as so many other of Lincolnshire's parishioners did forty years ago. It will be interesting to discover whether there are any landowners' documents or recollections among local inhabitants regarding this Lincolnshire airfield that never was.

APPENDIX O

Source Material and Research Methods

Broadly speaking, the material for this study has been gathered in four main stages: listing the airfields, locating them, tracing their operational histories and assessing changes in their physical character and condition. For the benefit of those readers who believe they have found errors in the text, or who intend embarking on a similar project, the following account may help to explain how the information was gathered and interpreted for use in this survey.

The first task was to ascertain which airfields have belonged to the historic county of Lincolnshire since the earliest days of organised aviation. This apparently simple exercise proved more difficult than expected since no comprehensive listing of airfields has ever been compiled for all periods. The nearest document to meet this requirement was P. H. Butler's *British Isles Airfield Guide* (published by Merseyside Aviation Society), which provides the names and approximate locations of all military and civil airfields which have existed since about 1930. From subsequent investigations, however, it was discovered that Lincolnshire contained three landing grounds — Holbeach Range, Ludborough and Theddlethorpe — which do not appear in Butler's *British Isles Airfield Guide*, presumably because they were not listed in the Air Ministry Index which formed the basis of that guide, and these were accordingly incorporated into the present study.

For the First World War it was necessary to consult original documents at the Public Record Office (Classes AIR 1 and AIR 2) in order to ascertain which airfields existed in Lincolnshire at that period. This was done from a combination of listings and synoptic maps, the most useful being the *Quarterly Survey* dated September 1918 (reference: PRO/AIR 1/452 and 453) and the *Map showing Areas, Groups and RAF Stations* dated November 1918 (reference: PRO/AIR 1/2107/26131). In a few instances, e.g. Blyborough and Willoughby Hills, the existence of a landing ground did not become apparent until several files of earlier dates had been consulted and it is still not absolutely certain that every airfield of that period has been included in the study. In two cases — Buckminster and Gainsborough — it was not initially clear which county each actually stood in, and as it turned out both of them lay in a different county from the settlement of the same name. The special case of the 'Handley Page Field' at Lincoln was derived from published research by John Walls.

On the civil side, Butler's *BIAG* proved to be at its most useful since it provided a cumulative record of all civil airfields listed in *UK Air Pilot* from the early 'thirties onwards. Without Butler's civil listing it is quite probable that several minor civil airfields, such as Cleethorpes Beach, Scunthorpe and Spalding, would have been missed out altogether. Private airstrips, which are not included on the main survey (Part Two) but are listed in Appendix J, were derived from two independent sources: *Pooley's Air Touring Flight Guide* and Hardy's *Directions to British Aerodromes*, both of which documents are regularly revised and therefore of considerable historical value. As airstrips are very numerous and in many cases short-lived, only those which have remained active for a sustained period have been considered worth recording at all.

Moving on to ground locations, those for the Second World War were initially derived from *Air Maps* of the period, ranging in scale from $1:633\,000$ (ten miles to the inch) to $1:250\,000$ (four miles to the inch). The circular symbols were sufficiently precise to indicate which tracts of land should be followed up on larger-scale maps, but several smaller landing grounds were not shown and therefore had to be tracked down from other sources. In the case of Theddlethorpe the exact site happened to be shown on the Lindsey County Development Plan (1954), but the Holbeach Range field could only be located in detail by direct communication with the present administration at RAF Holbeach.

The formulation of six-figure grid references was done from the Seventh Edition of the Ordnance Survey One-Inch Series as revised in the late 'sixties. This particular map series provided the best available record of Second World War airfield sites and it is perhaps worth mentioning that popular O.S. scales have not always yielded equivalent information for other dates. Immediately after the war the Sixth Edition concealed all airfields for security reasons by showing instead the pre-war landscape features. The earliest seventh Edition maps began by showing white blanks overprinted with the word 'Airfield' and moved on gradually to distinguish between 'Airfield (Disused)' and active stations, e.g. 'Manby Airfield'. During the 'sixties the full runway layouts were introduced, providing a useful indication of which stations were paved or grass, but with successive revisions the grass type have tended to be deleted altogether where they are no longer clearly identifiable in the landscape. The new $1:50\,000$ Series has continued to exclude mention of airfields after they have been largely demolished or redeveloped and this now applies to a fair number of the originally large and paved type. The point to make here is that popular O.S. Maps no longer provide a reliable indication of the distribution of wartime airfields and a good deal of research into obsolete editions had to be carried out in order to compile a comprehensive record of the sites.

During this stage of the research a number of interesting anomalies and inconsistencies in the Ordnance Survey were discovered, for instance on the 1954 edition of Sheet 113 (Lincoln and Grantham) the North Aerodrome at Cranwell was shown as an 'Airfield' whereas the more important South Aerodrome was not indicated at all. Likewise on the 1967 edition the disused grass station at Coleby Grange was explicitly indicated whereas the identical site at nearby Wellingore could only be inferred by the configuration of its perimeter track. Finally, for reasons which are not at all clear, the disused paved station at Faldingworth (Sheet 104 Gainsborough) has never been shown in layout whereas the most strategic strike bases in the county are clearly visible by their published runway arrangements.

For the First World War, it is impossible to glean any exact locations from O.S. maps since layouts were not published at that period and most of the physical evidence has in any case been eradicated by the passage of time. The locations of aerodromes and other main air stations were fortunately available from the aforementioned *Quarterly Survey* (September 1918) which contains a 6-inch scale site plan of every establishment. Landing grounds, however, are only described in written form and no compass directions were provided from the nearest railway stations. In the case of Gosberton, a huge Fenland parish, the airfield was vaguely described as lying 3½ miles from the local railway station. With the aid of symbols on the *Map of Areas, Groups, etc.* (November 1918), plus listed telephone numbers, most landing grounds could be found within a few hundred metres but the precise sites were only discernible from official records if a sketch map happened to have been left on correspondence in a Home Defence file. In two cases, New Holland and Winterton, the exact fields in question were pin-pointed with the assistance of elderly residents who remembered aeroplanes landing there, while at Market Deeping the parish council and the local branch library had some existing historical material to offer. By a combination of documentary research, field work and eye witness accounts all the First World War airfields were successfully traced in the end, but it might be as well to forewarn those investigating other counties that there is no short cut to the smaller landing grounds of this early period.

Civil airfields, though more recent than the First World War, remain oddly elusive in many cases with pre-war fields ironically proving much easier to find than some of those dating from the early post-war period. Whereas complete copies of the pre-war *Air Pilot* reside in many aeronautical libraries today, the post-war equivalent is constantly up-dated by additions and deletions and in consequence contains no maps or details of defunct fields such as Cleethorpes, Scunthorpe and Spalding. Fortunately Spalding Aerodrome happened to be included in the *County of Holland Development Plan* (1953) and the exact site could be derived from that published source. With Cleethorpes Beach, however, the memory of the staff at the Town Hall had to be jogged, while for Scunthorpe the British Steel Corporation and the local planning department between them were able to provide quite detailed maps of the site. An interesting discovery from this phase in the research was the fact that the Civil Aviation Authority appears to hold no complete collection of old aerodrome plans for the benefit of anyone interested in the development of regional civil aviation.

Private airstrips proved even more difficult to pin-point and had to be sought in the field with the aid of written descriptions (longitude and latitude, road directions, the nearest farm, etc.). In some cases the local authority provided information where applications to develop hangars had been received, though for the most part there are no official site plans available other than the actual landowner's property deeds. Airstrip buildings are sometimes shown on large-scale O.S. maps (1 : 2500 Series) but this is not a great deal of help until the location is already known in some detail.

Turning now to operational histories, the military ones were initially gleaned from J. Rawlings' *Fighter Squadrons of the RAF* and P. Moyes' *Bomber Squadrons of the RAF* which are both standard works and until recently the only published sources listing wartime airfields systematically. Eventually, however, these proved to be limited in what they covered and excluded some important flying functions in Lincolnshire such as training and aircraft supply. Dozens of other narratives were therefore read in order to pick up other material about units known or believed to have been based in the county, and much of the same material was published in T. Hancock's *Bomber County* in 1978.

The bulk of the Second World War information relating to particular RAF stations was obtained directly from the Ministry of Defence's Air Historical Branch, from the independent research society Air-Britain and from files recently acquired by the Public Record Office. With regard to the last mentioned source, the files AIR 10/4038 and 4039 provided categorical evidence of resident units in 1943 and 1944, while Classes AIR 28 (Station Records) and AIR 29 (Miscellaneous Units) revealed the sort of details necessary to fill out a specialised survey of this kind. For the period since 1945 there has been no shortage of operations reports in the various journals and magazines listed elsewhere.

First World War operations were more difficult to relate to particular airfields as official records were so much less sophisticated and eye witness accounts naturally more difficult to obtain in retrospect. The official history of the period, *The War in the Air* by Raleigh and Jones, contains few specific references to airfields and certainly no mention of all the minor landing grounds which played a vital part in Home Defence patrols. Similarly the standard squadron histories do not refer to landing grounds for the simple reason that these were not aeroplane bases as such. Far greater reliance was therefore placed on files at the Public Record Office than was even the case for the Second World War and most of the squadrons and aeroplane types using landing grounds were inferred from what is known to have been stationed at the parent aerodromes. In many cases, however, local recollections confirmed what could be assumed from documents and it seems likely that a fairly accurate and comprehensive record has been compiled.

Fortunately Lincolnshire contains as many as eight First World War stations which survived in active form until after 1945, and several of these, notably Digby and Scampton, have individually published histories which greatly amplify what is generally known about First World War military aviation in eastern England. These, plus the three booklets on aircraft manufacturing firms in Lincoln (by John Walls), provided what was probably the best coverage of the period for any county up to the recent publication of *Bomber County*.

Civil flying operations, for which published sources are generally weak, were pieced together mainly from airline histories, occasional articles in the county journal *Lincolnshire Life* and the personal records of Mr. Peter Green and Mr. John Walls whose primary interest this aspect is. It proved very difficult to establish exact dates when the various commercial operators, clubs and private fliers were active at particular aerodromes and airstrips and a great deal of information had to be acquired directly from those operators concerned. One of the hallmarks of civil aviation in Lincolnshire has been its non-commercial nature, which probably accounts for the difficulty in finding any central source of historical material.

Having built up a reasonably comprehensive profile of flying operations over the years, the last stage of the study was to assess the main physical characteristics of each airfield, i.e. the runway arrangement, boundary, acreage, building stock and current use pattern. In some respects this was most easily done for the First World War, when all the fully-equipped stations were detailed in 6-inch map form on one set of files, now at the Public Record Office (AIR 1/452 and 453). The landing grounds for their part usually coincided with one or two agricultural fields, had no installations to speak of and have left little permanent mark on the landscape. One distinctive feature of First World War records is the listing of airfield acreages. This information was not subsequently provided and has been of considerable assistance in establishing the boundaries of landing grounds in retrospect.

Unfortunately Second World War, and indeed inter-war, stations have no consolidated file of medium-scale plans or listed acreages. The nearest thing is the invaluable AIR 10/4038 and 4039 file, which contains air photos of most, but not all, the aerodromes in Lincolnshire towards the end of the last war, plus a host of written details about runway lengths, hangars and other installations. The only thing missing in this document, apart from acreages, are the exact Air Ministry boundaries of the stations from which it would now be possible to calculate the amount of land actually taken up. After much searching it has been possible to obtain wartime airfield boundaries, most notably from the Imperial War Museum, the RAF Museum, local authority offices and directly from the Ministry of Defence Lands Branch (now the Property Services Agency of the Department of the Environment). In addition some data on the acreages of current active stations was gleaned from the report of the *Defence Lands Committee (1971-73)*.

As indicated earlier, civil airfield plans were more difficult to obtain than one might expect. Most of them were extracted from the pre-war *Air Pilot*, and post-war *Development Plans* prepared by local authorities, but others had to be ascertained by writing to current operators or to owners of the land where airfields are now defunct. Since no acreage information appears to exist in official files, the boundaries once ascertained were transferred onto a set of 6-inch maps and their areas calculated afresh for the purpose of this study.

Once boundaries and acreages had been individually calculated it was then possible to add these up for the various periods and to come to some conclusions about trends in airfield size and their impact on the Lincolnshire landscape. With the precise sites of the eighty-six airfields known, there were few difficulties in relating them to such factors as geology, slope, agricultural quality, neighbouring settlements, local communications and countryside amenity, and further lessons could be drawn about the position of wartime airfields in the geography of the county.

The final exercise was to evaluate the current state of the airfields, both in terms of their own physical decay and the long-term impact they have had on the traditional environment. This could only be done by a combination of field survey and approaches to land-owners, firms and planning authorities who hold all the relevant information about industrial activities and the further economic potential of vacant buildings, etc. When this research was being concluded there was nothing yet published on airfield construction and architecture, consequently the level of detail attempted was somewhat less than might be expected today by societies such as the Airfield Research Group. For that reason the emphasis in this study has been on the pattern of alternative uses which airfields have tended to gen-erate, rather than a purer historical appreciation of the buildings themselves, and hopefully this viewpoint will become an integral part of airfield studies in the future.

Finally, in order to help local historians take more serious note of airfields it was decided to provide not only the grid reference for each site but also the districts and parish(es) in which it lies. This was done by reference to the 1 : 100 000 scale Administrative Map for the county as revised at the major reorganisation of local government in 1974. For each airfield there are two successive districts, plus a parish which has not changed, and a set of unique O.S. co-ordinates (see explanation in the introduction).

Footnote: Since this note was compiled, *After the Battle* maga-has begun a series of facsimile airfield plans; the following Lincolnshire airfields have been published so far: Bardney, Digby, East Kirkby, Fiskerton, Metheringham, North Killing-holme, Skellingthorpe, Spilsby, Waddington. The majority of airfield plans are also supplemented by additional plans of the dispersed accommodation sites.

Addenda

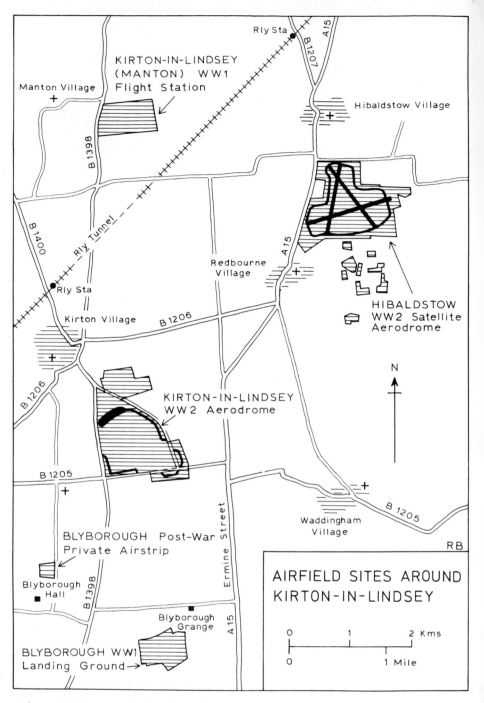

A late addition....to clarify the airfield sites around Kirton in Lindsey over which considerable confusion has existed in the past.